IDEOLOGY AND STRATEGY

POLITICAL ECONOMY OF INSTITUTIONS AND DECISIONS

Editors
Professor James Alt, Harvard University
Professor Douglas North, Washington University in St. Louis

Other books in the series
Gary W. Cox. *The efficient secret: the Cabinet and the development of political parties in Victorian England*
Mathew D. McCubbins and Terry Sullivan, editors. *Congress: structure and policy*

IDEOLOGY AND STRATEGY

A *century of Swedish politics*

LEIF LEWIN
Department of Government
University of Uppsala

Translated by Victor Kayfetz

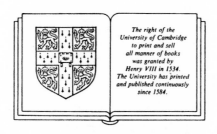

The right of the
University of Cambridge
to print and sell
all manner of books
was granted by
Henry VIII in 1534.
The University has printed
and published continuously
since 1584.

CAMBRIDGE UNIVERSITY PRESS

Cambridge
New York   New Rochelle   Melbourne   Sydney

Published by the Press Syndicate of the University of Cambridge
The Pitt Building, Trumpington Street, Cambridge CB2 1RP
32 East 57th Street, New York, NY 10022, USA
10 Stamford Road, Oakleigh, Melbourne 3166, Australia

Originally published in Swedish as *Ideologi och strategi: svensk politik under 100 år*, by
Norstedts Förlag, Stockholm, 2d edition 1985.

Now first published in English, edited for an international audience, by Cambridge
University Press, 1988, as *Ideology and Strategy: A Century of Swedish Politics*.

Library of Congress Cataloging-in-Publication Data
Lewin, Leif, 1941–
Ideology and strategy.
(Political economy of institutions and decisions)
Translation of: Ideologi och strategi.
Includes index.
1. Sweden – Politics and government – 1872–1907.
2. Sweden – Politics and government – 1905–
I. Title. II. Series.
DL658.8.L4513   1988   320.9485   88–2615

British Library Cataloguing in Publication Data
Lewin, Leif, 1941–
Ideology and strategy : a century of
Swedish politics. – (Political economy of
institutions and decisions).
1. Sweden. Politics, ca. 1880–1985
I. Title II. Series
320.9485

ISBN 0 521 34330 5

Transferred to digital printing 2004

Contents

Tables

Series editors' preface

The Cambridge series in the Political Economy of Institutions and Decisions is built around attempts to answer two central questions: How do institutions evolve in response to individual incentives, strategies, and choices; and how do institutions affect the performance of political and economic systems? The scope of the series is comparative and historical rather than international or specifically American, and the focus is positive rather than normative.

Leif Lewin uses rational political models to analyze significant political events. His models explain the interactions of rational agents pursuing their goals in a political context constrained by the goal-seeking activities of other rational actors. His events are taken from the last century of Swedish political (especially parliamentary) history, but readers will easily find parallel episodes elsewhere. Lewin employs both formal reasoning and careful analysis of historical materials to analyze cases that range across the conflict between free traders and protectionists in the late nineteenth century, the introduction of universal male suffrage and electoral reform in the early twentieth century, cooperation between social democratic and bourgeois parties on the planned economy in the late 1940s, and the decision to utilize and develop nuclear power plants in the late 1970s.

Lewin's game-theoretic analysis focuses on the choices of political actors. Many of these readily found winning strategies. However, Lewin also looks closely at the diverse activities of potential losers, whose appeals to outside authority, logrolling, vote trading, and coupling of previously separate issues to forge new coalitions of issues are but some of the strategic manipulations resorted to by those seeking to create some advantage out of apparently hopeless political situations.

Thus Lewin's political economy perspective reveals the benefits of insights gained from formal analysis and a close understanding of important, politically significant episodes from recent Swedish history.

Author's preface

In this work I have attempted to fulfill two purposes. The first was to write a basic textbook on Swedish politics during the past one hundred years. Rather than provide an exhaustive description, my account has focused on a handful of the most important controversies, beginning with the tariff dispute of the 1880s, that saw the birth of the modern party system. It examines the turn-of-the-century conflicts on suffrage reforms and the introduction of parliamentary government, then analyzes the crisis agreement of the interwar years – which laid the groundwork for the Swedish welfare state and its expansion of the public sector – and continues with studies of the postwar political battles on the economic planning issue and the compulsory supplementary pension system. The book closes with the present-day controversies on nuclear energy and government-run employee investment funds.

My second purpose was to present a theory of politics that has attracted increasing international interest – rational choice theory. Without denying the importance of other theories, it calls attention to the aims, calculations, and maneuvers of political actors; in game theory, it has found a concise format for summarizing its research findings. My own contribution has primarily been intended to show how rational choice theory can be applied empirically, because the disputes included in my book serve to illustrate various political strategies, games, and decision rules discussed by the theoreticians.

Rational choice theory has provided the framework for a research program called "Politics and Rational Action," which has been in operation since the mid-1970s at the Department of Government, University of Uppsala, Sweden. This book is the final contribution to the program. I am grateful to the following participants in the program for their constructive criticisms and many years of stimulating company: Nils Elvander, Sverker Gustavsson, Axel Hadenius, Roger Henning, Barry Holmström, Weine

Author's preface

Johansson, Barbro Lewin, Lennart J. Lundqvist, Lennart Nordfors, Olof Petersson, Evert Vedung, and Jörgen Wedin, as well as many others inside and outside the department, of whom I would particularly like to mention Jörgen Hermansson. The Bank of Sweden Tercentenary Fund has generously financed this research program.

The translation to English is the work of Victor Kayfetz, SCAN EDIT, San Francisco.

Leif Lewin
Uppsala, July 1988

1

The problem of rationality

1. THE VOTER'S PARADOX

In more than seventy years, only one political party has succeeded in attracting a majority of the Swedish electorate during peacetime: In 1968 the Social Democrats received 50.1 percent of the vote. Two years later, their share of the total vote fell by nearly 5 percent. Whereas democratic theory has been based on the assumption that the majority makes decisions, political practice has meant government through coalitions or other agreements between various minorities. As a result, politics has largely become a tug-of-war among parties with differing views. Those who currently belong to the winning coalition must constantly weigh their positions on a variety of issues. How far can they pursue their own policy without destroying their cooperation? How valuable is their coalition as such? How should parliamentary successes, extracted at the cost of concessions on substantive issues, be weighed against the voters' reward for pursuing a consistent policy? The level of political drama was heightened in the 1970s by the Swedish constitutional reform, which introduced a unicameral system and strictly proportional representation. Under these circumstances, the Swedes have seen their politics increasingly turn into a game of bargaining among minorities. Politics has become a series of deals and compromises, surprising initiatives and sudden shifts in the structure of majorities, agonized indecision and sweaty press conferences. Politics is not just official party programs, election campaign promises, and reform proposals – in short, ideology. Politicians also make use of strategy in an attempt to carry out their wishes.

Let us apply this realization to an introductory textbook example. Let us imagine that three party chairmen – C, M, and F – are negotiating on the distribution of government funds in various areas of politics. C would prefer to use the money for social welfare programs, M for defense spending, and F for cultural programs. None of them is opposed to any of these

1

areas, but all of them assign relative priorities to them in different ways, in keeping with certain general principles that guide the actions of their political parties. Let us assume that C assigns defense spending second priority after social welfare programs, but ahead of cultural programs; M's preferred ordering is defense–culture–social welfare; and F's preferences are culture–social welfare–defense. In artificial examples, it is easy to assume that political parties have such sets of priorities. In reality, they can be determined only after extensive analysis of their ideologies. Official party programs rarely contain unambiguous statements about how they rank different issues. And if they do, they are frequently limited to specific policy areas. The researcher must consequently be aware of the goal conflicts that may arise when interests from different sectors of society collide. In other words, the task of analyzing ideologies is to bring to light that which is latent in the material, but which obviously has to be there; the researcher has to be careful not to attribute to politicians a set of beliefs that they lack in reality. By showing what area or issue politicians consider the most important, and what they put in second place, in third place, and so forth, we demonstrate their preference ordering. A systematic compilation of a party's preference orders spanning the entire political field illustrates that party's central principles or, to use a more popular term, its ideology. Ideological awareness in the sense of the ability to rank one's preferences is a first step in determining rational political action.[1]

What, then, is the decision reached in our textbook example? Attempts to reach a decision using majority rule lead to deadlock; each of the three areas receives one vote. We have to look more closely at what the parties "actually want." If we begin by comparing social welfare and defense spending with each other (Table 1.1), we find that social welfare is preferred by two actors (C and F) to defense, which is only preferred by one actor (M). If we then compare social welfare and culture, we find that culture is preferred by two (M and F) against one (C) who favors social

[1] Herbert Tingsten, "De politiska ideologierna i vetenskaplig debatt," in *Åsikter och motiv. Essayer i statsvetenskapliga, politiska och litterära ämnen* (Stockholm: Aldus, 1963), pp. 19–52 (first published in 1941); Georg Lichtheim, "The Concept of Ideology," in *The Concept of Ideology and Other Essays* (New York: Random House, 1967), pp. 3–46; Leif Lewin, "Om studiet av de politiska ideologiernas innehåll och funktion," *Statsvetenskaplig Tidskrift* (1972): 437–468; Barry Holmström, "When Are Decision-Makers Irrational? Some Methodological Problems Related to the Analysis of Political Decision-Making," in *Politics as Rational Action: Essays in Public Choice and Policy Analysis*, ed. Leif Lewin and Evert Vedung (Dordrecht: Reidel, 1980), pp. 133–151; Evert Vedung, *Det rationella politiska samtalet. Hur politiska budskap tolkas, ordnas och prövas* (Stockholm: Aldus, 1977); Philip E. Converse, "The Nature of Belief Systems in Mass Publics," in *Ideology and Discontent*, ed. David E. Apter (New York: The Free Press, 1964), pp. 206–261; Karl Mannheim, *Ideology and Utopia* (London: Routledge & Kegan Paul, 1960) (the German edition, *Ideologie und Utopie*, was first published in 1929); Arne Naess, *Democracy, Ideology and Objectivity* (Oslo: Oslo University Press, 1956); David Spitz, *Patterns of Anti-Democratic Thought* (New York: The Free Press, 1965) (first published in 1949).

Table 1.1. *The voter's paradox*

	Vote of party chairmen between					
	Welfare–defense		Welfare–culture		Defense–culture	
C (welfare–defense–culture)	1		1		1	
M (defense–culture–welfare)		1		1	1	
F (culture–welfare–defense)	1			1		1
Total votes	2	1	1	2	2	1

welfare. The third comparison – between defense and culture – leads to a surprise. Even though culture was placed ahead of social welfare, which in turn was ahead of defense, culture loses when compared with defense! Two actors (C and M) prefer defense to culture, which receives only one vote (F). The rankings seem to go around in circles. Such a preference ordering is said to fail the test of transitivity. In other words, if someone prefers x to y and y to z, he must also prefer x to z. When individual preferences are to be turned into collective decisions, no rule guarantees that a decision will be rational, even though the individual actors act rationally. This is the famous voter's paradox.

Known as early as the end of the eighteenth century, the voter's paradox was discussed by Borda and identified as the phenomenon of "cyclical majorities" by Condorcet. Subsequently the paradox was neglected by scholars in the field of political theory,[2] until Kenneth Arrow reemphasized its fundamental importance. More specifically, Arrow states that there is no decision rule that guarantees collective rationality. Arrow presents two axioms for the preference orderings of individuals. The first is that given two alternatives, a person either prefers one to the other or is indifferent. The second is the previously described axiom of transitivity.

The problem is now to design a preference ordering for a group of people that satisfies the axioms. Arrow does not demand that these decision rules should achieve fairness, freedom, happiness, or other ambitious goals. On the other hand, he believes they should satisfy certain minimum requirements. Arrow formulates five conditions that decision rules should fulfill, and about which he believes that all reasonable people should agree. First, there should be no limit on the ways individual actors may rank

[2] The history of the voter's paradox is sketched in the second half of Duncan Black, *The Theory of Committees and Elections* (Cambridge: Cambridge University Press, 1971), pp. 156–238. The book was first published in 1958. The fact that J. Salwyn Shapiro is silent about the voter's paradox in his major biography, *Condorcet and the Rise of Liberalism* (New York: Harcourt, Brace & Co., 1934), indicates how neglected the paradox was for many years in scholarly thinking on politics.

Table 1.2. *A logrolling strategy*

C	*defense–welfare–*culture
M	defense–*welfare–culture*
F	culture–welfare–defense

their preferences. Second, a change in individual preferences must either leave the collective decision unchanged or lead to the same kind of change; the collective decision may not be changed in a way different from the individual changes. Third, the collective decision may not be made on the basis of irrelevant alternatives: The decision may not be changed if individual preferences have not changed. Fourth, a collective decision may not be forced on the actors from outside ("citizens' sovereignty") and, fifth, may not be dictated by any single actor ("nondictatorship"). These conditions, however, are inconsistent goals. They cannot all be satisfied at the same time by any one decision rule.[3]

There is no generally accepted solution to the voter's paradox today. Nor can the paradox be dismissed on the grounds of being a numerical game without political significance. It undeniably singles out an essential feature of political reality. Identifying decisions in real life that involve the voter's paradox is easy. Because the paradox touches a vital nerve in a democratic system of decision making, political scientists have occasionally been completely frustrated by this "confrontation between the theory of democracy and rational choice theory," as William Riker has put it.[4]

But what, then, *can* the three participants in the textbook example do? No matter how they manipulate the order in which the three areas of policy are compared, the application of the majority rule seems to lead nowhere except to cyclical majorities.

In fact, there is a lot they can do. One possibility is to change preferences. For example, C says that he does not attach such great importance to social welfare, but moves defense into first place instead. M changes his mind and moves culture down to last place instead of social welfare (see Table 1.2; preferences that have changed places are italicized). This change of preferences occurs by means of an agreement between C and M. One departs from his real preference ordering in return for the other's making the corresponding sacrifice in another area. Defense now defeats culture

[3] Kenneth J. Arrow, *Social Choice and Individual Values* (New Haven, Conn.: Yale University Press, 1963). The book was first published in 1951.

[4] William H. Riker, "A Confrontation between the Theory of Democracy and the Theory of Social Choice," in *The Frontiers of Human Knowledge. Lectures held at the Quincentenary Celebrations of Uppsala University 1977* (Acta Universitatis Upsaliensis: Almqvist & Wiksell, 1978), pp. 215–227.

by 2 to 1 according to the majority rule. After the change of preferences, social welfare is the second priority of all three actors. But because it is conceivable that in this vote, F will support his first choice – which was defeated in the first vote – social welfare beats culture by the same 2-to-1 margin. In concrete terms, the agreement might conceivably mean that defense and social welfare grants are approved while cultural grants are defeated.

Maneuvering for the purpose of getting at least something when you obviously cannot get everything is called strategic action. The particular method illustrated here, of departing from one's original preference ordering in exchange for similar behavior by one's counterpart, is called logrolling. According to some scholars, logrolling is the way out of the voter's paradox. Contrary to the image of cheating and fraud associated with this concept, logrolling is a method of bringing about collective decisions that are as close to the actors' preferences as possible. If this were not the case, logrolling would not have occurred, because everyone's decision to participate is voluntary.[5]

We can now make another determination of the concept of rational action in politics. Rational political action means that a person does not always cling to his original preference ordering. In a confrontation between the desirable and the possible, he instead maneuvers in such a way that as many of his wishes as possible are realized at the present time without thereby worsening his long-term prospects.

Strategic action thus enables a person to realize part of his preferences – assuming his strategy is successful. But it need not be. We will now continue to the third step in the textbook example – the analysis of the decision itself. Given the progression of events described in the example, it is unlikely that F will remain passive and merely let himself be shunted aside; numerous counterstrategies are available. Let us assume that the following takes place. F admits that there appears to be a majority for C's and M's "defense and welfare reform package" and a total indifference to culture. But how will this package be financed? F reminds the others that all three have agreed that the income tax is already so high that it poses a danger to productive work in the country. In keeping with their election promises, they should thus find financing alternatives other than a higher income tax. They should try to devise special fees earmarked for financing these reforms. F presents two concrete proposals and at the same time says that he is prepared to vote in favor of C's and M's package if these financing methods are approved. Under his proposal, the increase in defense outlays will be financed by a higher capital gains tax on shares and the expansion of social welfare services will be financed by user fees.

[5] See n. 17 below.

5

These are cleverly crafted financing proposals that require both C and M to do some thinking before voting. Let us systematize the preference of the parties as follows. Support for one's original first preference is assigned a value of +1 (approval of the social welfare program would be given +1 by C, defense spending +1 by M, and the cultural program +1 by F). Another policy besides one's own is valued at 0. If no decision is made, this is also valued at 0.

The financing issue, as structured by F, awakens stronger ideological feelings in both C and M. F has managed to touch on their most fundamental principles. The financing of social welfare services through fees might be the first step toward a market approach to the welfare state, something that – we will say in this example – M would like more than anything else and thus values at +2. As far as C is concerned, let us say, this represents a step toward dismantling the social welfare system and is the least acceptable of all proposals, −2. Raising the capital gains tax on shares, on the other hand, would be a step toward the kind of social leveling that C is primarily seeking, because it will only affect the wealthy. C thus rates this as a +2. To M, such a penalty on savings and investment appears the least acceptable of all alternatives and is valued at −2.

As mentioned previously, F opposes an increase in the income tax to finance the defense and welfare reform package (−1). But F believes, let us further stipulate, that imposing both a user fee for social services and higher taxation of capital gains on shares to finance defense expenditures is a reasonable and fair measure (+1). On the other hand, we can assume, although it has no practical importance to this case, that financing the defense and welfare reform package either by increasing user fees or raising the capital gains tax on shares alone would appear less fair and thus be valued at 0.

Table 1.3 summarizes the way the three actors may be thought to evaluate the various financing methods. The proposals framed by broken lines in the upper left-hand area of the table are the only ones that the majority bloc of C plus M has any reason to consider.

As we see, even in a simplified textbook example such as this, decision making becomes rather complicated. It is therefore customary to use a special aid – known as a game matrix – to make the analysis of collective decisions easier to follow. A game matrix consists of rows and columns. In the simplest case, it includes only two players: the row player and the column player. Each player's values – or, to use the customary term, utilities – resulting from various alternative decisions are written in the quadrants formed by the table. The row player's utility numbers are always written first in the quadrant and the column player's utilities last. In Table 1.4, the utilities of C and M according to Table 1.3 have been written into the respective quadrants according to the two alternatives being consid-

Table 1.3. *Evaluation of financing methods*

	C	M	F
+2	Defense: capital gains tax on shares; welfare: income tax (y)	Defense: income tax; welfare: fees (z)	—
+1	Defense and welfare: income tax (x)	Defense and welfare: income tax (x)	Defense: capital gains tax on shares; welfare: fees
0	Defense: capital gains tax on shares; welfare: fees	Defense: capital gains tax on shares; welfare: fees	Defense: capital gains tax on shares; welfare: income tax or Defense: income tax; welfare: fees
−1	—	—	Defense and welfare: income tax
−2	Defense: income tax; welfare: fees	Defense: capital gains tax on shares; welfare: income tax	—

Table 1.4. *Making a decision using a game matrix*

		M	
		x	z
C_x	x	+1, +1	−2, +2
	y	+2, −2	0, 0

ered by the majority block: raising the income tax to finance both reforms (x) or various combinations of earmarked special fees (y and z). An important prerequisite for this game is also that F be entitled to vote according to the majority rule on the issue that C and M are bargaining about. The upper left-hand quadrant signifies an outcome in which the income tax is increased to finance both reforms. The upper right-hand quadrant means that the income tax is raised to finance the defense reform while user fees

7

Table 1.5. *The "prisoners'*
dilemma"

		Prisoner 2	
		Silence	Confession
Prisoner 1 Silence		−2, −2	−20, −1
Confession		−1, −20	−10, −10

are employed to finance the social welfare reform. The lower left-hand quadrant signifies higher taxation of capital gains on shares and a higher income tax to finance the welfare reform. The lower right-hand quadrant means higher taxation of capital gains to finance the defense reform and user fees to finance the welfare reform. A game matrix does not give us any new knowledge, but it is a convenient and concise way to summarize information.

What decision will now be made? In the literature of game theory, the matrix we have drawn is a well-known decision-making situation, usually identified as the "prisoners' dilemma" because it is based on the following hypothetical case (Table 1.5). Two suspects, accused of having committed a crime jointly, have been locked up in separate cells so that they cannot communicate with each other. Their alternatives are to confess or remain silent. The judge then gives them the following choices. If both of them confess, each will be sentenced to ten years of prison. If one should confess and the other not confess, the one who confesses will have his sentence reduced to one year, whereas the one who refuses to confess will be given the maximum sentence allowed by law, twenty years. If both should remain silent, they will still be sentenced to two years each on a lesser charge for which there is ample evidence against them. (The example was designed on the basis of the way American courts work.) A prisoner who would like to act rationally in order to receive the shortest possible sentence, and who thus refuses to confess, always has reason to fear that the other prisoner will confess, thereby subjecting him to the maximum sentence. But the possibility of receiving the mildest sentence is also an argument against refusing to confess. If both of the prisoners follow this line of reasoning and confess, however, they will end up in the lower right-hand quadrant and each receive a ten-year sentence, which is exactly what the judge was counting on.

The logic of rational action always leads to the same solution to the "prisoners' dilemma" – the quadrant that constitutes the so-called equilibrium point of the matrix. As we will see, the lower right-hand quadrant is also the solution to Table 1.4, to which we will now return.

C has his agreement with M on the alternative known as x – that is, raising the income tax, which gives both C and M a utility of +1 (upper left-hand quadrant). But if C instead chooses alternative y, he has a chance to increase his utility to +2 (lower left-hand quadrant). And it is not only the prospect of this improvement that persuades C to move to alternative y. His fear of a −2, which would be the outcome for him if C stuck to alternative x and M switched to alternative z, also persuades C to choose y. The same reasoning applies to M. But if both of them reason in this way, they will end up in the lower right-hand quadrant. And this quadrant yields poorer utilities for both of them than if they had stuck to x. Yet both of them acted rationally – that is, they chose the alternative that would maximize their utility. This matrix provides yet another illustration of the rationality problem: Rational action by individual actors is no guarantee that a collective decision will be rational.[6]

To put it differently, in our example the vote will yield the following result. On the issue of financing the defense reform, raising the income tax will receive one vote (M) whereas a capital gains tax on shares will receive two (C + F). On the issue of financing the social welfare reform, the income tax increase will receive one vote (C) against two in favor of financing the reform from user fees (M + F). In other words, the reform package will be paid for as F wants but neither C nor M wants, by means of capital gains tax on shares and a social welfare user fee.

The decision reached in this way, using majority rule, thus does not correspond to any majority opinion among the actors responsible. In the final round only F manages to enact his financing proposal, but neither of the winning issues is at the top of F's preference ordering. Nor would the decision have reflected the preferences of the actors better if F had failed in his counterattack and if the logrolling strategy of C and M had won. This outcome occurs because the ranking defense–welfare–culture, which the reform package contains, is not among the original preferences of any of the actors. And if the actors had abstained from strategic action and stuck to their ideologies in all respects, no individual preference would have been satisfied. Instead, a deadlock would have ensued, with no decision at all.

In this example, I have attempted to summarize the perspective on Swedish politics that will be presented in this book. Politicians are driven by a desire to implement their ideological preferences. If they have no

[6] The "prisoners' dilemma" will be applied empirically in Chapter 2. One solution of the "prisoners' dilemma" is for the actors to apply a cooperation strategy by which they stick to the upper left-hand quadrant and thus to the best outcome. The game that such cooperation results in – the so-called assurance game – is discussed in Chapter 6.

majority in favor of their preference ordering, which is almost always the case, strategic action is necessary. The success of the strategy chosen will depend on the game situation when the decision is made. There is no rule that guarantees that individual ideological preferences will be transformed into collective decisions, no matter how consciously the actors rank their preferences and how rationally they subsequently behave in order to maximize their utility values. But ultimately, the political struggle centers on ideological preferences. Strategy should facilitate, not work against, the implementation of ideology.

2. RATIONAL CHOICE THEORY

Within our research project, "Politics as Rational Action," we have not developed any normative theory on how politicians ought to act in order to escape from the voter's paradox. Our purpose is different. Rational choice theory has made today's political scientists once again emphasize what politicians themselves have always known. Strategic action is often possible in politics. You cannot understand how political decisions are reached if you do not also systematically study the decision makers' strategic motives for their action.[7] Explanations for political decisions can be sought in the form of the goals, deliberations, motives, and calculations of decision makers. Or to rephrase the line of reasoning in the previous section: Collective decision can be explained by means of an analysis of the ideological preferences and strategic motives of politicians.

Strategic assessments are always present in politics. A politician who does not achieve a position of influence will soon lose his or her importance. No matter how carefully thought out an ideological program may be, it is of no use in a democracy if it is not supported by many people. We thus assume that behind any decision are actors equipped with their own will; that these actors are capable of ordering their preferences; and that they try to maximize their utility – that is, as indicated previously, they behave in such a way that as many of their preferences as possible are implemented at once, without thereby worsening their long-term prospects. This type of theory is referred to as rationalist or – because it explains decisions on the basis of decisions by various actors – intentional. Its philosophical premise is methodological individualism: Individual actors are the active participants, whereas collective actors such as political parties, special-interest organizations, government agencies, parliaments, or nations are always represented by more or less appropriate individual actors. The assumption of rationality is in the nature of a postulate; it will be an open question how much we can explain with this supposition.

[7] Riker 1978, p. 222.

10

The problem of rationality

Structural theory is often presented as an alternative to rational or intentional choice theory. This is an umbrella term for those theories that are not based on rationality. Those scholars who work with structural theory thus do not focus on the deliberations of the actors. Instead, they try to explain a political phenomenon by using structures on different levels – from psychological microstructures that determine a person's ability to utilize complex information to social macrostructures such as urbanization and emigration that are often what triggers the intervention of politicians.

The difference between rational choice and structural theory thus concerns the explanatory factors: In the first technique the researcher focuses on the ideological and strategic motives of decision makers, whereas in the second he looks at structural conditions of various kinds. An actor's motives may be the reason for a political decision, just as an economic downturn may be. In one case researchers try to depict how the economic downturn fits into the calculations behind a decision maker's behavior; and in the other they try to determine a direct correlation between the downturn and politics, regardless of how the actors view economic conditions.[8]

Thus, rational choice and structural theory are merely different perspectives from which a researcher may view politics. Modern political scientists are usually cautious about claiming that one of these perspectives is truer or more correct than the other. The need to study economic conditions in analyzing political decisions is often just as obvious as the fact that which alternative is chosen within the framework of available resources depends on the ideas and judgments of politicians.

In principle, the rationalist approach is a purely theoretical model that requires no assumptions about reality. In principle it should be possible in a rationalist study to conclude that there is no room for the actors to maneuver and that structural factors explain everything. But in practice, a researcher also makes certain assumptions about how reasonable an approach is. If there were reason to believe that no maneuvering room existed for the actors, it would be pointless to apply rational choice theory – for example, in trying to explain why Robinson Crusoe did not return to his home country. In our judgment, it is fruitful to use rational choice theory in analyzing political decisions, because we assume that the politician has some maneuvering room.

With this as our point of departure, let us look at two assumptions about politics that, though diametrical opposites, seem equally incorrect. One is the assumption that politicians are like fireflies who perform their dance freely without any restrictions whatsoever on their freedom of

---

[8] This is a controversial issue in rational choice theory. For another view, see Georg Henrik von Wright, *Explanation and Understanding* (London: Routledge & Kegan Paul, 1971).

movement. This assumption frequently underlies abstract textbooks on game theory and rational choice theory. In reality, politicians cannot move as freely around the game matrices as these mathematics books presume. Politicians are limited by economic resources and political traditions. Sudden ideological or strategic switches would destroy people's confidence in them, which is their greatest asset in the political game. An evaluation of what can be done without overburdening government finances or straining a coalition is thus also part of the calculations of a rational actor. Such evaluations provide a framework that sets limits on a politician's room to maneuver. Given the current state of research, the greatest contribution a scholar can make in conducting empirical research on rational choice theory is thus to work out a decision maker's alternatives, while taking into account the limits on his maneuvering room resulting from economic, political, and other constraints.

But it would be equally incorrect to portray the actors as totally controlled by structural factors, as mindless puppets entirely manipulated by outside forces. It is possible to distinguish alternatives for the actors to choose between, no matter how narrow their room for maneuvering may seem. A freedom of choice in politics enables politicians to act in a particular way instead of another way, thereby improving their chances of implementing some of the ideology their voters have entrusted them to represent.

3. STRATEGIES

In concrete terms, what can a politician do to further his or her ideological goals? What strategies are available?

When we read historical accounts, we often encounter a way of writing that, in its ambition to explain what happened, piles so many explanations on top of each other that in the end, the poor reader really believes that history is predetermined. How could World War I possibly have been avoided when all the factors discussed are presented as possible explanations: economic rivalry among the great powers, the personality of Kaiser Wilhelm, the German national character, the expansion of the German Navy, France's desire to reconquer Alsace-Lorraine, Russia's decision to carry out a general mobilization, Serbia's nationalism, Russia's unwillingness to restore its treaty of friendship with Germany, the French–British attempt to shut German interests out of Morocco, the diplomatic alliance system, the anachronistic structure of the Austro-Hungarian monarchy, and so on?[9]

[9] Various explanations for the beginnings of the war can be found in Dwight E. Lee, ed., *The Outbreak of the First World War: Problems in European Civilization* (Boston: Heath, 1958).

Borrowing a term from statistics, we might call this an "overdetermined explanation": The researcher is providing far too much information when it would have sufficed to identify the crucial factors. But despite this wealth of information, the explanation is insufficient, because it lopsidedly selects those factors that "fit" what happened, while other phenomena that might have given rise to alternative courses of events are passed over in silence.[10]

The modernization of scientific methods often moves in the same direction in different disciplines, but at different rates and under various conceptual labels reflecting the separate traditions of each subject. Just as political scientists have become interested in alternative courses of action during recent years because of rational choice theory, professional historians have debated what are called counterfactual explanations. How would it have changed history if something had happened differently than it actually did? How much lower would U.S. gross national product have been in 1890 if the country had not developed its railroad system but had instead continued relying on its canal system?[11] In counterfactual theory as in the political scientist's use of game matrices, it is necessary to work out plausible and realistic alternatives to what happened or was decided.

In this book on Swedish twentieth-century history, we reject the notion that history is deterministic and that the political decisions that were made were the only ones possible. We try to avoid delivering overdetermined explanations. In order to give the greatest possible pedagogical impact to the concept of maneuvering room, within which the actor may choose among a number of alternatives, we will view history from the standpoint of the potential *loser*. To the loser, of course, the important thing is to use one's willpower in an attempt to steer history on a different course than it seems to be taking. What options are open when you are losing? That is the question we will now examine.

To illustrate our point more clearly, let us look at a meeting of an association. Before the meeting starts, some of the members are pondering what they can do to avoid defeat when an issue comes up for a vote. Table 1.6 distinguishes eight strategies for the potential loser. This is not an exhaustive chart of all conceivable strategies. Devising such a system is a research task still awaiting its author. The chart lists eight strategies illustrated later in this book by actual events in modern Swedish history.

Nor is it true that only *one* strategy is generally applied in each indi-

[10] I would like to thank Anders Westholm of my department for his valuable opinions on this problem. As for the statistical approach to the overdetermination problem, see J. Johnston, *Econometric Methods* (New York: McGraw-Hill, 1972), pp. 352–365. The book was first published in 1960.

[11] R. W. Fogel, *Railroads and American Economic Growth* (Baltimore: Johns Hopkins Press, 1964).

13

Table 1.6. *What can you do if you are losing? Eight strategies for the potential loser*

1. Is the organization qualified to make
   a decision?   →No   (1)
     →Yes → Refer to another body   (2)

2. Can the agenda be approved?   →Nondecision   (3)
     →Yes → Amend the agenda   (4)

3. Are deliberations completed?   — →Yes → Adjournment → Logroll   (5)
     → Bind oneself   (6)

4. Are the motions properly understood?   — →Yes → Adjustment of motions   (7)

5. Decision: → Choose the least evil   (8)
     → DEFEAT

vidual issue. A skilled politician uses a multiplicity of methods to achieve his goals. The following account of some pivotal decisions in recent Swedish history nevertheless concentrates on the main outlines of action – on the most characteristic and striking aspects of how a potential loser acts. These strategies are arranged in Table 1.6 to fit the logic of an agenda of the association's meeting. They comprise answers to questions regarding the qualifications of a decision-making body, the approval of an agenda, the completion of deliberations, and any adjustments in the motions at hand before a final decision is made.

If you notice that you are in the process of losing, the first strategy is to try to *deny that the body is qualified* to make a decision on an issue. The powers of different bodies are often carefully regulated. For example, the legislative work of the highest decision-making body in the Swedish government, Parliament, must conform with constitutional rules. If we wish to find examples of this strategy, we can look at the political controversies around 1970 concerning decisions by certain municipalities to supply aid to liberation movements in the Third World. The decision by the Municipality of Borlänge to appropriate five thousand Swedish kronor as a contribution to a National Liberation Front fund drive for Vietnam was thus struck down by Sweden's Supreme Administrative Court because it was regarded as violating the rule that a municipal government's jurisdiction was limited to handling its own affairs.[12]

It is uncommon to be able to argue in this purely legal sense that a body is not constitutionally qualified to make a given decision. More frequently, political reasons are cited against such qualifications. Someone will say that a body is not qualified to make a decision because it has no mandate to do so. The voters have not expressed an opinion on the matter. In the early 1980s this was a common argument used by those who did not want the Swedish Central Organization of Salaried Employees (TCO) to take a stand in favor of employee investment funds. Members who felt this way argued that TCO should not take a stand because the organization was not qualified to express its views on the subject.[13]

If you do not believe that you can deny the qualifications of a decision-making body, you can attempt a second strategy – to argue that it would still be suitable to *refer the issue to another body*, and then of course to a body that can be expected to follow your own policy instead. This strategy probably explains the reasoning of the Moderate (formerly Conser-

[12] *Kommunal biståndsverksamhet* (Statens Offentliqa Utredningar, reports from commissions of enquiry [SOU] 1974:86), p. 19. The work of this government-appointed commission of inquiry resulted in some new legislation entitling municipal and county governments to provide disaster relief in the form of medical equipment no longer regarded as necessary at home.

[13] For example, see Gunnar Williamson, "Privat tyckande i fondfrågan – kan vi lita på Lennart Bodström?" in *Dagens Nyheter*, 29 Mar. 1981.

vative) party in 1979 when the question of passing an omnibus clause against tax evasion arose during negotiations to form a new government. In this government, the Moderates found themselves in a minority vis-à-vis the Center (formerly Agrarian) and Liberal parties, which supported the idea of such an omnibus clause. The Moderates succeeded in having the issue referred to the Draft Legislation Advisory Committee. The Moderates attributed a reliable judicial conservatism to the prominent jurists on this council. Their condition for allowing the passage of an omnibus clause against tax evasion was that "an examination by the Draft Legislation Advisory Council shall not give reason for other action." It is, again, another matter that this Moderate strategy failed. The Committee did not strike down the omnibus clause, as the Moderates had apparently expected them to.[14]

If you succeed neither in denying that a body is qualified nor in having an issue referred to another body, you can try a third strategy – to prevent the issue from being included in the agenda. Political science theorists call this the *nondecision* strategy. This concept was launched in two famous journal articles during the early 1960s, in which two scholars argued that political scientists would never be able to depict the real face of power if they only analyzed those issues that came up on the agenda. Crucial power rests in the hands of those who set the agenda and thereby determine what issues will be brought up for consideration at all. Power shows its true face when it can prevent certain issues from advancing far enough to be considered for action by any decision-making body.

The nondecision theory has been criticized for its vagueness and the notorious difficulties that always arise when you are trying to make a conspiracy theory operational. Broadly defined, most of the points in Table 1.6 could be called nondecisions. It is more reasonable, however, to concentrate on attempts to prevent an issue from coming up on the agenda. The way the Social Democratic party leadership treated demands for higher taxes on capital around 1970 has been mentioned by political science researchers as an example of nondecision in this sense. A radical shift of opinion took place within the Social Democratic party during these years. Delegates to the party congress called for heavier inheritance and wealth taxes, even though they knew that such taxes were insignificant from the standpoint of government finances and would provide insignificant funds for improving the living standards of low-income earners. Raising these taxes was "an urgent demand for social equality, which is of great importance from the standpoint of justice." The party leadership found such a policy risky; it warned that it would result in the closure of

---

[14] Cf. Gösta Bohman, "Därför säger vi ja nu," in *Svenska Dagbladet*, 13 Oct. 1980. See also the editorial in *Svenska Dagbladet* of the same day.

companies, tax evasion, and negative effects on Sweden's foreign currency reserves. Using various methods, the party leadership managed to prevent these radical demands from proceeding further. The party's executive board and the Stockholm local branch concurred with the general aims of the radicals in a vaguely worded fashion but sidestepped their actual demands by suggesting that they await the results of ongoing research; they were, however, unable to stop a proposal to amend the declaration of the party congress.

Closely related to attempts to prevent an issue from coming up on the agenda is the act of removing an issue that is already there. Again, the vagueness of the concepts in question makes it uncertain whether such behavior should be classified as a nondecision in the strict sense. One example of the removal of an issue from the agenda when its sponsors expected to lose occurred in Swedish politics during 1967, when the Social Democratic minority government withdrew its bill to abolish rent controls. The government thought it had assured itself of a majority through an agreement with the Liberal and Center parties. When this turned out not to be the case, it avoided defeat by removing the bill from consideration.[15]

Blocking an issue or withdrawing it from the agenda is thus a strategy to enable a potential loser to avoid defeat. An equally successful strategy may be the opposite – *making additions to the agenda*. This fourth strategy is designed to divide one's opponents by bringing up a new aspect on which they disagree. This was the classic Roman strategy of divide and rule. In Sweden the Social Democrats successfully employed this strategy for decades to maintain control of the government by dividing the non-socialist opposition. In our introductory example, we allowed actor F to use this strategy when he succeeded in breaking up the arrangement between C and M by tabling an amendment on different ways of financing the proposed defense and social welfare reform.

We can see a concrete example of the strategy of amending the agenda by looking at the way Prime Minister E. G. Boström sought to end opposition to a reform of the army in the early 1890s. For years, the reform had failed because farmers were eager to keep costs down, but the prime minister believed that the reform's margin of failure was shrinking, because a growing number of opponents were being persuaded to change

---

[15] Prop (government bill) 1967:174. This government bill, in which the Social Democrats clearly state their strategic motives, is an excellent example of how much information Swedish public documents can provide. Parliamentary publications are a frequently underrated source for studies in rational choice theory. Incidentally, the same strategy was also used in December 1983, when the Social Democratic government withdrew a proposal to phase out widows' pensions after it had become clear that it had misjudged parliamentary support for this proposal.

their minds. Boström then took the bold step of summoning an extra session of Parliament. A revised army reform bill was submitted, with an important amendment in the form of a government assurance that the income requirements of the state would not be covered through consumption taxes, but instead through direct income and wealth taxes. This bill now won the approval of Parliament. Joining such prodefense groups as large landowners, high civil servants, and the owners of major companies were a number of small freeholders, who admittedly had a lukewarm attitude toward defense issues but found the bill attractive because it spread the tax burden more evenly. Opponents of the reform, consisting mainly of urban radicals and farmers from western Svealand (the region northwest of Stockholm) and the southern part of Norrland (the northern three-fifths of Sweden), became the minority.[16]

Adding items to the agenda is not necessarily intended as a way of dividing your opponents. This strategy may also be used to free your own side from a group that may otherwise be a liability. As the March 1980 referendum on nuclear power drew near, the Social Democrats found it uncomfortable to be perceived as closely allied with the Moderate party (formerly the Conservatives), the other main supporter of atomic energy. Formal cooperation with the Moderates would create internal problems in the Social Democratic party. It would probably also make it more difficult for the Social Democrats' own referendum alternative to compete with the opponents of nuclear power for the votes of those blue-collar workers and low-ranking white-collar employees who had still not decided how to vote. So the Social Democrats requested that the agenda of the referendum be amended. The voters would take a position not only on the issue of nuclear power but also on the issue of whether nuclear power plants and other major facilities for generating electricity should "be owned by the state and municipal governments." Of course the Moderates could not accept this. The more pronuclear camp split, and the result was three alternatives instead of two. This gave the Social Democrats a better competitive position than if they had been allied with the Moderates. In the end, the referendum represented a success for Line 2, the alternative sponsored by the Social Democrats and Liberals. Initial forecasts in January had indicated that Line 2 enjoyed the support of only 30 percent of the electorate. In the actual referendum, it got 39.1 percent of the vote.[17]

Even if you fail to influence the agenda in your favor, the battle is by

---

[16] Sten Carlsson, *Lantmannapolitiken och industrialismen. Partigruppering och opinionsförskjutningar i svensk politik 1890–1902* (Stockholm: Lantbruksförbundets Tidskriftsaktiebolag, 1953), pp. 81–110.

[17] Sören Holmberg and Olof Petersson, *Inom felmarginalen. En bok om politiska opinion sundersökningar* (Stockholm: Liber, 1980), p. 171.

no means lost. You can ask for adjournment and use the time for various kinds of bargaining. *Logrolling,* a fifth strategy for avoiding defeat, already has been illustrated in our textbook example. Like the nondecision strategy, logrolling has been extensively studied by political science theorists. As already stated, it has been presented as a way out of the voter's paradox and a way of bringing about collective decisions that reflect the preferences of the individual actors as closely as possible.[18]

Logrolling should not be confused with compromising and is probably less common. A compromise means that each actor meets the others about halfway on an issue, or on every issue if they are bargaining on more than one. Logrolling means that you exchange two issues with each other: In principle, you get your way on the issue you consider more vital and you give in on the issue that the other actor considers more important.

An example of logrolling is the so-called December Agreement of 1906 between the Swedish Employers' Confederation and the Swedish Trade Union Confederation. It guaranteed employers the right to direct and distribute work and freely hire and fire workers, and in exchange they pledged to respect their employees' unlimited right of association, something that the trade union movement had been trying to implement for many years. The two sides exchanged issues with each other. They recognized each other's rights on their respective favorite issues.[19]

If you notice that you are losing, an exchange of preference on an issue of secondary importance may thus be a method for achieving the upper hand. Remarkably, a statement to the exact opposite effect may also be an equally successful strategy – that is, a declaration that under all circumstances you are going to adhere to your preference – just as it is occasionally the wisest choice to remove an issue from the agenda, and occasionally wisest to add one to the agenda. In the literature of political science, declaring your unwillingness to depart from your preference ordering, a sixth strategy, is called *binding yourself.* The technique is to commit yourself early, publicly, and in a fashion that ties you completely to that preference. A politician who binds himself adheres steadily to his original preferences, like Odysseus, who had himself tied to the mast so he would not be lured off course by the sirens.[20] This strategy is usable because even your opponent knows that a politician who changes preferences despite

[18] James M. Buchanan and Gordon Tullock, *The Calculus of Consent: Logical Foundations of Constitutional Democracy* (Ann Arbor: University of Michigan Press, 1962). But cf. William H. Riker and Peter C. Ordeshook, *An Introduction to Positive Political Theory* (Englewood Cliffs, N.J.: Prentice-Hall, 1973), pp. 112ff., and Robert Abrams, *Foundations of Political Analysis: An Introduction to the Theory of Collective Choice* (New York: Columbia University Press, 1980), pp. 103–138.

[19] Axel Hadenius, *Medbestämmandereformen* (Uppsala: Alqvist & Wiksell, 1983), p. 21.

[20] Jon Elster, *Ulysses and the Sirens: Studies in Rationality and Irrationality* (Cambridge: Cambridge University Press, 1979).

having publicly committed himself not to do so is in danger of a serious crisis of confidence.[21]

This strategy was employed by Prime Minster Tage Erlander in the 1960s during the process of reforming the Swedish Constitution when he tried to break down the nonsocialist parties' opposition to introducing a system of simultaneous national and local elections. In Sweden it is traditional for changes in the Constitution to be approved by the broadest possible consensus. To make it easier to achieve a consensus, the Social Democrats expressed their willingness to bargain on a number of issues. "We don't want to bind ourselves on any issues except where it's absolutely necessary to take a clear stand," Erlander told the Social Democratic party congress of 1964. "And we believe it's necessary to take a clear stand on two issues: first we don't want a new election system that reduces the potential for creating viable parliamentary majorities. Second, we feel that the link between local and national elections should be emphasized by enabling voters in local elections to influence not only local politics but also national affairs." The party "would be doing something very serious if we eliminated all links between local and national government. I don't believe it would be suitable to make a bargaining point out of something to which you assign such high value."[22]

In a seventh strategy to avoid defeat, a potential loser can *adjust his motion*, taking into account his opponent's views and thereby increasing his chances of winning the vote. One example is the action of the Liberal party minority govenment, which controlled only 39 out of 349 seats in Parliament during its one-year term of office in 1978–1979, on the issue of changing the law on ground leases. All the political parties said they wanted to strengthen the position of lessees. The Liberals and Moderates argued that land tribunals could not ignore market prices when determining rental amounts. The Social Democrats and Center party wanted to go a step further, completely rejecting the market principle and determining rental amounts solely on the basis of a property's economic yield. The Liberals knew a defeat was coming: They had a parliamentary majority consisting of Social Democrats and Center party members against them.

[21] Thomas C. Schelling, *The Strategy of Conflict* (Cambridge, Mass.: Harvard University Press, 1960); Knut Midgaard, *Førhandlingsteoretiske momenter* (Oslo: Istitutt for statsvitenskap, 1971), pp. 23–24.

[22] *Protokoll frånSocialdemokratiska Arbetarepartiets tjugoandra kongress 1964* (Stockholm, 1964), pp. 372 and 397, also p. 417. Eventually the Social Democrats had to give up their demand for guarantees of strong governments. Under the pressure of their 1966 electoral losses, the Social Democrats accepted a strictly proportional election method, which the preface to a major annotated edition of the Constitution describes as "a bombshell" and a change of view whose causes have still not been satisfactorily explained. Erik Holmberg and Nils Stjernquist, *Grundlagarna* (Stockholm: Norstedts, 1980), p. 12.

The problem of rationality

To a government that wished to be perceived as firm and decisive, there was nothing to be gained from thus ending up in the minority on an issue of peripheral importance to the Liberal party, and with the Moderates as company to boot. Hiding behind a verbal smokescreen designed to conceal the party's unilateral acceptance of the majority position, the Liberals abandoned their views in the course of the parliamentary committee hearings, joining forces with the Social Democrats and the Center. They left the Moderates alone to defend the Liberal government's original proposal.[23]

But even if you have failed on all counts, including an attempt to appease your opponent by adjusting your motion, you need not be passive at the moment of defeat. A defeat often means that your opponent gets his way on important principles, but that as the loser, you are able to influence the details. Some would argue that this is particularly true in Sweden, where people do not want anyone to be a genuine loser. The culture of consensus is considered a major asset and can be preserved, for example, by not letting the winner take all, but instead making sure the loser gets something.[24] *Choosing the least evil* is thus an eighth strategy of great practical importance to a loser, allowing at least part of his preference ordering to be included in a decision too.

One example of this strategy is the outcome of the negotiations that took place within a government-appointed commission of inquiry on traffic policy in the mid-1970s. By this time the pendulum of public opinion had swung from the enthusiasm of the 1950s and 1960s for highway traffic to a growing concern about the plight of the public transit network, the biggest problem being the continuing shutdown of railroad lines. The Social Democrats presented a proposal for tough administrative regulation of heavy long-distance truckers, aimed at shifting more hauling work to the National Railways. The proposal ran into strong opposition from representatives of the three nonsocialist parties; even the chairman of the transport workers' union supported the nonsocialist camp. An alternative was proposed – introducing an eighteen-meter (fifty-nine-foot) limit on trailer trucks. All parties could now agree on this proposal. Rather than face a majority proposal for strict regulation of the road haulage business, the nonsocialist camp chose a limitation on the length of trucks. Given two evils, they chose the lesser.[25]

[23] Barry Holmström, *Äganderätt och brukningsansvar. Idéer och intressen i svensk jordpolitik* (Uppsala: Almqvist & Wiksell, 1983), pp. 106ff. and 215–216.

[24] Thomas J. Anton, *Administered Politics: Elite Political Culture in Sweden* (The Hague: Nijhoff, 1980), pp. 173–174 and passim.

[25] Jörgen Wedin, *Spelet om trafikpolitiken* (Stockholm: Norstedts, 1982), pp. 241ff.

4. DECISION RULES

The line of reasoning in our introductory example on the voter's paradox was based on two tacit assumptions – that the actors enjoyed equal voting rights and that the actors disagreed. If their voting rights were different, enabling one actor to prevail over another, no voter's paradox would arise. This actor's wishes would be law for the group. There would be no problem of collective rationality. His preference order would also be that of the group. The last of Arrow's conditions – the requirement of nondictatorship – would then not be fulfilled and the voter's paradox would thereby be avoided.[26] Historically speaking, this is the most common decision-making rule we have had. Louis XVI's "L'état, c'est moi" is the best and most concise description of the method by which humanity has tried to wrench itself loose from the voter's paradox. The power that is the origin of laws, according to Jean Bodin, the theoretician of autocracy, cannot simultaneously be bound by laws. The sovereign power of princes is the best form of government.[27]

Nor, of course, would there be any voter's paradox if the actors were unanimous. They would then approve the policy on which everyone agreed. But in practice, total agreement almost never happens. It is, admittedly, possible to find examples of issues on which the leaderships of a country's political parties agree on a joint policy. But it is probably impossible to gain support for this policy from all citizens. Solving the voter's paradox by creating unanimity among actors has nevertheless occupied political philosophers for centuries. The greatest contributor to this debate was Jean Jacques Rousseau. His distinction between the "will of all" and the "general will" implies that a minority should not see itself as defeated when losing a vote, but instead consider itself enlightened about what the general will is and thereby prepared to give up its views and support the majority policy.[28] In our example – but only in an example with this constellation of preferences – this decision rule does not work, however: No matter what voting method we use, we can distinguish no majority policy and thus no embryo of a general will. As we know, this situation leads one individual actor to step forward from among the minority opinions and proclaim himself the correct interpreter of the general will, as has occurred from the time of Babeuf's conspiracy during the

---

[26] On Arrow's conditions, see pp. 3–4.
[27] Jean Bodin, *Six livres de la république* (Paris, 1576).
[28] Jean Jacques Rousseau, *Du contrat social* (first published in 1762). Beginning with Arrow himself (Arrow 1963, p. 81), it has become common in rational choice theory to refer to Rousseau's doctrine of the general will as a way out of the voter's paradox. For a discussion of Rousseau's distinction in the light of Arrow's paradox, see Jörgen Hermansson, *Rousseau and the Theory of Social Choice: Escaping the Dilemma* (forthcoming).

French Revolution to Lenin's and Hitler's takeovers of power in our own century. By means of this logical somersault, along with a goodly portion of violence, Rousseau's doctrine of the general will as a way out of the paradox of voting has been perverted in such a way that the greatest disunity has turned into the greatest unity – on the dictator's conditions. In practice there are thus important similarities between autocracy and the general will as a decision rule.

A decision rule is a method of making collective decisions on the basis of individual preferences. In societies of our type, we are never called upon to use either of the two methods presented here; the decision rules we use in practice fall somewhere between the lone voice of the dictator in an autocracy and the 100 percent unanimity of the general will. The most common decision rule in case of disunity falls exactly between these extremes – simple majority rule. It is usually called "simple" to distinguish it from various kinds of qualified majorities sometimes required for decision making. Simple majority rule makes it possible to handle a situation where the actors have equal voting rights but disagree. The rule stipulates that if 50 percent plus one of those entitled to vote support a proposal, it is approved. This decision rule need not be associated with any profound ethical conviction, although such a conviction is often forthcoming. From the standpoint of principles, it is fairly irrelevant whether we draw the line for the necessary support at 40, 50, or 60 percent; under any circumstances, individual preferences are suppressed in case of disunity. The widespread use of majority rule is instead probably based on pragmatic reasons: It has turned out to be of practical use and appears, at least viewed superficially, to be legitimate in the eyes of citizens.

But as mentioned, other decision rules besides majority rule also occur in Western constitutions. On certain constitutional issues, for example, it is customary to require some sort of qualified majority to adopt a proposal (two-thirds, three-fourths, four-fifths). A decision rule based on a qualified majority gives a minority the right of veto against the majority, permanently or for a limited period. In other contexts we are satisfied with substantially less than 50 percent support for a decision. This may apply, for instance, to the question of whether an issue will be submitted to a referendum or whether a government will be subjected to a vote of no confidence. This decision rule, allowing a small percentage of the people to impose their will on a completely dominant majority in certain procedural issues, was designed to reduce the risk of oppression of minorities, which majority rule otherwise easily creates.

If we look at history from the perspective of the potential loser, simple majority rule is not of great interest. After all, if you have a majority in favor of your opinion, you are instead a potential winner. In the same way as we attempted to identify some strategies for the potential loser, we will

Table 1.7. *Who is to govern? Eight decision rules for the minority*

The king alone (autocracy)		
Disagreement		
Between king and people	Division-of-power rule	(1)
Between parties and voters	The imperative mandate	(2)
	Referendum	(3)
	The proportional representation method	(4)
Among political parties	The Condorcet method	(5)
	The party discipline method	(6)
	The weighting method	(7)
	The rights method	(8)
The people alone and united (general will)		

introduce some decision rules with whose help those who find themselves in a minority still have a chance to influence collective decisions.

Before we consider these decision rules, we should first merely observe that in modern societies there are intermediate structures, between individual preferences and collective decisions, by which preferences are organized. The most important are political parties, which form a connecting link between preferences and decisions – representing, sorting, influencing, and weighing them together. In every stage of the decision-making process among political parties, where internal disagreements often precede what is later declared to be the party's official view, strategic action may occur. Because of the central role of the political parties today, in practice it has become the primary function of decision rules to serve as regulations governing the relationship of the parties to the voters and to each other.

Table 1.7 lists the decision rules that will be discussed in this book. The table thus ignores autocracy and the general will, because we will occupy ourselves with issues in which the actors, with few exceptions, have equal voting rights and disagree with each other. Nor does it single out simple majority rule, because we are not interested in those who are winning but in those who are in the process of losing.[29]

The first decision rule in Table 1.7, the *division-of-power rule*, enjoys a special position because it is not based on equal voting rights but instead gives one actor, the king, greater influence than others. This decision rule

---

[29] But if we had wanted to mention majority rule, its place in my table would have been in parentheses after the word "disunity." I would then have signified the "normal" decision rule in the case of equal voting rights and disunity, whereas the rules we will be discussing are instead to be regarded as "exceptions to the norm."

enables the king to assert his will even though he is in a minority. His influence is not based on individual preferences. It is an echo of the theory of autocracy; God, history, or other principles higher than the citizens were regarded as giving a prince his power. But when we moved from absolute autocracy to the principle of dividing power between a king and his people, the question of how to organize this division of power arose. How should the power of the king and that of the people be balanced against each other? That question bears the blame for much of the bloodshed in Western history. Perhaps we arrived at an answer – because the executions of an English monarch in 1649 and a French one in 1793 were soon followed by the restoration of the monarchy – only when the Continental European monarchies collapsed at the end of World War I and the division-of-power rule gave way to the principle of popular sovereignty. In the history of Sweden, too, disunity between the king and the people has been a fundamental cause of disputes. It was in no way resolved by the revolution of 1809 and the subsequent constitutional rules on division of power. Instead the issue was merely shunted onto a more peaceful track, retaining its explosive potential and creating tensions in our constitutional development for more than a century.

The other decision rules in Table 1.7 all assume equal voting rights for the actors involved and are all intended to regulate disunity involving political parties, either between party leaderships and the voters as in rules 2 and 3 or between different political parties as in rules 4 through 8.

Disunity between the citizens and the leadership of a state can, of course, also occur in a country where the king has exhausted his role. Early in the history of democracy, people realized that general meetings of all citizens or continuous referendums were not practical decision-making methods. They tried out representative democracy as a working method, using elected deputies, which led them to ask what was the proper relationship between voters and elected representatives. A number of decision rules were possible. One alternative to the decision rule based on the majority opinion among the representatives is decision making by most of the electors, whose views might sometimes possibly diverge from those of their representatives. This rule means that a minority in the decision-making assembly does not immediately need to consider the battle lost. This minority can argue that it has public opinion on its side. This second decision rule is called the *imperative mandate*. It states that representatives should make decisions in keeping with instructions or other directions from the voters. If these are not followed, their position of trust may be terminated.

Developments took a different path, however. To achieve their aims, politicians had to enjoy a freer position than the imperative mandate allowed them. But this also laid the foundation for government by small numbers of people in democracies. Leaders became specially trained, independent. They had great power concentrated in their hands and enjoyed a unique overview of the political battle lines.[30] This situation can lead to disunity between the leaders and the people. Representative democracy, with its technique for choosing political leaders, is not always a sufficient guarantee that the voters and their elected representatives will come to share the same views. Under such circumstances there may be reason to appeal directly to the voters, using a third decision rule, the *referendum*, to solicit their opinion on a political issue. Like the imperative mandate, referendums are an alternative to having a decision-making body reach decisions using majority rule. Decision-making power is returned to the people themselves.

The most important conflicts in politics, however, are those that arise between political parties. These are based on the principle of disunity. The task of a party is to defend interests that it believes other parties are neglecting. But how can we decide which party will get its way? As we shall see, resorting to simple majority decisions is often insufficient. We must specify when and in what way the majority will be allowed to rule. By using different qualifying rules, we can respond to minority interests to a greater or lesser degree. Here we will present five such decision rules, ranked mainly according to the extent to which minorities are favored compared with what would be the case if we used the simple majority rule: the proportional representation method, the Condorcet method, the party discipline method, the weighting method, and the rights method.

The fourth decision rule in Table 1.7 is thus the *proportional representation method*. Simple majority rule prescribes that the winner gets all and the loser gets nothing – whether we are referring to economic aid, political offices, or the number of seats in a decision-making body. This result may sometimes appear unfair. Instead, many countries distribute their parliamentary seats according to proportional representation; the minority is represented in Parliament in proportion to its strength in the respective election districts, instead of being entirely excluded. The supporters of majority rule, on the other hand, counter this fairness argument by saying that if the proportional representation method is used in a parliament, for instance, a division into a large number of parties may result, making it difficult to achieve a consistent and deliberate policy. There has thus been heated debate as to which rule is best. But beyond any doubt, the proportional representation method is more favorable to a minority group.

The fifth decision rule, the *Condorcet method*, bears the name of the great French philosopher who originally pointed out the phenomenon of

---

[30] This is how Robert Michels depicts the emergence of oligarchy in the German trade union movement in *Zur Soziologie des Parteiwesens in der modernen Demokratie* (Leipzig: Klinkhardt, 1911).

Table 1.8. *The Condorcet method*

A	x	y	z
B	y	z	x
C	z	y	x

cyclical majorities and was thus one of the founders of rational choice theory. Just as in the case of the voter's paradox, there may be situations where a tabulation of the votes of decision makers according to their first preferences does not yield a simple majority for a given proposal. If we look more closely at the actors' preference orderings, however, it nevertheless turns out that they prefer one alternative to another, as indicated by the example in Table 1.8. In this example, which for the sake of simplicity will be made entirely abstract, we imagine three actors (A, B, and C) and three alternatives (x, y, and z). The actors rank these alternatives in the following preference orders: A ranks them x, y, and z; B ranks them y, z, and x; and C ranks them z, y, and x. A simple majority decision as to their first preference leads nowhere, because each alternative receives one vote. In such a situation, Condorcet argued, the winner should be the alternative that receives a simple majority over every other alternative in a pair-by-pair comparison. In the example, B and C prefer y to x and A and B prefer y to z. In other words, a majority prefers y to any other alternative and it is thus the Condorcet winner. Unlike the proportional method, the Condorcet method does not favor the minority in general terms. Only certain minorities benefit from the use of this decision rule instead of simple majority rule, depending on the composition of the actors' preference orderings.

The same thing applies to the sixth decision rule, the *party discipline method*. First the parties decide on a policy. Then the Parliament makes a decision. When a party has determined its policy, party discipline generally applies – that is, the party leaders prescribe how their M.P.'s will vote. On certain issues, of course, the members are left free to vote their consciences. But this is the exception and is never true of highly politicized, controversial issues. Sometimes the party discipline method enables a minority to stand up to a majority. Let us imagine that a governing majority is split. Forty percent of the party's members share the views of the opposition. Sixty percent support the party line but make up only a minority of Parliament. But within their own party, they of course constitute a majority and thus win the first stage. The whole party then supports one policy. They are thus also victorious when Parliament votes as a whole.

The *weighting method* gives the minority a stronger position. The reasoning of this seventh decision rule is very simple. If a minority is intensively committed to a particular issue, it should get its way. In that case, the lukewarm majority should abstain from imposing its will. In other words, the influence of a person with a strong commitment is accorded special weight. To a greater degree than their numbers would justify, minorities are entitled to leave their mark on those decisions that are especially important to them. This decision rule works well in everyday life. If one member of a family is very intensively committed to a particular food and the other members are fairly indifferent but lean mildly in another direction, for the sake of domestic peace they will often allow the intensively committed person to get his way. In politics, this decision rule is not as easy to enforce. For example, wealthy capitalists are strongly committed to maintaining the right to own their companies, whereas the general public, judging from public opinion surveys and election results, has a cooler attitude toward nationalization. But allowing the intensity of people's commitments to decide the influence of various social classes on the issue of nationalization is a decision-making rule that a socialist, for example, would oppose. The question of where to draw the line on the use of the weighting method – between fairly innocuous collective decisions on shared meals and highly politicized nationalization campaigns – is a controversy in which any shift works either for or against minorities.[31]

The very strongest protection for minority interests is provided by the *rights method*. This eighth decision rule means that certain issues are specifically exempted from the jurisdiction of majority rule. In Western constitutional systems, this is usually the case with such "human rights" as freedom of opinion and speech, which a majority constitutionally cannot abolish. The right to strike and the right of ownership are more controversial. As with the weighting method, where the lines are drawn is of decisive importance to the special interests of minorities. To John Locke, it was clear that the popular will with which he wanted to replace autocracy could not, in practical terms, mean anything but majority rule. But this entailed a risk of tyranny by the majority, and Locke thus energetically defended the rights of minorities. This marked the birth of the fundamental issue of deciding which political rights should be excepted from majority decisions. How far can we follow Locke's path before it becomes meaningless to speak of government in the name of a majority of the people?[32]

In the following chapters, we will examine more closely the eight deci-

---

[31] Robert A. Dahl, *A Preface to Democratic Theory* (Chicago: The University of Chicago Press, 1956).

[32] Willmoore Kendall, *John Locke and the Doctrine of Majority Rule* (Urbana, Ill.: Illinois Studies in the Social Sciences, 1941).

sion rules that have been listed. Neither Table 1.6, with its list of strategies, nor Table 1.7 claims to present an exhaustive chart of all conceivable decision rules that can be regarded as possible alternatives to simple majority rule in resolving conflicts between actors with equal voting rights and differing opinions. We have instead singled out those decision rules that will be discussed in the following account of actual events in modern Swedish history.

5. STRUCTURE OF THIS BOOK

The purpose of this book is to explain the decisions on some of the major issues in Swedish politics during the past hundred years. The theory used to do so is rationalistic – that is, explanations are sought in the ideological and strategic motives of individual actors. The results will consistently be summarized in game matrices. The issues are viewed from the perspective of the potential loser. Looking at each substantive issue, we distinguish a main strategy with whose help this potential loser attempted to turn defeat into victory. In connection with each issue, we also discuss the decision rule applicable in that case.

This study consistently links together ideological assumptions, strategic action, decisions on the issue, and decision rules. In contrast, textbooks in rational choice theory generally assume that the actors first reach agreement on the decision rule, preferably in the idealistic manner that John Rawls has developed: One should introduce the decision rules that people would devise if they had no idea in what position they themselves would end up in the political system. This "veil of ignorance" is the guarantee of fair decision-making rules.[33] After this, the actors are presumed to use these decision rules to resolve their disagreements on concrete issues.

In the real political world, however, decision rules are continuously being questioned by various groups wishing to improve their position. This process is eminently true of the political conflicts discussed in this book. For it is characteristic of major issues that these conflicts are so fierce that they undermine the sense of shared values. They are crisis issues. Even the decision rules themselves become the object of reexamination.[34] The model for this inquiry is thus not something quite as simple as explaining political decisions by reconstructing the ideological and strategic motives of the actors. The decision rule discussed in each individual case also becomes a dependent variable whose relevance to the power struggle requires clarification. Table 1.9 provides a schematic model of the inquiry.

[33] John Rawls, *A Theory of Justice* (Cambridge, Mass.: Harvard University Press, 1971).
[34] I would like to thank Sverker Gustavsson of my department for presenting this view with his usual constructive imagination.

Table 1.9. *The model of this study*

Explanatory variables	Dependent variables
Ideology	Decision on issue
Strategy	Decision rule

This is not to say that linking ideology to strategy to decisions to decision rules is something desirable. Rawls's recommendation for working out decision rules without the opportunity to favor one's own position appears ideal, of course. It is also obviously in the interest of clarity that the political scientist be sure to make an analytical distinction between decisions and decision rules. But to provide the reader with as concrete an understanding as possible of the conditions of political life, I have subordinated the discussion of decision rules to the ideological and strategic explanation of decisions on the various issues at hand. Thus, the sections on strategies and decision rules in this chapter have not been written in a theoretically exhaustive fashion. I have focused on those strategies and decision rules that have arisen over time in connection with the most important ideological disputes of modern Swedish history, when actors with different views have struggled for the right to leave their mark on collective decisions.

Table 1.10 brings together ideological issues with strategies and decision-making methods. There is no column for decisions, because it is not possible to summarize them in this way.

What, then, have been the biggest issues in Swedish politics in the past hundred years? Swedish political scientists have given remarkably unanimous replies when I have asked this question over the years. Naturally, I do not wish to claim that the issues to be discussed here are the most important in any objective sense; one can always question whether a particular issue should be replaced by another. Nor have I found it worthwhile to define my criteria of selection in detail. I have simply made my choices in a way that well-qualified observers consider reasonable.

We will begin with the *tariff dispute* of the 1880s, which laid the groundwork for the modern party system and awakened the Swedish people from their political apathy. In a predemocratic society this awakening was a threat to the independence of the members of Parliament, and we shall see how they attempted to shield themselves from the new demands of the people.

The tariff issue was succeeded by the *suffrage issue* as the main litmus test in Swedish politics. The Conservative party had no doubts as to who would be the loser if voting rights were extended to the army of radical

Table 1.10. *Ideological issues, strategies, and decision rules in this study*

Ideological issue	Strategy	Decision rule
Tariffs	Avoiding a decision	The imperative mandate
Suffrage	Amending the agenda	The proportional representation method
Parliamentary government	Choosing the least evil	The division-of-power rule
The crisis agreement	Logrolling	The Condorcet method
Economic planning	Denying of qualifications	The rights method
The supplementary pension system	Referring to another body	The referendum method
Nuclear power	Binding oneself	The weighting method
The employee investment fund system	Adjusting one's motion	The party discipline method

industrial workers, which was growing larger every year. We shall follow the Conservative party's moves in response to the demand for voting rights.

At the same time as the Left was struggling with the Right on the suffrage issue, the Left was struggling with the king on *parliamentarism* as the basis for forming a government. This was the period when monarchies were being replaced by republics. What could the Swedish monarch do in this situation?

After the triumph of universal manhood suffrage and parliamentary government, Sweden went through a period of ideological confusion and party splits. But during the worldwide economic depression of the early 1930s, the Social Democrats won an important election victory on the basis of a remarkable *crisis program*. This victory did not, however, give them a parliamentary majority. The Social Democratic program was on the verge of being rejected when the Social Democrats succeeded, through strategic action, in assuring its implementation despite their own minority position.

The Social Democrats took advantage of their new position of power to continue expanding the role of the state in the business sector, a policy that even during the 1930s but especially during the 1940s led to the dispute over *economic planning*. The nonsocialist parties and the business community regarded the *Postwar Program of the Swedish Labor Movement* as a threat both to freedom and democracy, and they mobilized all their resources to prevent such economic planning, which enjoyed the support of a majority in Parliament even after the 1948 election. Yet economic planning along these lines never materialized.

The major dispute of the 1950s concerned the compulsory *supplementary pension system*. The nonsocialists tried to use this issue to force the Social Democratic government out of office. This put the Social Democrats in a serious plight. They lost their coalition partner, the Agrarians, and support for their supplementary pension policy was soft even among their own voters. What actions helped them to escape from these difficulties?

Nuclear power dominated Swedish politics in the 1970s. This is the story of how the Center party, as the representative of a minority view, attempted to prevent a continued "march into a nuclear power society."

In the mid-1970s the Swedish Trade Union Confederation presented its proposal for *employee investment funds,* which the Social Democratic party also came to support. A majority of the Swedish people opposed the proposal. The Social Democratic party leadership nevertheless succeeded in pushing it through Parliament.

There will be a chapter devoted to each issue in the chronological order just listed. Each chapter is structured in the same way, with four sections – one for each of the key terms in the study as indicated in the model in Table 1.9. The first section of each chapter depicts the ideological dividing lines on an issue, against a broad backdrop. The second section analyzes the choice of strategy. The third section summarizes the explanation of each decision in terms of game theory. The fourth section deals with the relevant decision rule.

After these eight empirical chapters I will discuss the problem that usually dominates the perception of politics by the public, the media, and literature, but which we have not considered in this chapter – the problem of whether strategic action in politics is acceptable at all. What arguments can be used to defend it? All things considered, is the only decent policy never to surrender your ideology?

2

Tariffs

1. FREE TRADERS AND PROTECTIONISTS

During the first half of the nineteenth century, free trade made its European breakthrough. For a limited period following the Napoleonic Wars, the mercantilist tarriff-and-rule system was fully restored. However, in the industrial society that was now emerging, with its vibrant activity, increased production, population growth, urbanization, and improved communications, there was no place for economic restrictions. A steadily growing quantity of goods was being permitted to flow more and more freely among peoples.

For a long time, Sweden did not share the economic growth of the Continent. It was a poor, backward agrarian country with a number of restrictive regulations governing trade and business. But a few reforms during the mid-nineteenth century resulted in full economic freedom, even in rural areas. A crucial factor in this development was that the United States and certain European states began to carry out a policy of retaliation toward Sweden's extensive tariff system. Another crucial factor was the intensive economic boom of the 1850s. Prices climbed very rapidly. It became necessary to suspend tariffs on both grains and animal feed. The reform was originally intended as a temporary measure. But circumstances made it permanent.

In theory, the doctrine of free trade was universal. In practice, the world was viewed from a European perspective. When people called for division of labor and exchange of goods between countries, they were primarily thinking of relations among the industrialized countries of Europe. Overseas were the colonies that served as Europe's granaries.

After a few decades of flourishing world trade, it was the exchange of goods with only two of these countries that eventually led to the end of free trade. During the late 1870s there was a general decline in the price of agricultural products due to large-scale grain imports, especially from the United States and Russia. Because of new transportation technology on land and at sea, the small states of Europe were subjected to overwhelming competition from the vast agricultural lands of these two countries, which were well endowed with resources and would emerge as the global superpowers of our own century. The price of rye and wheat in Sweden fell dramatically. Soon the popular American pork also posed a threat to Swedish livestock producers. The agricultural crisis deepened. Many a Swedish farmer had to leave the land.

These consequences of free trade were unacceptable to many people. Once again there were calls for tariffs to protect Sweden's farmers. In 1880 the "Friends of Swedish Labor" was formed to promote protariff ideas; local tariff associations throughout Sweden joined this organization. Under the slogan "Sweden for the Swedes!" they demanded protection for the country's main source of livelihood. Free traders responded with the slogan "No starvation tariffs!" from their own propaganda organizations, among them the Association Against Tariffs on Food. The dispute was mainly a clash between producers and consumers. But because of the changing nature of agriculture in different parts of Sweden, the geography of public opinion on the tariff issue was somewhat more complex than a simple division between rural and urban areas.

The major tariff dispute of the 1880s profoundly changed the political culture of Sweden. The Swedish people, who had previously taken part in elections only to an extremely limited extent and shown little interest in politics, woke from their political apathy. Political debate achieved an unprecedented level of public involvement. The voters took a position on the issue itself, not just on the personal reputations of the political candidates. The foundation of the current party system was laid. The tariff dispute marks the beginning of Sweden's modern political life.[1]

When free traders defended the prevailing system during the period of the tariff dispute, they based their arguments on the doctrine of economic harmony.[2] Freedom of trade and business spurred people to do their very best.

---

[1] Arthur Montgomery, *Svensk tullpolitik 1816–1911* (Stockholm, 1921); Montgomery, *Industrialismens genombrott i Sverige* (Stockholm: Skoglunds, 1947), pp. 152–177 (first published in 1931); Torsten Gårdlund, *Industrialismens samhälle* (Stockholm: Tiden, 1942), pp. 9–60; Eli F. Heckscher, *Svenskt arbete och liv* (Stockholm, Aldus/Bonnier, 1963), pp. 246–329 (first publsihed in 1941); Sten Carlsson, *Lantmannapolitiken och industrialismen. Partigruppering och opinionsförskjutningar i svensk politik 1890–1902* (Stockholm: Lantbruksförbundets tidskriftsaktiebolag, 1953), pp. 65–81; Leif Lewin, Bo Jansson, and Dag Sörbom, *The Swedish Electorate 1887–1968* (Stockholm: Almqvist & Wiksell, 1972), pp. 40–49.

[2] On the views, arguments, and behavior of the actors during the tariff dispute, see Leif Kihlberg, *Den svenska ministären under ståndsriksdag och tvåkammarsystem. Intill 1905 års totala ministerskift* (Uppsala: Almqvist & Wiksell, 1922), pp. 337–359; Edvard Thermaenius, *Riksdagspartierna. Sveriges riksdag XVII* (Stockholm, 1935), pp. 69–76 and 91–95; Torsten Petré, *Ministären Themptander* (Uppsala: Almqvist & Wiksell, 1945); Olle Gellerman, *Staten och jordbruket 1867–1918* (Uppsala: Almqvist & Wiksell, 1958), pp. 17–43; Per Sundberg, *Ministärerna Bildt och Åkerhielm. En studie i den svenska parlamentarismens förgårdar* (Stockholm, 1961), pp. 9–16. Also Montgomery 1921, pp. 135–169.

Tariffs

"The principle of free trade is the principle of freedom and . . . the principle of freedom is the only one that fosters strong lungs, strong muscles and sinews in the body politic."[3] Protective tariffs undermined those efforts that resulted in economic progress. Tariffs "will presumably have about the same effect as alcohol; for as we know, alcohol has a momentary awakening and life-giving effect but as a rule this is followed by an even greater laxity."[4] "Instead of fostering hothouse activities in our country that are suitable for industry in other countries, let us create our own (industries) exposed to the open air."[5]

As far as the government was concerned, this conviction as to the advantages of a free exchange of goods and free competition could only lead to one conclusion: The state should keep its hands off economic activity. Any intervention and regulation, any decision to protect or forbid, any attempt to hamper or help different business sectors only harmed productive activity. Prime Minister O. R. Themptander declared, "We free traders . . . reply both to protectionists and socialists: . . . the state wishes to leave production in freedom, not trespass in its area, for example by intervening in and arranging the conditions of production and labor."[6]

If the protectionists did not want to accept these theoretical agruments, they at least had to recognize the evidence of history. During the age of economic freedom – the decades that had passed since the mid-nineteenth century – the business sector had flourished in extraordinary fashion. By applying the principles of economic freedom and free trade, "our businesses have undergone a growth that should be a source of joy to every Swedish man and that is unmatched by any equally long period in Swedish history." The emergence of a mechanical engineering industry was an outstanding example. "In free competition with other countries, without any kind of protection, during this 30-year period they have built up such standing that they are now a source of pride and a credit to the Swedish business community."[7] One could go through industry after industry and see that economic progress had been achieved in fields where there was foreign competition, not in fields protected by tariffs. "It is thus not at all true that we could not have any industry in this country without tariff protection. Our most vigorous industrial firms have arisen and grown without such protection."[8]

The fact that an economic crisis was now affecting Sweden did not

---

[3] FK (Proceedings of the First Chamber) 1886:13, p. 6 (Borg).

[4] AK (Proceedings of the Second Chamber) 1866:14, p. 6 (Johansson i Noraskog).

[5] J. H. G. Fredholm, *Om spannmåls- och industritull* (Särskildt aftryck ur Industritidningen Norden, 1886), p. 46.

[6] AK 1887 A:13, p. 42.

[7] AK 1887 A:11, p. 29.30 (Fredholm).

[8] Hugo E. G. Hamilton, *Hvad protektionisterne säga och hvad frihandlarne säga* (Stockholm: Norstedts, 1887), p. 6.

mean that there was anything wrong with the free-trade principle. This principle meant, of course, that an individual country continuously had to adapt itself and reassess its production system in the light of global economic change to be able to offer improvements to its citizens. And such adjustments always had an impact, declared one parliamentary committee in 1885, when free traders repulsed the first serious protectionist onslaught in Parliament: "The fact that competition from one country occasionally compels another to change the nature of its production to a greater or lesser degree does not, in the view of this Committee, entail any real national loss to the latter country, even though the actual transition from one kind of production to the other cannot take place without more or less sizable costs and other inconvenience." The increased imports of fall-sown grains, for example, were partly due to an improvement in the Swedish diet: In recent years rye and even wheat had begun to be consumed on a large scale by social classes previously satisfied with oats and barley. Such a shift to better nutrition, the committee felt, had to have a strengthening effect on the labor force and should not be resisted by means of tariffs.[9]

Crises (or recessions, to use the modern term) were a recurring feature of the global economy. They were not the product of chance but were a part of the world order. We could learn from them where improvements were needed in the production system. The desire to relieve the suffering of individuals was understandable, but it was also necessary to make sure that tariffs or other "artificial means did not shift this suffering from one to the other – that we did not take one evil and create from it something much worse."[10] The industrial revolution might cause hardship to individuals. Many a conscientious craftsman had suffered the consequences of mechanization. "It is now the turn of farmers. May they accept their fate, may they try vigorously to save what can be saved, may legislation come to their aid by providing well-ordered credit institutions, good schools, and carefully prepared laws well suited to their aims, but may they not persuade us to attempt (through tariffs) to divert the broad course of human civilization."[11] The same views were expressed by the so-called Welfare Commission, which the Themptander government had appointed. It proposed steps of the kinds mentioned in the previously quoted speech, but rejected the concept that agriculture should be protected by building up a tariff wall around Sweden's borders.[12] "The poor man may cry for help," a member of the First Chamber declared, "but he

---

[9] BevU (Proceedings of the Ways and Means Committee) 1885:3, pp. 13 (quotation) and 17.
[10] FK 1886:11, p. 3 (Bennich).
[11] AK 1886:14, p. 11 (von der Lancken).
[12] Petré 1945, p. 110, n. 2; Sundberg 1961, p. 14.

who practices Sweden's principal industry ought to be a good man capable of helping himself; if he is not, may he be ruined."[13]

Imposition of tariffs would not only obstruct the necessary restructuring of Swedish agricultural production but would also unfairly affect the poorest classes. This view, the most powerful argument of the free traders, was used with great energy. "They want to lift a burden from the landowners by using grain tariffs to place it on farmers and other workers, including the poorest of these."[14] Introducing this kind of "starvation tariffs" was grossly unfair to people of small means, who were the least able to bear indirect taxes.[15]

But even if the protectionists, in their blind selfish interest in shielding Swedish agriculture, did not allow themselves to be swayed by these appeals to justice and fairness, it was nevertheless in their own interest not to take such provocative action as to make the poorest people pay for the landowners' and independent farmers' unwanted agricultural products through indirect taxes. Such a step would lead to dangerous protest actions. "But there is one thing that the chamber ought to consider," a baron warned Parliament in 1886, "and that is the fact that the people standing outside these walls are the ones who will have to pay by far the bulk of the tax in question here. If I wished to promote universal political suffrage or some other radical upheavals in our social conditions, I do not believe I could do it better than by voting for the Committee's proposal today. For it seems that nothing is more likely to give agitators a weapon in their hands and provide an impulse for political pressures than if people are of the opinion that those who make the laws do so for their own purposes and for their own utility."[16]

With such a view of recessions and of their long-term beneficial function, the free traders had no difficulty sticking to the doctrine of economic harmony, even during the prevailing agricultural crisis. Adherence to this view did not keep them from sympathizing with its victims, but they nevertheless considered it important not to let such feelings persuade them to make a bad thing worse by introducing tariffs. Tariffs would mainly hurt Sweden's genuine poor, whose welfare could only be improved by means of continued industrialization in an atmosphere of economic freedom and free trade.

Measured by the standards of that age, this consistent Manchester liberalism was the more radical of the two camps during the tariff dispute. The free traders now feared a conservative tide of the German type following a victory by protariff forces. They tried to protect their general

[13] FK 1888:4, p. 20 (Hedlund).
[14] FK 1886:13, p. 2 (Almén).
[15] Sundberg 1961, p. 15.
[16] FK 1886:11, pp. 24–25 (Ericson). Also Gellerman 1958, p. 29.

principles of freedom and their continued striving for cultural liberalism against such tendencies.[17] Adolf Hedin expressed his concern about an imminent wave of political reaction in 1886: "In combination with the (new tariff system) I see another new system in another field where we want no change. I hear how the (German) magpies laugh; they are expecting company."[18]

The protectionists found it amazing that the free traders stuck to an ideology that had pulled Sweden straight into a profound European agricultural crisis. They thought they understood where the free traders had derived their basic principle – from biological science and Darwinism. "Here it is called 'the struggle for existence' and the way it works is that the strong removes the weak, the big eats up the small. . . . The economic struggle is the struggle for existence based on ownership rights and by means of free exchange." In both cases "the law is the same: the strong wins, the weak succumbs or must give in."[19] There was a word that expressed the true nature of free trade better than "freedom." It was "selfishness." "The economic doctrines portend and anticipate the Darwinist hypotheses. According to these, the stronger is fully entitled to oppress and crush the weaker, who is disfavored by nature. In such an order of existence, selfishness becomes the only motive of practical life."[20] The main advantage of free trade was "the great attribute of beginning with the word 'free.'" This gave its ideology a "magic power," which made people believe that free traders were fighting for freedom, when actually they were attacking Swedish workers and Swedish labor. The fundamental principle of free trade was "to leave the individual isolated, alone and without support in the struggle for existence."[21]

On the basis of this negative assessment of the free-market economy, the protectionists formulated a theory of the state that was the direct opposite of the free-trade position. Precisely because there was *no* harmony between self-interest and the general interest, the state must accept its responsibility for economic policy and intervene to protect industries with problems. The protectionists thus now wanted to "break with a system that, if continued, will unconditionally lead our country to destruction."[22] The state had to safeguard the interests of the entire public against self-interest and restore "a sense of social community and solidarity."[23] In

[17] Petré 1945, pp. 139, 157–158, and 165.
[18] AK 1886:19, p. 46.
[19] Pontus Fahlbeck, *Den ekonomiska vetenskapen och näringsskyddet. Några ord för dagen* (Lund, 1887), quotations from pp. 6–7.
[20] FK 1886:13, p. 20 (Casparsson).
[21] AK 1886:14, p. 29 (Sparre).
[22] Ibid., p. 24 (Sparre).
[23] FK 1886:13, p. 20 (Casparsson).

the end, a ruthless economic struggle brought suffering to everyone. "If one of the country's major industries is suffering distress, this has repercussions on nearly all the others."[24] There were, of course, parts of the country with special economic structures that, at least in the short term, could benefit from free trade. But now people should consider their responsibility for the best interests of the whole. One baron gave his reaons: "Now that I have decided to take this step in a protectionist direction, I am thinking neither of the people of Skåne (province) nor those of (the) Norrland (region), but of the country as a whole. I want to protect my native country and I want to keep its workers at home instead of sending them away."[25] Confronted by national need, the state could no longer remain indifferent. "Confidence and hope have finally died. Thousands upon thousands of landowners, farmers, country people and farm workers now demand that Parliament take another path."[26]

It was, of course, possible to follow the urging of the free traders and look at the evidence of history. But then you also saw something entirely different from what the free traders depicted in their propaganda. Everywhere in Europe, people had been hurt by the crisis – even in Britain, the leading free-trade country. The terrible poverty in that country showed what happened when the state left people to themselves in the struggle against overwhelming economic forces. "The inevitable consequence is also the awful pauperism that one finds in the cities of Britain."[27]

But in other countries the leaders knew how to protect themselves. Everywhere in Europe, tariff barriers were now being erected. Only the Swedish free traders wished to resist this trend. It showed that the Swedish free-trade principle had lost its way and been transformed into a doctrinaire belief lacking contact with political realities, according to one protectionist leader in the Second Chamber. "In the 1850s when Baron Gripenstedt removed the tariff barrier, he was nevertheless so practical that he did not do so before it had been removed in all other European countries. . . . But now, when the gentlemen are fighting to maintain free trade, now we should keep it even though all other countries have abandoned this tariff system!"[28] A count declared rhetorically: "I ask you: When Russia, Germany, France and to some extent Norway, Denmark, Holland and Switzerland have protection for their farm products, is it right for this small country alone to do without it?"[29]

But would tariffs not have an especially heavy impact on poorer consumers, as the free traders claimed? The protectionists tried to respond to

[24] FK 1886:12, p. 11 (Strömfelt).
[25] FK 1886:12, p. 27 (Barnekow).
[26] FK 1885:18, p. 24 (Strömfelt).
[27] AK 1886:14, p. 29 (Sparre).
[28] AK 1887 A:11, p. 49 (Boström).
[29] FK 1886:12, p. 11 (Strömfelt).

this critique in a number of ways. Their main view was that consumers were also workers, and their jobs – the basis of their buying power – were now being threatened by continued free trade. It had to be considered "more important to have access to steady and fairly well-paid work than to a low price for the necessities of life."[30]

A second argument was that Sweden's workers would also derive great advantages from the economic upswing that the change of system was expected to bring. Agricultural workers would benefit directly from the improvement in the economic situation of farm owners. And urban workers, too, would stand to gain. Competition for jobs would be less acute in urban occupations if the farmers did not have to fire their workers. Further, greater buying power among farmers would stimulate industry and trade.

A third argument was that tariffs would not have to be paid for in their entirety by the consumer. They would not result in any actual increase in food prices. Based on German experience, protectionists argued that a large proportion of tariffs were paid by the foreign exporters and middle men – something that caused free traders to make jokes about a trade system that was "so wonderfully well arranged that prices rise for the seller but . . . not for the buyer."[31]

Free traders also claimed, of course, that the introduction of a tariff system would provoke radical, "socially destructive" protest actions among the poorest consumers. This accusation was indignantly rejected. A wave of resentment arose among conservative protectionists when their action was compared with radicalism. This claim was a complete distortion of cause and effect. The market economy and free trade had created mass poverty in the major cities of Europe, and this pauperism "is what generates the concept of communism."[32] It was the free traders, with their political base among poor urban people, who were responsible for socially destructive propaganda.

The tariff controversy was the beginning of a conservative renaissance. As one researcher has shown, this conservatism differed greatly from the old, backward-looking patriotism with its devotion to the monarchy and historical memories. The new conservatism focused on contemporary society, devised a political action program and sought to awaken the self-esteem of the Swedes vis-à-vis other peoples.[33] When the new system, in turn, was criticized, it was consequently more than just its tariff principles that were in danger. Other values, too, were threatened. People should not

---

[30] FK 1886:11, p. 9 (Dahl).
[31] Petré 1945, p. 110; Sundberg 1961, p. 16. Sundberg quotes AK 1888:5, p. 11 (Herslow).
[32] AK 1886:14, p. 29 (Sparre).
[33] Nils Elvander, *Harald Hjärne och konservatismen. Konservativ idédebatt i Sverige 1865–1922* (Stockholm: Almqvist & Wiksell, 1961), pp. 30 and 32–33.

forget, the newspaper *Svenska Dagbladet* warned a few years after the tariff dispute, "that if this structure is eliminated it will not only spell the end of protective tariffs as such but also all the patriotism and good sense that have characterized the policy of the new system. For free trade is closely related to radicalism and superficial cosmopolitanism. The fruits of today's seeds flourish under its cover: government by the masses, worker oppression, the destruction of industries in small states, a taste for foreign things in intellectual and material terms, lack of patriotism and so forth."[34]

2. STRATEGIC SILENCE

Throughout Sweden – in free-trade organizations and in tariff associations, in parish halls and public meetings, in farmers, clubs and urban workers' associations – the tariff issue was discussed with a level of involvement unprecedented in Swedish political history. But for a long time, an amazing silence prevailed in Parliament and in election campaigns. Research has consistently indicated that members of Parliament were reluctant to make official statements on the tariff issue.[35] What was the reason for this silence?

The members of Parliament had their reasons. According to the then-prevailing doctrine of government, M.P.'s were supposed to assume an independent stance toward their voters. The Parliament Act stated that a member could not be bound by any instructions other than the Constitution. It thus rejected the so-called imperative mandate, which meant that the voters gave their M.P.'s instructions on how to act on different issues. Without stealing any glances at the special interests of his voters or his election district, an M.P. was supposed to form an independent opinion of what was best for the country as a whole. As a contemporary authority on constitutional law put it, "When the act of election is completed, all legal links between the electorate and the elected cease; his relationship to his election district is no different than to any other part of the people; his calling is that of *munus publicum*. Representatives are not obliged to execute a higher will that stands above them. What is referred to as the popular will or public opinion develops among the representatives with inner freedom. . . . It is this assembly that shall make the laws, but neither the people nor the electorate."[36]

---

[34] *Svenska Dagbladet*, 21 June 1893, quoted in Staffan Björck, *Heidenstam och sekelskiftets Sverige* (Stockholm: Natur och kultur, 1946), p. 14. In the terminology of that period, "worker oppression" meant oppression by workers.

[35] cf. Kihlberg 1922; Thermaenius 1935; Petré 1945; Gellerman 1958.

[36] Christian Naumann, *Sveriges statsförfattningsrätt III* (Stockholm: Norstedts, 1881–

No, an M.P. could not thoughtlessly give in to the resolutions now being submitted on the tariff issue. "A few hundred people, mainly workers in industrial occupations within the election district that I have the honor to represent, have sent me addresses with the request that I should vote against grain tariffs. But because I find that the conditions upon which they base their opinion are invalid, I thus cannot allow myself to be bound by them."[37] Another M.P. gave this advice: "Weighing all such protests against each other would, however, be a difficult task, so I believe it is better to ignore them entirely."[38]

At public meetings, you could persuade people to support whatever opinion you wished, one count declared. One day a free trader was applauded, another day a protectionist. If you then asked how those attending the meeting could act this way, the answer would be, " 'Well, we don't understand all that, we only thought it sounded good.' Strange things happen at these meetings, and if we now cast our votes on this issue based on them, it will be all wrong."[39]

It was necessary to resist the hasty expressions of opinion emanating from public meetings. "It is peculiar to see how these major issues are resolved at so-called public meetings by means of a few minutes of discussion, when we know that Europe's greatest statesmen and economists have not been able to agree on them even after years of study and lengthy disputes. I will, of course, admit the great good intentions of those workers and other people who gather at these meetings in order to give the most cocksure statements on the most intractable of social issues after a few hours or minutes, but we must not accord their statements the decisive importance that some of them would like to claim for themselves."[40]

A member of Parliament had to follow his own opinion on political issues, and the voters consequently were wisest not to try to exercise the imperative mandate. "In my opinion, election to Parliament should mean that the voters are confident of the goodwill and judgment . . . of the person elected, and as a consequence of this, they should leave him with full freedom of action as a representative."[41]

1883), p. 327. The book was first published in 1863. P. O. Gränström quotes Naumann in "Om regionalism och enhetssträfvande i vårt riksdagsskick. Till historisk belysning af senare tiders imperativa valmanstendenser," *Statsvetenskaplig Tidskrift* (1915): 285, n. 1. He himself categorically rejects the imperative mandate (p. 285): "The imperative mandate, or a membership in Parliament limited and bound by the special regulations (instructions) of the electorate, is thus irreconcilable with all modern representational theory."

[37] AK 1886:15, p. 24 (Unger).
[38] AK 1886:17, p. 7 (Farup).
[39] AK 1886:18, p. 48 (Sparre).
[40] AK 1886:19, p. 34 (Larsson).
[41] AK 1887 A:17, p. 10 (Lönegren).

You were not a better representative of the Swedish people merely because you yielded to special interests or temporary opinions. On the contrary, you could often be a better representative if you followed your convictions and said no to the demands being presented. "You consider yourselves to be the representatives of the people in the real sense, their true friends. But you are not entitled to do so. We too are just as much representatives of the people, and the time will come when we will see who are its true friends – those who have caressed them and merely shouted yes and amen to the demands of the crowd, who have not been able to understand the scope of the issue now before us, or those who had the courage to say, 'If you do not get what you want, you will get what is better and more useful to you.' "[42]

Yet these arguments against the imperative mandate did not prevent certain M.P.'s from yielding to it. One researcher has gone through the Swedish election campaigns of the late nineteenth century with this issue in mind. He can, of course, quote many an insolent farmer M.P. who stuck to his guns against the imperative mandate. "You gentlemen speak of public opinion. What exactly is that? Where I come from, it's me." But he also observes that there were parliamentary candidates who gave in to the demand for a "public candidacy" enabling voters to examine their views, and that some of them expressly corrected their votes on the basis of resolutions they had received from their voters.[43]

It was feared that if the tariff issue was presented to the voters, they would inevitably demand that candidates for Parliament should declare their views on it. The imperative mandate would go into effect. The independence of M.P.'s would be undermined. Members of Parliament therefore followed a nondecision strategy on the tariff issue. They avoided raising the issue in the 1884 election campaign. Our interpretation is that the long-time silence of M.P.'s in Parliament and in election campaigns was strategic. An issue as complex as tariffs, which had caused headaches among Europe's leading economists and statesmen for years, was hardly suited for decisions by means of short-lived majority opinions that could easily be manipulated at public meetings. The broad popular anxiety generated by agitation on the tariff issue was harmful to the country. The best solution to this issue and others would be achieved if the M.P.'s, who were elected to represent the Swedish people, could make their decision uninfluenced by voter mandates and resolutions.

But when the new Parliament assembled after the 1884 elections, all the barriers collapsed. The big tariff dispute was immediately launched in Parliament when the protectionists submitted bills that called for grain tariffs

---

[42] AK 1886:16, p. 8 (Boström).
[43] Carlsson 1953, pp. 34–52, quotation from p. 50.

43

of one krona and fifty öre per hundred kilos.[44] After years of farm crisis and popular agitation, and five years after the formation of "The Friends of Swedish Labor," the issue of a new tariff system had now been placed on the parliamentary agenda. Members of Parliament now had three years before the next election to the Second Chamber.

These three years witnessed the development of all the arguments for free trade and protectionism – often expressed in brilliant, rhetorical speeches. They repeated the popular arguments for and against tariffs, albeit on a stylistically higher level.[45]

As the tariff dispute became more intensive, it had far-reaching consequences on the party system. The previous, more or less loosely organized parliamentary parties fell apart under the pressure of the new political dividing line that emerged from the tariff dispute; even the powerful Rural party *(Lantmannapartiet)* split into free-trade and protectionist factions. Another novel feature was cooperation between the two chambers; the newly established protectionist party was an organization of M.P.'s from both the First Chamber and the Second Chamber. Its first known meeting was held in Stockholm in March 1885, with Count E. J. F. Sparre as its chairman and sixty to seventy M.P.'s present. Also of the greatest importance to later developments was the fact that both new parliamentary parties had their corresponding national organizations – "Friends of Swedish Labor" and "Association Against Food Tariffs." The modern party system was being born.[46]

The government also reexamined its role. Quite contrary to the custom of the period, the government headed by Prime Minister Themptander became energetically involved in the parliamentary debate, which is believed to have strengthened the position of the free traders greatly. The protectionists reacted sharply against what they regarded as this completely unwarranted interference by the prime minister. They felt that Parliament should be allowed, as before, to decide such fiscal issues as tariffs without pressure from the government; the issue had, moreover, arisen in the form of individual members' bills *(motioner).*[47]

A change in the political climate was clearly under way. Ideologically closely knit parties with organized support around the country and a government engaged in party politics were something new in Sweden. Would the M.P.'s succeed in their strategy and preserve their independence against these new, powerful forces? That King Oscar II was acutely aware

[44] Mot (members' bill) FK 1885:23 and mot AK 1885:60.

[45] No one has yet written the content analysis of the extensive propaganda material from the tariff dispute that Elis Håstad calls for in "Tullstridens val och folkmeningen," in *Festskrift till professor skytteanus Axel Brusewitz* (Uppsala: Almqvist & Wiksell, 1941), p. 106, n. 1.

[46] Thermaenius 1935, pp. 70, 72, 91ff., and 96ff.

[47] Petré 1945, pp. 66–67.

of the threat to the traditional Swedish governmental system posed by the tariff issue is well documented.[48] He was not, however, destined to remain inactive during the tariff dispute.

The first attack against the free-trade system was easily beaten back. The call for grain tariffs was rejected in both chambers during 1885. The following year, the protectionists had strengthened their position. The Second Chamber now approved the grain tariffs, but the First Chamber rejected them and the proposal was defeated in a joint vote of the chambers.

The third assault on the free-trade system in Parliament during 1887 marked the culmination of the tariff dispute. The First Chamber defeated the proposed rye tariff by 70 to 68, then in keeping with the "all or nothing" principle it rejected all other proposed tariffs. The Second Chamber, in contrast, approved the rye tariff by a vote of 111 to 101. The country excitedly looked forward to the joint vote. Adding together the votes, it seemed as if the protectionists would now finally triumph.

But before the tariff issue could go to a joint vote, the king – backed by the prime minister and his government – took the extraordinary step of dissolving the Second Chamber and calling a new election. The king was pleased to be able in this way to demonstrate his political power and use the dissolution prerogative, which the 1809 Swedish Constitution gave him but which until then had seemed a dead letter.[49]

The members of Parliament were apparently losing control of developments. Most of their scheduled term in office had passed without any final decision on the tariff issue. Now an extra election had been called on the very issue that the M.P.'s, who opposed the concept of an imperative mandate, would have preferred not to ask the public to decide on.

---

[48] Sundberg 1961, p. 4.

[49] Was the dissolution of the Second Chamber an expression of strategic action, for example, of the strategy described in Chapter 1 as "referring the issue to another body"? In other words, was the Chamber dissolved in order to avoid a defeat on the tariff issue at the first joint vote and instead let the issue be resolved by means of a parliamentary election, which the free traders thought they had a better chance of winning? Although it may seem that way superficially, a more detailed analysis does not support this interpretation. First and foremost, Prime Minister Themptander does not at all appear to have been determined to try to win the tariff dispute through strategic action. On the contrary, he was fairly resigned to defeat and had, as mentioned previously, asked to be allowed to step down on account of growing protectionist opinion. In addition, Themptander does not seem to have believed the free traders would win the upcoming election; in other words, he overestimated the strength of protectionist opinion. In his world view, the people were by no means a more reliable decision-making body than was Parliament in bringing about a free-trade victory. As for the other key actor representing government power, King Oscar II, he was admittedly a moderate free trader. But the primary motive for his action was, as mentioned earlier, constitutional rather than related to tariff policy per se. He wanted to assert his authority against dangerous modern tendencies by invoking his prerogative to dissolve the chamber. See Petré 1945, pp. 131–156, esp. p. 155, for the king's attitude.

Ideology and strategy

The election campaign during the spring of 1887 was intensive. When we speak of how the Swedish people were politically awakened by the tariff controversy, the main evidence available is the sharp increase in the number of people who voted in this election. After the parliamentary reform of 1866, a maximum of 25 percent of eligible voters had used their franchise. Now the level jumped to 48 percent. From this time on, we can speak of elections to Parliament based on political views and national parties in the modern sense. The strengths of the parties in this "tariff election" would also remain remarkably stable in geographic terms. Studies have indicated how the regional patterns of free traders and protectionists visible in the spring of 1887 can be seen in the distribution of socialist and nonsocialist votes well into our own age; for example, a systematic comparison with the 1968 election has been made.[50]

The protectionists came out unexpectedly badly in the election. Only 85 protectionist M.P.'s were elected, whereas the free traders obtained 136 seats.

After the election, when Parliament resumed its work during the summer of 1887, time was short for those who wished to preserve what little freedom of action politicians still enjoyed on the tariff issue. Some M.P.'s then tried the classic method for bringing about a nondecision: They proposed that the government appoint a commission of inquiry on the tariff issue. The proposed commission received the express support of the prime minister himself, who apologized for once again breaking with the custom that members of the government should refrain from taking part in deliberations of this kind.[51]

But it was too late to pour oil on the waters. The nondecision strategy suffered yet another defeat when the proposal to appoint a commission was rejected. A protectionistic count expressed his burning indignation at the idea of a commission: "This proposal, a proposal that postpones the issue, a proposal that completely mutilates our demands, this proposal was intended to calm the excitement in our country. . . . No, gentlemen, it appears as if the lighted torch will be allowed to burn until it has burned out and one view or the other has been suppressed."[52]

In the regularly scheduled election during the fall of 1887, the protectionists gained ground. They increased their representation to 97 against 125 for the free traders. At that point, a sensational event occurred. It was discovered that 1 of the 22 free traders from the city of Stockholm, a steam

---

[50] Lewin 1972, pp. 191ff.; Carlsson 1953, p. 396; Pär-Erik Back, *Det svenska partiväsendet* (Stockholm: Almqvist & Wiksell, 1967), pp. 3, 13ff., and 77–92.

[51] FK 1887 B:16, pp. 27ff., quotation from p. 28 (Tamm), and FK 1887 B:17, pp. 21–22 (Themptander). The event is mentioned by Per Sondén, *Hugo Tamm till Fånöö. Hans liv och åskådning* (Stockholm: Svenska kyrkans diakonistyrelsens bokförlag, 1925), p. 317.

[52] FK 1887 B:16, pp. 31–32 (Strömfelt).

kitchen manager named Olof Larsson, owed 11 kronor and fifty-eight öre in unpaid municipal taxes. According to the Parliament Act, this misdeed not only disqualified "Ångköks-Olle" (Steam-Kitchen Olle) himself, but all the candidates on any list that included his name. A Supreme Court ruling resulted in the replacement of 22 free traders with 22 protectionists, thereby giving the protectionists a majority in both chambers.

A quirk of fate had thus decided a dispute in which the nation's most important political forces had been embroiled for three years. Could such a result be described as the result of rational political action? Even if we political scientists have now learned from rational choice theory not to have any illusions when looking at the ability of decision rules to turn individual preferences into collective decisions, the regulation in the Parliament Act that now decided the matter seems "preposterous" – to quote one researcher.[53]

Or did the new protariff majority created by the disqualification of the Stockholm free-trader election slate actually mean that Parliament better reflected public opinion? Elis Håstad asked this question in a study of election statistics. His cautious answer is: "Although the votes cast indicate that the free traders probably had a slight edge, it may be argued that the protectionists had a somewhat stronger position, among other things considering the higher population figure in their election districts and because the number of votes for free traders, now as always, was favored by a higher election turnout in the cities. In any case the composition of the Chamber before the disqualification of the Stockholm slate was hardly an adequate reflection of the public mood; again, it cannot be definitely stated that seating 22 protariff M.P.'s in place of free traders was a wondrous act of statistical justice, but it is undoubtedly within the realm of possibility.[54]

The free-trader government submitted its resignation. The king tried to prevent this. To change governments now would be "to accord far too much immediate significance to the verdict of the ballot box," the king argued in his letter of reply to the government. "Sweden's form of government according to the 1809 Instrument of Government is constitutional, but not parliamentary in the modern sense of this word."[55] But in the end, the king had to give in and a new government was formed. The change of system thus took place during the 1888 session of Parliament. Tariffs were imposed on a long list of goods, both foods and industrial products.

The members of Parliament had failed in their nondecision strategy on the tariff issue. They had tried to protect their constitutional right to find

---

[53] Sten Carlsson and Jerker Rosén, *Svensk historia II. Tiden efter 1718* (Stockholm: Bonniers, 1961), p. 561.

[54] Håstad 1941, pp. 123–124.

[55] The king's letter, reproduced in Petré 1945, pp. 295ff., quotations on pp. 296 and 295.

solutions that were in the best interests of their country, freely and independently of popular opinion. As late as the 1884 election campaign, they had avoided discussing tariffs. They were thus not bound by campaign promises when the new Parliament immediately tackled the tariff issue. But this process generated forces that the M.P.'s could soon no longer control. The voice of the people genuinely reached them for the first time, and many of them were not unwilling to listen when the country was in need. The call for tariffs was not just any old issue; it revealed a profound ideological conflict about the responsibility of the state for economic activity in the country. In their ambition to persuade and their unwillingness to compromise, the M.P.'s were finally driven to a point where they were compelled to ask for the views of the people in what, in practice, was a referendum on tariffs. During the campaign for this extra election, the Swedish people showed an unprecedented interest in politics; what was more, this interest had come to stay. In the future, the will of the people would be accorded a decisive influence on the policies approved by Parliament. In other words, the M.P.'s not only failed to keep the tariff issue away from a public decision. They also helped bring about a change in the rules of the political game, in which their traditional independence vis-à-vis public opinion disappeared. It is hard to imagine a more spectacular political collapse than the defeat of the nondecision strategy of Swedish M.P.'s on the tariff issue.

3. THE BREAKTHROUGH OF THE POPULAR WILL

Why did the tariff dispute establish the principle that the popular will would determine the position of Parliament, despite the fact that this principle not only went against the Parliament Act but was also heartily disliked by both free traders and protectionists?

We will attempt to answer this question by summarizing and clarifying the previous discussion, using a game matrix. According to our interpretation, in principle there were two alternatives for the M.P.'s to choose: *to be silent* or *to speak out*. Silence was their original strategy during the tariff dispute. This prevented M.P.'s from becoming bound by campaign promises on the tariff issue and protected their independence vis-à-vis popular opinion. If, on the other hand, the M.P.'s expressed their ideological conviction by speaking out, this would lead to a public debate that would commit the M.P.'s to these views, and the popular will would ultimately determine the position chosen by Parliament. Both free traders and protectionists wanted to avoid the latter scenario. Nevertheless, this was the outcome of the dispute.

The game matrix in Table 2.1 attempts to show how developments could be pushed to this point, completely contrary to the wishes of the

Table 2.1. *The tariff game: the independence of M.P.'s versus the popular will*

	Protectionists	
	Remain silent	Speak out
Free traders Remain silent	0, 0	−2, +2
Speak out	+2, −2	−1, −1

actors. If both free traders and protectionists chose the alternative of remaining silent, the prevailing conditions would be preserved. Things would change for neither better nor worse, and the outcome in the upper left-hand quadrant of the matrix can thus be labeled with a utility value of 0 for both parties. If both of them spoke out, the constitutionally guaranteed independence of M.P.'s would be gambled away, and, as indicated earlier, both parties considered this a worse outcome. In the lower right quadrant we thus assume a utility of −1 for both players.

But what would happen if one of them was silent and the other spoke out? When their silence was broken, it was as if a dam had burst. The tariff issue rapidly became the dominant political litmus test. When the voters were finally asked what the composition of the Second Chamber should be, they allowed the candidates' position on the tariff issue to determine how they voted in the election. Any attempt to remain silent on the tariff issue in the election campaigns of 1887 would have entailed a very sizable risk of incurring the displeasure of the voters and being defeated by the opposing candidate. Expressed in utility values, this outcome would have meant −2 for the loser and +2 for the winner. These figures thus also imply the conclusion that, in the end, the M.P.'s became more intensively committed to implementing their actual program in the increasingly heated tariff dispute – a new tariff system or not – than to scoring points with an abstractly phrased critique of the imperative mandate.

The mathematical structure of this game matrix is the same as in the example in Chapter 1. In other words, we see yet another example of the "prisoners' dilemma."

During the tariff controversy, M.P.'s were driven by the logic of the situation inexorably toward a point of equilibrium that was not the best choice for either party. Both the prospect of increasing the utility number to +2 and the risk of reducing it to −2 made the M.P.'s vacate the best quadrant at the upper left-hand corner in Table 2.1, which they originally occupied. But when both sides reasoned this way, they ended up against their will in the lower right-hand quadrant in Table 2.1. Yet each of them had acted rationally, that is, in such a way as to maximize their respective utilities. Individual rational behavior is no guarantee that the collective decision will also be rational.

The dilemma of the M.P.'s during the tariff dispute was the same as that of the prisoners. They ended up in a decision-making situation they could not control. When an attempt was made in the summer of 1887 to escape from the dilemma by removing the tariff issue from the agenda and appointing a commission of inquiry, this proposal was indignantly rejected. The torch that had been lit by the tariff dispute had to be allowed to burn until it faded away and one side or the other had been defeated. When the tariff controversy flared up in earnest, there was no longer any chance of the kind of cooperation between the two sides that could have resulted in an agreement to stick with the alternative found in the upper left-hand quadrant, which represents the collectively rational decision.[56] In practice, there was just as little opportunity for communication between the two sides in the tariff dispute as in the illustration using prisoners locked in solitary confinement. Without any discussion, the M.P.'s remained fixed in their ideological convictions. "All or nothing" became the guiding principle of parliamentary work. But in this way, against their will, they helped bring about the breakthrough of the popular will in Swedish politics.

4. THE IMPERATIVE MANDATE

Until the very end, it had been unclear who would win the tariff dispute. The members of Parliament had tried to estimate the relative strengths of the two sides. Diaries and letters from 1887 that are preserved today contain "the calculations on our positions that were undertaken almost daily within both parties."[57]

Because it was conceivable that either side might win, there was reason to consider whether the tariff dispute could finally be decided with the help of any decision rule other than a simple majority. People thought of the imperative mandate. Instead of allowing the issue to be decided by an uncertain vote among M.P.'s, it was possible to let the opinions of the voters decide the issue. This view was expressed by free traders in particular as the protectionists gained strength. Faced by the danger of losing on the issue itself, they were prepared to jettison their independence. There was a conflict between the choice of strategy and the choice of decision rule, which illustrates with extreme clarity the dilemma of the M.P.'s during the tariff dispute.

[56] As for this solution to the "prisoners' dilemma," see Chapter 6.
[57] Petré 1945, p. 141.

Tariffs

Two arguments against the imperative mandate are usually presented. The first concerns respect for national unity. If an M.P. is regarded as representing only his own election district or certain special interests, there will be no one who takes responsibility for the country as a whole; if key decisions have to be confirmed by instructions from their principals, national power is undermined.

The second concerns the need for a Parliament capable of action. "A Parliament . . . with the imperative mandate is qualified to act only as far as the instructions to its members extend. Even this is enough to make the imperative mandate unreasonable in a modern state – all the more unreasonable the more powerful the Parliament is. For in our age, it may often be especially necessary for the will of the state to be expressed rapidly."[58] The voters do not have the same political overview as M.P.'s. They cannot know in advance how the parliamentary agenda will look. They cannot foresee what strategies are possible. In short – to use a term from rational choice theory – the imperative mandate makes strategic action impossible. As the danger of a dissolution of Sweden into regions diminished, this latter argument grew in importance.

It is not true that the principle of the imperative mandate triumphed during the tariff controversy, despite everything that people said along these lines at the time. The ban on the imperative mandate in the Parliament Act remained in force until the major overhaul of the Constitution in the 1970s. The fact that the ban was then removed is not considered to have changed anything in practice.[59] As earlier, however, there continued

---

[58] Gränström 1915, p. 323.

[59] Both the report of the government-appointed commission of inquiry on the Constitution, SOU 1963:17, pp. 312–313, and the report of the constitutional drafting committee, SOU 1972:15, p. 19, proposed that the rule be retained. The minister responsible, however, was influenced by the criticism presented by the Svea Appeals Court in its official comments, to the effect that the stipulation was of no practical importance today. The issue at hand, instead, was to what extent M.P.'s should be considered bound by the views adopted by their parties. Because the reports themselves had emphasized the great importance of political parties in Sweden's democratic system, the appeals court felt it was inappropriate to state "fictions" such as those contained in the constitutional rule. It was also possible to point out that the rule might give the impression that M.P.'s were not bound by ordinary law. The minister added that the proposal had not considered the fact that in deciding on appropriation issues, M.P.'s have to take into account expenditures authorized by existing law. Prop 1973:90, pp. 261–262 and bil (appendix) 3, p. 183. One comment on the constitution states: "The absence of the rule from the Parliament Act has probably not actually changed anything. The fact remains that M.P.'s not infrequently actually vote against their party's policy and that they sometimes do so on matters very important to the party. The party's weapon against a member who deviates too much is to exclude him from the work of the party in Parliament and, ultimately, to make sure he is not reelected. The party has no right to withdraw his mandate. And it is certainly proper that in performing their tasks the members are bound by law, and likewise that they must respect the obligations the state may have on such matters as expenditures. But no sanctions may be enforced against a member who does not feel bound by these in a vote." Erik Holmberg and Nils Stjernquist, *Grundlagarna* (Stockholm: Norstedt, 1980), p. 176.

to be certain tendencies toward imperative mandates, especially in periods of strong political conflicts such as in the extra election of 1914, when the imperative mandate was once again rejected.[60]

The change in the relationship between M.P.'s and the voters brought about by the tariff dispute is best described in other terms. The break-through of popular will triggered a change in the Swedish theory of representation itself.[61] Until then, the assumption was that M.P.'s were representatives – that is, they took the place of and played the part of the entire Swedish people and could speak on its behalf on all occasions with full sovereignty. The appearance of the party system inevitably meant that the candidates who were elected to office represented special interests – those of free trade or protectionism, later those of liberalism, socialism, or conservatism. It was not meaningful to say that an M.P. belonging to a particular party represented the entire Swedish people. The modern M.P. represents his party and the voters who cast their ballots for it. From this, it follows that the independence of M.P.'s vis-à-vis the will of the people cannot be maintained. A member of Parliament achieves his position because of the trust he enjoys from his party. Formally, he is entitled to vote differently from his party, and his mandate cannot be recalled. But if he loses the trust he enjoys from his party, he loses his political platform. The tariff controversy brought an end to the independence of M.P.'s. But their new dependence on the popular will would be different from what people generally assumed at the time when they spoke of the imperative mandate. It became a dependence on the popular will as expressed through political parties, which are the organizers of political life in our century.

The tariff dispute triggered a crisis for the political system. It not only led to a major change in practical policy when tariffs were introduced. The controversy also introduced a new decision rule that, in the long term, would undermine the traditional means by which deliberative bodies arrived at collective decisions. The assumption that an M.P. represented the Swedish people, whether his voters expressed any opinions or not, could no longer be maintained. The M.P. of the future would be compelled to subject himself to the values of his voters and his party. A death-blow had been aimed at the system of independent M.P.'s, who autonomously formed their own opinions on social issues. The age of democracy and of the party system was about to begin.

[60] P. O. Gränström, "Om tendenser till imperativt mandat under oppositionen mot Karl XIV Johan," *Statsvetenskaplig tidskrift* (1915): 145–146.
[61] Cf. Bengt Owe Bergersson and Jörgen Westerståhl, *Den svenska folkstyrelsen* (Stockholm: Liber, 1979), pp. 161ff.

3

Suffrage

1. UPPER-CLASS RULE OR POPULAR RULE?

The tariff dispute was over. For the first time, the people had let their voice be heard.The actual opinion they had expressed was a matter of debate. But one thing was clear: The issue of the people's right to play a part in governing the country had irrevocably arrived on the political agenda.

The tariff issue was depoliticized soon after the 1888 law was adopted; it was like a flame that had flared up quickly in the forecourt of Swedish parliamentism.[1] Succeeding it as the new, dominant political litmus test was the suffrage issue. With their roots among broad categories of urban consumers, free traders were usually supporters of expanded suffrage, whereas the protectionists, with their base among prosperous rural free-holders, feared the urban masses and opposed a broader franchise. But as we have seen, there were also free traders who opposed radical reforms of voting rights.[2] During a transitional period there is thus reason to count not only the Left (mainly Liberals and Social Democrats) and the Right (mainly Conservatives, who coalesced into a modern party soon after the turn of the century) but also a third party. In this case it was "the moderate free traders," who in the two-dimensional Swedish domestic politics of the early 1890s combined support of free trade with opposition to universal manhood suffrage,[3] before the voting rights issue overshadowed all other issues. All attempts to broaden the franchise failed, however, because no reform policy was able to gather the requisite majority. Para-doxically, it was a Conservative government that later ended upper-class rule by pushing through the 1907–1909 constitutional reform and intro-

---

[1] The expression is taken from Per Sundberg, *Ministärerna Bildt och Åkerhielm. En studie i den svenska parlamentarismens förgårdar* (Stockholm, 1961).

[2] FK 1886 (Ericson).

[3] Leif Lewin, Bo Jansson, and Dag Sörbom, *The Swedish Electorate 1887–1968* (Stockholm: Almqvist & Wiksell, 1972), pp. 215–216.

ducing universal manhood suffrage to the Second Chamber of Parliament. In 1918–1921, voting rights became truly universal when women also gained the vote; universal and equal suffrage was also applied for the first time to local elections.

The Conservative party's opposition to broadening the franchise entailed a defense of the existing rules. These had been created when Louis De Geer's parliamentary reform of 1866 replaced the four estates with a bicameral Parliament. Just as the De Geer government – by virtue of Finance Minister Gripenstedt's free-trade reforms – was at the root of the tariff dispute, its reform of Parliament also created the starting point of the suffrage dispute. But whereas this government inspired a radical ideology on tariffs, it furnished arguments to the conservative camp on the second issue.

According to the Parliament Act of 1866, the First Chamber was elected by the county councils and by the municipal councils of Sweden's largest cities; local voting rights, in turn, were graded by income and wealth. Because of extremely restrictive regulations, only a very few people could run for public office. The Second Chamber was elected by majority vote, with each voting district outside of the major cities electing one M.P. The right to vote in Second Chamber elections was open to men aged twenty-one or older who owned property with an assessed value of at least a thousand riksdaler, leased agricultural property assessed at six thousand riksdaler or more, or had an income of at least eight hundred riksdaler. Another restriction on voting rights was that a person had to have paid his local taxes. This requirement also applied to candidates for public office, and, as we have seen, it played a fateful role in the tariff dispute.

In the lengthy and fruitless debate on the suffrage, some people called for a tightening of the requirements on voters: payment of national as well as local taxes for the past year or, in other proposals, up to three years; restrictions related to compulsory military service, poor relief, and bankruptcy; double voting rights for all men aged forty or older and also for all married men, and so on and so forth. A multitude of rules made it possible to devise clever proposals on voting rights by lowering or raising the various restrictions. But in all essential respects, the rules spelled out in the Parliament Act of 1866 remained in force.

In 1866 rules gave the franchise to 5.5 percent of the Swedish population, or roughly 21 percent of all legally competent men. Only a few new people gained the right to vote during the next few decades due to inflation and rising salaries and wages. Louis De Geer's intention had been to place power "in the hands of the middle class." But this was not at all the case. The First Chamber became even more dominated by high-born aristocrats and plutocrats than the Estate of the Nobility before 1866. The new bicameral Parliament turned into much more of an instrument of upper-class rule than De Geer had foreseen.[4]

De Geer tried to create a Second Chamber with approximately the same rules that had previously applied to the two lowest estates. No one who had been entitled to vote for these estates would be deprived of his franchise. New categories of citizens had become eligible to vote. But within the categories already eligible, the suffrage would not be broadened.[5]

Suffrage would thus continue to be limited, "because to ensure a calm social order, it may be important to restrict the right to vote to persons with living conditions that may be regarded as leaving some time and inclination free for independent participation in political life." De Geer regarded wealth as the best basis of qualification. "Ownership of property may generally be assumed to indicate a more secure and independent position than that of an ordinary wage earner, even if the latter has a good income for the moment, and to result in a great interest in the improvement and welfare of society." The property requirement was thus set relatively low, the income requirement relatively high.[6]

Two lines of reasoning emerge from the text of the 1861–1862 government bill we have quoted here. The right to vote should be granted on the basis of wealth and ability. On the one hand, wealth is presented as a reason in itself for the franchise, because it provides a secure, economically independent position. On the other hand, wealth generates a greater interest in the welfare of society. One researcher has pointed out how the emphasis in De Geer's arguments alternates between one line of reasoning and the other. "Wealth is sometimes portrayed as having its own intrinsic value and being the bearer of interests that entitle people to vote, sometimes as the representative or indicator of certain conceptual values."[7] Thus, for example, De Geer had said he wanted the First Chamber to represent "the conservatism of wealth." But a few lines later, he spoke of the greater ability possessed by the wealthy. "It is likely that higher education and more extensive experience are generally also to be sought within these categories."[8]

Members of the estate of the Clergy, which had had everything to lose from the parliamentary reform, had denied that wealth was a sign of ability. The "golden pale of money" – not education, experience, or maturity – was now being granted political power.[9] But in the industrial society

---

[4] Georg Andrén, *Tvåkammarsystemets tillkomst och utveckling. Sveriges Riksdag* II:9 (Stockholm, 1937), p. 73.

[5] Andrén 1937, p. 61.

[6] Prop 1862/63:61, p. 41.

[7] Andrén 1937, p. 61.

[8] Prop 1862/63:61, p. 43.

[9] KU (Proceedings of the Constitution Committee) 1862/63:7, p. 31.

that was now beginning to emerge, victory went to capital's claims to guarantee conceptual values. It has been aptly stated that capital "was not only mobilized during the first golden age of European liberalism; it was also nobilized."[10]

During twenty years of suffrage debate between the time of the tariff dispute and the introduction of universal manhood suffrage in elections to the Second Chamber of Parliament, opponents of universal suffrage adhered to the De Geer's dual principle of limiting the franchise with regard to wealth and ability. Let us now examine the parliamentary debates more closely to see how the Right developed its arguments.

The first main feature of opposition to broader voting rights was thus a defense of what were regarded as the legitimate interests of wealth. The 1866 reform had not placed power in the hands of the middle class but in those of landowners, especially the large landowners. Their political position was threatened by demands for extending the franchise. Without being concealed in any ideological reasoning, the class interests of rural property owners were presented as arguments in the suffrage debate. In 1902, for instance, the Constitution Committee of Parliament justified its rejection of suffrage demands with the following words: "The committee wished to prevent the representatives of landowners' important interests from being reduced to an insignificant minority in the Second Chamber in order to make room for an overwhelming majority of representatives of the so-called working class."[11] Some years earlier, a professor and member of the Second Chamber had tried to explain what a broadening of voting rights would mean from a class standpoint. It meant "no less than that those classes that from time immemorial had been the bearers of political life, would completely hand over power to another class that has not previously had any political rights – they would simply abdicate completely."[12] In the major suffrage debate of 1906, when the Left had gathered an increasing number of supporters even among farmers, one M.P. expressed his "amazement and surprise that so many among Sweden's farmer class are really working with hands and feet to bring about the political downfall of their class," and he quoted De Geer's words about the importance of landowners to the peace and improvement of the country and their role as a secure counterweight to anarchism, communism, and socialism.[13]

The conservatism of wealth was thus regarded as guaranteeing that the country would develop calmly. There were "special reasons why those

---

[10] Andrén 1937, p. 65.
[11] KU 1902:6, p. 99.
[12] AK 1894:30, p. 49 (Boethius).
[13] AK 1906:54, p. 47 (Hermelin).

who posssess the property of the realm should enjoy a decisive word. This is because in time of danger, they cannot take it with them and depart for other places; they have to stay where they have their property and suffer what happens to them. Yet he who has no such thing, but is entirely unattached, he can much more easily remove himself from danger. This circumstance provides a guarantee that those who have something to lose and are tied to their property must be more eager for calm development and must not easily participate in things that may bring about upheavals or dangerous shifts in the development of national life."[14] The Swedish Parliament should continue to rely on "the permanently domiciled population," and "not on the loose classes to whom people are now trying to extend voting rights."[15] The broadening of the electorate entailed the risk of tearing down Christian culture and legal order. Again, the guarantee against such an eventuality would be "to accord a preponderant political influence to the landowning class of our country."[16]

The parallels between land ownership and social calm were sometimes pushed even further. Debators formulated arguments that not only attributed social calm to property ownership. Farmers themselves were portrayed as especially calm and quiet, in sharp contrast to the supporters of voting rights, "these popular speakers, these agitators and these chairmen of demonstrations. . . . Can it be proper and right to let these people come to power? Power now belongs to the thoughtful, quiet Swedish country people, who in all ages have placed themselves under the shelter and protection of laws and constitutions and religion."[17] These are words that hark back to Edmund Burke, the ideologist of classic conservatism. Burke, too, had believed that representation should be based on wealth and ability: "But as ability is a vigorous and active principle, and as property is sluggish, inert, and timid, it never can be safe from the invasions of ability, unless it be, out of all proportion, predominant in the representation."[18]

Assuming that wealth was a sign of ability, one might think that wealth could defend itself. This, it was feared, would not be the case if universal suffrage were combined with majority rule in a decision-making body, because the lower classes would then be able to attack wealth without listening to arguments.

More concretely, some debators justified the overrepresentation of the wealthy by pointing to the structure of tax policy. Because the wealthy paid more taxes, they should also have more of a say.[19] Replying to

---

[14] AK 1890:28, p. 32 (Redelius).
[15] FK 1888:21, p. 36 (Casparsson).
[16] FK 1902:35, p. 24 (Rodhe).
[17] AK 1890:28, pp. 22–23 (Jansson).
[18] Edmund Burke, *Reflections on the Revolution in France,* with a foreword by Conor Cruise O'Brien (London: Penguin, 1969), p. 140. The book was first published in 1790.
[19] FK 1893:32, p. 45 (Billing); AK 1894:30, p. 51 (Boethius).

57

demands by workers for voting rights without having to pay taxes, they introduced the principle that people who make spending decisions should also know what it feels like to pay the costs.[20] It was only fair that "those who pay much more in taxes should have more of a say than those who pay less in taxes or nothing at all."[21] The Right could show how even the father of liberalism had wanted to make voting power contingent on the amount of taxes paid. In a 1906 debate in Parliament, Liberal party chairman Karl Staaff was thus played off against John Stuart Mill by M.P.'s who triumphantly quoted Mill's words to the effect that giving the vote to those who did not pay taxes was a violation of the fundamental priciples of a free constitution.[22]

Others pointed out that a change in suffrage rules was unnecessary because inflation and wage hikes continuously pushed new groups over the minimum. Was "it not enough under current circumstances to let this uniform growth under the system of government approved in 1865 continue?"[23] Suffrage rules did not need to be changed "when the natural trend is such that a steadily greater number of people come to enjoy the right to vote and when the suffrage thus grows by itself,"[24] an excellent example of what the conservatives called "development based on existing conditions."[25] A modern reader cannot suppress the reflection that the emphasis in this phrase lay on the second part. For when the Constitution Committee presented arguments against changing the suffrage rules in the form of statistical data, it could only show an increase in the number of eligible voters averaging 0.5 percent for each parliamentary term of office during the period 1872–1893.[26] Of course the Conservatives could be criticized for so stubbornly adhering to the limits that had once been established, one Conservative admitted. But if changes were permitted, it ought to be possible not only to make modifications "forward" but also "backward, as we have also recently seen in the kingdom of Saxony, where in order to save the social order it was considered necessary to push back voting rights, which had been expanded there, inside the permissible limits."[27]

The other main point in the Conservative opposition to universal suffrage was that wealth was a sign of ability. Year after year the Constitution Committee rejected the call for broadening the franchise. "A fairly secure economic position provides the likelihood, if not the certainty, of

[20] AK 1899:34, p. 29 (Ivar Månsson).
[21] FK 1902:35, p. 18 (Billing).
[22] FK 1906:48, p. 73 (Nyström).
[23] FK 1899:27, pp. 25–26 (Åkerhielm).
[24] FK 1888:21, p. 36 (Casparsson).
[25] FK 1893:32, pp. 58–59 (Nyström).
[26] KU 1899:14, p. 9.
[27] FK 1896:23, pp. 45–46 (Treffenberg).

a more independent participation in political life, as well as of the maturity of judgment and experience without which the stability of the social order can easily be upset."[28]

In conservative ideological debate, the arguments against universal manhood suffrage became increasingly sophisticated. A few years later, the Constitution Committee prefaced its rejection with an ideological argument on the rights of the individual and the interests of the state, in which it attempted to refute the Left's main argument that every legally competent citizen should be entitled to vote regardless of his economic position. As the committee saw it, the issue of individual rights was not relevant in this connection. The franchise should be given to those who had shown signs of general worthiness by means of their wealth. "For in the opinion of the Committee, it is not primarily the rights of the individual that should determine the issue of broadening political voting rights, but the best interests of the state. It is thus both the right and duty of the state to ensure that suffrage regulations are designed not to accord a preponderant influence to those members of society who have the smallest prerequisites for attaining the independence, the maturity of political judgment and the experience that should be found among those to whom influence on matters of state should be entrusted."[29]

Now, of course, those who had acquired their wealth through inheritance also enjoyed the right to vote. Could an inherited fortune also be a sign of ability to serve the public? Yes, this was the case: "If it is inherited money, it often means education and an interest in public affairs; if it is earned money, it often means thrift, industriousness and energy."[30] One proposal for certain changes in the minimum tax level for voting was rejected because it was not considered fair "that a person who inherited a large fortune in money and other chattels and who did not have the right to vote on other grounds was deprived of this for at least two years while a person who acquired property of comparatively small value immediately gained the right to vote."[31] Here the committee's conservative majority forgot what it otherwise always argued – that it was the owners of fixed assets who guaranteed stable social development.

A wealthy person had more time and interest to devote to social issues. He should thus be given the right to vote. The same concept could also be expressed negatively: A poor person had to devote all his time to working, had no time to form an independent opinion on social issues, and was thus not ripe for the suffrage. "The hard work with which our workers

---

[28] KU 1890:9, p. 6 is quoted here. Similarly worded statements are found in the official recommendations of the Constitution Committee throughout the 1890s.

[29] KU 1899:14, p. 5.

[30] FK 1902:35, p. 65 (Palmstierna).

[31] KU 1896:11, p. 19.

are occupied, insolvency, shortages, poverty, the uncertainty of their whole existence, in short all these weighty concerns that every man with a heart would very much like to lift from them if he could, must necessarily limit their political range of vision to comparatively narrow conditions, but on the other hand make their senses open and receptive to the teachings of those social improvers who single out the existing social order as the root and origin of all evil. It is thus also to be feared that if they ever came to power, they would exercise it without recoiling from the violent overthrow of social conditions, which overthrow they naturally feel they have nothing to lose from, but everything to gain."[32]

This fear of the leaders of the working class ran like a red thread through the conservative opposition to broadening the suffrage. When they spoke about "independence" of political judgment, it was independence in relation to socialism and other movements based on collectivism that they were mainly thinking of. They argued that the interests of the workers would not be furthered by the broadening of voting rights. It would only benefit "a bunch of party leaders,"[33] "these leaders of the crowds of workers,"[34] "the agitators,"[35] "certain professional politicians."[36]

The Conservatives considered it indisputable that an extension of voting rights would primarily hurt those who had shown the greatest ability to serve their native country in a responsible way. In 1893 one member of the First Chamber attacked with eloquent passion the demands of the Left, which he regarded as an obstacle to recruiting the most qualified people to the Swedish Parliament. As a warning lesson, he pointed to "the promised land of universal suffrage, America." There "corruption had spread" and "the label politician, which should be a title of honor, has become a term of abuse." The speaker examined one occupational group after another in detail, showing how their representation would be affected if the Left's demands for a broader franchise were approved. His conclusion was unequivocal: "It is thus those groups who represent education, wealth and a firm, independent social position who would lose influence and the loose, amorphous social classes that would gain increased influence." It was thus important now to make sure that reforms of voting rights did not exclude qualified people. "It is a general experience that the more voting rights are extended, the lower the level of representation."[37]

The notion of giving greater decision-making rights to the talented was developed into an advanced, so-called organic theory, especially in the

---

[32] FK 1896:23, p. 40 (Säve).
[33] FK 1896:23, p. 30 (Nyström).
[34] AK 1899:34, p. 30 (Ivar Månsson).
[35] Ibid., p. 42 (Lindblad).
[36] FK 1902:35, p. 24 (Rodhe). See also n. 17 above.
[37] FK 1893:32, pp. 51–52 (Casparsson).

speculations of political scientists. According to this theory, the state was an organism whose various body parts corresponded to different social classes. The monarch and the upper classes corresponded to its head and higher functions, the working classes to its lower functions. Progress had to follow the laws of this social organism, assuming the form of the quiet growth of the organism without sudden changes. This state organism had its own goal and its own will. Because the people consisted of past, present, and future generations, the will of the people could not be ascertained by asking only the generation now living.[38] Rudolf Kjellén, a professor of political science, maintained that universal suffrage was against "the order of nature and the organism of the people." In order to uphold its will, it was necessary to "demand barriers against the murky flood of private interests to prevent it from pouring over the whole state and undermining its unity. Such barriers are called suffrage guarantees, and in our age a patriotic association must devote itself to opposing such campaigns for broader voting rights which fundamentally aim at depriving us of all guarantees of our native country's unity and organic structure."[39] In Parliament, another political scientist rejected universal suffrage because it was a way for popular opinion to make itself heard only "through a numerical–mechanical advantage," "not an organic, but a temporary collection of numbers."[40]

Organic theory thus provided a way of rejecting views even when they were supported by a majority and of arguing that they conflicted with the ideology of the public organism. This doctrine, which was constantly being cited, was extremely influential because it was taught as part of the curriculum in philosophy and political science and became something of a bureaucratic philosophy for Sweden's higher civil servants. The mutual status and rights of the various social classes were postulated. It was not necessary to investigate whether such a harmony of interests among the classes existed. "In this way," writes Herbert Tingsten, "the prevailing philosophy became a coulisse of suggestive concepts fitted together into an artistic pattern that concealed personal interests and social struggles."[41]

The class interests of farmers would seem to have little in common with this subtle academic metaphysics. But the consequences of both arguments were the same: Suffrage rules should be designed in such a way as to assure the members of the ruling class in society greater political influence than others. Wealth had its own interests that deserved to be represented. It

[38] Herbert Tingsten, *De konservativa idéerna* (Stockholm: Bonniers, 1939), pp. 93–97; Nils Elvander, *Harald Hjärne och konservatismen. Konservativ idédebatt i Sverige 1865–1922* (Stockholm: Almqvist & Wiksell, 1961), pp. 10ff.

[39] Rudolf Kjellén, *Om uppgiften för ett fosterländskt förbund* (Gothenburg, 1896), p. 7.

[40] FK 1893:32, p. 57 (Nyström).

[41] Herbert Tingsten, *Den svenska socialdemokratiens idéutveckling I* (Stockholm: Tiden, 1941), p. 29.

was also a sign of the ability to form an opinion on public issues in an independent, responsible way.

The Left rallied around the demand for universal manhood suffrage. "One man – one vote" was the slogan. A citizens's rights should not depend on his economic positon. Everyone must personally participate in electing the representatives of the people. As time went on, this view was expressed more radically: not merely a lowering of all barriers but their elimination, not only an equal franchise to the Second Chamber but also in local elections, not only universal and equal voting rights for men but also for women.

The Left justified its opinion mainly by citing the so-called personality principle. From among numerous prosuffrage arguments, this principle emerged as the rallying point for the Left. It had pretensions of representing a morally higher view than the Right's defense of monied interests. The personality principle had been introduced as early as 1840 by Erik Gustaf Geijer, who had argued at the time that representation should be based on individual personality. The day was long past when the interest groups in society could be represented in other ways – for example, through the four estates. The individual himself was best qualified to safeguard his interests. Each citizen should thus be given the right to vote, provided that he had a minimal understanding of Christianity and other knowledge required by the public schools. Geijer had warned that a "slave class" lacking in rights was emerging in Sweden. Rather than respond with violence, it was better to show justice to all people by granting them the right to represent their own personal interests in politics.[42]

Adolf Hedin had expressly used the personality principle to justify his suffrage demands immediately after the 1866 parliamentary reform. With others, he turned the New Liberal Society into a meeting place for those who did not regard De Geer's reform as having gone far enough. In his letters to the members of the reformed Parliament, entitled "What the people expect of their new representatives," he had attacked "the worship of money" with radical arguments, using a vocabulary reminiscent of the arguments that members of the estate of the Clergy had aimed at the reform from their conservative perspective.[43]

S. A. Hedlund had advocated the personality principle in his famous members' bill of 1880, in which he persuaded the Second Chamber to begin supporting a move to cut voting requirements in half. Opposition

---

[42] Carl Arvid Hessler, *Geijer som politiker II. Hans senare utveckling* (Stockholm: Gebers, 1947), pp. 280ff.

[43] Adolf Hedin, "Hvad folk väntar af den nya representationen. Femton bref från en demokrat till svenska riksdagens medlemmar," 1867, in *Tal och skrifter*, ed. Valfrid Spångberg (Stockholm: Bonniers, 1904), pp. 15, 32, and 54.

from the First Chamber killed his proposal, however. According to Hedlund, the broader the basis for representation, the greater the chances that everyone's rights would be observed. The happiest society was one where animosity between the powerful and the weak was reduced by means of concessions by the powerful, so that the lower classes could also assume their rightful place in political life.[44]

Now that the suffrage issue had entered a new phase as a consequence of the tariff dispute, and the chances of reform seemed much better than previously, the men of the Left once again embraced the personality principle. Julius Mankell introduced bills annually during the period 1890–1896 calling for the introduction of universal manhood suffrage. According to Mankell, the most obvious injustice in society was that all citizens could not help choose the representatives who were supposed to look after their interests. The 1866 reform had only shifted power from one favored social class to another; instead of being ruled by estates, Sweden was ruled by monied interests. The country would continue to be ruled by the privileged few as long as each citizen could not personally influence the composition of Parliament.[45]

Outside Parliament there was a suffrage movement, with Mankell as chairman.[46] Petitions supporting universal manhood suffrage gathered several hundred thousand signatures. In 1893 and 1896, elections to a so-called people's parliament *(folkriksdag)* took place on the basis of universal suffrage for both men and women. In 1893 Prime Minister Boström refused to receive a deputation from the people's parliament on the grounds that he did not know any representatives of the Swedish people "appointed in ways other than our constitution specifies." After this, the people's parliament issued a very strong condemnation of "the policy of presumptuous stubbornness" by "those who now rule." It demanded, "in the name of justice and civil equality," a system of representation based on personality, not money; this was referred to as "our holy, just cause, the people's right of self-determination over their own fate."[47]

David Bergström succeeded Mankell as the chairman of the suffrage movement.[48] In Parliament, too, he continued where Mankell had left off, submitting a members' bill demanding, among other things, a referendum on universal manhood suffrage.[49] He tirelessly defended the "principle of

---

[44] Mot (members' bill) AK 1880:146, p. 5.

[45] Mot FK 1890:46, pp. 1ff.

[46] On the suffrage movement, see Torbjörn Vallinder: *I kamp för demokratin. Rösträttsrörelsen i Sverige 1886–1900* (Stockholm: Natur och kultur, 1962).

[47] "Folkriksdagens manifest till svenska folket," in *1893 års folkriksdag. Handlingar och beslut* (Stockholm, 1893), pp. 31ff.

[48] Vallinder 1962, p. 173.

[49] Mot AK 1897:130; this made Bergström the first man to advocate a referendum system in Sweden. Vallinder 1962, pp. 185–186.

Ideology and strategy

one man, one vote" and "voting by number of heads," not by wealth. He quoted Geijer's words that "justice is the primary task of society."[50]

The suffrage issue now dominated the parliamentary party system. In 1895 a liberal party known as *Folkpartiet* was formed – with the suffrage issue as the main point in its program.[51] Following preparatory work by Sixten von Friesen and Hugo Hamilton, in 1900 the modern Liberal party *(Liberala samlingspartiet)* was formed and immediately seized the initiative on the suffrage issue.[52] Von Friesen did not allow conservative arguments against universal manhood suffrage to pass unchallenged. In a parliamentary debate during 1899, he replied to an attack on the personality principle by saying that everyone could agree with such concern for the best interests of the state, but what was the best interest of the state? It was not a superhuman concept, as conservatives tried to argue; and it was not the exclusion of the majority from the right to vote – a situation that created discontent that was dangerous to the state. The best interests of the state lay in the extension of the suffrage to all citizens.[53] Hamilton declared that "it cannot be denied that influence over our political life should be based on the personality principle and by no means on the power of money."[54] When a few years later, Karl Staaff succeeded von Friesen as the chairman of the Liberal party, he not only organized the party's work in Parliament but also traveled around the country and agitated for his cause.

Under the firm leadership of Hjalmar Branting, the Social Democratic party shifted from a revolutionary to a reformist policy, whose main expression was the struggle for universal manhood suffrage. During the 1902 parliamentary debate on voting rights, the Social Democrats underlined their demands with a three-day demonstration strike. "During the parliamentary debates on the subject, Branting sometimes spoke with surprising moderation," according to one standard work on the ideological development of the Social Democratic party. Branting justified "the demand for suffrage in a way that differed little from Liberal speakers; he based it on the personality principle and the value of 'the equal political rights of all members of society.' "[55] The Liberals and Social Democrats thus fought side by side to implement universal male suffrage.

In the evolution of liberal ideology in Sweden during the second half

[50] AK 1902:53, pp. 58–59; Erik Gustaf Geijer, "Om personlighetsprincipen i förhållande till samhällets utveckling," in *Om vår tids inre samhällsförhållanden i synnerhet med afseende på fäderneslandet* (Stockholm: Norstedts, 1845), p. 25.
[51] Vallinder 1962, pp. 132–133.
[52] Ibid., p. 211.
[53] AK 1899:33, p. 18.
[54] FK 1902:35, p. 47.
[55] Tingsten 1941 II, p. 61.

of the nineteenth century, from Adolf Hedin to Karl Staaff, the personality principle thus appears as the central justification for universal suffrage. It distinguished the "new" liberalism from the "old"; it had no patience with a system of representation based on the economic position of citizens. It was also critically watchful of the superhuman concept of the state, which denied people what the Left considered their civil rights in the name of the best interests of the state. According to liberal thought, the best interests of the state were nothing more than the sum of the best interests of individuals, and individuals were best at understanding what these were. Conservatives were quick to reply that the differences in human abilities could be observed continuously and that a high income might be a sign of talent that also ought to be applied in political life. The liberals seldom refuted this argument energetically. Condemnations took the place of arguments, morality the place of observations. The personality principle became the symbol of a just system of representation, a political credo that gave the Left power and inspiration in its daily political work on behalf of universal manhood suffrage.

The Left attached a number of other, partly contradictory arguments to their main one. We will touch on four of these complexes of ideas here. The first one concerned the impact of a suffrage reform on the social order. One of the chief rightist arguments was that broadening the franchise would disturb social stability. The leftists replied somewhat ambiguously. On the one hand, they tried to calm the Right. They depicted the suffrage as "a safety valve, which can forestall and soothe much social unrest. If only the great mass of people feel they possess this right, they calm down and think that the time will always come when they can assert their interests." Through practice, the mass of people would come to realize the necessary conditions of social stability, and "then this right to vote will only be used to further sensible reforms that will not harm the legitimate interests of any social class, but will be useful for everyone."[56] "Far from posing any danger to social order, a genuinely popularly elected Second Chamber ... would comprise a guarantee of stable, sound social development."[57] It was not true that universal manhood suffrage would lead to "an attack by unknown mobs who, like Huns, would throw themselves on society to devour everything they could devour." On the contrary, a suffrage reform would protect social stability.[58] Opposition to a broadening of the franchise was what subjected the social order to danger. It resulted in an increasing number of discontented people. "This evil grows, takes root and develops more and more in the very bosom of soci-

[56] Mot FK 1890:46, p. 7 (Mankell).
[57] Mot AK 1899:226, p. 2 (Bergström et al.).
[58] AK 1904:65, p. 63 (Lindhagen).

ety, from which it can thus no longer be excluded; this is when a real danger to the existing social order arises."[59]

Hjalmar Branting pledged with all his authority that universal manhood suffrage would not threaten the social order. Such a reform "would not result in any major upheaval in our country." A one-by-one review of countries that had already introduced universal manhood suffrage demonstrated this. The risk, instead, was that Parliament's repeated refusal would drive the working class to radical action, which it really did not want to resort to. By phrasing the problem in this way, Branting was able to depict the workers as representatives of social stability, whereas it was the "obstinacy" of the First Chamber that posed a risk of upheavals: the question was whether in the conflict "between Sweden's industrial working class and the Junker Chamber, the Second Chamber would like to put itself on the side of stable development" by agreeing to a broadening of voting rights.[60] Branting also tried to calm the Conservatives by saying not all workers were Social Democrats. The fears of the Conservatives as to the consequences of universal manhood suffrage were completely unjustified, representing an approach "that is entirely incorrect and that should be set aside, because it has no foundation in reality."[61]

On the other hand, it was stated almost as a self-evident truth that universal manhood suffrage would, in fact, have an impact on the social order. Its purpose was to abolish the glaring differences between social classes and bring about an economic leveling. A member of Parliament could argue on both sides with impunity – even in the same speech or member's bill. A few years after leading Liberals assured the Conservatives (in a members' bill) that universal manhood suffrage was not a threat but a guarantee of stable social development, they launched a polemic against the Conservatives saying that all their arguments on voting rights were based on respect for the class interests of farmers. The sponsors of the Liberal bill wanted "instead to emphasize seriously" the axiom that no special class interests should be favored and that all "outdated class differ-

---

[59] AK 1890:28, p. 16 (Bratt).

[60] AK 1899:34, pp. 20ff.; quotations from pp. 20 and 23.

[61] AK 1902:52, pp. 25ff.; quotation from pp. 26–27. The creation of myths about the radicalism of the early Social Democrats on this point continues in our own age. In the debate on employee investment funds during the 1980s, the central leadership of the party and that of the Swedish Trade Union Confederation were criticized for trying to calm the business community by saying that such funds would not lead to drastic changes: free trade, industrial restructuring, and profitability would remain objectives. "This is, of course, turning the concept of democracy upside down. It is as if when universal suffrage was introduced, the Social Democrats had assured their political opponents, 'Don't be afraid. Our members will vote for exactly the policy you are now pursuing. It is only the actual right to vote we want. Our members will, in fact, accept some things they used to grumble about, as long as they know that they themselves have helped approve them'" (Anna Christensen, "Löntagarfonder och demokrati," *Dagens Nyheter*, 30 Nov. 1981). What the author of this newspaper article depicts as an unthinkable absurdity is in fact very close to what Branting actually claimed.

ences" should, on the contrary, be eliminated. With this "main view" they justified their suffrage bill.[62] And when Hjalmar Branting was addressing a people's parliament, not the regular Parliament, his tone was different. "For the working class, the right to vote is not merely a matter of rights and of equality in principle, but very much a practical issue. The right to vote is the means by which evil will be averted and good will be created for the mass of people. . . . Only through its close links with the major issue of social welfare does the suffrage become a genuine popular issue." And Branting proposed that the people's parliament issue a statement "in which the role of voting rights as a weapon in the social struggle of the lower class against the upper class is expressly emphasized."[63]

Another problem was the principle that equal rights should be balanced by equal duties. The Left, too, adopted this line of argument but with an important difference: Unlike the Conservatives, they did not mean by duties the tax burden, with the resulting view that a person who pays more taxes should have more say in political life. By duties, the Left meant compulsory military service. During this period, the Conservative government was carrying out a major upgrading of Sweden's defenses, and the heavier burden of conscription was used as an argument for greater civil rights. The slogan "one man – one vote – one rifle" made an impression on the Conservatives. In the long term it would become the Left's main battering ram against rightist oppostion to a broader franchise. A person who was required in times of danger to "wear a bloody shirt for his native land" should also be entitled to participate in elections to Parliament. The right to vote was a clear consequence of the heavier defense burden on the individual.[64] Aside from material resources, the armed forces could also count on ideological factors. Among these was the feeling of solidarity among a people. But as long as the suffrage issue was unresolved, it should not be assumed that the working class possessed this feeling of national solidarity.[65]

On the one hand, the suffrage and defense issues were thus linked together. If universal manhood suffrage was introduced, you could count on the support of the Left for rearmament; if you were upgrading the armed forces, the consequence should be universal manhood suffrage. On the other hand, this link was denied. Militarism was criticized categorically, especially within the Social Democratic party. This party, of course, belonged to an international movement that believed in internationalism.

---

[62] Mot AK 1902:197, p. 8 (von Friesen et al.); cf. mot AK 1899:226 (Bergström et al.). Karl Staaff, Fridtjuv Berg, David Bergström, Oskar Eklund, J. Byström, Edvard Wavrinsky, Magnus Höjer, M. F. Nyström, and Curt Wallis cosponsored both bills.

[63] *1893 års folkriksdag. handlingar och beslut*, pp. 55–56.

[64] Vallinder 1962, pp. 268–269.

[65] AK 1899:33, p. 40 (Nydahl).

The proletariat had no native country to defend. You should never let yourself be fooled into helping the upper class arm for war, because these armaments were aimed primarily at the working class. The vacillation among Social Democrats on this subject was a premonition of the split on defense-related issues that the party would suffer during World War I.[66]

A third contradictory argument emerges in the debate on the ability of people to form an independent opinion on social issues. The Conservatives doubted that people in general possessed this ability; a person showed his abilities by creating a fortune. On the one hand, the Left rejected this approach but, as noted previously, without great energy and with qualifications such as "often" or "in many cases." The richest people were not best suited to rule; those who had undergone life's many trials were often wiser.[67] Wealth, in many cases, was better as a sign of selfishness than of ability.[68] Furthermore, a new situation had arisen after the 1866 Parliament Act had gone into effect: "The effects of our country's excellent public school system have turned out to be especially splendid. Information and knowledge have been disseminated to a growing proportion of the country's inhabitants. People's moral condition is generally good. Public affairs are followed by a broad circle of citizens with lively interest." In other words, the ability to participate in politics was now widespread.[69]

The Conservatives' concept of a correlation between wealth and talent was criticized more passionately in Swedish literary debate. The novelist and dramatist August Strindberg wrote that his generation had grown up in an age that respected faith and honesty; the new age, on the other hand, worshiped economic success at any price. It was an age of humbug. No one believed that success went to those who deserved it; virtue was no merit, and honesty was less important than practicality. There was thus no link between intellectual and moral qualities and economic qualities. It was not possible to maintain that certain groups had greater ability to participate in political life than others.[70]

On the other hand, the Left admitted that the mass of people were actually not very capable of taking a political stand. Again, this situation could also be cited as an argument for broadening the suffrage. In keeping with John Stuart Mill's doctrine of democracy as an educational process, they argued that individuals would develop a public spirit if they could take part in politics. Manual workers had poor knowledge of political issues, but such knowledge could be enhanced by exercising their voting

[66] Tingsten 1941 II, pp. 147–185.
[67] Johan Bergman, according to Vallinder 1962, p. 263.
[68] AK 1894:30, p. 53 (Schönbeck).
[69] Minority statement in KU 1896:11, p. 21 (Elowson). Also AK 1899:33, p. 20 (von Friesen).
[70] Andrén 1937, p. 282.

rights.[71] Extending voting rights to the broad mass of people would promote public spirit, Branting declared, because it was "correct to assume that there is a growing interest in the work of the state and people are becoming aware of its needs."[72]

Finally, there was a fourth constellation of arguments for universal manhood suffrage based on natural law and utilitarianism. When people invoked the personality principle, they often did so, as we have indicated, by using terms closely connected with natural laws; for example, they spoke of "our holy, just cause."[73] Others used arguments more directly based on natural law: The right to vote was not something that the state could hand out as it pleased but was a right comparable with the right to life, liberty, and property. Some people, however, advocated universal manhood suffrage because it was socially useful. There was nothing called "the public interest" next to or above private interests. And all these private interests were "best represented by means of universal (manhood) suffrage, but most poorly by means of rule by the few, which prevails due to current conditions."[74]

But if suffrage was a natural right, it did not have to be justified by pointing to its usefulness; a right should be respected regardless of its consequences. And if it was useful to society, it did not have to be justified by arguing that it was a natural right, because there would be reasons for the government to implement it in any event. But in the world of suffrage supporters, all good things coincided. It was not only "fair" but also "wise" to introduce universal manhood suffrage.

But no matter what arguments the Left resorted to, it was unable to overcome the Right's resistance to broader suffrage, not even after the Left had formed a government. A solid Conservative majority in the First Chamber resisted every reform proposal, "wisely slow in action but firm and strong in opposition." These words from the 1809 constitutional committee described a reality that leftist demands for suffrage reform were unable to overcome for decades.

2. ADDING PROPORTIONAL REPRESENTATION TO THE AGENDA

In May 1906, when Arvid Lindman became prime minister in a Conservative government, he made it one of his top priorities to resolve the suffrage issue. No matter how rigid the positions of the Right and Left might seem in this controversial issue, there was a definite trend: From one elec-

---

[71] Mot FK 1890:46, p. 7 (Mankell).
[72] Minority statement in KU 1902:6, p. 114 (Moberg).
[73] See the discussion of the 1893 People's Parliament in this chapter at n. 47 (Staaff).
[74] FK 1890:24, p. 38 (Mankell).

tion to the next, economic growth helped more and more industrial workers to fulfill the economic requirements to vote, and there was no doubt as to which side these new voters supported. The Conservatives were the losing party. One election district after another switched from a Conservative representative to an M.P. for the Left, represented by the Liberals and Social Democrats. In the rapid wave of industrialization that was now sweeping across the country, the political map was being repainted in red – this was the disturbing perspective that Conservatives had to face.

Could anything be done to change this trend? Could a skillful Conservative politician take any step that would prevent the party from becoming the victim of what appeared to be a major long-term disaster?

Of course much could be done. Lindman decided to use the strategy described in Chapter 1 as "amending the agenda." What was necessary, Lindman argued, was to find some aspect of the suffrage issue that would split the growing Left. It could not be assumed that demands for universal manhood suffrage would continue to be defeated in Parliament. There were now too many people who supported such a reform. Sweden would soon be the only country in Europe that did not allow all adult men to vote. No, the introduction of universal manhood suffrage was certainly unavoidable. But could this process take place in a way less harmful to the Conservatives than by embracing the suffrage ideas of the Left? If such a solution could be found, it was better to act now, while the Conservatives were in government and could direct the political game. If this opportunity were squandered, the Left would soon get a chance to implement *its* suffrage program.

When we try in this way to reconstruct Prime Minister Lindman's thinking on the suffrage issue, it provides yet another illustration of what we said in Chaper 1 about the implications of rational choice theory – that this theory by no means compels the researcher to ignore structural causes. As we noted, the difference between rational choice theory and structural theory is only that in the former case the researcher tries to state the role that an economic downturn, for example, plays in a decision maker's analysis of the alternatives. In the latter case he tries to establish a direct link between the economic downturn and politics, regardless of how the state of the economy is perceived by the actors. In explaining Lindman's suffrage proposal by means of rational choice theory, we very much have to take into account the structural conditions represented by industrialization, the general rise in wage levels, and the resulting increase in the number of industrial workers entitled to vote. But we are trying to present the issue as Arvid Lindman saw it. We want to show how he perceived the problem and how he reasoned in order to counteract the threat to the position of the Conservative party that these trends represented.

The election method turned out to be the aspect of the suffrage issue that Lindman was looking for. Staaff's rhetorical question about "upper-class rule or popular rule?" was not only arrogantly phrased. Lindman tried to show that it was also incorrect. Democracy was on the doorstep. Even the Conservatives had to accept universal manhood suffrage. But the question was whether the country – confronted by a militant Left that denied the throne, the sword, and the altar – should continue to elect its M.P.'s by a majority method in which the winner took all and the loser got nothing. This method would soon put the Left in a totally dominant position in Swedish politics. Given the new situation that had arisen in Sweden, there was good reason to ensure the minority some protection by switching to a proportional representation system of elections. This change would at least guarantee the country's conservative elements an influence equivalent to their strength in the electorate. Could any claims be more reasonable and fair than this? In this way an amendment on majority election versus proportional representation was added to the issue of universal manhood suffrage versus limited voting rights.[75]

Lindman was not the inventor of this strategy. As early as the 1890s, when some Conservatives began to speak of universal suffrage with guarantees[76] in response to the growing burden of defense expenditures, they had thought about proportional representation. As the labor movement grew, the Conservatives became increasingly worried. They became more and more skeptical about an election system that overrepresented the majority. After the turn of the century, the discussion of the majority method or proportional representation had received almost as much room in parliamentary debates as the ideological arguments for and against universal manhood suffrage.

Proportional representation had played a key role most recently during the 1906 session of Parliament. The so-called Påboda proposal, presented as an alternative to the government bill, called for the introduction of proportional representation in both chambers (so-called double proportionalism). By playing on the fear of socialism, the author of the bill, a leading M.P. and farmer named Alfred Petersson i Påboda, had picked up votes not only from a sizable number of Conservatives but also from some

---

[75] On the background of the suffrage reform and its implementation, see especially the extensive account in Erik Timelin, *Ministären Lindman och representationsreformen 1907–1909* (Karlskrona, 1928); also Andrén 1937, pp. 450–485; Axel Brusewitz, *Kungamakt, herremakt, folkmakt* (Stockholm: Prisma, 1964), pp. 17–32 (first published in 1951); Ivar Anderson, *Arvid Lindman och hans tid* (Stockholm: Norstedts, 1956), pp. 99–110; Leif Kihlberg, *Karl Staaff II. Regeringschef, oppositionsledare 1905–1915* (Stockholm: Bonniers, 1963), pp. 104–118. Unfortunately Lindman did not begin his diary, which has now been published, until after the suffrage reform. As we have earlier had reason to state – as regards housing policy in Chapter 1, n. 15 – the proceedings of Parliament are also rich in accounts of strategic deliberations. This is also the case with the suffrage reform, as is clear from the works cited and the government bill on suffrage summarized and quoted below.

[76] Kjellén 1896.

moderate Liberal M.P.'s A large majority in the First Chamber had voted for the Påboda proposal instead of Staaff's government bill; in the Second Chamber the government bill had won by 134 to 94.

The chambers had thus voted differently, and Staaff had approached the king to request the dissolution of the Second Chamber and a new election. Once again, as during the tariff controversy, Oscar II had been given a chance to show his political power by using his prerogative to dissolve the Second Chamber. But this time it would have been in the king's interest to refuse to dissolve the chamber. The king disliked Staaff, his belief in parliamentary government, and the majority election method. The king turned down Staaff's request with a reply that, ironically, had some merit. Oscar II argued that it was inconsistent with the parliamentary system of government to dissolve a chamber that had just voted for a royal bill. There could only be one result. The Staaff government resigned. After Petersson i Påboda turned down the opportunity to become prime minister and a second person did the same,[77] the king turned to Lindman, who accepted. In the same statement in which he rejected Staaff's request for dissolution, the king assigned his new advisers the task of resolving the suffrage issue in keeping with the Påboda proposal: "I urge you immediately to undertake a thorough and serious examination of the important suffrage issue so that as soon as possible, the time and opportunity may be given to the representatives of the Swedish people also to consider a fully crafted proposal for a proportional system of elections to both chambers of Parliament."[78]

"During the seven months that (Staaff) was prime minister, Mr. Arvid Lindman had patrolled the area below the Royal Palace every weekday while taking his strolls each morning and dinner time to and from his office (at the Board of Telecommunications) on Skeppsbron. He walked there like a young boy scout with the motto 'Be prepared!' All that was necessary was a signal from the Palace wall above him, and he would show up, ready to direct the battle for proportionalism and against parliamentarism." This caustic account, which appeared some years later in a newspaper,[79] is quite consistent with the opinions expressed in the literature about this successful forty-four-year-old naval officer, industrialist, public official, and M.P., who now stepped forward from the majority Conservative party in the First Chamber to become Sweden's prime minister. He was described as "the daring young prime minister,"[80] "a new, admittedly unknown quantity but a strong, energetic force,"[81] one of "the young con-

[77] Fredrik Wachtmeister.
[78] Timelin 1928, p. 104.
[79] Von Zweigberk in *Dagens Nyheter*, Oct. 1925, according to Timelin 1928, p. 88, n. 13.
[80] Anderson 1956, p. 106.
[81] Timelin 1928, p. 89.

servative activists, accustomed to fighting their way and running things."[82]
Lindman was a stranger to ideological debate. His strength was practical
and strategic action.

The starting point of Lindman's calculations when he began preparing
his government bill on the suffrage issue was the number of votes cast for
and against Staaff's bill in the spring of 1906. The figures indicated that
there was already a majority in favor of proportional representation in the
First Chamber. In the Second Chamber, on the other hand, at least twenty
M.P.'s would have to be persuaded to switch their allegiance from majority elections to proportional representation. In other words, it was necessary to phrase the amendment on proportional representation in such a
way that it attracted new supporters in the Second Chamber without
thereby losing its majority in the First Chamber.

By the late summer and early fall of 1906, there was already speculation
as to what "Boström maneuver" Lindman was planning on the suffrage
issue.[83] On 2 February 1907 the government submitted its bill to Parliament.[84] Its text represented the perspective of the potential loser. It was
completely natural, given the conflict between different interests and
views that comprised modern politics, that "the shortcomings of majority
elections should be quite imperceptible to those who are the rulers at a
given point in time. It is correspondingly stronger in the party or parties
that are at a disadvantage in the struggle and that often see themselves
entirely excluded from all influence due to the peculiar outcome of majority elections." It was no secret to anyone "who wants to see and admit
what he sees" that political developments gave reason for concern. As
long as the minority had, and was perceived as having, some control over
the majority, there was little threat to national development. "But if this
control ceases, there is undoubtedly a danger that in the struggle that
arises in society between different interests, each of them justified, the
party that is ruling at the moment will not take necessary account of the
opposing interest." The size of the concessions the winner was willing to
make certainly depended, the government assumed, "not only on the arguments the opposing party could offer but also, and to a significant degree,
on the voting strength at their disposal." To strengthen the position of the
minority, the government thus proposed that the introduction of universal
manhood suffrage be accompanied by a switch from majority elections to
proportional representation in both chambers.[85]

To win a majority in the Second Chamber, the government had added

---

[82] Kihlberg 1963, p. 97.

[83] Anderson 1956, p. 106.

[84] It was divided into three government bills, no. 28 (political voting rights), no. 29 (municipalities), and no. 30 (county councils).

[85] Prop 1907:28, p. 11.

three radical elements to its "double proportionalism" proposal: a lowering of the voting age from twenty-five to twenty-four; the extension of proportional representation to the county councils and big-city municipal councils, which served as the electors to the First Chamber; and a limit of forty on the number of votes one person could cast in local elections, where the franchise was linked to tax liability. Lindman was hoping that the last rule in particular would split the Left and attract the necessary twenty or so new votes. The rule was specially worded to take into account the farmers from the forested counties of northern Sweden, who had rather specific political sympathies. Because the forest product companies had bought so much timberland in their region during the early twentieth century, these farmers had a negative attitude toward "corporate Conservatives" and voted according to a more leftist pattern than most farmers.[86] Because of this middle position, they would probably be receptive to proposals that limited the influence of wealth on local government. Lindman did not hesitate to hold out this bait to the small farmers, even in the actual text of the government bill. These farmers were now being squeezed between the big companies and the labor movement. Limiting local voting rights to a maximum of forty votes per person would improve their standing in relation to the companies. Industrialization was now advancing into traditional agricultural districts. "With universal (manhood) suffrage and elections in one-man constituencies, the time will not be distant when the interests of farmers here and there in the country are not well represented in elected bodies." But because of the government bill on proportional representation, "the danger of a shift in the direction now indicated is very greatly diminished. Even if farmers are no longer in a majority, agriculture should nevertheless have a chance to enjoy its fair share of representation."[87]

The government bill was discussed during the general policy debate in both chambers. The First Chamber's reaction was severe. The proposal was criticized by two of its most conservative members, and no one defended it.[88] In the Second Chamber, the reception was more mixed. Because of the uncertain parliamentary situation, M.P.'s spoke very cautiously and it was not possible to draw any conclusions as to the bill's prospects.[89]

The bill was ready to be sent to committee. But to which committee should it be referred? The Constitution Committee would have been the

---

[86] Lewin, Jansson, and Sörbom 1972, pp. 38 and 79; Sten Carlsson, *Lantmannapolitiken och industrialismen. Partigruppering och opinionförskjutningar i svensk politik 1890–1902* (Stockholm; Lantbruksförbundets tidskriftsaktiebolag, 1953), pp. 16ff.

[87] Prop 1907:28, p. 13.

[88] FK 1907:6, pp. 6–18.

[89] AK 1907:8, pp. 4–33.

natural place. But Lindman did not intend to leave anything to chance. He wanted to keep the Second Chamber and local-government voting rights issues from being separated by being handled in two different committees. Above all, he wanted the body discussing the suffrage bill to have sufficient authority to pick up broad support for the bill in the parliamentary parties. The Constitution Committee was not suitable for that purpose: The top leaders of the Liberals were prevented from taking part in this committee, because it would also be examining their recent performance as government ministers. Lindman thus wanted a special committee. His plans were easy to see through. Both the extreme Right and extreme Left, which distrusted his reform plans on the suffrage issue, protested. Not dealing with an issue of this nature in the Constitution Committee was unconstitutional, the far Right exclaimed. Making it easier to fine-tune the government bill in such a way as to pick up those notorious twenty or so additional votes was the last thing Parliament ought to do, the Social Democrats maintained. But by mobilizing various forces between these two extremes, Lindman succeeded in pushing through the idea of a special committee. It had twenty-four members: nine proportionalists and three supporters of majority elections from the First Chamber, and the opposite constellation from the Second Chamber. Both Staaff and Branting were members of the committee.[90]

Aside from the government bill, the special committee was entrusted with examining no fewer than thirty-eight members' bills on the same subject. The main alternative to the government proposal was a Liberal bill cosponsored by a total of seventy-three M.P.'s headed by Staaff. This bill proposed universal manhood suffrage while retaining the majority method.[91]

Weeks of complex bargaining and compromises followed. One researcher summarizes the situation in this way: "The mood of the Second Chamber was still extremely unstable; rumors of defections in one direction or the other crossed each other."[92]

One name was missing from the Liberals' main bill: Daniel Persson i Tällberg, a farmer from northern Sweden. The explanation came as late as 16 April when Persson i Tällberg submitted his own members' bill on the suffrage issue, cosponsored by four other Liberal farmers. The brief bill, characterized as "a purely tactical move,"[93] began like many other leftist statements with a criticism of the long-time Conservative opposition to suffrage reform. "Only as a last resort these days, forced by circumstances, do they seem to have realized the serious importance and

---

[90] Timelin 1928, pp. 274–288; Andrén 1937, pp. 458ff.
[91] Mot AK 1907:203.
[92] Timelin 1928, p. 348.
[93] Ibid., p. 346.

implications of this issue." The political parties were peeking over each other's shoulders. This had brought the suffrage issue "into the foggy waters of mistrust, where the various parties cruise around the issue and, constantly colliding with each other, nearly forget their real task: trying to tow the issue to a safe harbor." Tällberg and his cosponsors now wanted to contribute to a solution. They wished to confess from the start that the government bill was "as far-reaching as we can reasonably ask at present, since it is based on the principle of universal (manhood) suffrage." The amendment on proportional representation was a shortcoming, however. It was now necessary to examine whether this was offset by its proposed reform of voting rights in local elections and thus indirectly in elections to the First Chamber. This analysis led to two more conditions that had to be fulfilled to make the government bill acceptable: Election requirements for members of the First Chamber had to be loosened, and members of the First Chamber must begin to be paid a salary.[94]

Where did Tällberg's bill originate? There has been extensive speculation. Nowadays researchers agree that it was not written without the government's knowledge. It resulted from an understanding, and perhaps after actual bargaining, between two farmers who were members of Parliament – Tällberg and Påboda, who had become the minister of agriculture.[95]

The defectors had stated their price. It was higher than Lindman had counted on at first. But he was also willing to pay it. The prime minister threw his support to the Tällberg proposals. To their dismay, Liberal party leaders saw the ranks of the Left in the Second Chamber divided over Tällberg's proposals, which the special committee had included in its published recommendation after backing the government bill.[96] In this way, the Left split in the Second Chamber exactly as Lindman had hoped, and the government won the vote by a large majority.

The situation was much more difficult in the First Chamber, which of course had strongly opposed the original government bill. Now Lindman had taken an additional step in a radical direction. Lindman was fully aware of what a sacrifice the majority Conservative party in the First Chamber, which he also belonged to, would be making if it supported the

---

[94] Mot AK 1907:252, quotation from pp. 1–2.
[95] Timelin 1928, p. 350; Andrén 1937, p. 463; Anderson 1956, pp. 106ff; Kihlberg 1963, p. 109.
[96] SäU (proceedings of the special committee) 1907:3 and 4. In the First Chamber, the government supported a members' bill that had been worked out by some First Chamber members headed by Olof Jonsson i Hov, which merely stipulated that Chamber members would be paid a salary. In the Second Chamber, where there was a bill by Hans Andersson et al. incorporating the Tällberg demands for both a salary and a lowering of property requirements, the government merely appealed for a decision that would pave the way for a final agreement.

Tällberg proposals. He understood the party's concern that the special constitutional role of the First Chamber was being undermined. This chamber had been an upper house representing education, wealth, and sensible judgment. Lindman's dislike of the "Second Chamber parliamentarism" of Staaff and other leftist leaders was as strong as that of any other member of the First Chamber. During 1906, when his defeat on the suffrage issue became clear, Staaff had spoken his mind in some bitter words to the effect that the actual right to make decisions should rest with the Second Chamber. This was the chamber whose task was to make sure that "the clock is running," whereas the First Chamber should merely tell "what time the clock says." Lindman concurred with a witty remark by a First Chamber member to the effect that no, the First Chamber should also make sure "that the clock is running properly."[97] In Lindman's view, the First Chamber should also continue to perform this task even if its roots, as he put it, were now sunk "deeper among the people."

In his speech initiating the First Chamber debate, Lindman asked what would happen if the First Chamber remained unchanged while the Second Chamber was now being reformed. Conflicts between the chambers would increase, perhaps becoming so great that the whole bicameral system would be damaged. There were, of course, those who wished to undermine or even abolish the First Chamber – the members certainly understood who Lindman was referring to. The government bill had proposed major changes, and the prime minister admitted that these should have been enough. But the additional adjustments that were now required to achieve agreement could not be considered so crucially important as to block the entire reform.[98]

After the prime minister finished speaking, a storm of criticism against him broke out. The dangers of government by the masses were painted in gaudy colors, the traditional role of the First Chamber was defended with great emotion, and the prime minister's tactical concession to Tällberg was condemned. The prime minister replied with a series of apt remarks. With disarming honesty, he confessed his tactical methods. As every military man knew, Lindman reminded the chamber, there was sometimes reason "to give up one position, without losing sight of your goal, in order to gain another." Everyone knew that the suffrage issue could not be resolved in the way proposed in the government bill. Should the government alone then stick to its old views? Should it sit as a silent witness and watch the chambers arguing about the proper solution? Among those who now condemned the government, were there men willing to form a new government that better understood the art of governing? Perhaps that art

[97] FK 1906:48, p. 43 (Staaff) and p. 48 (Blomberg).
[98] FK 1907:38, pp. 48ff.

would not be so difficult if, as the speakers seemed to be saying, it only meant sitting, with arms crossed, waiting for Parliament to decide matters.[99]

The threat of an imminent government crisis was now in the air. It is evident from the debate that the members of the First Chamber regarded the threat as very clear. In a bold fighting mood, the following day Lindman announced a vote of confidence – not on his own government bill but on the Tällberg proposal.[100] Some people regarded this as going a bit too far. It was "a new theory not only in Sweden but, I believe, in the rest of the parliamentary world, that a government uses the threat of resignation to persuade a chamber that wishes to approve that government's proposal to vote for a more far-reaching proposal."[101] But after the prime minister's message, the mood in the First Chamber began to shift. Immediately after the announcement of a vote of confidence, one member declared that he "had not heard a government called weak when it wishes to maintain leadership up to the very end."[102] The debate increasingly came to resemble an open vote, because speaker after speaker declared his support for Lindman. But it was a conversion in the face of the seemingly unavoidable. Finally the First Chamber approved the payment of salaries to its own members, while maintaining strict conditions for election to the First Chamber. The versions approved by the two chambers were not too far apart to permit a compromise to be reached. They agreed to lower the wealth requirement for election to the First Chamber to fifty thousand kronor and the income requirement to three thousand. Parliament approved the suffrage reform. Under the Constitution, it had to pass the identical bill again, with an intervening election. Final approval consequently came in 1909.

The suffrage issue was thus finally settled. With great strategic skill, though at a high price, Arvid Lindman had split the Left and won a prestigious victory on the Left's own pet issue. There was great bitterness among the leaders of the Left. Both Karl Staaff and Hjalmar Branting voted no when universal suffrage was introduced in Sweden.[103] Staaff was especially disappointed. As his biographer remarks, he was caught off guard by Lindman's resolute behavior during the many twists and turns of the suffrage issue. Staaff had reason to regret his lack of skill in dealing with the farmers in Parliament. None of them were members of his group of advisers. And of his friends, "several became so downhearted that they

---

[99] FK 1907:39, pp. 38–39.

[100] FK 1907:40, p. 20.

[101] FK 1907:40, p. 37 (Trygger).

[102] FK 1907:40, p. 21 (Tamm).

[103] When the bill came up for reaffirmation in 1909, Branting again voted no, while Staaff – whose party now aimed for women's suffrage and the complete democratization of local voting rights – voted in favor.

had a hard time maintaining their balance."[104] In the long term, too, Lindman's strategy of dividing the Left bore fruit: To lure back the right-wing Liberals who had supported the suffrage reform, Staaff partially shifted Liberal policy toward the right; the so-called Staaff laws of a few years later, which targeted antimilitary meetings and pamphleteers, were sharply criticized by the Social Democrats. But for Arvid Lindman, the suffrage reform was a parliamentary triumph that he always remembered with great satisfaction.

3. THE SUFFRAGE REFORM

Why was universal manhood suffrage introduced by a Conservative government theoretically opposed to this demand?

In keeping with the organization of this book, we now will try to answer this question by summarizing the previous sections as concisely as possible, using a game matrix. It perhaps bears repeating that this matrix is not a voting record that states all the proposals introduced; it is not even certain that a vote took place between the alternatives listed in the matrix. The function of the game matrix is, instead, to capture the essence of the issue at hand and to simplify and clarify it so that the big picture becomes evident.

For this reason we will simply pose two issues against each other: on the one hand, universal manhood suffrage versus a more limited suffrage; on the other, majority elections versus proportional representation. The actors are the Right and the Left, modeled on Lindman and Staaff respectively; the range of views in both camps makes such a specification necessary. The Left's alternatives are universal manhood suffrage or more limited suffrage. Leftist demands for universal manhood suffrage were what led to this becoming a major ideological issue in the lengthy debate on suffrage. The Right's preference was limited suffrage, the Left's universal manhood suffrage. As the Left's position among voters was becoming stronger, it became increasingly likely that its demand for universal manhood suffrage would be realized.

To soften the effects of this reform, the Right amended the agenda to include a shift to proportional representation. The new question posed by the Right was a choice between two alternatives, the majority method or the proportional representation method. The result was two intersecting questions, far more complex preference orderings by the actors, and a more interesting decision-making situation.

In this reconstruction, the Right's preference ordering is first, limited suffrage with proportional representation; second, limited suffrage using the majority method; third, universal manhood suffrage with proportional

---

[104] Kihlberg 1963, pp. 115ff.

Table 3.1. *The suffrage game*

	The Left	
	Universal manhood suffrage	More limited suffrage
The Right		
Majority method	−2, +2	+1, −1
Proportional representation	−1, +1	+2, −2

representation; and last, universal manhood suffrage with the majority method. The Left's ranking is first, universal manhood suffrage with the majority method; second, universal manhood suffrage with proportional representation; third, more limited suffrage with the majority method; and last, limited suffrage with proportional representation. In the game matrix, we assign the best alternative for each actor a value of $+2$, the second best $+1$, the second worst -1, and the worst -2. This gives us the matrix in Table 3.1.

Are there any problems in summarizing the preferences of the Right and the Left on the suffrage issue as we have done? As far as the Left is concerned, the answer is no. There is no doubt that the Left preferred universal manhood suffrage to more limited suffrage and majority elections to proportional representation, while the issue of expanding the suffrage was accorded greater importance than the election method. As far as the Right goes, it is likewise obvious that the broadening of suffrage was the most important litmus test and that in terms of election methods, it preferred proportional representation to majority elections. But is it correct and fair to say that even some years into our own century, the Right preferred a restricted suffrage to universal manhood suffrage? Yes, our analysis of the ideological debate leads to the conclusion that this was indeed the case. There were, admittedly, a few firm believers in democracy among the Conservatives. But the dominant opinion among members of Arvid Lindman's majority Conservative party in the First Chamber was that a limitation of voting rights was still preferable, given the chamber's task of representing maturity of judgment and experience that guaranteed the stability of the social order. As risky as it may be to make statements about what an actor "wanted deep down" – as opposed to the position he adopted – there is sufficient evidence in the proceedings of Parliament, including Lindman's own speeches, to justify the opinion expressed in the Tällberg bill that it was the coercive force of circumstances, not any profound ideological change, that now persuaded the Conservative government to propose universal manhood suffrage. If we wish, as here, to list what game theory refers to as the true preferences of the actors, it seems proper to let the Right put limited manhood suffrage ahead of universal manhood suffrage.

The matrix we have produced has a number of interesting properties. We first notice that one actor's preferences are a direct mirror image of the other's. The game is a two-person zero-sum game, in which both players have dominating strategies. This means, first of all, that what one wins is exactly what the other loses; second, that for each player, one alternative course of action is always preferable to the other, no matter how the second player chooses. In this case, the Right always has reason to select "proportional representation," thereby achieving +2 or +1 instead of −1 or −2. Correspondingly, the Left always has reason to choose "universal manhood suffrage," thereby achieving +2 or +1 instead of −1 or −2. No type of game offers such powerful explanations for the actors' behavior as two-person zero-sum games with dominant strategies for both sides. If the two actors are rational, it is obvious how they should choose. The quadrant thus singled out is the solution of the game. In this type of game, it is usually called the saddle point and is defined as the quadrant from which neither player, given the other's choices, can move without lowering his utility. As we see, the combination of the rational choices of Right and Left leads to the lower left-hand quadrant, which is the solution and saddle point. "Universal manhood suffrage and proportional representation" was also the decision that was made in reality.

But this solution did not represent the first preference of any actor. The suffrage reform of 1907–1909 is an outstanding example of one of the main findings of rational choice theory: There is no decision rule that guarantees that a collective decision will be rational, even though the individual actors behave rationally – that is, they can both rank their preferences and then act in a way that optimizes their utility. There are thus opportunities for strategic action, in which they give up their original preferences. No one was really pleased with the suffrage decision; no one's first preference was adopted. But no one was left out completely, either. The Left's demands for broader voting rights were implemented, but the majority election method had to be sacrificed. The Conservatives finally accepted universal manhood suffrage but won acceptance for proportional representation, which they regarded as a guarantee against majority oppression.

Finally, the game matrix also gives us more precise information on the distribution of gains and losses between actors. Surprisingly enough, it turns out that Karl Staaff, who was very disappointed, received +1 while the triumphant Arvid Lindman received −1. Yet political successes are not judged according to what is ideologically desirable, but according to what is strategically possible. Even though Staaff got his way on the main issue of expanding the suffrage, he was deeply disappointed because his very first preference had seemed completely possible to achieve. And then he was caught off guard by his main opponent on the issue he felt most strongly about.

Arvid Lindman's greatness consisted of the fact that from the viewpoint of a potential loser, he intuitively understood the decision-making situation he was in, he knew what room for maneuvering he had, and he was able to manipulate the game in such a way that the outcome, in our terms, was -1 instead of -2. The former value here stands for a considerable ideological sacrifice, as Lindman himself was very much aware. The Tällberg proposals made the price of proportional representation high. The conservatism of wealth and an independent view of society contrary to all political parties were values that the Conservatives now had to sacrifice, after decades of struggle, in order to prevent the creation of a Parliament totally dominated by the Left. The age of upper-class rule was past. But the party that represented the upper-class interest had been given a chance to survive.

4. THE PROPORTIONAL REPRESENTATION METHOD

During the process of Swedish suffrage reform, politicians succeeded in consistently distinguishing between what was a decision and what was a decision rule. The decision was universal manhood suffrage using proportional representation. The decision rule was simple majority rule among M.P.'s. The fact that they, in turn, had been elected according to a method different from the one now introduced – according to limited suffrage and using a majority election method – was unimportant in this context. No impatient revolutionaries appeared in Sweden to demand that the new decision rule being introduced should be implemented immediately. Because it involved an amendment to the Constitution, it was also necessary to reaffirm it in 1909 following a regular election. Exactly as stipulated in the Constitution, Lindman's suffrage rules went into effect only in 1911.

Things had been different during the tariff controversy. At that time the new decision rule, the imperative mandate, had been put into effect immediately and the system consequently went into a crisis, resulting in the birth of the modern party system. The conflicts had been so dramatic that the decision rule itself was placed in question. At the time, reality had been far removed from Rawls's ideal of reaching decisions on rule-making issues under a "veil of ignorance" that would guarantee fair rules without regard to people's own interests in the issue at hand.[105]

[105] Chapter 1, Section 2.

Suffrage

It might seem as if the danger of decisions and decision rules being questioned simultaneously would have been greater during the suffrage dispute than the tariff dispute – and not only because it was so lengthy that the patience of the radicals was strained to the limits. The essence of the suffrage decision was a change in the decision rule – or, to use the terminology of rational choice theory, the decision was a "question of regulation." A "question of action" refers to a collective position on some policy area, such as the structure of housing subsidies, a ban on alcohol advertising, or choosing locations for institutions of higher education, in which the actors directly attempt to achieve the highest possible utility values. A question of regulation is instrumental and attempts to influence the rules of the game of political decision making, such as the rules for codetermination by employees at the workplace, referendums, and the formation of governments.[106] In the tariff dispute, tariffs were a question of action, the imperative mandate a question of regulation. In the suffrage dispute, on the other hand, the decision under debate was a question of regulation. The system nevertheless managed, as we have said, to distinguish between what, at the time, was a decision and what was a decision rule. The most far-reaching change in the Swedish political system in half a century could be implemented without jamming the decision-making machinery. The system reformed itself by applying the decision rules specified for this purpose.

The proportional representation system that was now introduced was a recent invention. The one-round majority election is, of course, the oldest method. Its simple principle is that the victor, whether an individual or a group, gets the prize and the loser gets nothing. Condorcet, father of the voter's paradox, is usually regarded as the pioneer of proportional representation. The first country to consider abandoning or modifying the majority election system was probably France, in the early 1790s. Condorcet presented a proposal to the national assembly, but the assembly rejected it and approved a system of majority elections in two rounds; this new constitution never went into effect, however. The first time proportional representation was used on the national level was in 1855, in an election to Denmark's upper chamber, the *Landsting*. This system had been devised by the finance minister, Carl Andrae. By the turn of the century, there was growing general interest in proportional representation around Europe. In many countries, fear of socialism led to the same development as occurred in Sweden.[107]

---

[106] William H. Riker and Peter C. Ordeshook, *An Introduction to Positive Political Theory* (Englewood Cliffs, N.J.: Prentice-Hall, 1973), pp. 276ff.

[107] Torbjörn Wallinder, "Majoritetsval eller proportionella val?" in *Modern demokrati*, ed. Pär-Erik Back and Agne Gustafsson (Lund: Liber, 1980), esp. pp. 86–87. The book was first published in 1963. This survey article provides extensive references to the literature.

There were thought to be good arguments for proportional representation. When debating a question of regulation, there are certain assumptions as to what good manners allow a person to demand. Rawls's work is an excellent example of this. Openly demanding a regulation that gives advantages to oneself is not considered proper – for a person who is already in a favorable position. It can be tolerated if a weaker party presents his reasons for getting out of a weak position. To the potential loser, it is thus acceptable for him to declare his personal interest in supporting the proportional representation system. The government's suffrage bill had expressly stated that it was now proposing a change to the proportional representation system in order to protect future minorities (that is, its own party) from emerging ruling parties (the Left). The loser can often awaken sympathy. It sounds better to say that you want to protect the small than to say that you want to support the stronger. The Lindman government was thus able to embellish the text of its bill with the statement that the proportional representation amendment was an expression of "justice" – justice required that elections be carried out using this representation method.[108]

For the potential winner, the arguments are more delicate. It is not considered good form to advocate the majority election method on grounds that it favors your own party, now that it has become large and powerful. In the long speech in which Staaff explained his "no" vote, he thus criticized proportional representation for other reasons. He began by maintaining that the method was unsuitable for Sweden; special conditions prevailing in the country made it sensible to keep the majority method. In his own city of Stockholm, majority elections had not noticeably paralyzed the minority, as the government claimed, by shutting it out of all power. On the contrary, the Conservative minority in the capital was a lively and energetic party. On the other hand, using a phrase that we would have expected instead from a Conservative, Staaff said he believed that sharper party conflicts would result from the change to proportional representation. Even more surprising was Staaff's next argument: The proportional representation method would lead to a complete takeover of the Swedish Parliament by the political parties, leaving no room for those who wished to form their own opinion without being affiliated with any party. This statement came from the man who, more than anyone else, had symbolized the modernization of the party system that had begun during the tariff dispute. In the same category was Staaff's remark that the proportional representation method would make it necessary for parties to have strong leaderships. And this, he continued, would mean that a particular class with special habits and traditions would fall between stools. Staaff was

---

[108] Prop 1907:28, p. 17.

now declaring that he wanted to protect the interests of the farmers on the suffrage issue – a bit too late, one might think. Staaff continued by detailing the heavy election costs he thought would result from the proportional representation system and the constitutional aspects: Double proportionalism would now put the two chambers on an equal footing in terms of political power, whereas Staaff wanted the Second Chamber to play the leading role in Swedish political life.[109]

If we go back two or more decades in time, the opposite opinions prevailed; the majority election method was defended by a large rightist camp, while the small leftist parties demanded proportional representation in order to win parliamentary seats more easily.[110] As late as during the 1902 election campaign, Staaff declared that proportional representation "by which minorities, too, would be given an opportunity to make their views heard and the electorate would thus be more faithfully reflected in the legislature, is a concept of profound, irresistible justice."[111]

Finally, if we turn our gaze to the most recent constitutional debate during the 1960s and 1970s, when the Liberals were once again a small opposition party, proportional representation was again depicted as the fairest election system. Indeed, the proportional system introduced by Lindman in 1907 was not only defended as the true Liberal view. It was taken a step further, with the party calling for "strict proportionality" – that is, a system guaranteeing complete national proportionality by means of extra seats. The Liberals' main opponents were now the Social Democrats, who by this time had become the ruling party and had a strong interest in an election method that produced "strong governments."[112]

In 1968, when Parliament was about to vote on proposals for a unicameral system and strict proportionality, former Liberal party chairman Bertil Ohlin claimed that this was what Swedish liberalism had always wanted. When it came to the one-chamber Parliament, this statement was undoubtedly consistent with what Staaff had once argued, but as we have seen, it hardly applies to the choice of representation method. According to Ohlin, however, "ever since before the turn of the century," the Liberal party had marched in the forefront of reform efforts. Most recently, it was the Social Democrats who had resisted changes in the election system, whereas the Liberals had particularly stressed "the importance of a fair distribution of seats. . . . I hope that no one will find it unwarranted if I also emphasize that those of us in the Liberal grassroots movement regard

---

[109] AK 1907:52, pp. 78–89.
[110] Douglas V. Verney, *Parliamentary Reform in Sweden 1866–1921* (Oxford: Oxford University Press, 1957), pp. 136–173; Rudolf Kjellén, *Rösträttsfrågan* (Stockholm: Hugo Gebers Förlag, 1915), pp. 70–185; Andrén 1937, pp. 306–354.
[111] Kihlberg 1963, p. 266.
[112] Erik Holmberg and Nils Stjernquist, *Grundlagarna* (Stockholm: Norstedts, 1980), pp. 1–18.

today's decision as a milestone not only in the history of democracy in Sweden but also that of liberalism. Liberalism has been a driving force behind all the most important constitutional decisions for three quarters of a century."[113]

Looking at the changing views on methods of representation in a long historical perspective, as we have done, it is difficult to take completely seriously the lofty words uttered at various times. They often look like fairly lame rationalizations after the fact. Behind the solemn phrases are party interests. Proportional representation is the loser's method of gaining some protection against the majority, whether that minority be the Liberals in the 1890s, the Conservatives in 1907, or the Liberals in the 1960s. In the same way, it is in the majority's interest to oppose proportional representation, whether the majority be the Conservatives in the 1890s, the Liberals in 1907, or the Social Democrats in the 1960s. As the relative strengths of the parties shift, their views and arguments change. What is true liberalism today is darkest conservatism tomorrow. There are, of course, objective reasons for the consequences of proportionalism on many aspects of the party system. But the crucial factor behind the official policy of a party seems to be what impact the election method will have on that party's number of seats. Debate on this question of regulation thus seems mainly to be a purely power-related tug-of-war in which the views of the winner and loser are known beforehand, regardless of their ideological abode.

[113] AK 1968:25, pp. 29ff.

4

Parliamentarism

1. FOUR CONCEPTS OF MONARCHY

Ever since the 1880s, the monarchy had shown newly awakened political ambitions. During the tariff dispute, Oscar II had taken the opportunity to demonstrate his power by using his constitutional prerogative to dissolve the Second Chamber, which had long been regarded as a dead letter.[1] Sweden's system of government, the king reasoned, was "constitutional but not parliamentary in the modern sense of this word." Consequently, the "verdict of the ballot box" alone should not determine the shape of the government.[2] During the suffrage dispute, the king had once again used his prerogative, this time negatively by citing the right of the monarchy in principle to refuse to dissolve the Second Chamber when there were good reasons for adopting such a position.[3] The new king, Gustaf V, who assumed the throne in 1907, shared his father's constitutional views in all essential respects.

The same period had also witnessed the emergence of a more and more ideologically conscious Left, with its roots in the political forces that members of Parliament had unwillingly helped unleash during the tariff dispute. Leftists advocated parliamentary government, as opposed to the division of powers specified in the Constitution. The controversy concerned the role of the king in the formation of a government. Did he have the right to choose his advisers freely, or did he have to yield to the wishes of a majority of Parliament? When the first election following the suffrage reform of 1907–1909 again made Karl Staaff the prime minister, a trial of strength between these two philosophies was inevitable. Sweden was thrown into a dramatic constitutional crisis whose high points were marked by the Farmers' March, the Palace Courtyard crisis, the resignation of the Staaff government, and the formation of a "royal government"

[1] Chapter 2, Section 2.
[2] Ibid.
[3] Chapter 3, Section 2.

the same year that World War I broke out, before parliamentary government was finally accepted by the king in 1917.

Division of power or parliamentarism – that was the original main match. But as the controversy intensified, an extreme version appeared in each camp: To the right of those who supported the division-of-power rule were the advocates of personal monarchy, to the left of the spokesmen of parliamentary government were those who agitated for a republic. In the ideological debate of the decade after 1910, we thus distinguish four concepts of monarchy.

The king, of course, based his defense of the division-of-power rule on the 1809 Constitution (or Instrument of Government). The power to govern was reserved for the king; to be valid, a royal decision had to be countersigned by the minister handling the matter, who was responsible before the estates for the advice he gave, primarily through the Constitution Committee. In case he violated the law, he could be tried before a court of impeachment; if he had not observed "the true interests of the realm," the estates could demand his dismissal. Legislative power was divided between king and Parliament. The power of taxation belonged to Parliament alone. Judicial power was exercised by judges who could not be removed from office. There was no trace of parliamentary government. As one researcher put it, parliamentarism was neither intended nor foreseen by the 1809 Constitution.[4]

Since the tariff dispute, there had been a radical undercurrent in Swedish politics aimed at creating rule by political parties. But until the Staaff government, the king believed that in his choice of ministers he had generally succeeded in keeping the government above the party struggles in Parliament. This did not mean that the king could ignore the mood of Parliament. His constitutionally mandated dependence on Parliament to approve tax proposals prevented this. But the king had made an effort to appoint ministers who enjoyed the confidence of Parliament by virtue of their talent and general reputation, a practice somewhat different from appointing party hacks.

What evidence is there of the king's interpretation of constitutional developments? Gustaf V himself never presented his opinion in written form. But political scientists developed arguments to support the king's position. For a more detailed analysis of the ideology of the royal side, let us therefore examine some of their contributions.

The constitutional crisis we are experiencing, wrote Pontus Fahlbeck, professor of political science at Lund, is based on Karl Staaff's efforts to introduce "British parliamentarism," with a concentration of power in the hands of the prime minister, which "actually makes him an absolute ruler

[4] Nils Nilsson-Stjernquist, *Ständerna, statsregleringen och förvaltningen. Striden om makten över utgifterna 1809–1844* (Lund: Gleerups, 1946), p.424.

– as long as he enjoys public favor." But in Swedish politics, this doctrine was something foreign. The British monarch had no political functions, while the Swedish king had a constitutional duty to govern the country with the help of ministers responsible before Parliament. The British government was a government of parties, whereas the Swedish government tried to stay above parties. The British prime minister was a party chairman, whereas the Swedish prime minister – if he belonged to a party grouping – often soon broke off his intimate ties with his party in order to protect the independence of his government. The British government was based on a majority of Parliament, and fair treatment of different opinions was created in the long term by the so-called pendulum theory, which said that their relative strengths tended to shift back and forth. The Swedish government was not based on such clear majorities; achieving them would, moreover, become even more difficult now that a proportional representation system had been introduced. The Swedish government instead based its policies on a compromise "consisting of mutual concessions by each of two opposing parties and interests, thereby implementing the intended reform or measure." This was how the "correct compass" of Swedish politics worked. Above all, there was a major social difference between the British and Swedish party systems. With some exceptions, British voters were not affiliated with parties: One year they might vote liberal, another year conservative. This occurred because the parties were not based on particular social classes or even on opposing interests. The government consisted of elected representatives, and the nation was, admittedly, governed by and through a party, but never for a party. In Sweden, again, the political parties were class parties; the dominant Rural party of the late nineteenth century and the burgeoning Social Democratic party of the early twentieth century were the best examples of this. The importation of British parliamentarism would thus result in party governments that one-sidedly favored their class interests.

As natural as parliamentary government was in Britain, this doctrine was equally unnatural in Sweden. The king of Sweden should never lower himself to being "a mouthpiece of the parties, lacking in independence." A majority of Parliament could not dictate the king's choice of ministers. Only a government not bound by party concerns could ensure a fair balance between class interests, smoothing out conflicts by means of compromises and thereby bringing about decisions that benefited the country as a whole, not merely a particular party.[5]

[5] Pontus Fahlbeck, *Engelsk parlamentarism contra svensk. Ett stycke nutidshistoria* (Lund: Gleerups, 1916), esp. pp. 3, 42ff., 73, 78ff., and 84 (a collection of articles, mainly published in the political science journal *Statsvetenskaplig Tidskrift*); idem, *Sveriges författning och den moderna parlamentarismen* (Lund: Gleerups, 1904), pp. 178–184 and 205–219.

Another scholar who stressed the broad differences in the prerequisites for parliamentary government in Britain and Sweden was Carl Hallendorff, president of the Stockholm School of Economics and a professor of political science and economic history. Yet it should not be forgotten that parliamentarism "currently is, to some extent, in a state of decadence even in its own home country." Hallendorff was referring to the new parties representing Irishmen and labor. The weaknesses of parliamentary government were most clearly revealed, however, when it was exported. All around Europe today, Hallendorff said, you could see what damage had been done by "imitated parliamentarism." When countries with constitutional, party, and social conditions different from Britain tried to practice parliamentary government, chaos broke out: Small parties were united into blocs, usually to defeat a government, but these blocs often fell apart just as they were beginning to rule. Imitated parliamentarism thus achieved the direct opposite of what its British model was intended to create – strong governments. According to Hallendorff, we in Sweden should be the last to want such imitation. We had our bicameral system, our proportional representation, and, above all, our experience in dealing with governments under the king's leadership, independent of Parliament and until recently consisting of people with authority in Parliament but not elected for purely party reasons. We lacked a class of trained professional politicians, and our M.P.'s were not accustomed to submitting obediently to the dictates of a party government. The division of power between king and Parliament should continue. We should resist attempts by the Left "to transform the king into nothing but a government-appointing decoration and a rubber stamp between changes of ministers. The Age of Liberty had given us more than enough of parliamentary encroachment on government and of rule by political parties."[6]

The letter of the Constitution obviously supported Gustaf V's views. It was also clear that the prerequisites for party systems and parliamentary government were different in Britain and Sweden. But the question remains whether the royal side's interpretation of constitutional developments was correct. Was it true, as Fahlback claimed, that Swedish practice rejected parliamentarism, that governments generally enjoyed freedom and independence from the parties in Parliament? In an article in the journal *Svensk Tidskrift*, Gunnar Rexius, also a political scientist, set out to answer this question by analyzing statements and behavior during government crises following the 1866 reform of Parliament. No one could deny that a radical undercurrent had actually existed in Swedish politics since the tariff dispute. But many people, including Rexius, had certainly been surprised by the leftist claim that their current demand for parlia-

[6] Carl Hallendorff, "Parlamentarismen," *Svensk Tidskrift* (1911): 391–401.

mentary government was the natural end point of a domestic trend during the past half century. First and foremost, Rexius wished to establish the fact that every constitutional monarch obviously wished to create as good a working relationship with Parliament as possible. This wish might lead to parliamentary government – that is, a system where Parliament alone had the power to form a government, as was the case in Britain. But Sweden had not followed Britain's path. The main trend of development in Sweden since 1866 had been that the division-of-power rule had been respected, "admittedly with occasional deviations toward parliamentarism, but only as exceptions to the rule."

Rexius began his analysis by quoting Louis De Geer to the effect that his consistent desire was to keep the power of government above political parties. "In my nature I have always had an insuperable disinclination for any party system. . . . In particular, it has always been my aim that the government should stand above parties." De Geer had tried to keep his own government above parties by conciliation and coalition, preferably by means of agreements and compromises. A political party running the government while engaged in conflict with the other parties was something De Geer had found distasteful. Rexius noted "the immense difference between De Geer's and Karl Staaff's constitutional ideals."

After De Geer came Arvid Posse. He was a party man and was appointed prime minister in this capacity. But the Rural party refused to lower itself to being a passive supporter of the government. "We shall follow the Count to the cabinet room door," the famous words of Carl Ifvarsson, a prominent Ruralist, indicated the difficulty of introducing parliamentarism in Sweden. Posse's government also fell because his party refused to accept his defense program.

After this unsuccessful experiment in parliamentary government, Swedish political life returned to its main principle, the division-of-power rule. Boström followed De Geer's policy of coalition and compromise, elevated above party distinctions. He became Sweden's conservative "statesman," just as De Geer had been the liberal one.

Then Karl Staaff appeared on the scene. Sweden's young students had supported his ideas on suffrage, not as an indication of radicalism but because at the time of the breakup of Sweden's union with Norway, Staaff expressed the concept of national unity. But after only a couple of days, the youthful delegation received a reply. It was "that memorable May evening" when Staaff's words about upper-class rule and popular rule echoed from the government bench in the Second Chamber. "It was a blow to many youthful illusions." Staaff could not have emphasized more clearly his disapproval of the methods by which De Geer, Boström, and other earlier Swedish prime ministers had governed. "It was a signal to engage in battle against our old Constitution. . . . Now the British parliamentary doctrine, which had long circled around our system of government, would wrestle with it in earnest."

Rexius did not question Staaff's right to challenge the Constitution. But it was wrong to conceal what the struggle was about. The sensitivity to Parliament that ministers had shown since 1866 was in keeping with the division-of-power rule. "But the parliamentarism that the Left has strived for is, in essence, government by party, and this is profoundly alien to the spirit of our form of government, the intentions of the authors of our Constitution and of our political tradition." This tradition instead "appealed to the monarch to try to avoid a one-sided orientation toward one of the parliamentary parties when forming a government."[7]

Political scientists thus lent prestige and legitimacy to royal constitutionalism. When Gustaf V maintained that he was entitled, after duly considering parliamentary opinion, to choose his ministers on the basis of his own judgment, he could refer to a clearly reasoned doctrine that took into account both the letter of the Constitution and subsequent constitutional developments.

Gustaf V asked himself whether he should really capitulate completely to Staaff's demands for parliamentarism and voluntarily assume the pitiful role in the formation of governments that the political scientists had described as "a government-appointing decoration." As far as the king understood constitutional law and practice, he was neither required nor even entitled to do so. With the welfare of the nation being threatened by a prodisarmament government at a time when there was danger of war, he had to look for other advisers. The king thus went behind the back of the Staaff government, contacting moderate Liberal and Conservative leaders to study the possibility of finding a government more favorably disposed toward defense.[8] The men he now contacted also had different views than the leftist government on the issue of the monarchy; they rejected Staaff's parliamentarism and supported the division-of-power rule.

In Gustaf V's arguments and behavior there is an inner logic that inexorably undermined the king's credibility. Citing the division-of-power rule, the king attempted to defend his traditional position as an independent political power, standing above the popular assembly with its partisan battles. But in struggling for his independence, he committed himself to rightist views. At the same moment that the leftists presented their demands for a parliamentary system of government, the king saw them as his political enemies and allied himself with moderate liberal and conservative forces. With his articulate views on numerous political issues, the

---

[7] Gunnar Rexius, "Parlamentarismen och svensk tradition," *Svensk Tidskrift* (1917): 181–193.

[8] See next section.

92

king seemed to the leftists to be as obvious an opponent as any Conservative party chairman. Instead of standing above social controversies, to leftists the king symbolized precisely the upper-class state they wished to tear down.

But there were also people who believed that the king was not strong enough in his opposition to Staaff. Their wish was to see Gustaf V exercise personal monarchy. On the defense issue, which triggered the constitutional crisis, the explorer Sven Hedin published the pamphlet *A Word of Warning* (Ett varningsord) early in 1912. Hedin used suggestive phrases to describe how the Liberal government's lack of desire to defend the country caused a gnawing anxiety to spread among the Swedish people "like a heavy, murky fog in the dark autumn."[9] *A Word of Warning* helped rekindle traditional fears of Russia and gave the Conservatives a powerful propaganda weapon against the Staaff government.

Hedin propagandized on behalf of personal monarchy and essentially wrote the Palace Courtyard speech, which the king read to the crowd when the Farmers' March of 1914 took place. With rhetorical brilliance, the speech recalled the historical bonds between the king of Sweden and his people. "From ages so distant that they are hidden in the obscurity of sagas, the building of this realm has rested on a foundation of solid and unshakable trust between king and people." The fact that the farmers of Sweden were now turning directly and personally to the king out of concern for Sweden's defenses showed that this trust still existed. The king thanked the farmers for their support of defense in an age when some people did not consider it necessary to solve the problem of infantry service periods. His references to the Staaff government were clear enough. The king promised that, in keeping with his position, he would not accommodate himself to their opinion. "I will not retreat from the battle-readiness and war-preparedness requirements that the experts in my army regard as indispensable."[10]

The times were right for a Charles XII cult. On the two hundredth anniversary of the Battle of Poltava, a Caroline Society was formed, mainly at the initiative of Lieutenant Carl Bennedich, who also assisted Hedin in writing the Palace Yard speech, and two history professors, Arthur Stille and Harald Hjärne. The goals of the society combined their scholarly and political ambitions. Researchers fully rehabilitated the reputation of Charles XII as a military leader. Bennedich attempted to show that Charles XII had been close to a decisive victory at Poltava. If the Swedes

---

[9] Sven Hedin, *Ett varningsord* (Stockholm, 1912); quotation from p. 3.
[10] The Palace Yard speech is printed in Karl Hildebrand, *Gustaf V som manniska och regent II* (Stockholm: Svensk litteratur, 1948), pp. 115ff.

once again had a leader like Charles XII, they could accomplish great things.[11]

The advocates of personal monarchy also included Queen Victoria of Sweden, born as Victoria of Baden and a granddaughter of Wilhelm I. A genuine child of German monarchism, she embraced the Wilhelmian constitutional ideal of giving personal power to the king. She had a burning interest in politics and despised parliamentary government and Staaff – in this respect she went even further than her husband. The queen sought her own advisers among the extreme Right, where her political sympathies lay. Because of her willpower and intelligence, she exercised a strong influence on Gustaf V and took an active part in his deliberations on government issues.[12]

The royal court was more strongly affected by the queen's extreme ideas than by the king's moderate ones. This applied very much to the leading official of the court, Ludvig Douglas, who was appointed marshal of the realm when Staaff formed his government, in order to provide a source of support to the king in his dealings with Staaff. "When the unpleasant moment has arrived – I cannot describe it with other words – when sooner or later a leftist government must be formed, then the king needs a devoted and reliable man nearby with whom he can speak and seek advice, a man who has political and parliamentary experience," the queen wrote in order to persuade Douglas to accept the appointment as marshal of the realm. "I know that the king needs this help. Indeed you and I will work together, Count. I am interested in everything that has to do with the office that we wish you, Count, to take charge of."[13] Douglas replied that he accepted the appointment. The queen's letter had dispelled his doubts.[14] Douglas, who had also been described as Hedin's teacher in the art of propaganda,[15] was a loyal ally of the queen in the cause of personal monarchy.

The leader of the Conservatives in the First Chamber, Ernst Trygger, a professor of law and Supreme Court justice known for his elegant and sharp-witted repartee, occupied a central position in the ideological environment. Unlike the leader of the Conservatives in the Second Chamber, Arvid Lindman, who advised the king to use cautious tactics, Trygger consistently defended the position of the king as outlined in the 1809 Consti-

---

[11] Nils Elvander, *Harald Hjärne och konservatismen. Konservativ idédebatt i Sverige 1865–1922* (Stockholm: Almqvist & Wiksell, 1961), pp. 419ff.

[12] Olle Nyman, *Högern och kungamakten 1911–14. Ur borggårdskrisens förhistoria* (Uppsala: Almqvist & Wiksell, 1957), pp. 266–267.

[13] Queen Victoria to Ludvig Douglas, 17 Sep. 1911, quoted in Leif Kihlberg: *Karl Staaf II. Regeringschef, oppositionsledare 1905–1915* (Stockholm: Bonniers, 1963), p. 235.

[14] Ibid.

[15] Ibid., p. 263.

tution. This document simply did not permit Parliament to control the state in an autocratic fashion as the advocates of parliamentary government wished. "The monarchy of the Constitution" meant that "the king makes the decisions and the minister is not responsible for the decisions but for his advice." "Thus, the introduction of British parliamentary government" required an amendment to the Constitution. Was the Left willing to submit to this complex procedure, with repeated parliamentary voting and an election between? Trygger was not convinced of this. He feared "a revolutionary trend." Perhaps Staaff did not want a revolution in order to "impose his views regarding the king's position of power or, more correctly, position of no power." But the legal route seemed long, while the seriousness of the world situation required resolute action in the interest of national unity and rearmament.[16]

For his part, Trygger did not feel that a study of custom provided any information on how the constitutional crisis should be solved, because there were no universally accepted procedures related to the powers of the king. Consequently Trygger defended the king's constitutional right to assume political leadership, as he did with his Palace Yard speech – directly addressing the people without first consulting with his ministers.

The leading ideologist among the supporters of personal monarchy was Rudolf Kjellén, a professor of political science who was also a Conservative M.P. His geopolitical system-building and extreme conservative ideology made him famous far outside Sweden's borders, especially in Germany. Parliamentary government and the liberal view of mankind and the state on which it was based were profoundly alien to him. Kjellén built up his entire ideology around the concept of nationalism. The state was a biological organism in which people were arranged according to their functions.[17] The true will of the people was not expressed by the sort of party squabbles and tactical games that characterized parliamentary democracies, but was interpreted intuitively by their leader. Even before Gustaf V assumed the throne, Kjellén expressed his hopes for personal monarchy. "It is our innermost wish that the time might soon return when the occupant of the Swedish throne ... will know how to listen to the secret, perhaps only half-conscious desires of the nation; for only in such an intimate rapport with the mood of the people can the throne find the strength and determination to assume leadership of the people in awkward situations."[18] Kjellén later presented the idea that the people needed "a strong man to follow," a reference to the monarch. Obeying their

[16] Ernst Trygger, *Öfver allt och alla Sverige, dess ära och oberoende* (Stockholm, 1914); quotations from pp. 6ff.
[17] Elvander 1961, pp. 257–258, 309ff., 325, and 425.
[18] AK 1907:8, p. 28.

leader was "the deepest longing of all Germanic peoples." The Swedes in particular needed "a hard hand over them."[19]

The other main ideologue was Harald Hjärne, Kjellén's more moderate professorial colleague at Uppsala and a Conservative M. P. Hjärne did not subscribe to this kind of leader cult. As a historian he – unlike Kjellén – dissociated himself from the myth of Charles XII, although as one of the founders of the Caroline Society, as we have mentioned, he encouraged new initiatives to carry out scholarly research about this king. But at the same time he criticized Lindman for what he regarded as excessively compliant tactics toward Staaff.[20]

The propaganda on behalf of personal monarchy and the spectacular arrangements intended to promote it during the period around World War I – for example, the Charles XII commemorations, the Farmers' March, the Palace Yard speech – have a theatrical, almost mischievous air. But the concept of personal monarchy is worth taking more seriously, and not only because it emerged in a surprisingly short time. It can be placed in a larger context in intellectual history. It derives from the reaction to the ideas of 1789, which reemerged around Europe during the early twentieth century after the first stage of the industrial revolution, with its far-reaching economic, social, and political changes. During World War I Rudolf Kjellén published a brochure *The Ideas of 1914* (Die Ideen von 1914). The ideas proposed would now replace the liberal, Enlightenment concepts that had dominated intellectual trends since the French Revolution. Instead of liberty, Kjellén spoke of "order," referring to the disciplined incorporation of the individual into the national collective as opposed to the individualism of Enlightenment ideology. Instead of equality, Kjellén spoke of "righteousness," that is, the respective values of different parts based on their importance to the whole as opposed to the rule by mediocrities said to have resulted from the concept of equality. Kjellén responded to the concept of brotherhood, interpreted as internationalism, with "national kinship."[21] The future seemed bright for ultraconservatism; liberalism, its main ideological enemy, was pronounced dead. Only when the fortunes of war turned did people begin to suspect that this reaction would merely be a parenthesis in the history of Swedish political thought. In Continental Europe, national socialism would soon perpetuate this line of thought.[22]

[19] Elvander 1961, p. 285.

[20] Harald Hjärne collected a number of lectures and articles in the pamphlet *Från försvarsstriden 1914* (Uppsala: Askerbergs, 1914).

[21] Rudolf Kjellén, *Die Ideen von 1914. Eine weltgeschichtliche Perspektive* (Leipzig: Hirzel, 1915).

[22] After the upheavals of World War I, Kjellén no longer attached his hope to personal monarchy. He began to speak of a "chief" or leader from the ranks of the people in a way that anticipates the German and Italian dictatorships (Elvander 1961, pp. 285ff.).

Parliamentarism

When Karl Staaff developed his thoughts on the concept of parliamentary government, he made a distinction between the written Constitution and what he called "the living constitution." Constitutional documents were merely the external framework of a country's system of government; it had to be filled by constitutional developments and customs. As this occurred, imperfections and contradictions in the rules were often revealed; "this is true of state constitutions." "The solution will arise in such a way that the message or principle that derives its strength from political developments as a whole will achieve richer realization than the message or principle whose importance has declined during this process." In Staaff's opinion, political scientists and legal scholars should focus their attention on such matters instead of being "the handmaidens of personal monarchy," who "dutifully" cited "the rules supporting the supposed demands of this power."

These words are taken from Staaff's pamphlet *The Constitutional System of Government* (Det konstitutionella styrelsesättet), which appeared during the crisis year 1914.[23] It was later incorporated into the second main source for understanding Staaff's views on parliamentarism, an extensive work entitled *The Democratic Form of Government* (Det demokratiska statsskicket), which Staaff worked on for eight or nine years and which was published posthumously. This work deals primarily with developments in four major democracies – Britain, France, the United States, and Switzerland – but the presentation also includes a number of views that indicate Staaff's parliamentary ideals. In *The Democratic Form of Government,* Staaff again stressed the need to study constitutional custom, and he proposed a formidable research program in political science. According to Staaff, it is not enough to interpret constitutions and illustrate them with precedents. Not only the parts of the machinery but also its operation while the machinery is running should be studied by political scientists – "whether everything is running calmly and smoothly or its parts creak and the bearings are hot." It was necessary to penetrate deeply into conditions not mentioned in constitutions. Above all, the workings of the modern party system should be studied. Modern political science in fact regarded "the actual national constitution as a document that in

[23] Karl Staaff, *Det konstitutionella styrelsesättet* (Stockholm: Aktiebolaget Ljus, 1914), pp. 31–32. In the suffrage debate, Staaff had already declared: "The actual fundamental difference in opinion between the prime minister and myself is that he is speaking about the words of the Constitution, and I about the shape of constitutional life. A constitution is seldom more than a framework. How constitutional life is shaped therein, depends on numerous factors. Without there being the slightest change in the constitution, constitutional customs may develop within its given framework whose justification is no longer questioned by anyone, but which are respected by all; and obviously there may also be deliberate efforts to lead constitutional life in a certain direction or to move further toward goals already being pursued, without this in the slightest way entailing a conflict with the constitution itself." AK 1907:52, p. 87.

itself provided little information. It always asks: How do things really work?"[24]

It is possible to object to Staaff's words by pointing out that the rightists, as we have already noted, by no means neglected the study of constitutional custom. The interesting question, however, is whether Staaff found anything different from his opponents when he studied constitutional developments.

Staaff's method in this context may appear surprising. In *The Constitutional System of Government* he did not discuss developments in Sweden, but in Britain. He quoted a thirty-five-year-old essay written by "no less than one of Britain's most outstanding statesmen, Gladstone."[25] The same technique is used in *The Democratic Form of Government,* which consistently reflects Staaff's conviction of the superiority of British parliamentary government and its applicability to Sweden as well.[26] Staaff devoted much space to the specific problems of British parliamentary government. The British system provided him with proof to back up his Second Chamber parliamentarism: The House of Commons or its equivalent should dominate the other chamber in a parliamentary system, especially if the upper chamber was based on restricted voting rights. The Second Chamber should be given unrestricted initiative and leadership in national politics.

The government should also be based on the Second Chamber. Parliamentary government created a "fusion" between the first and second branches of government, Staaff wrote in the spirit of Walter Bagehot.[27] The government should answer to the popularly elected legislature, not to the monarchy. There must be complete agreement between king and ministers. "If differences arise between the sovereign and his ministers, it must be their will that prevails in the final analysis." Power must be accompanied by responsibility. In a parliamentary system of government, the people could demand responsibility on the part of their rulers. In countries ruled by monarchs, the responsible person was beyond reach.

The fact that the king subordinated himself to the will of a minister did not mean that he had lost his importance. Staaff assigned him a long series of tasks: during changes of government, trying to create a cabinet that corresponded most closely to opinion in Parliament; following government business and giving it the benefit of his experience, which could become rich over the years; representing Sweden externally, without thereby pursuing any personal foreign policy; representing the nation

[24] Karl Staaff, *Det demokratiska statsskicket. Jämförande politiska studier* I, ed. Nils Edén and Erik Staaff (Stockholm: Wahlström & Widstrand, 1917), pp. 28–29.

[25] Staaff 1914, pp. 5ff.

[26] This characterization is also found in Kihlberg 1963 II, p. 406.

[27] Carl Arvid Hessler, "Parlamentarismens begrepp," in *Studier tillägnade Fredrik Lagerroth* (Lund: Gleerup, 1950), p. 172.

internally on ceremonial occasions; and in times of unrest, using his high position to take steps that might encourage calm and reconciliation. In addition, the king might still exercise a purely political influence on the issues – but, please note, by means of persuasion, by arguing his point in the government. The king should not publicly disagree with his cabinet.

Anglophile that he was, Staaff did not want to abolish the institution. "Instead of abolishing the monarchy, parliamentary government wants kings to help bring about the smooth transition of real power to the people." Monarchs should voluntarily give up political power and withdraw into the shadows. If this happened, advocates of parliamentary government would not demand a republic. Instead, it could be argued, parliamentary government would forestall a nation's transition to a republican mentality. But further in the future, when a long period of parliamentary government had weaned all classes away from seeing any necessary protection in the monarchy and had made them realize that the function of the monarchy could be nothing but "formal and decorative," then perhaps the issue would be so ripe that no conflict would be needed to resolve it. A transition to a republic could take place amidst great calm.

Staaff discussed the problem of leadership in a parliamentary democracy with particular devotion. On the basis of British developments, he came to the conclusion that once the party system had adjusted to universal suffrage and Second Chamber parliamentary government had become well established, modern party governments could rule with greater authority than the royal cabinets of earlier days. All power would be gathered in the hands of the prime minister. But unlike royal autocracy, it was a form of power under responsibility. The parliamentary system provided a technique for demanding that leaders accept political responsibility.[28]

These were Karl Staaff's constitutional ideals. Like an architect who gains new impressions by traveling abroad, he wanted to introduce and re-create British conditions in Swedish national life. But how could Staaff claim that the development of the Swedish Constitution supported his parliamentary ideals?

The answer is that when it came to developments in Sweden, Staaff did not work by the empirical method. There are, admittedly, plenty of reflections on Swedish conditions in Staaff's works. But he did not publish any systematic historical background as Rexius did. Perhaps his method should instead be characterized as logical. He seized upon the radical undercurrent in Swedish politics, whose existence even Rexius acknowledged, demonstrated its growth and triumphs after the turn of the century, and attempted to draw conclusions as to what a fully developed parlia-

---

[28] Staaff 1917 II, esp. pp. 164–214 (quotation from p. 169), 253, 265–266, 349–354, and 359–373; Staaff 1914, p. 35.

mentary democracy should entail. In this context, the British example served as an ideal that we should strive for.

The age of royal autocracy was over, Staaff wrote in his 1914 pamphlet. Modern constitutions ensure greater and greater political influence for the people. If a monarch overstepped these constitutional rules, this was of course an unconstitutional act. "But it is customary to speak of an unconstitutional form of government in another sense aside from the one characterized by direct violations of specific constitutional regulations. This is when an unconstitutional form of government means the same as a personal form of government. And its opposite, a constitutional form of government, then means something different from the mere fact that the existing constitutional stipulations are not directly violated. What do these terms mean in the cases now referred to?" They meant, Staaff continued, that the popularly elected legislature had "a voice in the matter," that it could exercise "control" over the government. Both a personal and a constitutional system of government could exist without the king being guilty of unconstitutional behavior in the narrower sense. But in "a fully developed constitutional form of government," referred to in this discussion as parliamentarism, there was no room for personal monarchy.

We cannot say that this opinion is expressed especially clearly. When the pamphlet was incorporated into *The Democratic Form of Government,* this part of the text was reworked. It remained clear that royal violations of the Constitution had to be labeled unconstitutional behavior. "But in another sense, the expression in question may be used in such a way that a form of government deserves to be called constitutional only when the head of state listens to the opinion of his legally appointed advisers." Now, of course, it was customary to distinguish between a "constitutional" and a "parliamentary" form of government. "But in actuality, historically and logically they are extremely closely related. . . . For these advisers cannot stand up to the personal will of the head of state unless they know that they have the support of a parliamentary majority. From this standpoint we can thus say that parliamentarism is the necessary prerequisite to make a form of government . . . constitutionally secure, and that it is consequently the most perfect form of constitutionalism."[29]

In Karl Staaff's interpretation, the Swedish constitutional system thus evolved toward parliamentary government by logical necessity. He regarded a constitution such as Sweden's that prescribed a certain measure of personal governing power for the monarch as an absurdity, a self-contradiction. The living constitution showed that these written constitutional rules were not supported by political developments and thus had to give way. In this perspective, royal intervention in politics, such as the

[29] Staaff 1914, pp. 4–5; Staaff 1917 II, p. 165.

Palace Yard speech, appeared to be inconsistent with constitutional developments. This is why Staaff labeled the king's behavior unconstitutional.

Like no other Swede, Karl Staaff symbolizes the trend toward parliamentary democracy in Sweden. In lofty words, he depicted the intellectual tradition with which he identified. The first sentence of *The Democratic Form of Government* describes developments since the late eighteenth century as "a remarkable, indeed a wonderful stage in the history of human development." Staaff was referring to "the abolition of autocracy and the establishment of national statutes and constitutions." The latter exclusively meant laws that granted political influence to the people. This trend had begun early in Sweden. One forerunner of a modern constitution, one could say, was the form of government adopted in the Age of Liberty (1718–1771), after "Charles XII's exercise of an autocracy which humiliated the people and devastated the country"[30] (the contrast between Staaff's view of history and that of the ultraconservatives could not be formulated more clearly). Strongly influenced by British politics, as he interpreted it, he developed his parliamentary views with strength and consistency. To Staaff, British parliamentarism was a superior form of government. He was not, however, content to describe an ideal. He also attempted to persuade people that in Sweden, too, political developments were moving with logical consistency toward parliamentary government, even though it was hardly possible to speak of it as any main trend until then. Constitutions were unclear documents. Those rules that were in harmony with developments had precedence. Resisting the trend toward parliamentarism as the Conservatives and the monarchy had done was thus in conflict with the "living constitution" and must be labeled unconstitutional. Staaff selected from modern Swedish history those events that agreed with his own ideals and referred to them as "developments" or "the living constitution." But unlike his critics, he did not try to prove his thesis by any systematic account of Swedish constitutional development.

This way of trying to squeeze support for a particular constitutional philosophy from modern political history was also an unnecessary line of reasoning. Staaff could instead have argued as follows: Here is my constitutional ideal, and it is my intention to bring about a change in Sweden so that parliamentary government will be recognized. In the future, governments will be made to depend on the consent of Parliament (or possibly the Second Chamber), not that of the monarch. Using the language of this study, it would be possible to interpret Swedish political developments, in Staaff's perspective, as follows. The nondecision strategy suffered a temporary defeat during the tariff dispute but was soon revived and was successful for decades. Members of Parliament from various moderate-liberal

---

[30] Staaff 1917 I, pp. 1–2 and 4.

and conservative groupings, which from the standpoint of parliamentary democracy consisted of a single ideologically cohesive camp, managed to shift political controversy to issues other than those that threatened the prevailing division-of-power rule. By thus keeping the issue of parliamentary government off the agenda, they showed the true face of power. It was this community of values, whose centerpiece was the division-of-power rule, that Karl Staaff now attacked. Instead of maintaining that parliamentarism already existed in "the living constitution," he could have declared that his aim was a change of system that would replace the division-of-power rule with parliamentary government.

There were, of course, tactical motives for Staaff's way of structuring his argument, as is the case with all politicians. A declaration of intent to change the system might have been regarded by some voters as frightening. These tactical considerations should not be exaggerated, however. Staaff was honestly convinced of the correctness of his argument about "the living constitution" and built up a whole program of political science research around it. But he left it to others to find arguments for the viewpoint he represented. This research program was begun in Uppsala under Axel Brusewitz, a professor of political science who was a devoted supporter of Staaff's constitutional doctrine. Using a historical, source-critical method, Brusewitz and his students began to analyze one government after another. But no summary of this research program was written. Swedish political science is still waiting for some scholar who will step forward and draw conclusions from this research program – in favor of one interpretation or the other of what is actually the main trend of Swedish constitutional development from the parliamentary reform of 1866 until World War I.

Ever since its founding, the Social Democratic party had been republican in principle. But the demand for a republic was not included in the party program. Under Branting's leadership, the party had concentrated all of its agitational power on the struggle for universal suffrage. Branting stood just as loyally at Staaff's side in demanding parliamentary government. But arguing that the party had to avoid wasting its energy on demonstrations for such hopeless causes as republicanism, Branting defended the decision by the 1905 party congress not to demand a republic, even though "naturally ... in our hearts and souls we are all" republicans.[31] The king's refusal to approve Staaff's request for dissolution of the Second Chamber in 1906 strengthened the republican cause as the 1908 party congress approached. Monarchy should be dispatched in the same way as upper-class rule, Social Democratic newspapers wrote. "For good cause," the congress adopted a statement saying "that the Swedish Social Democratic

[31] *Sveriges Socialdemokratiska Arbetarepartis sjätte kongress* (Stockholm, 1905), p. 117.

party, like the entire international Social Democratic movement, is obviously a republican party."[32] The party program remained unchanged, however – but only after a vote that was as close as 164 to 124.

When the demand for a republic surfaced for the third time, at the 1911 congress, the Social Democratic party executive no longer wished to oppose it. Branting objected, however, because there had been change neither in the party's opinion nor in the actual situation. After a vote, the congress adopted new wording in the party program. It demanded "a revision of the Constitution to implement a republic and a democratic form of government."'[33]

As the constitutional crisis of the decade after 1910 unfolded, the Social Democrats had thus formally become a republican party. Backed by the decision of the party congress, in 1912 the demand for a republic was presented in Parliament for the first time, in a members' bill by Stockholm mayor Carl Lindhagen; its cosponsors included Rickard Sandler,[34] a leading representative of the youth movement. But the bill was sharply criticized even by the Social Democrats on the Constitution Committee. Branting, who wrote their opinion, argued that an issue such as this should not "be presented merely as an abstract topic of discussion" but only "when the inner logic of events has provided the necessary background" for "serious political action. Things should thus have developed to the point where the introduction of a republic seems to a substantial proportion of the nation not only theoretically right but also called for by the situation." But Branting added, "Such a state of events may come quickly enough if a monarch, obstinately insisting on his royal power, should raise stubborn resistance to the unambiguous and firm demands of the popular will."[35]

It may appear as though Branting's description was a direct anticipation of the Palace Yard crisis. But when this event occurred, he was not prepared to move from words to action – at least not to any far-reaching action. As a protest against the Palace Yard speech, he asked Parliament to vote against any government appropriation to the royal court. The demand for a republic, on the other hand, was rejected by the Social Democrats in the Constitution Committee with the same arguments as in 1912. In Parliament, Branting declared that there was no reason to debate continuously "the principle of monarchy itself. The growth of democracy in society is the important thing. Medieval views related to the monarchy

---

[32] *Sveriges Socialdemokratiska Arbetarepartis sjunde kongress* (Stockholm, 1908), pp. 226–227.
[33] *Sveriges Socialdemokratiska Arbetarepartis åttonde kongress* (Stockholm, 1911), pp. 34ff.
[34] Mot AK 1912:318.
[35] KU 1912:38, pp. 2–3.

fade away under the influence of time."[36] At the party congress, he criticized those who had sponsored the prorepublican bill in Parliament. The
issue of a republic would not reach maturity by means of constant members' bills. "Every parliamentary action that is to have any chance of success must be carefully weighed on the basis of the situation."[37]

A few years later, developments furnished Sweden's republicans with
new arguments. The Russian and German empires collapsed. Demands for
far-reaching constitutional reforms including complete democratization
and the introduction of a republic were also presented in Sweden. It too
seemed poised for a revolutionary situation. On 13 November 1918 the
leadership group representing all Social Democratic M.P.'s gathered for
an emergency meeting. A radical wing argued that it was time to "clean
up bourgeois society," among other things by introducing a republic. "If
these demands could not be carried out by voluntary means, the party
should be prepared for revolutionary action." But Branting "entreated"
his party colleagues not to consider revolution; developments in Russia
provided a frightening example and the situation in Germany was uncertain. His antirevolutionary policy finally won the day. It also prevailed
during the subsequent movement to reform the Constitution. A few days
after the M.P.'s met, Branting's policy was confirmed at a meeting of the
party executive, the editors of the Social Democratic newspapers, and the
executive board of the Swedish Trade Union Confederation. The issue of
a republic was postponed.[38]

Branting repeatedly voiced the Marxist concept that by natural necessity, the monarchy would wither away as the Social Democratic party
became stronger. In a major speech on the reform of the Constitution,
Branting declared in December 1918 that the Social Democrats indeed had
a program that "points beyond the framework of our present-day constitution in numerous respects. It points ahead toward an organization and
structure of national constitutions that quite clearly belong to a rather
near future when a democratic republic will be the general and common
pattern among civilized states in most countries both in Europe and on
other continents.... But anyone who wishes to see these things as they
are has to say that for the moment, these issues have not been thoroughly
discussed before our people and have not been so clearly presented that
one can say that there is a firm and pronounced public opinion in Sweden
that favors one or the other."[39]

The revolutionary storm passed. The monarchy survived. After the

---

[36] AK 1914 A:18, pp. 3ff.; mot 1914 B:250; KU 1914 B:18.
[37] *Sveriges Socialdemokratiska Arbetarepartis nionde kongress* (Stockholm, 1914), p. 196.
[38] Gunnar Gerdner, *Det svenska regeringsproblemet 1917–1920. Från majoritetskoalition
till minoritetsparlamentarism* (Uppsala: Almqvist & Wiksell, 1946), pp. 34ff.
[39] AK 1918 urtima riksdag (extra session of Parliament): 17, p. 29.

Social Democratic party split, it was the left-wing Socialists and Communists who introduced bills in Parliament calling for a republic. Why should people "make noise by talking about a republic" when there was "a strong monarchical feeling in this country?" asked Arthur Engberg, a leading Social Democrat, in 1920. The monarchy was a rallying point for reactionary movements; if it was threatened, it could catapult these forces into power.[40] The Social Democrats became less and less interested in republicanism. Things would go so far that a committee drafting the party program with the support of Prime Minister Per Albin Hansson, who by then had left his youthful radicalism far behind, proposed to the party congress in 1944 that the call for a republic be removed from the program.[41]

Throughout the decade after 1910, the Social Democratic Party was thus deeply divided on the issue of the monarchy. Only with difficulty did the moderate leadership of the party, more specifically Branting himself, manage to keep the radical opponents of the monarchy at bay. His arguments were continuously being undermined. When the conditions he specified for the introduction of a republic quickly materialized, apparently to his own surprise, he specified new conditions, which in turn also caught him off guard by rapidly coming true. In 1912 he said that if the king personally insisted on political power, this action would justify a change to a republic. When two years later the king did just that (according to any reasonable interpretation of his statement), Branting added that in order to succeed, any action had to be thoroughly weighed according to the situation. If this vague wording is regarded as anything but an evasion, it is difficult to imagine what "situation" would be more likely to further the republican cause than the one prevailing in the fall of 1918. But Branting also allowed this moment to slip past. He said the issue of a republic had not been discussed thoroughly enough; it was something for a future constitution, but "quite obviously in the rather near future." As we know, more than sixty-five years later this near future has not yet occurred.

It was obvious that the party leadership was not willing to act. Republicanism was not considered worth pursuing, in case it might sabotage more important issues. If the demand for a republic was pressed, this might bring the reactionaries to power. The party's view of history also provided some reason for confidence: There is a fatalistic tone to Branting's assertion that in the future, monarchist ideas would fade and the monarchy would wither as the Social Democrats became stronger. An analysis of the Social Democratic call for a republic during the 1910 dec-

[40] AK 1920:56, p. 33.
[41] *Sveriges Socialdemokratiska Arbetarepartis sjuttonde kongress* (Stockholm, 1944), pp. 111–119.

ade points toward the larger question of the determinism that, for decades, paralyzed the ability of Social Democratic M.P.'s to act on practically all issues except the suffrage issue. They found themselves trapped in a dilemma between what was ideologically desirable in the long term and practically possible to implement in the short term. This question will be discussed in greater detail on a more general level in the next chapter.

2. THE KING SEEKS A STRATEGY

After the Left had won the 1911 election, Gustaf V initiated a series of maneuvers aimed at preventing parliamentarist concepts from being put into practice. Like upper-class rule, monarchy appeared to be on the losing side of history. But the king was as little inclined as the Conservatives to give up his position of power willingly. In arriving at an overall assessment of how the king, as the potential loser, sought to avoid an expected defeat, it is striking that we cannot speak of *one* strategy on the part of the king and not even of a main strategy. Strongly upset at political trends but vacillating and irresolute, at times the victim of stronger wills than his own, Gustaf V was cast between different alternatives until finally, at the moment of defeat, he made a choice that meant that the least evil alternative, not the worst one, was implemented.[42]

The first possibility was simply to prevent Staaff from becoming prime minister. When the election results began to be known, the king was on a hunting trip in Skåne, Sweden's southernmost province. On the advice of Bishop Billing, a leading Conservative in the First Chamber whom the king contacted at the queen's suggestion, the king approached the governor of nearby Kristianstad County, Louis De Geer the Younger, and asked him to consider the possibility of forming a moderate Liberal government. Upon his return to Stockholm, however, the king realized that a Staaff government was unavoidable. But Gustaf V did not wish to

---

[42] The most penetrating scholarly work on the political game during these years is Nyman 1957. Other works include Axel Brusewitz, *Kungamakt, herremakt, folkmakt. Författnings-skampen i Sverige 1906–1918* (Stockholm: Prisma, 1964) (first published in 1951); W. M. Carlgren, *Ministären Hammarskjöld. Tillkomst, söndring, fall* (Stockholm: Almqvist & Wiksell, 1967); Gerdner 1946; Hildebrand 1948; Folke Lindberg, *Kunglig utrikespolitik* (Stockholm: Aldus/Bonniers, 1966) (first published in 1954); Knut Wichman, *Gustaf V, Karl Staaff och striden om vårt försvar 1901–1914* (Stockholm: Norstedts, 1967); Ragnhild Frykberg, *Bondetåget 1914. Dess upprinnelse, inre historia och följder* (Stockholm: Hörsta, 1959); Sten Carlsson & Jerker Rosén, *Svensk historia II. Tiden efter 1718* (Stockholm: Bonniers, 1961), pp. 617–626; Stig Hadenius, Björn Molin, and Hans Wieslander, *Sverige efter 1900. En modern politisk historia* (Stockholm: Bonniers, 1978), pp. 59–94 (first published in 1967); Henrik A. Olsson, "Om 'abdikationshot' och parlamentarism. Några uttalanden av Gustaf V från dennes tidigare regeringsår," *Statsvetenskaplig Tidskrift* (1962): 98–118; Jarl Torbacke, "Gustaf V och abdikationstanken. Ett meddelande," *Historisk Tidskrift* (1968): 296ff.; Sten Körner, "En ny källa till borggårdskrisens förhistoria," ibid. (1970); 208–218.

authorize Staaff to form a government with no strings attached. First, he expressed his reservations about a government that would rely to some extent on the support of a prorepublican party such as the Social Democrats. Second, the king refused to give Staaff carte blanche authority, now that the suffrage reform had been implemented, to dissolve the First Chamber, as Staaff requested. After their meeting, the king contacted the leaders of the Conservative party, who now began to play the role of "hidden advisers" they would have throughout Staaff's period as prime minister. A general delegation to the prime minister of the king's authority to dissolve the First Chamber was considered out of the question. Staaff had to specify the time period; the dissolution would take place during the fall. With that, the king was prepared to swallow the bitter pill and give Staaff the task of forming a government. The king bade the Lindman government an emotional farewell.

In keeping with Liberal election campaign promises, four committees were appointed in December 1911, to examine potential ways of saving money in the Swedish defense system. The king dictated a statement in the cabinet minutes saying he believed that the country's defense forces could not be cut without danger to the country. Such a royal statement, which the prime minister tried unsuccessfully to prevent, was of course directly contrary to Staaff's view that the monarch and the government should present a united front to the public – on the government's conditions. The king was demonstrating his displeasure with this doctrine. The Conservatives, too, were upset at the composition of the four defense-related committees: Aside from four Liberal ministers headed by Staaff there were thirteen other Liberal members, while the Conservatives and Social Democrats each had four representatives.

Two weeks later Staaff and his colleagues made another defense policy decision that the king found equally objectionable; the government decided to cancel construction of the F-boat, a dreadnought or large armored naval vessel that the Lindman government had ordered. The king noted his displeasure in yet another statement for the cabinet minutes. The government again failed to persuade him to abstain from this action. Private interests now started a campaign to collect voluntary contributions to assure the construction of the F-boat. Money flowed in much faster than expected – more than seventeen million kronor. The government accepted the gift and in 1915 the completed armored vessel was launched.

The four defense committees speeded up their investigations. By the fall of 1913 they were in the final stages of their task. Sven Hedin now gave a speech in the Dala Regiment officers' mess in Falun, north central Sweden, about a government that "plays ducks and drakes with our national independence" instead of following the proud traditions from the days of Charles XII. When the speech became known, it caused a great deal of controversy. The Liberals demanded that the commander of the regiment be punished, something that the king and his Conservative advisers found completely out of the question. The "Falun Affair" developed into a lengthy crisis between the king and the government. Feelings became even stronger when it turned out that the minister of war, David Bergström, had used the expression "by His Majesty's Command" in a letter without having discussed the matter with the monarch. The king and the Conservatives could see how the advocates of parliamentary government regarded the king as no more than a rubber stamp. The solution to the Falun crisis was suggested by Trygger. The colonel of the regiment himself requested a trial by court-martial. In his diary, Lindman describes what happened when the request was announced to the minister of war: "Upon this sudden news, David Bergström could not suppress a grimace apparently because his prey had slipped from his hands. It was really exceptional that a person should become angry because he could not condemn a man without a trial and create a conflict with the monarchy."[43] The colonel was later exonerated by the court-martial, hardly a surprise either to Trygger or the king.

No matter how insignificant the Falun Affair was in objective terms, it had far-reaching consequences. The relationship between the king and the government was now very strained; the king began eagerly looking around for a new prime minister; the ultraconservatives encouraged him to be increasingly combative toward the Staaff government.

It turned out that the Liberals in the defense committees were divided. There was no majority for such an antidefense attitude as the one they had campaigned for in 1911. The central committee of the Liberal party was also divided. After a long wait, the government announced its views to king and country by means of a speech that Staaff gave at Karlskrona, a naval base in southeastern Sweden, in December 1913. Staaff was fully aware of the crucial importance this speech would have on political developments; he agonized about it and postponed it several times. On a number of points, Staaff now moved in a prodefense direction. He also raised the possibility that the infantry might be given longer service periods but said that the voters should first be allowed to have their say on this issue. Many an orthodox Liberal was furious at this shift to the right. Staaff was viewed as a renegade.

From a tactical standpoint, the Karlskrona speech was a disappointment to the king. He had noticed how the defense issue had helped him along in the struggle against Staaff and his parliamentarism. In this struggle,

---

[43] Arvid Lindman, *Dagboksanteckningar,* ed. Nils F. Holm (Stockholm: Kungl. Samfundet för utgivande av handskrifter rörande Skandinaviens historia, 1972), p. 122.

aimed at a change of government, he would of course have had an even stronger argument if Staaff had pursued a consistent disarmament policy. How should he react now? The king and the leaders of the Conservatives began intensive deliberations. The king was advised not to accept the half-outstretched hand, but to exploit the defense issue to the limit and push the game further toward confrontation. Trygger told the king he should be more aggressive toward Staaff and demand that he no longer postpone the issue of the infantry's period of service. Trygger instructed the king on how he should react in different situations that might arise, depending on how Staaff answered. If Staaff refused to heed the king's demand, he should be dismissed. If he agreed to it, on the other hand, it was important to get him to commit himself firmly to a fixed timetable, including a final presentation of the matter before the king no later than 15 March and a declaration that the Second Chamber would be dissolved immediately after this date. In other words, Staaff should be forced either to capitulate immediately to the king or undertake an election campaign in which he would be in the hopeless position of defending his breach of the Liberals' 1911 campaign promises. Staaff gave no firm reply, even though "in all likelihood he leaned more toward a no than a yes."[44] But for the moment it did not prove possible to carry out Trygger's plan to replace the Staaff government, although Trygger himself declared his willingness to serve as prime minister.

The king's side now had the initiative, and the crisis rapidly moved toward its culmination. The Liberals were divided; the Liberal prodefense camp withdrew support from Staaff. Above all, public opinion around the country favored the king. The farmers around Uppsala began to prepare the Farmers' March; the movement quickly spread around the country. On 6 February 1914 more than thirty thousand farmers wended their way into the inner courtyard of the Royal Palace in Stockholm, where the king greeted them; an additional forty thousand sympathizers who could not participate in the march had signed petitions. The farmers declared their willingness to help resolve the defense issue that same year, as the experts had demanded and as the dangerous times required. It was time to refute the notion that Sweden's farmers did not wish to sacrifice anything for defense. In his reply, the king defended the right of a personal monarch to voice his political convictions without having to consult with or bend to the will of the government. The speech was repeated to those who could not fit into the inner courtyard by Crown Prince Gustaf Adolf on Slottsbacken (Palace Hill) and by Prince Carl in the outer courtyard. The issue of the infantry's service period must not be postponed, the king

---

[44] Brusewitz 1964 (1951), p. 70.

declared. "The defense issue as a whole should be discussed and decision should be made now, without delay and in a single context."[45]

A government crisis was unavoidable. When Staaff demanded a pledge from the king that in the future he would give the government advance notice of his political statements, Gustaf V replied that he did not wish to deprive himself of the right to address the Swedish people freely. As a result, the Staaff government resigned. It was succeeded by a "royal government," but one not headed by Trygger. The number of battle-ready Conservatives in Parliament was not sufficient for a government of the kind that Trygger would head. Instead, it became the task of a county governor, Hjalmar Hammarskjöld, in the words of *Dagens Nyheter,* to "play the role of the black knight in the joust."[46] Hammarskjöld formed a government of high-ranking civil servants with links to conservative groups and the business community.

Step by step, Gustaf V had moved away from the principles of the division-of-power rule and onto the path of personal monarchy. This had not been his original wish. His constitutional ideal had been a government that enjoyed the respect of Parliament and was something other than a political party government. But when the composition of Parliament made this impossible to achieve, he was persuaded by his advisers and by the generally positive trend of public opinion around the country to try a bolder strategy. Sources say that at first the king was skeptical toward the idea of a farmers' march, but as preparations proceeded and he heard more and more expressions of sympathy from Sweden's rural population, he snapped out of the lethargy into which the conflict with Staaff had led him, buoyed up by the thought of being able to demonstrate to the prime minister the strong ties between king and people. One writer summarized it thus: "The path to the Palace Yard crisis was certainly not the one Gustaf V would have taken of his own free will. It was staked out for him by strong wills in his immediate surroundings. The queen was bitterly irreconcilable in her distaste for the Liberal regime, and she exercised a strong influence on her husband. What she was aiming at was to activate the monarchy and make Sweden a power worthy of an alliance from the German standpoint. This implied both a shift in the constitutional balance of power and rearmament on the largest possible scale. No pronounced longing for power can be attributed to Gustaf V. He was compelled to play a part for which he basically had rather little inclination and for which in any event he was not well suited."[47]

The new government dissolved the Second Chamber and announced a

---

[45] Hildebrand 1948 II, p. 118.
[46] *Dagens Nyheter,* 15 Feb. 1914, quoted in Nyman 1957, p. 281.
[47] Knut Petersson, *En bondedemokrat. Alfred Petersson i Påboda* (Stockholm: Norstedts, 1965), p. 227.

new election. The ensuing election campaign during the spring of 1914 was characterized by extreme agitation and bitterness. It may be appropriate here to add a word to the reader, who may think that election campaigns are rather frequently described in this book as intensive. Let us recall that we have selected major controversies in modern Swedish political history for this study. It is thus natural that the elections with which they were associated were characterized by strong conflicts. Among these, in turn, it is probably possible to make a selection: The election campaigns of spring 1887, spring 1914, and 1948 appear more intensive than the others. And if, finally, we were to choose the roughest of all the election campaigns in modern Swedish political history, it was in fact the one that took place in the spring of 1914. The spitefulness of the campaign was genuinely extreme. Accusations of treason came from both sides; Staaff in particular was subjected to personal attacks. In his memoirs, Herbert Tingsten tells how the most incredible stories were widely believed: on how Staaff bought a house and tried to pay the workers in rubles; on how the ministers, in their insolence, forced the king to wait on them at government dinners.[48] In his biography of Staaff, Leif Kihlberg reproduces a photograph of a souvenir from the 1914 hate campaign: an ash tray in the form of Staaff's face, so that you could put out your cigarette in his eyes.[49] In its election program, the Conservative party gave the defense issue top priority and took advantage of the public mood created by the Farmers' March. The Liberals concentrated on the constitutional issue: As we have seen, in his campaign pamphlet Staaff accused the king of unconstitutional behavior. On the defense issue, the Liberals were divided. The Social Democrats rejected both rearmament and the king's behavior. The election turnout reached 70 percent, a record. The Liberals suffered a major loss. Most of the gains went to the Conservatives.

Hammarskjöld believed he had received a mandate to remain in office. His government submitted a bill to the new 1914 session of Parliament calling for large-scale rearmament. It would undoubtedly have been rejected by Parliament if World War I had not broken out during the summer of 1914 as the bill was being discussed. Staaff took the initiative of arranging a compromise between the Conservatives and the Left on the defense issue. The government completely rejected it. Given the new, more serious situation, there was no room for compromises. A week later Staaff wrote a letter to the prime minister and declared that the government bill could count on a majority in the Second Chamber. This position signified a total capitulation by Staaff.

At the regularly scheduled election in the fall of 1914 the trends evident

---

[48] Herbert Tingsten, *Mitt liv. Ungdomsåren* (Stockholm: Norstedts, 1961), p. 112.
[49] Kihlberg 1963 II, p. 321.

from the spring election continued: The Liberals suffered yet another defeat, while Conservatives and Social Democrats gained ground.

The Hammarskjöld government stayed in power for three years. There was a wartime truce among the political parties, which all supported the Swedish policy of neutrality. But by the spring of 1917 the Left had had enough of the Hammarskjöld system. Sweden's supply situation was very difficult. In its propaganda, the Left referred to the prime minister as "Hungerskjöld." A parliamentary vote to lower the government appropriation for defense preparedness from thirty to ten million kronor signified a vote of no confidence in the government, resulting in Hammarskjöld's resignation. The king became worried. Would he now be forced to accept a leftist government regardless? He dictated a statement for the cabinet minutes declaring that despite Parliament's clear rejection of the government, Hammarskjöld and his ministers enjoyed his full confidence. For the moment, the king could thus not accept their resignation. Attempts should be made to find a way out of the difficulties that had triggered the government's desire to resign. Associations that had been formed in 1914 once again stepped forward and tried to give Hammarskjöld the support he lacked in Parliament. A petition with more than six hundred thousand signatures indicating support of the government was presented to him. The government crisis became lengthy, and this was during one of the most critical stages of the world war. Brusewitz writes ironically, "The German U-boat war had begun, the United States was poised to enter the war, the Russian Revolution had broken out. In Sweden, public interest was captivated by the question of whether to keep Hammarskjöld or not."[50] When the king finally realized that it was impossible to keep Hammarskjöld, he approached the leaders of the Conservative Party. Trygger was prepared to take over, as usual. But in order to keep his appointment from seeming too provocative, the king and the Conservative leadership reached the following agreement. Carl Swartz, a moderate member of the First Chamber, would first be asked to assume the post of prime minister but would turn it down, after which the king would offer the job to Trygger. Lindman promised to become foreign minister and Swartz either finance or education and church minister. But Swartz and Lindman had second thoughts. In the end, Swartz became prime minister, Lindman was pressed into service as foreign minister in any event, and Trygger stayed out of the government. The king had succeeded in keeping the Left out of power. It has been said that "a government headed by the rightist Carl Swartz and with Conservative party chairman Arvid Lindman as foreign minister (could) hardly have lived up

[50] Brusewitz 1964 (1951), p. 96.

to its intentions."[51] But the Left regarded the Swartz government as a kind of caretaker cabinet until the regular fall election and was prepared to tolerate it until then. The 1917 election was a major victory for the Left. Nils Edén, who had taken over as head of the Liberal party after Staaff's death, and Hjalmar Branting reached an agreement on a government coalition. The king worked energetically to avoid a leftist government. He was particularly opposed to Branting. After the March 1917 revolution in Russia, Branting had visited the new rulers in Petrograd, who had his full sympathy. The king was well informed about the revolutionary currents that existed on the war-ravaged Continent. The government crisis took many twists and turns. One option was simply to let the Swartz government remain in power. The next alternative was a grand coalition government, but no prime minister to lead it was ever appointed. After that, the task of forming a government was offered to the Speaker of the Second Chamber, the moderate Liberal Johan Widén. The difficulties were too much for him, however: The Left was demanding more far-reaching promises on constitutional reform, and the Conservatives were unwilling to make any sufficiently prominent person available. The failure of these efforts signified a major defeat for the king. No other option remained but to give Edén the task of forming a coalition government of Liberals and Social Democrats, which would entail recognition of parliamentary government and the appointment of republicans as ministers. When he withdrew as a candidate for prime minister, Widén consoled the king with the observation that by joining the government, the Social Democrats would soon be cured of their republicanism. Apparently these words made an impression on the king.[52]

When Gustaf V finally made his offer to Edén, in his careful and correct fashion the latter initiated a detailed discussion of the future relationship between the king and his government. Edén made it clear that he was counting on the king's confidence and support in the struggle with the Conservatives that could be expected. In the event that the king lost his confidence in the government, this should be admitted openly so that "no others will come between him" and the government. The wording was so general that it could be regarded as including hidden advisers but also the queen. The king agreed to all this. The settlement reached between Edén and the king in October 1917 has been described as "a kind of guarantee agreement, almost . . . a capitulation document, which can be said to seal the breakthrough of parliamentary government."[53]

[51] Gerdner 1946, p. 9.
[52] Brusewitz 1964 (1951), p. 96.
[53] Ibid., pp. 103–104.

Table 4.1. *The parliamentarism game: "Shall power be shared?"*

	King	
	Yes	No
Staaff/Edén		
Yes	−1, +1	−2, +2
No	+2, −1	+1, −2

Since that government crisis, parliamentary government has not been questioned in Sweden. After the country survived an even worse shortage of supplies during the winter of 1917–1918, the dramatic end of the world war and the revolutionary events around Europe confirmed the king's belief that there was no longer any way of resisting parliamentary government. Not even the Conservatives could give him their support any more. The king honestly feared that continued controversy might result in an even greater loss – the loss of his crown. Accepting parliamentary government now seemed like choosing the least evil alternative. By finally approving the right of Parliament to decide on the shape of his government, the Swedish king gave himself better prospects than many of his colleagues to ride out the storm that was sweeping over the monarchies of Europe at the close of World War I.

3. PARLIAMENTARISM IS APPROVED

Why did the king finally approve parliamentary government? It had been neither intended nor predicted in the Constitution. The outbreak of World War I had shown that the Conservatives and the king had judged the international political situation more realistically than had the Left. There had been large-scale public support for the king not only in connection with the Farmers' March but also as late as the spring of 1917, when the existence of the Hammarskjöld government was threatened.

Let us try to summarize what we have said above in the form of a game matrix (Table 4.1) based on the main constitutional issue raised by the framers of the Constitution and emphatically repeated by Staaff: "Shall power be divided?" The actors are the king and Staaff, whose fallen mantle was assumed by Edén; let us call the king's opponent Staaff/Edén. Their alternatives are to answer yes or no to this question. As we shall see, the four conceivable outcomes of this game – the four quadrants – will coincide with the four concepts of the monarchy mentioned at the beginning of this chapter, which analyzed the ideologies in question. If both actors reply yes to the question of sharing power, so that they end up in the upper left-hand quadrant, they support the *division-of-power rule*. Division of power is precisely the main principle of the 1809 Constitution. This was also the concept that the king originally defended. In reality, the game of parliamentary government begins in this quadrant.

If Staaff/Edén, the row player, sticks to the yes alternative but the king switches his reply to no when asked if power should be shared – with the proviso that this power should revert to him – we are talking about *personal monarchy* (upper right-hand quadrant). The game was driven in this direction when the king began to apply a bold strategy involving the Farmers' March and the Palace Yard crisis.

If the row player shifts to the no alternative, meaning that power should revert completely to Parliament and not be shared, and the column player chooses the yes alternative, we end up in the *parliamentary government* quadrant at the lower left-hand corner; political power has been taken away from the king. This possibility is what eventually happened through the acceptance of parliamentarism in October 1917.

Finally, if both players say no to the question of dividing power and demand to keep all power for themselves, a confrontation undoubtedly arises. According to the king's calculations in the fall of 1917, the outcome of such a confrontation would be the introduction of a *republic* in Sweden (lower right-hand quadrant).

The following utility values are achieved by the actors. For the king, personal monarchy results in $+2$, division of power $+1$, parliamentarism -1, and a republic -2. For the Left, it was essential that power be in the hands of the people's representatives without having to be shared with the king. Parliamentary government was the most important thing, while republicanism on the other hand was no aim in itself for most supporters of the Left. The Left's utility numbers are thus preferably parliamentary government at $+2$ followed by a republic at $+1$; of the remaining alternatives, division of power at -1 was not quite as distasteful as personal monarchy at -2.

The biggest problem in this specification of the actors' preference orderings is the king's first and second preferences. What did the king actually prefer – division of power or personal monarchy? As we have seen, the king vacillated between these preferences and was strongly influenced by those around him to opt increasingly for the no strategy and personal monarchy. Under these circumstances, would it perhaps be better to do two separate analyses and draw a game matrix for the period before the Palace Yard crisis and one for the period after? The answer, in spite of everything, is no. As we see, a single matrix – and thus a structure symmetrical with the other chapters – can in fact capture the dynamics of the game: The game moves from the upper left-hand quadrant to the upper right-hand one, then ends up in the lower left-hand quadrant, thereby avoiding the lower right-hand quadrant containing the king's worst alternative. The reason for classifying personal monarchy as the king's first preference and power sharing as his second preference can be expressed as follows. At first the king never thought that personal monarchy, as we have defined this concept, could be an alternative. But as the king learned from his advisers that personal monarchy was not as unrealistic as he had thought, and the preparations for the Farmers' March gave him more and more evidence of the high regard a large proportion of the people had for the monarchy, this alternative appeared increasingly attractive to him. He abandoned the division-of-power rule in favor of personal monarchy when he understood that the latter existed as a realistic alternative. For a few short years, personal monarchy bloomed once more. Whatever was desired by the government and the legislature from which it derived, the king decided to push through his opinion as to what was necessary to strengthen "his" army and "his" navy. Personal monarchy was consequently the king's first preference, worth +2, and division of power second with +1.

If we look more closely at the game matrix, we find that the Staaff/ Edén side has a dominating strategy, which is to reply no to the question regardless of how the king acts. A utility value of +2 or +1 is better than −1 or −2. Under no circumstances should the people and its representatives yield any power to the king.

The king, on the other hand, has no dominating strategy. He can try to maximize his gains and reply no in order to get +2, which he did in February 1914. (There is, however, a danger that his losses will instead be maximized. In game theory, this is called the maximax strategy.) Or he can try to minimize his losses and answer yes in order to suffer a −1 in the worst case, which he did in October 1917. This eliminates the opportunity to achieve maximal gains, however. In game theory this is called the minimax strategy. Which one he chooses depends on the strategy of his opponent, and this strategy is generally not known during the game nearly as well as we can reconstruct it in retrospect. In other words, it is completely understandable that the king shifted between different strategies in the game of parliamentary government.

At the beginning of 1914, when the king switched to the maximax strategy, international events brought him success for a longer period than he had reason to expect. As the threat of direct Swedish involvement in the war gradually appeared to subside, the Left became less inclined to tolerate the king's government. It took the king time to realize that his maximax strategy was being undermined. He finally realized that Hammarskjöld had to be sacrificed. He shifted to a minimax strategy. Because the Left, in anticipation of the election a few months later, was still not willing to demand all power for itself, during a transitional period we saw a return to the division-of-power rule under the Swartz government, a government that enjoyed the confidence of the king and was tolerated by Parliament but was not based on a majority constellation of its political parties. During the government crisis following the election, the king also tried to carry out the ideals of the division-of-power rule. But now the time had arrived for the Left's no alternative. For some months, the king had become resigned to giving up his maximax strategy. In the situation that now arose when the Left followed its no strategy, his maximax strategy would only have rendered the king maximal losses. The minimax strategy was the only one remaining. Combined with the Left's no strategy, the game arrived at a clear solution in the lower left-hand corner. The acceptance of parliamentary government comprises the equilibrium point in this matrix. In our game theory terms, the king's final acceptance of parliamentarism can be explained by the fact that in vacillating between a minimax and a maximax strategy, he finally realized that the first of these was the rational choice when the opposing player had a dominating strategy that would cause him losses under any circumstances. When the king understood that the battle was lost, he chose his alternatives in such a way that these losses would be as small as possible – so that the least evil alternative, not the worst one, was implemented.

4. THE DIVISION-OF-POWER RULE

Why was there no revolution in Sweden at the end of World War I as there was in so many other European countries, which switched from monarchy to a republic at that time? At the beginning of the war, the Swedish king had hardly behaved in a more conciliatory way than his colleagues in other countries; he had pursued the path of personal monarchy. The ideological debate of the decade after 1910 did not concern just any political issue. There was disunity on a fundamental decision rule – the division-of-power rule. In this account, the struggle over parliamentary government has been portrayed as a serious constitutional crisis.

The question of whether the king acted unconstitutionally during the Palace Yard crisis – whether his behavior conflicted with "the living constitution" – stirred up a storm when it was asked. Over the decades it has continued to have a noticeable impact on Swedish political science, as happens when scholarly problems are fueled by political passions. In scholarly and political debate alike, the concept of parliamentarism has been stretched in a way that has made the term border on the meaningless.[54]

[54] Hessler 1950, pp. 172–182.

Making the conceptual confusion total, the ultraconservatives denied that they were aiming at personal monarchy. Trygger defined personal monarchy as "a monarchy independent of constitutional rules," and the Conservatives did not wish to promote this. With this definition, Trygger was guilty of changing the concept, presumably for polemic purposes; the other participants in the debate defined personal monarchy as the exercise of royal power entirely in keeping with the Constitution but independent of *the government's* opinion. This controversy is what the debate was about.[55]

Our own conclusions are clear from the preceding account. Staaff did not present any conclusive proof for his thesis that the king's behavior was contrary to "the living constitution," and not even Staaff tried to argue that it conflicted with the letter of the Constitution. In summary, it is difficult to reject Trygger's sarcastic comment: The king's behavior was not a violation of the Constitution – it was not even a violation of constitutional custom; perhaps one could speak of a violation of preparations for a change in constitutional custom.[56]

If we may be inclined to view the matter in this way, far removed as we are from the Palace Yard crisis (although our detachment should not be exaggerated), instead the question arises: Why did Staaff impose his doctrine of the state on historical developments? The most likely answer is that in those days, constitution and constitutional were prestigious terms that people wanted to adorn themselves with, in much the same way that during the postwar period, everyone wanted to use the word democratic for the most varied of philosophies.[57] And people were as little inclined during the 1910s to state their values as during the debate on democracy in recent decades. They also tried to prove the correctness of their terminology by referring to some form of empirical material, whether philosophical publications, formal rule systems, or public opinion or legal opinions among the citizenry.[58] Like shimmering soap bubbles, or rather speech balloons, these prestigious words floated upward from lecterns and demonstration processions and enchanted the audience with their magic aura. By calling the king's behavior unconstitutional, Staaff awakened political passions among the supporters of the Left while provoking the equally emotional royalism of the rightists.

The Palace Yard crisis actually represents a clash between two irreconcilable doctrines – the division-of-power rule and the principle of popular

[55] Trygger 1914, p. 5.

[56] FK 1914 A:22, pp. 21–22.

[57] Cf. Hjärne 1914, p. 1: "People think they have found a grain of gold in the mere word 'constitution' and its derivative and affiliated adjectives and nouns."

[58] Leif Lewin, *Folket och eliterna. En studie i modern demokratisk teori* (Stockholm: Almqvist & Wiksell, 1970).

sovereignty. The parliamentarism that Staaff and the Left advocated was irreconcilable with the division of power stipulated in the 1809 Constitution. There is, of course, no reason for the people to share their power if they are sovereign.

The conflict between the division-of-power rule and popular sovereignty was resolved when the division-of-power rule was abandoned and the king finally accepted parliamentary government. But it was an eleventh-hour capitulation. What would have happened, we might ask according to the counterfactual method of historiography, if Sweden had not had a leftist government fulfilling radical demands in the fall of 1918, but if the king had continued to resist parliamentary government? It is certainly likely that demands for a republic would have been even stronger. Now the leading Social Democrats were encumbered by the responsibilities of government. It thus became the task of the Left to tame the revolutionary currents in the country. The king's change to a minimax strategy and the transfer of government responsibility to the Left removed the prerequisites for revolution and a republic. After parliamentarism was accepted, the final democratization of the system of government was carried out extremely quickly. With remarkable speed, the Conservatives and the monarchy also embraced the new set of shared values that parliamentary democracy began to generate. An era had ended – the one sometimes referred to as "the good old days" with its industrial revolution and ensuing rapid rise in living standards, its bright faith in the future, its international peace, its bold spirit of discovery, its flourishing cultural life and brilliant literature. In the perspective adopted in this book, the three decades between 1887 and 1917 appear as one long prelude to democracy, during which the people slowly but surely asserted themselves against the authoritarian state in order finally to replace it as the only legitimate basis of political power.

During this rapid, peaceful, and in the end generally accepted transition, strangely enough, the division-of-power rule was allowed to remain undisturbed. No change in the 1809 Constitution was undertaken. It still specified that the king alone governed the realm. Generations of respectful students studied the dead Constitution and had to memorize its rules, with their beautiful, old-fashioned – and for many people undoubtedly incomprehensible – language. Political reality, on the other hand, was shaped by rules entirely different from those in the Constitution.

Not until the constitutional reform of the 1970s were politicians willing to take the consequences of the disappearance of the division-of-power rule and apply them to the wording of the Constitution. But not even then was the solution particularly straightforward. The division-of-power rule did, admittedly, give way to popular sovereignty. Instead of the old rule "The king alone shall govern the realm in the manner prescribed by this

Constitution," Section 1 of the 1974 Constitution states that "All public power in Sweden emanates from the people." But the rules concerning the head of state were the product of collective decisions characterized by remarkable compromises and could not have satisfied any individual who had careful, reasoned preferences. A commission of inquiry on the Constitution was appointed. Out of respect for the old Constitution, for a long time the commission considered carrying out a necessary modernization within the framework of the existing document. But there turned out to be insurmountable obstacles to "incorporating parliamentarism" properly in principle into a constitution characterized by the division-of-power rule. The government thus decided to work out a completely new constitution.[59] The proposal was based on the principle of popular sovereignty. It assumed, however, that the monarchy would be preserved. The king was given a more modest rule than had previously been the case but would still appoint the prime minister after having consulted with the Speaker and representatives of the parties in Parliament. He would also have certain powers in connection with major government issues and the dissolution of Parliament.[60]

There was vehement debate. Once again, the ghosts of the Palace Yard crisis were summoned forth. Conservatives were dissatisfied with what they considered the excessive downgrading of the monarchy. It was also thought to have been carried out in an inconsistent manner. The king had, of course, been allowed to retain certain powers and thus, wrote Nils Herlitz, a professor of constitutional law and a Conservative, in the future there might be "an unresolvable conflict between the king and his ministers, with the king taking advantage of his decision-making rights. He is entitled to do so. . . . Of course in a sharp conflict with his ministers on an issue he regards as vital, the king may conceivably take the greatest risks. The older generations may be reminded of 1914. But let us note that the commission of inquiry on the constitution certainly wishes to limit the king's opportunities for action but not entirely eliminate them. The great constitutional conflict of 1914, the most recent we have experienced, ultimately concerned an issue that according to the commission's proposal would also be dependent on a royal decision – an issue related to a proposed government bill. The king's power over the appointment and dismissal of ministers, in particular, combined with his power over extra-parliamentary elections, might leave room for a personally colored policy just as much as today. It thus cannot be claimed, to put it briefly, that the potential for pursuing a royal policy contrary to the government's policy

---

[59] Jörgen Westerståhl, "Författningsutredningen," *Statsvetenskaplig Tidskrift* (1976): 7; Erik Holmberg and Nils Stjernquist, *Grundlagarna* (Stockholm: Norstedts, 1980), p. 8.

[60] SOU (Statens Offentliga Utredningar, reports from commissions of inquiry) 1963:16 and 17.

is a reality that now exists but would be removed by the proposal of the commission of inquiry on the constitution."[61]

Leftists admitted that the proposal had these shortcomings but drew the conclusion that the monarchy ought to be weakened further. In a much-discussed pamphlet *Should the Monarch Be Strengthened?* (Skall kunga-makten stärkas?), Herbert Tingsten began with Staaff's distinction between the letter of the Constitution and "the living constitution" and argued that compared with the latter, if not the former, the commission's proposal would strengthen the monarchy. Tingsten said Herlitz was completely correct in asserting that the proposal brought us back to the legal situation of 1914. He was therefore justified in pointing out that in recent years, people had "generally assumed that according to common law and custom, the king is not entitled to behave as in 1914; the king kept his crown by following the rules of parliamentarism without changes in the Constitution being considered necessary."[62]

The republican cause had thus picked up support once again. In 1966 a Social Democratic members' bill called for the appointment of a commission of inquiry on the position of the head of state in a parliamentary democracy. The bill described hereditary monarchy as "one of the most antiquated elements" of the Constitution. Although the call for a republic had so far not been regarded as very urgent, there was reason to assume that soon enough, the situation might change, the sponsors wrote, alluding to King Gustav VI Adolf's advanced age (the king, then eighty-four, lived to be ninety-one). "To a large proportion of the Swedish people, even now it seems natural to change in the future to a republican form of government with a president as head of state."[63]

In the many tactical twists and turns that followed, representatives of the four largest parties in Parliament reached a different conclusion than the sponsors of the bill: There was no large proportion of the people who wanted to change to a republic. They viewed the matter in roughly the way Engberg had done in 1920: Why make a fuss about a republic when there was a strong monarchist feeling in the country? Social Democrats and Liberals were, however, not willing to incorporate in the Constitution those concessions to the division-of-power rule and the monarchy that Herlitz had pointed out. Popular sovereignty should be consistently observed. At the same time, the monarchy should be retained. The politicians had obviously maneuvered themselves into an impossible situation.

The parties finally reached agreement through the so-called Torekov

---

[61] Nils Herlitz, *1969 års regeringsform? Kommentarer till författningsutredningens förslag* (Stockholm: Norstedts, 1963), pp. 41–42.

[62] Herbert Tingsten, *Skall kungamakten stärkas? Kritik av författningsförslaget* (Stockholm: Aldus/Bonniers, 1964).

[63] Mot FK 1966:1 (Lennart Geijer et al.) and mot AK 1966:2 (Nancy Eriksson et al.).

compromise of 1971. It proposed that all of the king's official functions be abolished, except for ceremonial ones and those where he represented the nation.[64] In other words, they took away all of the powers that traditionally belonged to a monarch, but retained the term monarchy. Tactical considerations took precedence over intellectual stringency. In order not to trigger a storm of protest, the parties tried to conceal what had happened by continuing to speak of the "king" and the "monarchy."

Ironically, the task of introducing the government bill based on the compromise and proposing the preservation of the monarchy went to Lennart Geijer, who had once sponsored a members' bill calling for a republic but who was now minister of justice. Geijer's official arguments on behalf of the government bill were brief, if not reluctant. The monarchy was being preserved, the minister of justice admitted, but the king would only have representative and ceremonial tasks. "He will lack all political power.... Many people in our country believe that hereditary monarchy is out of place in a democratic form of government.... but I shall not go into more detail about the arguments for and against a monarchy or a republic. I will confine myself to stating that the members of the drafting committee have reached agreement not to depart from the current form of government in the new Parliament Act and that this view won very strong support from those who submitted official comments on the committee's proposal.... Otherwise I can confine myself to stating that the adaptation of the written Constitution to constitutional custom, evidenced by the fact that the head of state is losing the formal powers he now possesses, is generally regarded as a natural step in the work of writing a new Constitution."[65]

This marked the final act in the struggle for parliamentary government – the abolition of the division-of-power rule, appropriately enough under the supervision of two republicans, Rickard Sandler and Geijer, who proposed the preservation of the monarchy. Throughout the twentieth century, a lack of ideological principles had characterized the attitude of the Left toward the monarchy. This lack of principles received its most magnificent expression when it was elevated to the rank of constitutional law; in practice a republic was introduced, but as a concession to popular opinion, the system was referred to as a monarchy. The call for a republic was not high enough in the preference ordering of the radical parties to make them ready to accept the election losses that would most likely be the result of an attempt to abolish the monarchy formally as well. Once again, the threat of a republic was overcome. Once again, the result of the game on the issue of monarchy was that ideology had to yield to strategy.

[64] Nils Stjernquist, "Grundlagsberedningskompromiss i statschefsfrågan," *Statsvetenskaplig Tidskrift* (1971): 377ff.
[65] Prop 1973:90; quotation from pp. 171–172.

5

The crisis agreement

1. DETERMINISM AND THE DOCTRINE OF HARMONY

The triumph of parliamentary government in Sweden was followed by a period of parliamentary crisis.[1] Just as Swedish public life before World War I had fallen short of the constitutional ideals of the Left, events after the introduction of universal suffrage and parliamentarism did not live up to leftist expectations either. Arvid Lindman's proportional representation formula preserved the multiparty system. In addition to the Conservatives, the Liberals (who had split in 1922 into a "Prohibitionist" and a "Liberal" party before merging again in 1934) and the Social Democrats, there were two comparatively new parties represented in Parliament – the Agrarians and the Communists; the latter had broken away from the Social Democrats. There was no parliamentary power base for a strong government. Short-lived minority governments came and went, including the Conservatives, the Prohibitionists (both with and without the Liberals as a coalition partner), the Social Democrats, and an occasional nonparliamentary government of senior civil servants. Under such circumstances, it was not possible to carry out a thoughtful and purposeful government policy. Politics became one continuous strategic game. In parliamentary committees, the parties were constantly looking over each other's shoulders with the aim of forming new coalitions to improve their positions, perhaps by unseating the government and helping form a new cabinet. The diminishing power of governments during an era of serious postwar economic problems was an international phenomenon; it compromised the new system of government based on parliamentary democracy. Although Swedish critics of the system were not as deprecating as some of their counterparts on the European Continent, who adopted a firmly antidemocratic stance

---

[1] This section is based on the first chapter of my doctoral dissertation, *Planhushållnings-debatten* (Uppsala: Almqvist & Wiksell, 1967). I refer the reader to this work for more detailed source references. For the most part, I have listed here the primary sources of direct quotations only.

as fascism emerged, people in Sweden were dissatisfied with "this damned system in which one day you're arm in arm with Admiral Lindman and the next day arm in arm with Per Albin Hansson, and where no Swedish citizen has any idea what will happen next."[2]

The political party scene changed. When the constitutional reforms sought by the Liberal and Social Democratic parties had been achieved, ties between the two parties weakened. When the latter party now declared its wish to go a step further and add "economic democracy" to "political democracy" – that is, advocate the socialist concepts it had embraced most recently in its 1920 program – the Liberals were driven into the arms of the Conservatives. Once again, the political parties realigned. Just as the dispute between free traders and protectionists over tariffs during the 1880s had given way to the struggle between Right and Left over suffrage, there was now a gap between Social Democrats and the nonsocialist bloc. The issue of the state's role in the business sector was the litmus test between the two.

The nonsocialists were successful in defending economic freedom during the 1920s. The Social Democrats had neither the ideological nor the parliamentary prerequisites to pursue an explicitly socialist policy on a day-to-day basis. The private business sector was also expanding rapidly. After a temporary slowdown at the end of the war, production curves again pointed upward. Conditions admittedly varied from one industry to another; agriculture in particular continued to have problems despite state subsidies. But successes dominated the picture. Sweden showed faster growth than most other industrialized countries. People firmly believed in the future. In a reference to Sweden's seventeenth-century foreign military adventures and trans-Baltic territories, they even spoke of Sweden's second Great Power period; a pamphlet by this name was published in the late 1920s by a liberal entrepreneur and social critic. Just as King Gustavus Adolphus (Gustav II Adolf) and Charles XII had put Sweden on the world map, the country had once again gained renown, this time not because of its battlefield victories but through its matches, ball bearings. telephones, and cream separators.[3]

In broad terms, this is the background in terms of party politics and economic history to the liberal economic ideology of the nonsocialists during the 1920s.

Just as freedom was the central theme of Edén's reflections on political philosophy, it became a rallying cry for all nonsocialists in Sweden. "Freedom is the source and sustenance of progress," said Arvid Lindman, the Conservative party chairman. "Liberty enables the entrepreneurial and

[2] *Sveriges Socialdemokratiska Arbetarpartis trettonde kongress* (Stockholm, 1928), p. 115 (Lövgren).
[3] Lewin 1967, pp. 10ff.

ambitious to carve out new settlements, start new companies, utilize the country's natural resources and create new jobs and means of livelihood." But like Edén, Lindman stopped short of advocating unlimited freedom. When freedom was misused, the state ought to step in and exericse its corrective powers. In similar fashion, the chairmen of the two parties into which Edén's Liberals split in 1922 – Prohibitionist leader C. G. Ekman and Liberal leader Eliel Löfgren – enunciated their belief in economic freedom, as opposed to the regulatory policies advocated by the Social Democrats, as a prerequisite for progress.[4]

The concept of freedom that the nonsocialists espoused was the classic doctrine of economic liberalism: freedom from the state, the absence of government coercion. Conservative party spokesmen, too, espoused this liberal concept. Gone were the days when the Conservative party could boast its own conservative, antidemocratic concepts of freedom and the state. By the 1920s, the Conservatives had embraced the liberal concept of freedom and even defended it emphatically against Social Democratic attempts to control and regulate the business sector.

But when freedom was being misused, the nonsocialists wanted to impose limits. On such occasions, the state should intervene to protect the individual. How to create the proper balance between individual liberty and the state's protective powers was regarded as the main philosophical problem of modern liberalism. As luck would have it, there was actually a principle that provided guidance in this delicate balancing act. The idea was that the state would be allowed to expand as long as it did not harm the country's "wealth-generating forces." As Finance Minister Gripenstedt and his fellow free traders had done in the nineteenth century, the nonsocialists now based their doctrine on Adam Smith's doctrine of economic harmony. They were thus ideological heirs to the free-trade movement. What passed for leftist philosophy in the 1880s had become the Conservative thinking of the 1920s.

The conventional wisdom among nonsocialists was thus that a harmonious interplay prevailed in the economy; while working for his own gain, the individual was guided by a kind of invisible hand to promote common goals that were not his own. It became the main task of nonsocialist politicians to protect this delicate mechanism against the regulatory and socialistic ambitions of the Social Democrats, whose intervention would upset natural market forces. Sweden's foremost liberal spokesmen

[4] Arvid Lindman, *Utveckling i hägn av fred och frihet. Tal i Laholm, Bökeberg och Övedskloster den 14 och 15 augusti 1926* (Stockholm: Allmänna valmansförbundet, 1926); C. G. Ekman, *Penningvälde, klassvälde, medborgarvälde. Tal i Filipstad, Kil och Arvika den 25 och 26 augusti 1928* (Stockholm: Politiska dagsfrågor, no. 9, 1928); Ekman, *Jordbrukslagstiftning, skuldsättning, nykterhetsprinciper. Tal i Ulricehamn den 18 augusti samt i Kinna och Borås den 19 augusti 1928* (Stockholm: Politiska dagsfrågor, no. 8, 1928); Eliel Löfgren, *Det nya partiet. Föredrag den 22 oktober 1923* (Stockholm: Liberal politik, no. 2, 1923).

of that age, Eli Heckscher and Gustav Cassel, wrote brilliant pamphlets defending the market economy and the right of private ownership. If the wealth-generating forces were harmed by far-reaching expansion of the state and by social leveling, everyone would suffer the consequences. Referring to the right of private ownership, Heckscher and Cassel warned against killing the goose that lays the golden egg. The class-leveling policy of the Social Democrats would only mean that a large quantity of capital now used for investment would instead go toward consumption – "as desperate an undertaking as destroying a large and valuable building in order to obtain some fuel for the day."[5]

When the nonsocialists held power, an important task for the government was to pursue a "positive economic policy." This did not primarily mean support for specific sectors (except for agriculture). It referred instead to economic relief measures of a general kind, mainly reductions in taxes and other fees imposed on the business sector. They regarded increased production as the only sure way out of all economic difficulties. A positive economic policy was also the country's best social welfare policy.

The three basic ideas that formed the framework of this presentation of nonsocialist economic policy in the 1920s – the liberal concept of freedom, the doctrine of harmony, and a positive economic policy – were of course closely interrelated. A positive economic policy primarily meant attempts to ease the levies on the business sector and, when implemented, was a way of applying to daily politics the principle of calling for freedom from the state. This demand, in turn, was pursued so adamantly because of the assumption that harmony would prevail on the economic scene in the absence of state involvement. Of course, there would be occasional disharmonies in the market requiring state intervention. But such actions might very easily hurt the wealth-generating forces and the state would then have harmed, rather than helped, the situation. The newspaper *Göteborgs Handels- och Sjöfartstidning* interpreted this philosophy in the following pregnant words: "The free interplay of economic forces, their mutually limiting effects on each other and stimulation toward unremitting effort are the indispensable tonic without which the creation of useful objects would stagnate and bog down. The ties between economic and personal freedom and the liberty of expression and thought are closer than many people imagine. They can be misused, and they are being grossly misused. But the sharp, bracing air of freedom is healthful. It spurs people to action. The atmosphere of coercion is drowsy and enervating."[6]

[5] Eli Heckscher, *Gammal och ny ekonomisk liberalism* (Stockholm: Norstedts, 1921); Gustav Cassel, *Understödspolitikens urartning* (Stockholm: Norstedts, 1930); Cassel, *Socialism eller framåtskridande* (Stockholm: Norstedts, 1928); *Svenska Dagbladet*, 31 Aug. 1928 (quotation).

[6] *Götesborgs Handels- och Sjöfartstidning*, 16 Aug. 1924.

The crisis agreement

The Social Democrats, however, could not see any signs of harmony in Sweden's economy. On the contrary, in their opinion, social conditions were marred by conflicts between different interests, which they analyzed according to Marxist ideology. They saw in capitalist society an ever-increasing exploitation; they saw wealth being gathered into the hands of a privileged few; they saw the proletarianization of the working class. Each year, as the number of workers grew, they sank deeper and deeper into misery. The capitalists sought new markets for their growing array of products, but regardless of how many new markets they conquered, they were unable to sell the goods they were producing at an increasingly frantic pace. *The Communist Manifesto* compared the capitalist production system to a sorcerer unable to control the forces that he himself had brought forth from the underworld. In its highly developed state, the capitalist system was thus plagued by crises caused by this very exploitation of the working class: Because their wages were so low, the masses could not afford to buy the goods they helped manufacture. Thus, the root of these crises was a shortage of buying power: "The ultimate reason for all real economic crises always remains the poverty and the limited consumption capacity of the masses versus the capitalist drive to develop the productive forces, as if their only limit were the absolute consumption power of a society."[7] But eventually, Marx prophesied, the proletariat would rise against the capitalists during the final desperate crisis of capitalist society. The expropriators would be expropriated in a violent revolution, the means of production would be transferred to public ownership, and a classless socialist society would ensue.

Swedish political reality diverged in many ways from the image projected in these Marxist theories: No disaster materialized, and instead of being exploited and proletarianized Swedish workers saw their wages rise in tandem with the upswing in the national income; an increasingly powerful middle class emerged between capitalist owners and workers. For these reasons, within the Swedish labor movement Marxist theory was revised on a number of points; this was also the case elsewhere in Europe. But the basic features of Marxism remained the official ideology of the party. A social philosophy based on Marxist analysis was said to be what divided the Social Democrats from the nonsocialist parties.

Marxist theory caused problems for the Social Democrats. What, if anything, would be the role of the party if capitalism was indeed caught in an inexorable trend toward crisis? Should the party bother to seek short-term reforms in social welfare policy? Such reforms would, of course, improve conditions for workers and give them buying power – that is, counteract exploitation and thereby eliminate the prerequisites for a long-

[7] Karl Marx, *Kapitalet. Kritik av den politiska ekonomin* III:2 (Stockholm: Tiden, 1931), pp. 460–461.

127

term trend toward crises and disasters for capitalism. Based on this dilemma between the long-term and the short-term perspective, Herbert Tingsten provided a penetrating analysis of the ideological evolution of the Social Democratic party in a famous work. "Why this passionate struggle for what was inevitable at a certain stage? . . . How could the big prediction (of a disaster for capitalism) become a reality if the call for political work was successfully heeded?"[8]

In numerous public statements, leading Social Democrats sought to escape from this dilemma. They claimed it was possible to disregard the economic determinism that might be considered implicit in Marxism, without their party losing its socialist soul and turning into just another party that advocated social reforms. Social Democratic spokesmen said that what Marx and Engels had "really" meant was something different, and they went on to reinterpret, soften, and dilute Marxism. Of course, ideas and party work, not just conditions of production, could influence developments: It would be wrong to sit down now with your arms folded and wait for a socialistic future; the entire forecast was based upon the premise that everyone would follow the same principles as before. Of course, there were reasons to fight for moral ideas, but where did these ideas come from? The answer: They emerged from the working-class principle of solidarity, which developed during the class struggle. To spur people toward liberation from the dominance of impersonal capitalism was meaningful and significant, because those ideas were based on material conditions. By necessity, the social process continued to be controlled by economic factors, while at the same time comprising the history of freedom. "The strongest lever of social common sense" was to be found in the ambition of the working class to put all its energy into replacing the current production system with a socialist one.[9]

As we can see, there was much talk of freedom in these statements, which were characterized by fuzzy thinking and metaphysical assumptions. What kind of approach to freedom is hidden in these articles? The liberal foes of the Social Democrats would surely have denied that these thoughts expressed a concept of freedom, because the socialist concept of freedom is totally different from that of liberalism. To the socialists, freedom meant freedom not from the state but from capitalist oppression, economic misery, and the material limits of production. They consequently pinned their hopes on the state. The state's coercive powers would prevent the capitalists from exploiting the working class, and a nationalized pro-

[8] Herbert Tingsten, *Den svenska socialdemokratiens idéutveckling* (Stockholm: Tiden, 1941), pp. 154–155.

[9] Presented in greater detail in Lewin 1967, pp. 22ff. The statements summarized here were made by Wigforss, Lindhagen, Oscar Larsson, and Engberg.

duction system would increase return on equity so much that poverty would be abolished; from being a "land of need," Sweden would become a "land of freedom." In contrast to the liberal call for freedom from the state, the socialist concept of freedom, we can say, means freedom *through* the state. State intervention would free workers from the oppression they were now subjected to in the capitalist society.

When the Social Democrats formed the one-party government that succeeded Edén's cabinet in 1920, they became increasingly absorbed by social reform work and political strategy. Every time they tried to initiate a more theoretical discussion of the ideological future of social democracy, they ran into the issue of determinism: What were the chances of nationalizing the means of production when developments seemed to be moving in a different direction than anticipated? On the one hand, given this situation some people proposed following the path of "gradual socialization"; nationalization would not take place through a single large action but would be implemented bit by bit. On the other hand, the importance of economic determinism was strongly emphasized – for example, when the Social Democratic party program was being revised: Nationalization could only be implemented after the capitalist disaster and the assumption of political power by the working class; a gradual nationalization process was impossible; political power was considered a weapon, either in the hands of the exploiters or the exploited.[10]

The softening of Marxism continued. One member of Parliament declared that nationalization could only take place in the long term and after winning a clear parliamentary majority in support of the socialization concept. Owners of nationalized companies should receive compensation, but higher inheritance and property taxes would gradually recover this money. Another participant in the debate declared that various combinations between liberal and socialist economic policies were conceivable in the future. All Marxist theory could really be reduced to the hypothesis that cooperation in the economic sphere was better than strife and competition. There was continuous emphasis on the need to approach economic policy in an undogmatic and experimental fashion. *Socialism Faces Reality* and *Everyday Socialism* were typical titles of books published as part of this debate. Socialization was regarded as meaning "everyone's mutual sharing of the good things owned by society." It was a matter of finding the system best suited to allow all citizens to benefit from the riches of the country. In this context, collective forms of production would show their superiority. The market philosophy of the liberals would be replaced by what Nils Karleby called "working-class econom-

[10] Lewin 1967, p. 32.

ics," a suggestive phrase which was nevertheless not defined more exactly.[11]

By now the fading belief in economic determinism had become a mere rhetorical device to avoid giving straight answers, and this further compounded the ideological confusion. People said that the course of events itself would set the limit on how far-reaching industrial democracy could become, because nobody could expect the Social Democrats to provide complete proposals in advance for the structure of nationalized enterprises.[12] It sometimes seemed as if the entire socialist philosophy was about to collapse. People complained about the shortcomings of the party's ideology: "Only those who hide from the true face of reality, out of laziness, cowardice or ignorance, can deny that social democracy today is in the midst of a crisis."[13]

It would be wrong to maintain that the Marxist belief in determinism characterized Social Democratic policy during the 1920s.[14] Its position within Social Democratic ideological debate can instead be explained as follows. The belief in determinism came to play an increasingly secondary role for the party. Politicians had their hands full with everyday politics. But now and again, the need for a long-term ideological argument made itself felt; occasionally it became necessary to emphasize that the Social Democratic party was based on ideas predicated on principles different from those of the nonsocialist parties. On such occasions, there was little choice but to resort to increasingly half-hearted references to the dethroned Marxist theory and its economic determinism. The Social Democrats looked back with nostalgia at what Tingsten called the Marxist dream castle; but despite extensive and increasingly more ambitious exegeses of basic Marxist writings, they did not succeed in developing them into any program for day-to-day politics. The unclear socialist economic policy with its fatalistic evolutionary elements was totally incapa-

---

[11] In greater detail in ibid., pp. 34–42. The statements summarized here were made by Möller, Wigforss, Karleby, and Lindström.

[12] Ibid., p. 40. Summary of *Ny Tid* and Per Albin Hansson.

[13] Rickard Lindström, "Partiet och tiden," *Frihet* no. 7 (1929): 7.

[14] This viewpoint is emphasized by some of the reviewers of my doctoral dissertation; they do not believe that determinism played as large a part as I have indicated. See Nils Elvander's review in the political science journal *Statsvetenskaplig Tidskrift* (1967): 358ff.; Diane Sainsbury's review in *Statsvetenskaplig Tidskrift* (1968): 110ff.; Herbert Tingsten's review in *Tiden* (1967): 464–465. It still seems wrong to me, however, to underestimate the ideological dilemma in which determinism placed the Social Democrats, even though most of the party's energy was thus devoted to concrete reform work by this time. Here I repeat and I hope clarify my thesis that *on those occasions* when leading party figures gathered for ideological discussions, Marxism and its economic determinism were the only original ideological heritage that distinguished the Social Democrats from the nonsocialists at the time. But the party was incapable of applying this heritage to practical politics. On the contrary, theoretically speaking, successful reform work undermined the prerequisites on which the theory of nationalization was based.

ble of competing with the prevailing liberal doctrine of harmony. The entire 1920s passed by without a concrete solution to the general talk of a political program of action reconcilable with Marxism. The Social Democrats were unable to work out any "working-class economics."

The young radicals were not the only ones disappointed with this ideological situation. When party chairman Per Albin Hansson opened the 1928 Social Democratic congress, he called upon the party to examine its ideological plight in a self-critical fashion, but he also encouraged them to work on new, clear policies: "Except for taxation issues, our party's contributions to economic policy have thus far not been positive to any significant degree. We must undertake a radical change. Our general views have been explained in our programs. What we need is a practical working program that translates our economic policy demands into concrete proposals."[15]

The chronic high unemployment of the 1920s was a challenge to both the harmony doctrine of economic liberalism and the determinism of the Social Democrats. The nonsocialists might reasonably be asked to explain how they reconciled their belief in a prevailing harmonious interplay between economic forces with the fact that so many people willing to work could not find jobs during that decade. And the Social Democrats, who claimed to represent the interests of the working class better than any other party, might be asked how – to the extent they in fact did – they could try to duck responsibility by claiming that events were merely following their course.

A well-organized Swedish state unemployment policy dated from 1914, when a government agency called the Unemployment Commission had been set up because of the country's rapidly growing joblessness. Because unemployment remained high even after the worst of the postwar depression had been overcome, the agency remained in existence for a long time. The mere establishment of this agency was of course incompatible with both nonsocialist and Social Democratic ideology. If, according to the harmony doctrine, unemployment need not exist in a liberal economy, then a government agency to resolve the problem was somewhat absurd; and if, according to determinism, day-to-day political action was still in vain, then the Unemployment Commission was an exercise in futility. During the recurring parliamentary debates about what directives the Commission should be given for a task that was thus considered either absurd or meaningless, both sides had a chance to think about their peculiar ideological conceptions. The unemployment debate of the 1920s

[15] Per Albin Hansson, *Inför partikongressen. Hälsningstal och parentation* (Stockholm, 1920), p. 19.

therefore became a powerful driving force behind the evolution of Swedish economic ideology.

In keeping with their doctrine of harmony, the nonsocialists blamed unemployment on high wages, which made it too expensive for companies to hire all job applicants. If wages were lowered, everyone could be offered a job. This wage theory became the predominant theme of the unemployment debate of the 1920s, both as a basis of explanation in economic analyses and as a guideline for unemployment policy as actually practiced. This wage theory argument was constantly cited in parliamentary unemployment debates. The belief was that unemployment could not be overcome by "artificial means," that is, via political measures. It would disappear only if wages were adapted to the natural equilibrium between the supply of labor and companies' demand for employees.

For humanitarian reasons, however, there was a desire to alleviate the hardship that the individual suffered while unemployed. Jobless people were offered so-called emergency work, which was solely of a social welfare nature. State-sponsored emergency jobs could not involve any productive, socially useful activity. If they did, they would be competing with private industry and would prevent market wages from adjusting to their "natural level." Emergency work wages thus had to be set at a lower level than those paid in the open market. Unemployment was "the unavoidable regulator of wage levels, in accordance with elementary economic laws on price formation. . . . Just as surely as the sun rises and sets, further upward pressure on wage levels would result in increased unemployment."[16] If emergency workers were paid the equivalent of open-market wages, "that would only be an act of false humanity, which experience now very unquestionably shows is likely to increase and exacerbate unemployment."[17]

The Social Democrats did not have to let their determinism prevent them from abandoning this unemployment policy. By this time, of course, determinism had been reduced to little more than a phrase, a stylistic embellishment in various ideological declarations. But the problem was that when it came to unemployment, as well as other areas of economic policy, there was nothing else to put in its place. Because the Social Democrats did not feel that their Marxist theories provided any practical political guidance, they had no other recourse but to endorse the nonsocialist unemployment policy. They were compelled to admit that only wage cuts could eliminate unemployment: They could object to the fact that emergency workers were paid less than employees in the open market, but they

[16] Gerard De Geer, *Sveriges andra stormaktstid. Några ekonomiska och politiska betraktelser* (Stockholm: Bonniers, 1928), pp. 55–56.
[17] *Stockholms-Tidningen*, 6 May 1929.

supported this policy and practiced it themselves when they were in power.

But the argument based on wage theory greatly troubled the Social Democrats. Incapable of refuting it intellectually, they responded to it on emotional grounds. Wasn't it outrageous to lower the wages of the poor working class? Was the state justified in paying its workers starvation wages? Did the nonsocialist majority in the Unemployment Commission possess any honest desire to help the jobless? Or as Gustav Möller, a leading Social Democrat, put it after leaving government and returning to the opposition, shouldn't there be an end to the entire discussion of wage theory? The nonsocialists were sharply critical of such whims. They wanted to protect "the Swedish system" and promised the Social Democrats that they would put up a tough fight against these attempts – to quote the liberal *Dagens Nyheter* – "to undermine the basically successful Swedish unemployment policy of recent years."[18]

The Social Democrats were in a bind, trapped between their desire to alleviate need and their assessment of what could possibly be done. The argument based on wage theory seemed irrefutable. "The principle that relief wages have to be lower than open-market wages is recognized by everyone. Even we Social Democrats admit that this principle must be maintained in the interest of normal production. But the principle only means not making emergency jobs more attractive than the available industrial jobs. To achieve this result, even the slightest difference between emergency-work wages and the wages offered by private employers is sufficient."[19] The contorted phrase, "the slightest difference," highlights the ideological dilemma of the Social Democrats during the period. The nonsocialists also made ironic comments about the ambivalent attitude of the Social Democrats.[20]

Finally, a few words about the unemployment policy advocated by the Communists. They bitterly attacked the "starvation policies against the unemployed" practiced by "all nonsocialist parliamentary parties, also including the Social Democratic party." They put greater faith in Marxist theory as opposed to the reformism of the Social Democrats. Instead of showing exaggerated concern toward private monopolists, they said, the unemployed should be given genuinely productive work. The natural solution would be for the state to nationalize companies that could not maintain employment. But because the Communists realized that there was no political support for such a program, they instead proposed that very large sums be paid for productive work at market wage levels. Such an arrange-

---

[18] *Dagens Nyheter*, 15 Jan. 1927.
[19] *Socialdemokraten*, 3 Feb. 1922.
[20] *Dagens Nyheter*, 27 Jan. 1925; *Nya Dagligt Allehanda*, 28 Jan. 1925.

ment should replace the system of emergency jobs. When someone asked what would be the purpose of increasing production when there would be no market for these products, the Communists replied by again citing Marx and his theory of underconsumption. If workers were only enabled to consume more goods through better-paid jobs, the demand for industrial goods would also increase.[21]

Without paying any heed to the Communists' ideas, the nonsocialists and the Social Democrats continued to support the existing unemployment policy, legitimized by liberal wage theory. But unemployment persisted. Toward the end of the 1920s, a certain fatigue began to pervade the political debate. "It is a system on the brink of collapse," the Social Democratic newspaper *Ny Tid* said of this unemployment policy, without indicating what should replace it.[22] "Political leaders have never been so helpless in tackling the multitude of economic problems and difficulties besieging postwar developments in the country as they have been on the issue of unemployment," wrote the liberal *Göteborgs Handels- och Sjöfartstidning*.[23] And the conservative *Nya Dagligt Allehanda* expressed hopelessness at the fact that "both sides remain stuck in their positions, that the battle is not being fought to achieve real improvements in the labor market situation and that the two sides had ended up in trench warfare which can benefit neither the unemployed nor the country."[24]

Neither the doctrine of harmony nor determinism seemed capable of passing the acid test of unemployment.

However, unemployment was not an intractable issue for everyone. Ernst Wigforss, a Social Democratic ideologist, grappled with the problem more successfully than anyone else. His ideas could be followed in articles in the party journal *Tiden* and in parliamentary debates. He looked for other strategies besides those offered by academic economists and Sweden's economic liberals. In times of depression, according to Wigforss, "the amiable spendthrift who gives people jobs by throwing around his money" was "socially useful," whereas the "miser" who put his money under the mattress instead of investing it was preventing an economic recovery. When private enterprise hesitated to put its savings to use, it was up to the state to step in and provide public jobs for the unemployed. These jobs should pay market wages, because the goal was to pump buying power into the country. Public jobs would have a multiplier effect. "The fact is that if I want to create jobs for 100 people, it is not necessary for me to provide

[21] Lewin 1967, pp. 55ff.; quotation from mot AK 1927:452, p. 3.
[22] *Ny Tid*, 2 Feb. 1928.
[23] *Göteborgs Handels- och Sjöfartstidning*, 29 Aug. 1928.
[24] *Nya Dagligt Allehanda*, 13 Apr. 1928.

jobs for all of them. This world is so fortunately arranged that if I can find a job for an unemployed tailor, he in turn will have the chance to buy new shoes, and this generates work for an unemployed shoemaker."[25]

Amazingly enough, Wigforss worked out a program of action against unemployment several years before Keynes published his major work on the new economic theory. Wigforss also managed to win over the Social Democratic party to his new ideas. In 1930, the Social Democrats introduced a bill proposing a complete revamping of Swedish unemployment policy according to the new guidelines. The state should not conduct unemployment policy as some kind of social welfare policy, merely intended to alleviate the needs of the unemployed. The policy of providing productive jobs was intended to have an expansive effect on the entire economy.[26] The Communists welcomed the new ideas in Parliament, taking pleasure in the fact that the Social Democrats had changed their mind and had, in their view, endorsed a policy already proposed by the Communists. But the nonsocialist majority in Parliament could not support the proposal. It was too incompatible with the liberal doctrine of harmony that dominated their thinking.

Where did Wigforss get his program? He was familiar with British Liberal thinking, but his sensitivity to their theories had its own special prerequisite. It was based on his familiarity with the Marxist theory of underconsumption, which had also inspired Keynes. It can be said that on the basis of the Marxist theory of economic crises, Keynes and Wigforss developed parallel concepts that pointed toward the expansionist theory of economics. In an age when macroeconomists used microeconomic arguments even when talking about the economies of whole countries, Keynes revived Marx's more realistic macroeconomic thinking. Marxism was, admittedly, hobbled with an incorrect forecast: The working class did not become poorer and consequently Marx's disaster scenario did not materialize. But the important thing was Marx's theory about how unemployment resulted from underconsumption. On this point Keynes applied his mental dexterity and proved the expansionary multiplier effects in the national economy if the state pumped in buying power. This would be a way to overcome recessions and unemployment – and along with it the threat of socialization, according to the liberal Keynes. Not without self-appreciation, Keynes declared that he had written a book that would revolutionize the world's approach to economic issues within a decade. And

---

[25] Lewin 1967, pp. 59ff.; quotation from Ernst Wigforss, "Spararen, slösaren och den arbetslöse," *Tiden* (1928): 501ff., esp. 501 (quotation) and 504–505; AK 1932:55, pp. 70–79 and 101 (quotation).

[26] Mot FK 1930:108 and AK 1930:186.

he emphasized that, with this book, he had also destroyed the foundations of Marxism.[27]

The root of unemployment could thus be found where Marx claimed it to be, wrote one Swedish Social Democratic editor. "This early Marxist crisis theory was on the right track. Its faulty conclusions were not due to a fundamental misjudgment of the factors that were known; they were due to the fact that the actual course of events was influenced by unknown or unforeseen factors. As for the latter, we can first of all include the labor movement itself, with all its impact on the trade union and political fields. One might say that the agitational effect of the theory itself became one of the strongest means toward undermining its validity." But it had been a fruitful theory, he continued. It had taught us that responsibility for capital formation could not be left solely to private business. If we wanted to avoid future recessions and unemployment, the state would have to intervene in the economy, by creating such prosperity that the buying power of the masses would increase and by making sure that investments and consumption remained in step with each other.[28]

The most important impact of these ideas was on nationalization theory. The worldwide economic depression eventually also reached Sweden. Unemployment figures soared. Did this mean that the disaster for the capitalist system predicted by Marx had arrived after all, so that the time was now ripe for nationalizing the means of production? This question was asked by a couple of radical souls when the Social Democratic party congress met in March 1932, but the idea was rejected by the party's leading figures. The crisis was admittedly perhaps the worst thus far for capitalism, but there were no indications that capitalism would not also survive this period of trial. Naturally, campaign propaganda for the September 1932 election would make maximum use of the difficult times at hand, but the crisis would be overcome by means of the party's new unemployment policy program, not through nationalization.

As it turned out, the man who had been the driving force behind the new unemployment policy also succeeded in most clearly spelling out the ideological consequences of this policy. Ernst Wigforss asked for the floor when the nationalization issue was being debated at the party congress. He asked to be allowed to speak freely from his heart for a moment. Wigforss said he did not think it possible to conceal the fact that ideolog-

[27] Joan Robinson, *An Essay on Marxian Economics* (London: Macmillan, 1947), esp. pp. 1ff., 43ff., and 63–95. The book was first published in 1942. Cf. Shigeto Tsuru, "Keynes versus Marx: The methodology of aggregates," in *Post-Keynesian Economics*, ed. Kenneth K. Kurihara (New Brunswick, N.J.: Rutgers University Press, 1954), pp. 320–344; R. F. Harrod, *The Life of John Maynard Keynes* (London: Macmillan, 1951), p. 462; Lewin 1967, pp. 64ff.
[28] Karl Fredriksson, "Kapitalbildningens roll i konjunkturförloppet," *Tiden* (1933):74–75 and 88.

ical developments within the Social Democratic party had led to a situation where it was difficult to establish positive guidelines. This was because the party had two roots: Marxism and liberalism. The Marxist nationalization theory had been interpreted in such a way that one industry or perhaps one company after the other would be nationalized; this was the principle of step-by-step nationalization. But because of this Marxism, the Social Democrats had been shunted aside and become passive observers of events. Only when the disaster predicted by Marx broke out would the Social Democrats act. For this reason, the party's current policy had ended up being a form of economic liberalism. According to Wigforss, this policy had consistently blocked the Social Democratic party from adopting a more active economic policy. The Social Democrats had gone out of their way to act solely in accordance with so-called "wise, sound economic principles" – that is, avoid any kind of interference in the economy. Speaking with irony, Wigforss criticized this cowardly Social Democratic liberalism; he said he had heard and read Social Democratic statements "that showed such concern for what is called free enterprise that nowadays you can hardly find its counterpart anywhere in the world except among the most ossified economic liberals."

Wigforss then pointed out that there were two irreconcilable concepts in Social Democratic ideology – nationalization and economic planning. By economic planning, he meant "greater public-sector control of the economy," without any nationalizations necessarily taking place. Nationalization could occur without having a planned economy, just as "public-sector control of the economy" could be achieved without nationalization. Wigforss sought to clarify his ideas by giving a concrete example: "Nationalization can occur step by step. We can nationalize the Boliden metals company one year, we can build up a large shoe factory the second year, we can open a nationally owned commercial bank the third year, and we can let the public sector take over the entire forest product industry the fourth, and so on. But note that this will not remove our business sector from the free market and its chaos. The fact that we have the Swedish National Railways does not help us to keep railroad workers fully occupied when a recession arrives. We have to lay off 5,000 or 10,000 because we cannot control the economy in which these railroads play a part. We can nationalize one branch of industry after another, but we are connected to a large system of economic liberalism where free price formation in the market is the decisive factor. Nationalization is not necessarily the same thing as economic planning."

Wigforss's speech turned into a recommendation for economic planning at the expense of nationalization. In the name of economic planning, he advocated "central intervention on matters concerning the monetary system and the utilization of capital," even if this meant "to some extent, and perhaps not such a small extent, that we depart from what might be called the principle of gradual nationalization."[29]

This event marked the end of the Social Democrats' long and difficult emancipation from Marxist determinism. Wigforss's speech showed a way out of the ideological dilemma that the party had faced because of the conflict between the long-term and the short-term perspective within Marxism. Although the belief in a long-term trend toward disaster and nationalization was abandoned, the concept of establishing a socialist production system was maintained. But this would not be achieved through any kind of "gradual nationalization" company by company, industry by industry, such as the Social Democrats had previously speculated about when they were engaged in trying to soften Marxist theory. Instead, they sought a higher degree of state intervention in the economy without nationalization; the most immediate step would be to introduce the new unemployment policy with its state-sponsored productive jobs at market wages. Nationalization was no longer the essential thing, only an option. The ideology of economic planning replaced nationalization in Social Democratic ideological development. The socialist concept of freedom remained the touchstone of this new ideology. Now as before, the Social Democrats put their faith in the state's ability to intervene in the economy in order to free the masses and particularly the unemployed from the hardships of private capitalism. But now the Social Democrats had found a new, more efficient way of working toward these ideals.[30]

The new unemployment program permeated the entire Social Democratic propaganda effort during the 1932 election campaign.[31] With his usual pedagogic skill, Wigforss called his election pamphlet *Can We Afford to Work? (Ha vi råd att arbeta?)*.[32] The party's campaign was characterized by a self-confidence and sense of purpose that were in total con-

---

[29] *Sveriges Socialdemokratiska Arbetarepartis fjortonde kongress* (Stockholm, 1932), pp. 472ff.

[30] This is one of the central theses in my dissertation (Lewin 1967). In this work, I went against the generally accepted description of history, as established by Tingsten's *Den svenska socialdemokratiens idéutveckling,* in which the ideological renewal of the Social Democratic party in the 1930s was neglected. According to Tingsten, the party continued to live with the conflict between the long-term and the short-term perspective, increasingly evolving into a generally social–liberal party without any socialistic elements. Tingsten did not make any clear distinction between the concepts of nationalization and economic planning; he used these concepts as synonyms. He stated incorrectly that the new unemployment policy did not trigger serious objections form the nonsocialists; on the contrary, it gave rise to intensive criticism of economic planning during the 1930s, couched in ideological terms. In all essential respects, my thesis has been accepted – even by Tingsten himself; see his postscript to the new edition of *Den socialdemokratiska idéutvecklingen 2* (Stockholm: Aldus/Bonniers, 1967), pp. 379–394.

[31] Lewin 1967, pp. 78ff.

[32] Ernst Wigforss, "Ha vi råd att arbeta? Något om sparsamhet och offentliga arbeten," in *Från klasskamp till samverkan* (Stockholm: Tiden, 1941), pp. 304–320.

trast to the party chairman's weary words before the 1928 party congress, when he had stated that the party lacked an economic action program. Now Per Albin Hansson distanced himself from the old-fashioned passivity of the economic liberal camp in a way that almost seemed like a polemic against his party's own past, as a clear demonstration that the party had now overcome its determinism and agreed on an action program. "The Social Democratic view of reform work as a continuous development process does not entail any fatalistic belief that everything will take care of itself and that all we have to do is announce the coming of a new order. On the contrary, our approach will make us emphasize day-to-day policies and try in every separate situation to do the most and best for the people. In the current economic crisis situation, the Social Democrats see it as their foremost task to devote all their energy toward providing fast and effective assistance to those categories of citizens who, through no fault of their own, have suffered from the consequences of the economic crisis."[33]

The Social Democrats looked forward to the election with great expectations.

Even amidst the ravages of world depression, the nonsocialists remained faithful to their doctrine of harmony. Just as the free traders had not regarded the economic crisis of the 1880s as incompatible with their philosophy, the nonsocialists did not view the depression of the 1930s as contradicting the doctrine of harmony. Such crises were a recurring feature of economic development, when the price of a particular production factor had become inordinately high, as was now the case with wages. The crisis was the economy's reaction to the violation of economic laws that trade unions and Social Democratic politicians had attempted to commit. Downswings were part of the rhythm of economic life; they could not be prevented. During the economic housecleaning and purification process of a recession, economic harmony was inevitably restored and each production factor returned to its natural price level. It was thus consistent of the Unemployment Commission to implement what it called "significant reductions" in emergency work wages on 1 August 1932 in view of the general wage cuts caused by the depression. It was no longer possible to live above one's means. The economy demanded a tribute in the form of hard work and thrift. The economic crisis had arrived as a corrective to all the mistakes made during the previous period, and the state should not try to prevent economic forces from restoring balance by intervening in the economy. Only in the agricultural sector were the nonsocialists prepared to deviate from their doctrine of harmony.

[33] Per Albin Hansson, *Socialdemokratin inför valet* (Stockholm: Tiden, 1932), pp. 7–8.

2. THE LOGROLLING STRATEGY

The Social Democrats won the election and formed a government. But theirs was a minority government; they had received 41.7 percent of the vote. The main task of the government was to implement its so-called crisis policy, based on the new economic theory. It was introduced in the government's 1933 draft budget and in subsequent bills during the spring of that year. The government's position was precarious, Prime Minister Per Albin Hansson stressed when he addressed the Social Democratic delegation to Parliament. Still, the government hoped to implement the economic policy reforms it considered more important than any other issue at hand. If it should encounter resistance to its policies from the nonsocialist parliamentary majority, it would have to consider "what options the situation offers in order to assert the wishes of public opinion."

The nonsocialists maintained their sharply critical attitude. The government's bills were referred to an ad hoc committee to which the nonsocialists appointed their principal spokesmen: Lindman and Trygger from the Conservatives, Olsson i Kullenbergstorp from the Agrarian party, and as chairman, former Prime Minister Hamrin of the Prohibitionists. The panel called itself the Welfare Committee, the same name that had been used for an equivalent body during the tariff crisis of the 1880s. The nonsocialist majority looked forward with confidence to a parliamentary vote that would defeat the government's crisis program. There were already those who were prepared to shoulder the fallen mantle of the prime minister after the government's expected collapse.

In this situation, Per Albin Hansson managed to maneuver himself out from under this threat of defeat by striking a deal with the Agrarians: This party was persuaded to support Social Democratic unemployment policy, and in exchange the Social Democrats abandoned their traditional free-trade stance and adopted a protectionist position on the farm issue. This agreement is the classic example of a successful quid-pro-quo strategy in twentieth century Swedish politics.

The main principles of the government's proposal for a reorganization of unemployment policy were the abolition of the emergency job system and of the Unemployment Commission, the very large-scale creation of relief jobs at wages matching those of the open market, programs to stimulate the business sector, and the introduction of state unemployment insurance. Prime Minister Hansson initiated talks with the nonsocialist party chairmen in an effort to bring about a consensus solution. Minister of Agriculture Per Edvin Sköld invited both Prohibitionists and Agrarians to dinners during which he hinted that the government had come to realize that its free-trade policy was inadequate to solve the problems of agriculture; a system of protectionist support might be considered, but how

far the government was willing to go depended on nonsocialist concessions on other issues, especially unemployment policy.

These hints led nowhere, however. The work of the Welfare Committee
continued. On 4 May the nonsocialists had progressed so far in their negotiations that they abandoned their party positions and agreed on a joint
committee report that would be presented as a counterproposal to the
Social Democratic government bill.

The prime minister intervened in this situation. He asked that the Welfare Committee postpone its vote, because he wanted to make another
attempt to negotiate with the nonsocialist parties. The Committee felt it
could not reject the prime minister's proposal. From that moment, the
Welfare Committee ceased to be the center of the political power game.

The new round of negotiations led nowhere as well, despite the energetic efforts of the prime minister. At this point he threatened to dissolve
the Second Chamber and call new elections if positive results were not
achieved. Given the new farm policy ideas being floated within the Social
Democratic party, it of course did not seem impossible to reach agreement
on agriculture. Certain compromises on unemployment policy also
seemed possible. But on the issue of the scope of relief jobs and the principle of paying market wages for them, two ideologies collided. Here, it
was impossible to agree. On 23 May, the prime minister submitted a final
memorandum and declared that he now felt he had exhausted all possibilities for reaching an agreement; however, he would still be available if
there was any desire for further negotiations. The nonsocialist party leaders returned to their committee work.

Little did they suspect that the game was dramatically changing character because the Agrarian party chairman's position was rapidly becoming undermined. More and more Agrarians disagreed with Kullenbergstorp's views and were willing to come to an agreement with the Social
Democrats. They rallied behind Axel Pehrsson i Bramstorp, a farmer from
Skåne province. At a late stage in the game Professor K. G. Westman,
another leading Agrarian, switched to the group that favored an agreement. Westman, who was not as critical of the new economic theories as
the nonsocialist party chairmen, let it be understood that an agreement
between the Social Democrats and the Agrarian party would not be out
of the question if the Social Democrats would further water down their
demands. Per Albin Hansson, who was stubbornly determined to use every
opportunity to bring about an agreement, now decided to take advantage
of the recess in the Parliament's committee work to reach a separate crisis
agreement with the Agrarian party. Negotiations between them began on
26 May, with the government represented by Hansson and the Agrarian
party by Westman, who now emerged as the official representative of the
Agrarians and negotiated on their behalf; the party chairman had been

taken off the case and shunted aside. Despite what he had told the non-socialist party chairmen three days before, Prime Minister Hansson approved further modifications of the government's conditions. Thus the final sum allocated for unemployment policy purposes was reduced from 195 to 180 million kronor, a cut that exclusively affected the Social Democrats' pet project, public-sector jobs. Some additional compromises were made. The Social Democrats would allow the Unemployment Commission to survive, and unemployment insurance was left outside the agreement. No changes were made in the large-scale protectionist agricultural support system, which the Social Democrats had previously declared they were willing to accept. The agreement was approved by a large majority of the Agrarian party leadership and received the approval of the Social Democratic delegation to Parliament. This made it official.

Despite all the rumors, the agreement came as a surprise to the other nonsocialist party chairmen. Relations between the Agrarian party and the other nonsocialist parties became extremely irritable. A pointed correspondence between Lindman and Westman began. The latter made himself scarce on the important day the agreement became known and did not arrive in Parliament until after 3 P.M. The Agrarian party gave evasive and unclear information. Hamrin and his committee work had been rendered completely irrelevant; all the committee could now do was to expedite the agreement by the newly constituted majority.

After a few weeks the argeement was ratified by Parliament. Several Prohibitionist M.P.'s led by Ivar Österström and Ola Jeppsson[34] voted for the agreement, as did the Conservative Nils Wohlin. There was great satisfaction within both the Social Democratic and Agrarian parties. The

[34] This caused Bertil Ohlin to make the amazing statement in his memoirs that "three parties approved" the agreement; he claims that behind the decision "stood primarily not only the two 'logrolling' parties but also the Prohibitionist party." *Bertil Ohlins memoarer. Ung man blir politiker* (Stockholm: Bonniers, 1972), p. 216. Gunnar Hellström, *Jordbrukspolitik i industrisamhället med tyngdpumkt på 1920-och 30-talen* (Stockholm: Lts Förlag, 1976), p. 558, disagreeing with this version of history, points out that the entire dispute between the nonsocialists and Social Democrats "concerning wages for reserve jobs vanishes from the picture in Ohlin's account." Ohlin himself was a faithful Keynesian economist and would eventually lead the Liberal party over to the new economic theory. But when he tries to argue that this happened as early as 1933, he is too eager to vindicate his party. Speeches by Ekman, Hamrin, Sam Larsson, and the newly appointed Liberal party chairman Gustaf Andersson i Rasjön, printed in the proceedings of Parliament, contradict him. Furthermore, the latter writes in his memoirs, Andersson, *Från bondetaget till samlingsregeringen. Politiska minnen* (Stockholm: Tiden, 1955), pp. 120–121, regarding the situation within the Prohibitionist party, "that most (of its M.P.'s) relied on the fund of knowledge and authority possessed by the party's committee representatives (Hamrin, Sam Larsson and von Stockenström)." They supported "the Prohibitionist minority statement, with its defense of lower wages for reserve jobs." Cf. also a statement by Ohlin during the economic planning debate of the 1940s: "Let us Liberal party members not once again commit the same mistake as in 1933 and give the Swedish people the impression that other parties are more willing than we to do something effective [against unemployment]." See Chapter 6 below.

Agrarian party had gained the support of a majority in Parliament for very strong protectionist measures to help Swedish agriculture. The Social Democrats had admittedly been compelled to sacrifice free trade in this area – thereby breaking their election campaign promises – and had had to make significant concessions on their original demands regarding unemployment policy. But more important to them was that their basic principle of very large-scale relief work at market wages had won acceptance.

In strategic terms, the crisis agreement of 1933 paved the way for a transition from the minority parliamentarism of the 1920s to a majority parliamentarism; after a few years the agreement culminated in a genuine "red–green" coalition government between Social Democrats and the Agrarians under the leadership of Per Albin Hansson. By means of various government coalitions and similar arrangements, the Social Democrats would remain in power for forty-four years.

In ideological terms, the crisis agreement gave the Social Democrats a chance to begin practicing a new economic policy that gave the state a fundamentally different and more important role in the country's economic life than before. Exactly as the nonsocialist parties had feared, major government programs were not dismantled when the Depression had been overcome. State intervention was now justified with the argument that the state also had the responsibility to ensure that the business sector was run as efficiently as possible during good times – that it was running "at full power." The nonsocialists began to criticize economic planning from an ideological standpoint and argued on behalf of a liberal-market economy. But throughout the 1930s, the Social Democrats emerged from the battles supported by a growing number of voters and continued building the welfare state, which caused the rest of the world to speak about Sweden as a country midway between capitalism and socialism – "Sweden, the middle way."[35]

3. THE PARLIAMENTARY OUTCOME

Why did a Parliament dominated by a nonsocialist majority approve the new economic policies of a Social Democratic minority government, which went directly against the most fundamental principles of the nonsocialists' liberal free-market doctrine? The previous section has provided a general answer: because the Social Democrats were successful in their logrolling strategy vis-à-vis the Agrarian party. Buy why were they successful? How did the potential loser, Per Albin Hansson, manage to snatch victory from the jaws of defeat? Why did an agreement come about

[35] Lewin 1967, pp. 97–142.

between the Social Democrats and the Agrarians? Why did their crisis agreement assume the shape it did? This section will summarize the situation in 1933 in terms of game theory. In this connection there is reason to refer to the paradox described by Condorcet and Arrow and use the Swedish empirical material from the 1930s to examine in greater detail the conditions for rational political action.

Let us assign the following labels to the main alternatives that were considered:[36]

$$x = \text{expansionist unemployment policy}$$
$$-x = \text{rejection of expansionist unemployment policy}$$
$$y = \text{agricultural protectionism}$$
$$-y = \text{rejection of agricultural protectionism}$$

According to the majority principle, the result would be $-x$ and $-y$, because an expansionist unemployment policy would be rejected by the Conservatives, the Agrarians, the Prohibitionists, and the Liberals. Agricultural protectionism would be rejected by the Social Democrats, the Communists, the Prohibitionists, and the Liberals.

Let us also introduce the following labels for possible combinations of the main alternatives:

$$xy = M$$
$$-xy = N$$
$$x - y = O$$
$$-x - y = P$$

In simplified terms, the preference orderings of the Parliamentary parties may be described as follows (C = Conservatives, A = Agrarians, L = Liberals, P = Prohibitionists, S = Social Democrats, X = Communists):

C	A	L + P	S	X	Result according to majority rule
NPMO	NMPO	PNOM	OMPN	OMPN	P

The Conservatives' first preference was to reject the expansionist unemployment policy and support a protectionist Agrarian policy; their lowest preference was the opposite. If the party did not win approval for its first preference, its most important priority was the rejection of Social Democratic unemployment policy, even if this was at the expense of agricultural tariffs; the staunchest ideological supporters of economic liberalism's doctrine of harmony at the time were found in the Conservative party. P thus preceded M in the Conservatives' preference ordering.

---

[36] For background on this presentation technique, see Robert Abrams, *Foundations of Political Analysis: An Introduction to the Theory of Collective Choice* (New York: Columbia University Press, 1980), pp. 104ff.

The crisis agreement

The Agrarian party's preference ordering was similar to that of the Conservatives. It was identical as regards their first and fourth preference. But an analysis of the party propaganda used during the 1932 election campaign indicates that a reversal of the second and third preferences took place: Relatively speaking, the Agrarian party's demand for agricultural tariffs was stronger than its oppostition to the new economic theory behind the Social Democratic unemployment policy.

If we turn to the Prohibitionists and Liberals, we find another pattern. They opposed the expansionist unemployment policy, as did the other nonsocialist parties. But they also opposed agricultural tariffs; as we have seen, they favored supporting agriculture by other kinds of regulation. Looking at our preference formula, the result shows that rejection of both was their first preference, approval of both their last. As for their middle preferences, we can assume they would have found it somewhat easier to accept the rejection of expansionary unemployment policy combined with the approval of agricultural tariffs (N) rather than the opposite combination (O); this possibility became clear when the nonsocialists prepared their joint report in the Welfare Committee.

For the Social Democrats, their first preference was the approval of an expansionary unemployment policy together with rejection of agricultural tariffs; the reverse was their last preference. It was easier for them to sacrifice their views on agricultural policy than those on unemployment policy; M thus preceded P in their preference ordering.

Finally, when we look at the attitude of the Communists, it turns out to have been identical with the Social Democratic preference ordering. Yet there was a difference between Social Democratic and Communist ideology. If we wanted to identify it, we would have to use more finely calibrated scales than the ranking systems we have restricted ourselves to. On a scale of intervals, the distance between O and M would be considerably larger for the Communists than for the Social Democrats and would at the same time form the dividing line of what is politically acceptable. For this was the preference ordering of an extremist party: Only the ideologically best position could be accepted, whereas every strategic concession aimed at achieving something instead of nothing was condemned. This approach was made easier by the fact that the party's isolated position generally never allowed it to take part in strategic games.

The P alternative, which almost won, was thus the first preference of the Prohibitionists and the Liberals. No wonder Felix Hamrin prepared himself to become prime minister again.

But further analysis using game theory shows that P was an "unstable" solution, as the term is used. As we shall see, no alternative could win if they were compared with each other in pairs. There was no so-called Condorcet winner, but instead the voter's paradox prevailed.

$$M > P (A, S, X - C, P + L)$$
$$N > M (C, A, P + L - S, X)$$
$$N > O (C, A, P + L - S, X)$$
$$O > M (P + L, S, X - C, A)$$
$$P > N (P + L, S, X - C, A)$$
$$P > O (C, A, P + L - S, X)$$

Thus $M > P > N > O > M$. The ranking order was intransitive. There were cyclical majorities and thus opportunities for logrolling. By slightly changing their preference orderings, two parties could cooperate to improve the situation. The Social Democrats agreed to agricultural tariffs, and the Agrarians accepted an expansionist unemployment policy. They both agreed to bring M into first position. The new ranking order was as follows:

C	A	L + P	S	X	Result according to majority rule
NPMO	MNPO	PNOM	MOPN	OMPN	M

Comparing the alternatives in pairs, we also find:

$$M > N (A, S, X - C, P + L)$$
$$M > O (C, A, S - P + L, X)$$
$$M > P (A, S, X - C, P + L)$$

The M solution, arrived at after the crisis agreement, was the Condorcet winner, and the M solution was stable. According to majority rule, an expansionist unemployment policy could be voted through with the support of the Social Democrats, the Agrarians, and the Communists. Agricultural tariffs, in turn, could be introduced by attracting the votes of the Social Democrats, the Agrarians, and the Conservatives.[37]

If we compare the solutions before the crisis agreement (P) and after (M) with the parties' original preference orderings, we find that the Social Democrats and Agrarians taking part in the deal both moved up from third to second position: The Conservatives moved from second to third position, and the Prohibitionists and Liberals from first to fourth.

For that matter, the Conservatives had reason to be pleased about the fact that the agricultural sector would get better protection than would otherwise have been the case.

The greatest political loss befell the Prohibitionists and the Liberals, which seems symbolic considering that they had been the chief advocates of the minority parliamentarism that the crisis agreement had brought to

[37] The Conservatives actually joined a majority of nonsocialist leftists in abandoning the compromise reached in the Welfare Committee and presented a policy of their own on the farm issue, but this did not influence the result and is of no importance to our analysis.

an end. Hamrin personally found his miscalculation hard to bear. "I have been too optimistic," he wrote with bitterness. "Developments have shown this. My calculations did not prove right. Here I stand like a sinner."[38]

The position of the Communists improved by sheer chance, because their preference ordering coincided with that of the Social Democrats. But as they did not allow the slightest deviation from their first preference, they thus strongly condemned the crisis agreement as well as the entire parliamentary system that made such strategic games possible.[39]

At the beginning of this section, we asked why a nonsocialist majority could be persuaded to accept the economic policy proposals of a Social Democratic minority government. The answer provided by an analysis based on game theory is that there was intransitivity in the preference orderings and instability in the expected majority solution. By agreeing on an alternative majority solution, two parties could improve their positions.

Given this solution, could the other parties also have begun logrolling to arrive at a majority solution that would have benefited them? In theory, the answer is yes; endless proposals seem possible. In this case, however, the other nonsocialist party chairmen lacked information on how the Agrarians would act. Persuaded that the nonsocialist majority would win, they saw no reason to get involved in further negotiations.

Let us look at yet another alternative. Could the Agrarians have strengthened their position further during negotiations with Per Albin Hansson by giving the other nonsocialist parties a hint about the events that were actually occurring, thereby persuading them to be more favorable toward Agrarian demands than the Social Democrats were? Fresh approaches to agricultural policy found sympathizers in all parties. The Agrarian party could count on good support from other nonsocialist parties on their pet issue. In other words, the analysis leads us to the question of why, under these circumstances, the Agrarians entered into any agreement at all with the Social Democrats and not with the nonsocialists. In brief, the answer is that the Conservative party was certainly reliable from an Agrarian point of view, but the Prohibitionists were not. The Agrarians therefore preferred to reach an agreement with the emerging Social Democratic party rather than with the nonsocialist parties, among which the Prohibitionists would continue to hold a key position. If the powerful Social Democrats could be persuaded to condone the Agrarians' agricultural policy ideas, this would be much more valuable than an unpredictable alliance with other nonsocialist parties. The Agrarians, like the Social Democrats, wanted stable majority conditions that could provide a long-

---

[38] Svante Thorell, "Felix Hamrin och krisuppgörelsen 1933," *Statsvetenskaplig Tidskrift* (1960): 282.

[39] Lewin 1967, pp. 96 and 115–116.

Table 5.1. *"The battle between the sexes"*

	Wife	
	Restaurant	Theater
Husband Restaurant	3, 2	0, 0
Theater	0, 0	2, 3

term guarantee of the policies they advocated. From a strategic viewpoint, the Social Democrats were a superior coalition partner.

That is how an agreement between the Social Democrats and the Agrarians came about. But why did it go no further than it did? The phenomenon known as "endless bidding" may well occur in a situation like this. The prerequisite for an agreement is that both parties choose the same alternative for action. If they choose different positions, so that no agreement is reached, this outcome is worse for both parties than abstaining from their first preference. The mathematical structure of this dilemma is usually illustrated in a game called "the battle between the sexes," depicted in Table 5.1.

To celebrate their anniversary, a husband and wife plan to go out together in the evening. There are two alternatives: going to a restaurant, which the husband prefers; or to the theater, which the wife prefers. They can afford only one alternative and would consider the evening ruined if they do not spend it together, given the occasion. Thus, neither of them can make the decision alone and let his or her own preference determine the outcome, or there is a risk that the evening "will be ruined." It is necessary to make a strategic calculation about the partner's reactions. As it turns out, the husband is not totally uninterested in theater; although he does not consider it as nice as going to a restaurant, it is still better than staying home. And the wife has the same attitude toward going to a restaurant. Their matrix thus contains the utility values shown in Table 5.1. The husband makes the following calculation: I know that my wife prefers going to the theater. So I should choose this alternative (lower right-hand quadrant) rather than getting nothing at all (upper right-hand quadrant). But, the husband says after further reflection, if I make this choice on the basis of what I know about my wife's preferences, then she should reason in the same way about my desire to go to a restaurant; she will prefer the upper left-hand quadrant to the lower left-hand quadrant. And so the couple endlessly continue to adapt to each other's preference without arriving at a decision.

The crisis agreement

The preferences of the parties went around in circles without reaching equilibrium when it became time to make a decision on Sweden's crisis policy. The Social Democrats and the Agrarians realized that it was in their interest to reach an accord based on both parties' second preferences, because neither party could implement its first. But what would the agreement look like? Both parties understood that cooperation was necessary. In other words, it was in the interest of the other party to support a relatively unfavorable solution rather than to reach no solution at all. But if this applied to one party, it also applied to the other. Just as in the case of the battle between the sexes, there was an inherent risk that the decision-making process might be prolonged ad infinitum.

Two circumstances enabled the parties to reach a final agreement. One was the time element. When we leave behind the textbook examples and analyze real politics, we find that this factor is a very clear reality. Parliament had a timetable to follow. It was necessary to reach a decision within a limited period. Per Albin Hansson nevertheless showed considerable patience, openness, and innovative thinking during the negotiations. Time and time again, he resumed discussions when they seemed to have reached an impasse. In his final deliberations with Westman, he was tireless in his willingness to continue making compromises and negotiating until they could conclude an agreement in time for approval by Parliament before its summer recess.

As discussed earlier, the second factor was the relatively strong position of the Agrarians. Let us make the game matrix a little more complicated. In theory, of course, we could present an endless number of combinations of unemployment and agricultural policy measures that the parties might conceivably talk about. Let us limit ourselves to two, because our purpose is not to exhaust all possibilities but to describe the basic decision-making problem: One alternative is the bid of 23 May, which was more advantageous to Hansson; the other is the bid of 26 May, which was more advantageous to Westman. One might question the choice of numbers; as usual, I only wish to indicate the structure of their preference orderings. The premise remains that both parties must choose the same alternative in order to come to an agreement. But who should adapt to whom?

As the reader will notice in Table 5.2, there is no longer a 0,0 in the upper right-hand and lower left-hand quadrants, but a 0,1. These numbers indicate how the parties might have regarded a breakdown in the negotiations. To Per Albin Hansson, a breakdown would have meant 0: His expansionist unemployment policy would have been rejected; the nonsocialist position on unemployment policy would have received parliamentary approval; and a new election might have been called.

But for the Agrarians, the outcome would not have been as bad. The Agrarians would have secured good support for their agrarian policies

Table 5.2. *The crisis policy game: the crisis agreement as an example of "the battle between the sexes"*

	K. G. Westman	
	May 23	May 26
Per Albin Hansson May 23	3, 2	0, 1
May 26	0, 1	2, 3

even without an agreement with the Social Democrats, although in the long term this support did not seem as reliable and valuable. Based on utility value, an agreement with the Social Democrats was worth a 3 or a 2 depending on the concrete outcome, while an agreement with the non-socialists was worth a 1.

But on the other hand, a 1 is better than a 0, which signifies the loss Per Albin Hansson would have suffered if negotiations had failed. Westman could thus negotiate from a position of strength. In the final round, Westman was the one who made demands while Hansson granted concessions. The appropriation for unemployment programs was cut, whereas the appropriation for agriculture stayed the same. While again emphasizing that the figures only indicate preference orderings that cannot be 100 percent accurate, our conclusion is that the lower right-hand quadrant best describes the contents of the crisis agreement. Time pressure and the Agrarians' more favorable position vis-à-vis the other nonsocialist parties broke the chain of endless bidding and caused the Social Democrats to agree to further concessions.

There is nevertheless no doubt that Per Albin Hansson emerged as the winner of the political game that was played during the spring of 1933 – in the same way as Arvid Lindman had once triumphed on the issue of suffrage – even though according to our analysis his opponent earned higher utility numbers. Compared to what was to be expected from a minority government, Hansson's victory was undisputed. There are, incidentally, great similarities between Per Albin Hansson's behavior in 1933 and Arvid Lindman's in 1907. Both politicians possessed the same determination, the same firm desire to take the initiative, the same refusal to be sidetracked by new tactics or closed committee doors. Instead, they had the flexibility to adapt in an unconventional manner to new circumstances and were prepared to pay even a high price for the solution they wanted. Both men had the same ability to surprise people and present their opponents with a fait accompli. Having started out as a potential loser, Per Albin Hansson provided a brilliant example of political and strategic gamesmanship, which greatly strengthened his authority and the power of the Social Democratic party.

4. THE CONDORCET METHOD

The value of consensus solutions was a recurring theme of the major speech in which Prime Minister Hansson defended the crisis agreement before Parliament in June 1933. The prime minister began by reminding his audience that there was one issue to which the government had a more intense commitment than any other – its economic crisis policy. As soon as it had assumed power, the government had stated "that it regarded trying to find ways to help the victims of the crisis as its main domestic task." It had also made it clear that it would not willingly accept a majority decision to reject its crisis proposals. If confronted with such a threat, the government would consider other ways of asserting what it interpreted as the will of the people. The constant negativism of the nonsocialist parties had now made this approach necessary. It had not been a matter of "the government being shunted aside without further ado. . . . Considering the outcome of the fall elections, it would not be reasonable to manipulate forth a situation where the Social Democrat government without further notice would say thanks and goodbye. Such a step would have triggered a very strong reaction throughout the country and would probably have contributed to a further increase in the public distaste for parliamentary activity which is so often discussed here."

For these reasons, the government had begun negotiations with the nonsocialist parties in an effort to reach an agreement on a crisis policy. The Social Democrats had gone to the negotiating table "with the utmost sincerity and with an honest desire" to find a consensus solution. The objective had been to enlist the support of all parties for a crisis policy. "I wish that a unanimous Parliament stood behind this policy." Hansson did not think it would have been impossible to achieve unanimity, because everyone agreed that vigorous measures had to be implemented against the crisis. When he examined the numerous proposals that had been presented, he felt that "actually, the entire Parliament agrees on most points." No efforts had been spared to arrive at a consensus. Even after three weeks of fruitless negotiations, when the prime minister had submitted his final memorandum, he had declared himself available to the other parties if they wished to continue. The ball was thus in the nonsocialist court. Was it unreasonable, Hansson asked rhetorically, "that after doing this, I did not afterward run and ask Mr. Lindman if he had anything to say to me? The other parties had received our offer. In normal negotiations, offers must be answered." But only one party had replied – the Agrarians. The party wanted to know if the government might consider further concessions. Among other things, these discussions had led to a reduction in the appropriation for unemployment programs from 195 to 180 million kronor and had thus finally resulted in an agreement between the Social Democrats and the Agrarian party.

The government had thus been only partially successful in trying to broaden support for its crisis policy. The discussions with the Agrarian party had led to an agreement but not to unanimity in the Swedish Parliament. Hansson nevertheless found a negotiated solution such as this one preferable to the negative decision that would result from a consistent application of the majority principle. As we have seen, Hansson even described the latter as a way of "forcing a situation by manipulation," which would further deepen the crisis of parliamentary government. Negative decisions and minority parliamentarism of the kind previously practiced by the Prohibitionists would not adequately reflect the will of the people. Looking below the surface of the arguments publicly expressed by the parties, one could detect the prerequisites for a broader consensus on vigorous crisis measures. Hansson could have concurred with Condorcet that if we looked beyond the first preference at the second, the third, and the fourth, it turned out that a crisis policy of the kind now proposed was preferred by the majority over any other alternative action.

Hansson indignantly rejected all the expressions of moral condemnation that were now directed against him. In his view, there was nothing reprehensible about the kind of strategic action that had been necessary to reach the agreement. This action had nothing whatever to do with tactical maneuvers in Parliament. "I am one of those members of Parliament who have never believed in political intrigue and lobbying. . . . I also base my political actions on another principle: I do not believe in tactical feints." This was why he had invited all the nonsocialist parties to negotiations on possible compromises in their original positions. He had only negotiated through the parties' official representatives. At no time had he taken advantage of his connections with individual members of other parties, in order not to harm the atmosphere of confidence that was a precondition for successful negotiations. He was not two-faced by nature. "I know that I have played a straight game all along." It was regrettable that the agreement was not unanimous, particularly because he had thought that the practical prerequisites for this had existed. The prime minister could only assure Parliament that he had done his utmost to find a consensus solution.

Otherwise, how would the nonsocialist parties have reacted to a negotiated solution as a method of decision making if unanimity had been achieved? "Imagine what would have happened if the agreement on the unemployment issue had been unanimous. Wouldn't the parties that took part in this agreement have demanded that the Social Democrats support measures to benefit agriculture? If this had been the case, would we not have been complimented on being so accommodating? I assume that if the agreement had been unanimous, it would have been regarded as our obligation to do what we have done, and for which we are now being morally condemned." The give-and-take of negotiations was no expression of political immorality. If the solution had been unanimous, Parliament would not now be hearing such unreasonable statements, with the non-socialists condemning the Social Democrats for supporting a proposal on the agricultural issue that the nonsocialists themselves considered useful to the country.[40]

The major speech in which Per Albin Hansson defended the crisis agreement thus resembled a plea for the Condorcet method instead of simple majority rule. A strict application of majority rule did not always provide the best picture of people's preferences. It was often more reasonable to consider that the parties had various degrees of commitment to different issues and also had second, third, and fourth preferences when facing a decision.

This view would be repeated thirty years later in a work that has become a classic of rational choice theory. In their book *The Calculus of Consent,* James Buchanan and Gordon Tullock demonstrated how the application of economic science could provide a pattern for each study of collective decision making. Economists assumed that each human being tried to maximize his or her utility, whereas political scientists attributed idealistic motives to people, such as the desire to find "truth." Using this method, social scientists not only failed to explain the collective decisions that were made. On the normative level, they also overlooked the fact that the theory of maximization of utility by individuals could provide a basis for "the Politics of the Good Society."

As Per Albin Hansson had done, Buchanan and Tullock began by pointing out that people were more committed to some issues than to others. Majority rule, based on the simple concept of one man–one vote, was not capable of recording this. In contrast, decision making by means of logrolling was based on this particular variation in intensity. If two people decided to resort to logrolling, both could improve their positions. One person's "welfare can be improved if he accepts a decision contrary to his desire in an area where his preferences are weak in exchange for a decision in his favor in an area where his feelings are stronger. Bargains among voters can, therefore, be mutually beneficial."

What happens to those who do not take part in logrolling? The authors

[40] AK 1933:49, pp. 6ff. and 35ff.

conceded that this was a problem. But if logrolling became sufficiently widespread that everyone became involved in this method of making decisions, everyone would benefit in the long run. On those issues that were really important to a person, he would have to pay a price to see his wishes come true, whereas in a majority-rule situation he would run the risk of losing everything.

The very best protection for those in danger of being left out of the logrolling process would be to combine logrolling with consensus solutions. Using arguments that often coincided even word for word with Per Albin Hansson's statements, Buchanan and Tullock advocated the rule of unanimity. If people tried to achieve unanimous decisions, no costs could then be imposed on a third party, because this person could stop the agreement. Under the rule of unanimity, people would make compromises so that everyone could finally accept the solution agreed upon, knowing that others would display the same accommodating attitude the next time around. Decisions should be made collectively in the good society through comparisons between pairs of different alternatives for action and through mutual respect – not by applying a majority principle, which mechanically compared all preferences regardless of how important they were to each of the participants.[41]

Buchanan and Tullock had a polemic purpose. They wanted to reevaluate logrolling as a decision-making tool. Until then, the term had been pejorative, associated with tactical maneuvering and political amorality. In their book, the authors wanted to show the advantages of logrolling. This reevaluation has been successful. Buchanan and Tullock have had great influence on the formation of the rational choice theory. A whole literature has emerged that points out the advantages of this kind of decision making. Some of these works have also argued that logrolling is a way of avoiding the voter's paradox, because it brings about a change in the preference orderings that lead to the paradox.[42]

As we know, the Swedish crisis agreement of 1933 did not involve all parties; some were left out. We will soon have a closer look at this particular circumstance, which is, of course, a central issue in evaluating the logrolling process. However, there is no reason to doubt that Per Albin Hansson really believed that unanimity would have been preferable and that he had tried to arrive at a consensus solution. It is tempting to speculate about how such an agreement might have looked. Especially considering the Conservatives' ideological commitment to liberal wage theory,

---

[41] James M. Buchanan and Gordon Tullock, *The Calculus of Consent: Logical Foundations of Constitutional Democracy* (Ann Arbor: University of Michigan Press, 1965); quotation from p. 145. The book was first published in 1962.

[42] For an overview of the literature, see Steven J. Brams, *Game Theory and Politics* (New York: The Free Press, 1975), pp. 129ff.

it is nevertheless difficult to imagine that they could have been persuaded to accept an expansionist unemployment policy unless the negotiations had been broadened to include some issue that was close to their hearts. Let us imagine, for instance, that defense policy had been brought into the bargaining and that the Social Democrats had declared their willingness to give up their disarmament policy in exchange for a united front on the new unemployment policy. Perhaps the parties could then have reached unity on an unemployment–agricultural–defense policy package. This is, of course, only speculation, but from counterfactual historiography, we have learned that it can be fruitful to speculate in order to illustrate a theoretical argument. And we would like to add that the hypothesis is not totally unreasonable, given our knowledge of Hansson's general consensus ideology and the menacing developments that were underway in Continental Europe during the 1930s.

So let us imagine, to use Per Albin Hansson's own words, that unanimity had been achieved. Wouldn't the Social Democrats then have been complimented on their concessions? Wouldn't everyone have been satisfied?

Recently, however, logrolling has come under criticism even though it is compatible with the rule of unanimity. Two objections will be mentioned in this chapter. The first is the proof of the so-called logrolling paradox. We saw that once the Social Democrats and the Agrarians had decided to reach an agreement, there was no obvious level where they should stop. The negotiations were characterized by endless bidding – time pressures and Westman's strong position finally led to a (theoretically arbitrary) decision. The literature has included case studies where there are motives for the participants to engage in logrolling but where they reduce their utilities by such cooperation; but each participant who withdraws from the logrolling process runs the risk of an even greater loss. The participants find themselves in a kind of "prisoners' dilemma"; even though each individual acts rationally, logrolling leads to collective irrationality.[43]

The second objection is that the rule of unanimity prevents radical reforms. The rule of unanimity admittedly prevents one participant from suffering when other participants shift their costs onto him. But in many cases, of course, this may be a political objective – for example, the objective of an income-equalization policy. There is thus a built-in conservative tendency in the rule of unanimity, which is controversial.[44]

So not even in principle or in general form do logrolling and the rule

[43] William H. Riker and Steven J. Brams, "The Paradox of Vote Trading," *The American Political Science Review* (1973): 1235–1247; cf. Gordon Tullock, "Communication," ibid. (1974): 1687–1688.

[44] Douglas W. Rae, "The Limits of Consensual Decision," ibid. (1975): 1270–1294.

Table 5.3. *Logrolling and the*
Condorcet method

				s	M′	M	N′
				b	M	N′	M′
h	+	f	+	1	N′	M	M′

of unanimity seem to represent a totally acceptable decision-making system.

After this digression into the field of political philosophy, let us return to our evaluation of the Swedish crisis agreement of 1933. Using the analytic language and symbols presented in the previous section, we might render Per Albin Hansson's calculation as follows. The majority constellation known as P, which was about to emerge and which among other things would have spelled the end of the prime minister's policy, was not stable. It was thus possible to achieve another solution, M, by means of logrolling. This meant that his policy would receive approval in exchange for his support of the Agrarian party's agricultural policy. During the negotiations, several alternatives quickly disappeared from the agenda: O, P, and N. The remaining alternatives were a modified N, which represented the nonsocialists' compromise of 4 May on the agrarian issue and which we refer to here as N′, plus different variations of M, of which for the sake of simplicity we will mention only two: the proposal of 23 May, here called M′, and the proposal of 26 May, here called M. At this stage of the game, the constellation of preferences was as described in Table 5.3. The Social Democrats' first preference was the solution of 23 May, their second preference the solution of 26 May. Their lowest preference was the nonsocialist agrarian compromise, which would have resulted in a rejection of their unemployment policy. The Agrarian party favored the solution of 26 May, followed by the nonsocialist compromise and in third place the alternative of 23 May. The Conservatives, Prohibitionists, and Liberals had by this time joined forces with the Agrarian party chairman in an agricultural compromise; their second choice was the solution of 26 May, their third the solution of 23 May.

We once again see that an application of simple majority rule leads to an impasse, because the three alternatives M′, M, and N′ each receive one vote. However, a more sophisticated decision rule, which takes into account the intensity of the participants' feelings, as exemplified by their second and third preferences, indicates that M most accurately reflects "the will of the people": A and C + P + L preferred M to M′, S and A chose M over N′. In other words, M was preferred over every other alternative. According to the Condorcet method, M should therefore be the collective decision.

Per Albin Hansson regretted that the other nonsocialist parties did not join in the agreement. He himself had, of course, agreed to sacrifice his first preference for his second – to give up M' for M – and had, among other things, cut the proposed unemployment appropriation from 195 to 180 million kronor. Was it too much to ask the other nonsocialist parties to give up their first preference for their second choice, that is, to move from N' to M? Then unanimity would have been achieved.

The answer is yes, it was too much to ask, because the nonsocialists now expected that N' would be the majority decision. At this stage in the game, they had no reason to abandon their first preference. There is no denying that the crisis agreement caught them napping. No matter how eager Per Albin Hansson had been to achieve a consensus, he finally gave up after making sure he had a majority. Attempts at broadening his base by putting out feelers to Hamrin were interpreted by the Prohibitionist chairman only as an offer to capitulate, an "empty gesture." Nor did Hansson think he had any reason to run to Lindman once again and ask if he had anything to say.

The Condorcet method is undoubtedly a decision rule that pays greater attention to the intensity of the participants' preferences than does simple majority rule. But in the final analysis, this attention only benefits the participant who gets his way as a consequence of the change in decision rules. In each given situation, one decision rule favors one participant and the second favors another. There is no agreement as to whether a particular rule should always be recommended; in the crisis agreement of 1933, the Prohibitionists and the Liberals – whose first preference would have been approved by a strict application of majority rule – had every reason to regret that the Condorcet method was now tried out. Given the shortcomings that have been discussed in this chapter, the Condorcet method cannot be accorded a higher moral status than the majority method. Instead, it should simply be included in the arsenal of decision rules for which a potential loser can try to gain acceptance under the appropriate circumstances when he is trying to snatch victory from the jaws of defeat.

As we have seen, during the negotiations leading to the crisis agreement, decisions and decision rules were questioned at the same time. As we can expect on the basis of one of the hypotheses that guide this investigation, the system experienced a crisis. Or to use a language that better reflects the values of most of the actors, the system underwent a change that provided a way out of the parliamentary crisis that followed the victory of the parliamentary form of government. During the 1920s, the wishes of minorities had collided in such a way as to prevent a forceful policy from being pursued by a strong government. When the Great

Depression arrived, this impotence in the decision-making process became alarming. If we study the complete preference orderings of the parties, simple majority rule did not seem capable of satisfactorily reflecting the parties' wishes. Comparing pairs of alternatives using the Condorcet method provided some hint at what might constitute a better decision from a collective standpoint. After a decade that failed to live up to the high expectations of the Left when the parliamentary system made its breakthrough, the Social Democrats created the prerequisites for a new system of majority parliamentarism and a long-term, ideologically based welfare policy.

6

Economic planning

1. PLANNING FOR THE POSTWAR PERIOD

The outbreak of World War II brought a pause in the debate on economic planning.[1] The ideological dispute on the role of the state in the business sector gave way to a truce as wartime regulation was imposed on the economy. Under the leadership of Per Albin Hansson, a grand coalition government was formed. It included representatives of the Social Democrats, Conservatives, Liberals, and Agrarians. The detailed regulation of the country's economic life that now took effect was supported by all social classes. Employees refrained from demanding extra pay to compensate for high wartime prices. Consumers felt called upon to accept a rationing system, manufacturers went along with price freezes and government direction, and special-interest organizations relinquished their independence and participated in the wartime economy as administrative bodies.[2] To express this consensus, different groups chose stylistic approaches that best suited their varying traditional world views. In the conservative camp, it seemed natural to appeal for national unity in the face of danger and to call on special interests to subordinate themselves to the best interests of the country. In the Social Democratic camp, leaders preferred to describe the necessary economic regulation in terms that might conjure up the image of an economy dedicated to meeting social needs, which had always been the ideal of socialism. Concealed behind these various modes of expression, however, was a strong desire for consensus. These shared

[1] Like the first section of Chapter 5, this section and the following one are based on my doctoral dissertation, *Planhushållningsdebatten* (Uppsala: Almqvist & Wiksell, 1967). I refer the reader to this work, pp. 176–262, for more detailed source references. For the most part, I have listed here the primary sources of direct quotations only.

[2] Karl Åmark, *Kristidspolitik och kristidshushållning i Sverige under och efter Andra världskriget I och II* (SOU 1952:49 and 50); Gunnar Heckscher, *Staten och organisationerna*, 2d rev. ed. (Stockholm: Kooperativa förbundets bokförlag, 1951), pp. 231–248. The book was first published in 1946.

values were also a psychological necessity in coping with the strains of war. Economic researchers have emphatically argued that perhaps the most important requirement for the success of the government regulation policies of World War II was precisely the fact that all circles regarded these measures as necessary in order to achieve generally accepted goals.[3]

Under the surface, however, fundamental ideological differences survived. When external pressures diminished toward the end of the war, economic policy disagreements once again came to the fore. All sides began to make plans for the postwar resumption of everyday political activity that more closely matched their ideological beliefs. After years of sacrifices and suppressed opposition, political parties and interest organizations cast longing glances toward the prospect of peace. Everyone had high hopes for the postwar period.

The end of the war coincided with important changes in political ideas and in the leaderships of the nonsocialist parties. A new generation had emerged whose political philosophies had been shaped during a period when the Social Democrats had successfully pursued an expansionist economic policy. The younger generation believed in the doctrine of full employment, which had gained widespread support in the industrialized world following the good experience of wartime employment policy. Briefly, this doctrine meant that the state was regarded as having both the ability and a responsibility to keep employment high. When young Conservative and Liberal party politicians accepted this concept, they were thus rejecting the nonsocialist arguments of the interwar period on the unemployment issue, which were based on wage theory, and they were embracing the principles behind the unemployment policy launched by the Social Democrats in 1930. Just as the Manchester liberals had been deserted by the economic liberals of the interwar period, the latter were now deserted by a new generation who wanted to give even greater room to the state in the national economy.

This conflict of generations emerged clearly when the Conservatives began to discuss a revision of their party program. Their existing program had been put together as early as 1919. The major changes that had occurred during the interwar period, not least in the economic and social welfare fields, had fundamentally altered the political agenda. The younger generation set the tone for the program revision process. Their leader, Jarl Hjalmarson, became the chairman of the program revision

---

[3] Erik Lundberg, *Konjunkturer och ekonomisk politik. Utveckling och debatt i Sverige sedan första världskriget,* 2d ed. (Stockholm: Konjunkturinstitutet and Studieförbundet Näringsliv och Samhälle, 1958), p. 436. The book was first published in 1953. The consensus that prevailed during World War II becomes instantly clear when we study the introduction of a general wage and price freeze in the fall of 1942. See Lewin 1967, pp. 176–186.

committee. In the long, intensive debate at the national party conference, his ideas were seconded mainly by Gunnar Heckscher and Elis Håstad. Against them stood a whole raft of politicians who had dominated the party during the interwar period, led by party chairman Gösta Bagge. When Bagge resigned in 1944 and was succeeded by Fritiof Domö – a man of compromises and the middle way – the journal *Svensk Tidskrift*, edited by Håstad, wrote that Domö was assuming "the leadership post in a period of transition. Of the conservative generation who dominated the scene during the previous war, hardly any are still in Parliament. A new generation has emerged whose view of life, especially on controversial social welfare issues, reflects the philosophies of our own age. Elsewhere, the gigantic problems of reconstruction are forcing people to think and behave in a social and collective manner that has also influenced people's opinions in our country, which was spared from war. Our report on the Conservative national conference showed how this new generation of conservatives, in particular, is calling for a positive social action program."[4]

The younger generation won passage of their "positive social program." Strangely enough, the Conservatives did not revise their party program. But the new concepts were expressed in a separate action program and in a more detailed commentary to it entitled *Freedom and Progress* (Frihet och framsteg). In this document, the party expressly recognized the responsibility of the state for ensuring "high, uniform employment." The Conservative party accepted the economic policy that it had so frantically resisted in the early 1930s.

Svensk Tidskrift's comment on the Conservative change of leadership could just as well have been written about the Liberal party. During the same year, Liberal party chairman Gustaf Andersson i Rasjön also resigned. He was succeeded by Bertil Ohlin. By choosing a leading Keynesian economist, the Liberals made it quite clear that they too had adopted the Social Democratic unemployment policy of 1930. If there were an economic downturn, Ohlin wrote in a 1943 article, the country should pursue an expansionist unemployment policy. Ohlin attacked "doctrinaire liberals" who criticized the expansion of public expenditures during the early 1930s in general terms as a "policy of waste." He urged the party to abandon such rigid economic liberalism. "Let us Liberal party members not once again commit the same mistake as in 1933 and give the Swedish people the impression that other parties are more willing than we to do something effective [against unemployment]."[5]

There is a striking difference between this article and an article that the

---

[4] "Kring ett ledareskifte," *Svensk Tidskrift* (1944): 664.
[5] Bertil Ohlin, "Ett ekonomiskt och socialt handlingsprogram för efterkrigsåren," *Folkpartiet* no. 4 (1943): 3 and 14ff.

retiring Liberal party chairman wrote at the same time. Ohlin emphasized that it was the duty of the state to keep employment and production up; his polemic against "state socialism" seemed rather vague in comparison. The opposite was true of Rasjön's approach. His main argument was an attack on Social Democratic plans for nationalization; only in a few subordinate clauses did he say that, in an abnormal situation, the state must take steps to safeguard employment. At the same time, however, he stressed that earlier employment crises should not be blamed on the business sector but on the state, which had created obstacles to free enterprise and thereby caused unemployment.[6] Ohlin would also later write antinationalization articles similar to Rasjön's. But the contrast between the two articles summarized here, which were written before the postwar debate on a planned economy had even started, is indicative of the difference in general political philosophy between the retiring party chairman and his successor.

It took the selection of Ohlin as party chairman to replace the Liberal party's decade-long vacillation in employment policy with a clear position. The clearest and most authoritative expression of this position is found in the booklet *Postwar Society,* (Efterkrigstidens samhälle), as the Liberals called their postwar program. This document gave no reason to doubt the party's support of the full employment doctrine.

As for the Agrarians, finally, we can say that their shift to the new employment policy had already taken place when they reached their crisis agreement with the Social Democrats in 1933. But it should be emphasized that the Agrarians' shift in positions had been an expression of strategic action, whereas during the final war years the Conservatives and Liberals were codifying a genuine ideological change.

Consequently, all three nonsocialist parties now accepted the approach to employment policy previously put forth by the Social Democrats. The role of the state in the economy should not be as passive as the theory of economic harmony prescribed. As an ideological principle, the liberal concept of freedom from the state was not satisfactory in all situations. "Freedom is not worth much to a person suffering long-term unemployment and poverty."[7] If the private labor market failed, employment should be maintained by using government funds.

The nonsocialists were, however, eager to avoid the conclusion that this change of opinion meant that liberalism was being softened. They argued emphatically that an expansionist economic policy was only intended for exceptional situations, for periods of depression. During normal periods, the state should leave the business sector in freedom. "The claim that pri-

[6] Gustaf Andersson, "Inför ett nytt år," *Folkpartiet* no. 1 (1944): 3 and 18.
[7] See n. 5 above (Ohlin).

vate demand for labor would never be sufficient, even under normal circumstances or in boom periods, is incorrect," *Freedom and Progress* argued.[8] And *Postwar Society* warned of the damage that would occur if the government intervention that was justified in an economic crisis was also used during periods of better economic conditions. "The decentralized type of society, with a free business sector within the framework of public legislation, is a prerequisite for the maintenance of civil liberty as well as a condition for the full utilization of people's talent and ability. A state socialistic society that has taken over the means of production and centralized power over politics and the economy, is a danger both to freedom and to economic progress."[9]

Despite this distinction in the role of the state between periods of economic crisis and more normal times, it is hard to deny that there was a genuine departure from the doctrine of harmony and that liberalism actually *was* being softened. The nonsocialists were also aware of the dangers to their ideological credibility that these new signals might pose, and they consequently made an effort to explain their economic policy views in detail and with great care. Their situation was actually much more complex than that of the Social Democrats in the 1930s. For the latter, their ideological tradition and the new unemployment policy program had coincided; indeed, this unemployment policy had solved the Social Democrats' ideological dilemma and had led the party out of its paralysis into a feverish desire for action. For the nonsocialists, however, the situation at the end of the war was the opposite. The doctrine of an active employment policy did not fit into traditional liberal philosophy at all. If the nonsocialists began to accept more and more of a state role in the business sector, this might have dangerous consequences. The new unemployment policy instrument obviously had to be used with extreme care; caution was necessary when interfering in the play of economic forces. The possibility of transforming the capitalist system by way of unemployment policy, which prominent Social Democrats around 1930 considered the party's big chance, represented a dangerous risk as far as the nonsocialists were concerned at the end of the war. Under such circumstances, it became absolutely necessary for the nonsocialist parties to declare that their support for the doctrine of full employment did not imply a break with any other principles of liberalism. Aside from their program publications, the nonsocialists and the business community thus repeated in innumerable articles, pamphlets, and books their belief in the welfare-generating ability of market forces and their critique of the Social Democrats' freedom-suffocating and apathy-inducing doctrine.

[8] *Frihet och framsteg* (Stockholm, 1946), p. 56.
[9] *Efterkrigstidens samhälle* (Stockholm, 1944), pp. 8–9.

The very best protection against individual hardships was to use a "positive economic policy" to make conditions easier for private enterprise so that no economic slowdown occurred, the nonsocialists repeated in the language of the 1920s. "Companies themselves are our first line of defense against unemployment. . . . The last line of defense . . . is public jobs initiated by society, supplemented when necessary by cash support."[10] In the future, too, prosperity would increase most rapidly if the business sector were left free to try to improve its productivity through its own power of initiative and inventiveness and through economic rationalization measures stimulated by competition.

When the nonsocialists defended the interests of private business and advocated the freedom of economic liberalism from state coercion, they were led to some rather specific conclusions at the end of the war – a call for the dismantling of wartime economic regulation. They suspected the Social Democrats of wanting to keep the wartime rules in effect for an unnecessarily long time and for ideological reasons. The nonsocialists now tirelessly repeated their demands for a dismantling of price controls, exchange controls, import and other trade regulations, and the numerous rules for the distribution network. The burgeoning paperwork required by the agencies administering these emergency rules also came under fire.

By issuing declarations of principle on the vitality of private enterprise and calling for a dismantling of emergency economic regulations as part of their day-to-day political work, the nonsocialists were thus attempting to dispel any doubts about their fundamental ideological stance that their acceptance of an expansionist unemployment policy may have raised. And whether any state expansion would take place at all depended, of course, on economic developments. They had, so to speak, abolished economic liberalism's doctrine of harmony only during recessions. If economic growth was favorable, it was unnecessary to accept any expansion in state activity.

The economic forecasts of the nonsocialists and of the business community differed from those of the Social Democrats. The latter were deeply pessimistic; we will discuss this at greater length later. The former had much greater faith in the ability of private business to resolve postwar problems. In their contributions to the debate, various business leaders presented their assessments of different industries and – in the words of one plant manager in Åtvidaberg – found reason for "budding optimism."[11]

The Swedish Industrial Institute for Economic and Social Research (IUI) also reported that the business sector was in fine shape: Employment

---

[10] *Frihet och framsteg*, p. 56.
[11] *Östgöta-Tidningen*, 12 May 1943.

opportunities were considered good in the mining, iron and steel, forestry, chemical and mechanical pulp, and paper and board industries. There would be some employment problems in the engineering sector. As for overall capital spending, the IUI study showed that Swedish industry had plans for sizable investments. The survey also reported heavy investments in construction and full employment in the building supply industry, as well as in the tanning, shoe, and textile and apparel industries.[12]

At a 1944 conference, the chairman of the Swedish Employers' Confederation rejected the Social Democratic tendency to evoke an "atmosphere of dread" about the postwar period. After this speech, five representatives of major companies reported on the postwar planning process in their firms. As a general rule, it would be possible to maintain employment, they believed.[13]

The Federation of Swedish Wholesalers and Importers also stated in its booklet *Postwar Planning* (Efterkrigsplaneringen) that the country would be able to maintain its employment level even if economic conditions deteriorated.[14]

Although the nonsocialists were aware of the risk of a postwar depression – the whole postwar planning process was a conscious attempt to avoid one – they regarded the economic pessimism of the Social Democrats as harmful. It was wrong to assume that a depression would occur. In a book edited by Eli Heckscher during the 1920s, *Old and New Economic Liberalism* (Gammal och ny ekonomisk liberalism), one debater had used a phrase that adequately characterized such behavior: It was like committing suicide for fear of death.[15]

The Conservatives and Liberals agreed with the bright economic forecasts of business leaders. When peace came, it would be a major task to replace the capital destroyed by war, Ohlin argued.[16] Difficulties might occur, but not on a scale large enough to justify extensive public-sector intervention, Bagge believed.[17] Domö contributed a booklet *Swedish Busi-*

[12] According to an agreement with the government, a decision had been made that industry would also participate in the official postwar planning process. For this reason, the study was published in SOU, the government's official series of reports from commissions of inquiry. *Industriens sysselsättning under åren närmast efter kriget* (SOU 1944:7), pp. 45–96. A summary of its research findings is provided in Gustaf Söderlund's speech at a Stockholm conference on postwar planning; see the following note.

[13] *Näringslivet inför freden. Anföranden vid konferens i Stockholm den 28 januari 1944* (Stockholm: Industriens utredningsinstitut, 1944), pp. 51–70.

[14] *Sveriges Grossistförbund om efterkrigsplaneringen* (Stockholm, 1944), p. 21.

[15] Arthur Montgomery, "Industrien och efterkrigsplaneringen," *Svenska Dagbladet*, 17 Nov. 1944; Eli Heckscher, *Gammal och ny ekonomisk liberalism* (Stockholm: Norstedts, 1921).

[16] Bertil Ohlin, *Ekonomiska efterkrigsproblem*; repr. *Studier i svenskt näringsliv, tillägnade Jacob Wallenberg* (Stockholm, 1942), p. 6.

[17] Gösta Bagge, "Högerns väg. Tal vid Högerns riksstämma i Örebro den 18 juni 1944," in *Tal 1943–1945* (Stockholm, 1945), p. 207.

ness in Wars and Crises (Svenskt näringsliv under krig och kriser) that expressed complete agreement with the findings of IUI.[18] So the nonsocialist members of the government-appointed commission of inquiry on postwar planning were being entirely consistent when they issued a minority statement recommending far lower relief work appropriations than the Social Democrats wanted. The latter proposed 100 million kronor, whereas the nonsocialists thought that 25 million was enough.[19]

The nonsocialists and the business community tried to defend themselves against the conclusion that their support of expansionist unemployment policy necessarily meant state expansion. They argued that the private business sector was so flexible that peacetime problems could be avoided without state intervention. Forecasts and value judgments tend to become intertwined in arguments of this kind. An ideological defense of the market economy led to a belief in the ability of the business sector to cope with postwar problems. The economic pessimism of the Social Democrats was regarded as a way of justifying ideologically motivated state intervention and the prolongation of emergency regulations.

Good economic growth makes state intervention unnecessary; there were also purely technical objections to expansionist policy, according to the Liberal program booklet *Postwar Society* (Efterkrigstidens samhälle), which counseled government restraint, not the frantic overspending of public funds that the nonsocialists believed the Social Democrats were aiming for. First, priming the pump with consumer purchasing power led to inflation; the price increases of 1936–1937 were regarded as proof of this. Second, capital spending had an important role in the business cycle: "A more detailed analysis of the business cycle seems to indicate that it is not consumer demand that occupies the central position. Depressions do not occur because consumers suddenly refuse to buy. On the contrary, we can say that consumer demand is reliable. If their income is maintained, on the whole we can depend on consumers to continue their purchases. The sensitive factor, instead, is demand in areas other than consumption. We may call it purchases by private companies and public agencies for investment purposes. Such purchases include buildings, machinery, inventories and much more. If this investment demand and consequently the production of such capital goods is maintained at a suitable level, employment there will also be good. . . . In short, the main task in the work of safeguarding a good volume of employment is to achieve some degree of stability in purchases and production of capital goods for investment purposes."[20] The booklet also criticized the Social Democratic concept of

---

[18] Fritiof Domö, *Svenskt näringsliv under krig och kriser* (Stockholm, 1944), pp. 30ff.
[19] *Utlåtande den 10 maj 1944 över investeringsutredningens betänkande den 3 april 1944 med förslag till investeringsreserv mm* (SOU 1944:5), p. 34.
[20] *Efterkrigstidens samhälle*, pp. 21–22.

varying the size of cash support according to the severity of the depression. Once sizable grants began to be disbursed, the nonsocialists did not think it would be possible to revert to lower payments. The Social Democratic model of the cash support principle did not fulfill the requirement that it should be possible to vary an economic policy instrument depending on whether times were good or bad.

Because the nonsocialists accepted the doctrine of full employment, there might have appeared to be a chance of a rapprochement with the Social Democrats in economic policy. But such was not the case. The reason was that the Social Democrats, too, radicalized their program at the end of the war, so that the ideological distance between the nonsocialists and Social Democrats by no means narrowed, but instead became even wider than before. An expansionist unemployment policy had only been the first step in implementing the economic planning ideology. After overcoming the Depression of the 1930s, the Social Democrats had continued to expand the role of the state in economic life, with the aim of making the business sector more efficient and rational even in good times. The outbreak of the war had stopped these plans. Now they once again raised the idea of a more ambitious effort than before to rationalize the structure of the business sector. They were, of course, prepared to pursue an active unemployment policy to combat the threat of a postwar depression; they emphasized very clearly that they would fulfill the "honorable traditions" of the 1930s, which were already starting to acquire a patina of legend within the labor movement.[21] But this policy no longer had an equally central role in Social Democratic ideology.

This development was described in a parliamentary speech by the Social Democratic economist Gunnar Myrdal, intended as a general reflection following a series of votes approving public-sector measures to prepare for a postwar depression. "These decisions of course mean," Myrdal said, "that practically without protest, criticism or discussion, Parliament is adopting a policy that was so controversial in the 1930s, namely that unemployment and depression should be combated with public-sector jobs. Many people who advocated such views in the 1930s – as I did – were considered much too radical at that time. It is undeniable, at least I have the feeling, that we have been too victorious. There is a danger that in the next unemployment crisis, we will be too willing to pursue a policy of public-sector jobs and that we will do too little to maintain normal production in the business sector. In case there is unemployment and we resort to public-sector jobs, this has some rather harmful effects compared with the situation that would arise if we could keep normal production

[21] For example, Karl Fredriksson, "Medelvägens ekonomi," *Tiden* (1942): 589.

going. Workers are moved from their workplaces and from their families. They are moved from jobs in which they are skilled to jobs where they often have no skills, and real capital in normal industry has to stand unused so that we can prepare for a corresponding return of workers when the crisis has been overcome."[22] Like the nonsocialists, the Social Democrats thus preferred normal production to public-sector jobs. But this similarity was confined to the verbal level. To the nonsocialists, "normal production" implied an opportunity to avoid state intervention. The Social Democrats, on the other hand, believed that far-reaching public intervention was needed to keep normal production going.

The Social Democrats launched their new economic policy doctrine in *The Postwar Program of the Swedish Labor Movement* (Arbetarrörelsens efterkrigsprogram), which was published in 1944 after two years of preparations. At the 1944 party congress, Prime Minister Hansson introduced the postwar program and the draft of a new party program with these words: "In these documents, one can learn practically everything about our intentions and our plans."[23] The postwar program was received with praise by the entire Swedish labor movement.

The fear of a postwar depression runs like a red thread through the postwar program. Economic crisis and stagnation had followed in the wake of earlier wars. The primary task of government economic policy had to be the prevention of mass unemployment at the end of World War II. In 1944 Gunnar Myrdal's *Warning Against Peacetime Optimism* (Varning för fredsoptimism) appeared. It painted the dangers of a depression in garish colors; the book's influence on the attitude of the labor movement to postwar problems cannot be overestimated.[24] All steps should be taken to combat an expected economic downturn. In doing this, wartime economic regulations could also assume a new task. The success of planned economic coordination during the war was tantalizing to Social Democratic theoreticians. As during the 1930s, the Social Democrats now wanted to retain regulations even after overcoming the conditions that led to their adoption.

But above all, the postwar program contained long-term plans. Its task must not be limited to overcoming economic crisis during the initial postwar period. In many ways, there would have to be changes in the world where the Swedish people would live after the war. Untrammeled free enterprise, with overproduction and underconsumption despite the fact that people's real needs were far from fulfilled, along with the resulting continuous economic crises, had to give way to more far-reaching eco-

[22] FK 1944:26, p. 29.
[23] *Sveriges Socialdemokratiska Arbetarepartis sjuttonde kongress* (Stockholm, 1944), p. 8.
[24] Gunnar Myrdal, *Varning för fredsoptimism* (Stockholm: Bonniers, 1944), esp. pp. 151–170.

nomic planning than the Social Democrats had been able to implement during the 1930s. In the postwar economy, all the productive capacity that was now being used for destructive purposes would be placed in the service of a program of social and economic improvement.

This ideological vision was spelled out in twenty-seven points, followed by arguments. These points, in which short-term demands for steps to combat the postwar depression were mixed together with more long-term plans for realizing economic planning, were in turn classified under three headings. Under the first heading, "Full Employment," the program repeated the principles of expansionist unemployment policy. Under the second, "Fair Distribution and a Higher Living Standard," the program called for a continued expansion of social welfare programs and socio-political advantages for the working class, based on the central Social Democratic belief in social equality.

Under the third heading, "Greater Efficiency and More Democracy in the Business Sector," the postwar program presented new, far-reaching demands for a structural rationalization of business in cooperation with the government. The authors of the program were aware that this was an extremely inflammatory issue: They had not forgotten the nonsocialist critique of economic planning during the 1930s; and they knew quite well that the difference between the socialist and liberal views of what was the proper relationship between government and business was the ideological powder keg of Swedish domestic politics. Both the prime minister and the finance minister reminded the 1944 congress of the painful experiences of the past: The slightest unclearness on this point had been taken by the nonsocialists as the excuse for scare propaganda claiming that the Social Democrats were aiming at nationalization of the entire economy and a dictatorship over intellectual and political activity. But this time they would be prepared for such attacks: They could refer to their postwar program and to the new party program.

To make the business sector more efficient, the Social Democrats called for greater government influence on the credit system. There were demands for a state commercial bank and the nationalization of the insurance system. To maintain the level of company investment activity, they recommended long-term planning of capital spending in a coordinating body in which the government would also be represented. Export-oriented industry would not only be given credit guarantees; foreign trade would be coordinated under government supervision to promote the exchange of goods and services. The state would, moreover, help bring about a lowering of costs and other efficiency-raising measures in the construction trade; in connection with housing policy, the need for labor saving in the home would also be satisfied. A major rationalization program for agriculture, with government financing, was presented. Private monopolies would be combated; a special investigatory agency would supervise cartel contracts and other price agreements among companies.

What role did the labor movement's postwar program assign to the private business sector? Now as earlier, the Social Democrats stated that an expansion of the government's economic activities would only take place in areas where private enterprise led to mismanagement. The postwar program did not make any categorical demands for nationalization, except for the insurance business. As during the 1930s, the decisive factor now should be the efficiency of the national economy. If private businessmen were able to put all productive forces into use by themselves, their right of ownership would not be threatened. Before any public-sector intervention took place, the structural conditions in various industries should be analyzed. "It is the task of practical economic policy to determine at any given point in time to what extent and in what ways society needs to expand its own operations or otherwise intervene.... It is well known that the Social Democratic party wishes to use the growing influence of the state on the business sector to ensure complete and efficient utilization of the country's productive forces, but this does not mean that it intends for all property to be in state hands and all economic activity to be directed by a central economic agency. The economic operations of the state are a means of achieving the greatest possible efficiency and are justified only to the extent that they promote this aim."[25]

The experimentalistic ideology of economic planning was recommended in a direct polemic against the abandoned, doctrinaire theory of nationalization. "The whole concept of economic planning is so obviously one of proceeding by trial and error amidst the shifting conditions of the business sector that any schematic demand for a particular distribution of private and joint ownership, and likewise for the economic powers of particular groups and of society as a whole, is out of the question from the start."[26]

In an editorial in the main Social Democratic newspaper, *Morgon-Tidningen*, Rickard Lindström described the Social Democratic view of the relationship between the state and the business sector as follows: "The primary goal of the Social Democrats for the future is to create economic security for working people. This policy is simple and clear. We must ensure that people obtain work to the greatest extent possible, so that they can support themselves. If private business falls short of this, the public sector should intervene. This has to be a goal of state policy. If the private business sector can handle the task in a reasonable way, there is no reason for the state to get involved.... The future goal of the Social Democratic

[25] *Arbetarrörelsens efterkrigsprogram* (Stockholm, 1944), pp. 198 and 188.
[26] Ibid., pp. 197–198.

170

party must be to create a livelihood and economic security for the people of Sweden. It will not achieve this by means of any theoretical speculations about using the state to intervene dramatically at any price in what have so far turned out to be practicable methods. Swedish workers do not support nebulous ideas about the miracles resulting from state intervention here, there and everywhere."[27]

The second principle presented in the industrial policy section of the labor movement's postwar program, more democracy in economic life, was rather vaguely defined. Sometimes the party's welfare policy as a whole was presented as a democratization of economic life: The theory of underconsumption was regarded as an argument for more equal distribution; there was a call for a guaranteed minimum living standard in cases of lost income and subsidies to people of unproductive age. The program also mentioned "nationalization from the consumer side," achieved by keeping the country's consumption up to a certain level. It recommended standardization and controls on quality and price. But under the heading "democracy," there were also straightforward demands for greater employee influence on decision making in companies.

As mentioned previously, a proposed new party program also was presented for the approval of the Social Democratic party congress when it met toward the end of World War II. As in the case of the Conservative program, the Social Democrats felt that the economic transformation of Sweden during the interwar period made a review of its old program necessary. It had been written in 1920 under the impact of post–World War I radicalism and reflected the Marxist spirit that dominated the Social Democratic party for some years around that time. It was characterized by Marx's long-term forecasts of historical developments, without indicating any concrete plan for immediate action. In short, it was full of Marxist determinism. The previous party congress had approved a proposal to revise the program. Among other things, doctrinaire demands for nationalization were labeled as antiquated; instead, the party should emphasize giving the state "supervision and influence over the business sector." Now there was a new draft version of a party program, written mainly by Ernst Wigforss.

If we compare it with the 1920 program, the following changes are particularly noticeable. In the sections stating its general principles, which were made longer, the party presented the lessons it had learned from the transformation of bourgeois society toward more economic planning, with the participation of the labor movement. Marx's theory of class struggle was pushed into the background; the key concept of economic exploitation, on which the 1920 program had based its critique of the cap-

---

[27] *Morgon-Tidningen*, 1 Dec. 1944.

italist system, was eliminated. The higher living standards enjoyed by the working class, even in relative terms, made the exploitation concept unclear or misleading. Marx's theory of accumulation was presented in watered-down form; the concept of a proletarianized working class squaring off against a few millionaires had no basis in Swedish reality in the 1940s. The new program focused especially on accomplishments since the Social Democrats gained power in 1932. Their new economic policy had indicated the possibility of realizing socialism without it first being necessary to fulfill the prophecy of the collapse of the old society. The pivotal importance of employment policy in Social Democratic ideology was also expressed by presenting it in a separate, newly written point in the political program.

The most significant change affected the concept of nationalization. The old unconditional demand for nationalization was replaced by a conditional and more generally worded demand for an increase in the economic influence of the state. The planned economy was actually the new element in the program; this term summarized the lessons that the authors of the program wished to include in the draft program.

Ernst Wigforss presented the proposal to the party congress. He discussed the relationship between the nationalization and economic planning concepts and spoke in a way that closely coincides with his address to the 1932 congress. He repeated that nationalization and economic planning were not the same thing, and that one of these phenomena could occur without the other; when it opted for economic planning, the party was pursuing a partially different policy than the one expressed by the term nationalization.

Two opposition groups spoke at the congress. The same radical minority who in 1932 had viewed the Depression as the crisis prophesied by Marx and had thus advocated the nationalization of the business sector was strongly critical of the proposal. Economic planning was not enough. It was also necessary to demand nationalization. Some of the authors of the 1920 program were critical for another reason. They felt that the proposal, coming in the midst of a raging war, was unsuitably timed. But if the 1920 program were revised, they admitted, the party would end up with something resembling Wigforss's proposal.[28] In all essential respects, however, the congress approved the draft proposal.

The debate I have summarized here and the new party program of 1944 expressed the main thrust of the Social Democrats' economic philosophy with great consistency. They confirmed the economic planning ideology and declared the death of the nationalization ideology. The aim was to further by pragmatic means the form of production that best satisfied the

---

[28] *Sveriges Socialdemokratiska Arbetarepartis sjuttonde kongress*, pp. 90–91.

values of the labor movement. Before carrying out any demands for state intervention, a survey of the structural conditions of the business sector was necessary, so that it would become clear where the problems lay. In terms of principles, there was no difference between the Social Democratic ideology of the 1930s and that of the 1940s. But on the day-to-day political level, the Social Democrats now displayed a far greater readiness for action than previously. The Social Democrats clearly mistrusted the business sector's ability to cope with both the general economic situation and structural problems during the postwar period. They expected that their economic policy survey would lead to findings that would justify a substantial increase in the government's role in the economy. On the day-to-day political level, the Social Democratic postwar program was thus perceived as a radicalization. Abstract socialist ideological debate had been succeeded by concrete plans for economic policy action.

The Communists, who enjoyed their strongest voter support in Swedish history following the Soviet Army's successes against the Axis powers in the final stages of the war, also came out in favor of *The Postwar Program of the Swedish Labor Movement*.[29] New directives were in force within the international Communist movement. Instead of the interwar period's total subordination to Moscow and criticism of Social Democratic class cooperation and logrolling, the Communists supported "the national path to socialism" and "the popular front concept," which meant that there should be attempts to achieve cooperation between Communists and Social Democrats. Together, these two parties would introduce a socialist order in Sweden at the end of the war. Just as bourgeois democracy was implemented at the end of World War I, socialistic democracy would now be introduced at the end of World War II. "We are actually experiencing a new 1918."[30] At their 1944 party congress, the Communists adopted a resolution declaring themselves prepared to fight for the realization of the program together with the Social Democrats. There was no reason for the Communists to present a postwar program of their own, according to a typical argument in one contemporary pamphlet, because *The Postwar Program of the Swedish Labor Movement* contained a long list of positive and important demands that the Communist party had supported for many years. It was now better for the labor movement to join forces behind *one* program instead of splitting itself in two.[31]

---

[29] Aside from the standard reference, Lewin 1967, pp. 234–241, the reader is referred to Jörgen Hermansson's dissertation at the Department of Government, University of Uppsala, entitled *Kommunism på svenska?*

[30] AK 1945:34, p. 57 (Hagberg).

[31] Nils Holmberg, *Tomma löften eller verklighet? Hur skall det bli med arbetarrörelsens efterkrigsprogram?* (Stockholm, 1944), p. 7.

Strangely enough, the Communists believed that they could reconcile this support of the Social Democratic postwar program with continuous criticism of the economic planning ideology, which was the fundamental principle behind this program. They felt that the Social Democrats had not drawn the logical conclusion of their own critique of capitalism. The situation reminded the Communist party chairman, Sven Linderot, of a medieval German custom. If a person was accused of a serious crime but there was no conclusive proof, sometimes he was condemned to have his head cut off, but with the vital distinction that the defendant was placed in the sunlight, whereupon the executioner cut off the head of his shadow. In the same way, the Social Democrats had now symbolically chopped off the head of capitalism. They had not demanded nationalization, as they should have, but had satisfied themselves with economic planning.[32]

Another leading Communist, Hilding Hagberg, also painted a lucid image to illustrate what he felt was the far too cautious attitude of the Social Democrats toward the business community. The Social Democratic abandonment of the nationalization doctrine in favor of the economic planning ideology reminded him of the fable about the young man who went off to steal the troll's gold but instead was spirited away and ended up being the man who guarded this gold.[33]

C. H. Hermansson, the most prominent Communist ideologist on economic matters, emphasized the same line of thought in a series of articles in *Ny Dag,* the party's main newspaper. The postwar program of the Swedish labor movement was an excellent basis for action during the next few years, but its theoretical framework was wrong. It was "pure, sheer utopianism" to believe that the goals of the labor movement could be achieved without nationalization.[34] And the Communist press was upset, as one newspaper put it, because the Social Democrats were carrying on "a swindle on the nationalization issue."[35]

The revision of the Social Democratic program naturally gave rise to additional criticisms from the Communists. They supported Social Democratic critics who wanted to retain the nationalization doctrine of the 1920 party program. When the Communists revised their own party program in 1944, they took the basic principles from the 1920 Social Democratic program, amazingly enough, and inserted them in their own program. Those who wished to follow "the national path to socialism" and at the same time be loyal to the doctrine of nationalization felt that there

---

[32] Sven Linderot, *Kommunisternas dagsprogram* (Stockholm, 1944), pp. 17–18.

[33] Ernst Wigforss and Hilding Hagberg, *Duellen. Den ekonomiska politiken under och efter kriget* (Stockholm, 1944), pp. 36ff. and 66–67.

[34] Lancet (C. H. Hermansson), "Arbetarrörelsens efterkrigsprogram," *Ny Dag*, 16 June, 21 June, 3 July, and 10 July 1944.

[35] *Ny Dag*, 9 Oct. 1944.

was no better starting point than the set of principles the Social Democrats had now abandoned.

Did this mean that the Communists ended up in the same ideological dilemma that characterized the Social Democrats before their transition to the economic planning ideology? Did the Communists now become caught in the contradiction between the short-term and the long-term perspective within Marxism? No, the Communists saw no obstacles to immediate nationalizations. They pointed out that the Social Democrats and Communists together had the parliamentary majority needed to carry out a nationalization drive, preferably through a coalition government between the two parties. Developments had progressed very far in Sweden, declared the commission that had worked out the new party program. Despite the labor movement's conquests, however, monopoly capitalism had only increased its power. At the same time, there had been a trend toward state socialism, especially due to depression and wartime economic regulations. "When capitalism has developed this far, there is no further stage that must be passed historically before socialism is achieved. This means that Swedish capitalism has reached such a degree of development that no progress in the historical sense can be achieved any longer within the framework of bourgeois society. The material prerequisites for a socialistic transformation have been reached." The program commission was eager to emphasize that developments need not be bloody. "Such state leadership of society by the working class can be exercised in very democratic forms. It need not assume the same means of expression as during its first years in Russia, for example. This is determined entirely by the current situation, by the power and strength of the revolution and the counterrevolution."[36]

The Communists thus believed that a series of ideological somersaults could get them out of the iron cage where Marxist doctrine imprisoned its supporters as long as its conditions were not fulfilled. They did not mention that the disaster postulated by Marx as a prerequisite for their nationalization drive had not occurred. They characterized the economic crisis policy they had previously condemned as a step toward the realization of socialism. They took over the program of principles of the party they had previously attacked as "social fascist." They shifted the responsibility for any violence from themselves to their victims' desire to defend their property.

A study of the ideology of the Swedish Communists during the 1940s is of interest primarily because it contrasts so clearly with the Social Democrats' codification of the economic planning ideology. By depicting the

---

[36] *Kommunisternas nya program. Programkommissionens förslag*, Dagspolitik, no. 19 (Stockholm, 1944), pp. 19–20 and 22–23.

Social Democrats as a party that had only symbolically cut off the head of capitalism, the Communists provided a vivid but skeptical interpretation of postwar Social Democratic plans. They criticized Social Democratic pledges to leave the market economy intact if private business, contrary to expectations, managed on its own to satisfy the requirements of the labor movement. In other words, an analysis of the Communist ideological debate casts additional light on the postwar ideas of the Social Democrats. And these ideas are what the economic planning debate of the early postwar years was all about.

To the most influential groups in Sweden – the nonsocialist parties and the business community as well as the political and trade union branches of the labor movement – planning for peacetime now seemed the most important domestic political issue of the day. The government appointed a commission of inquiry on postwar economic planning, whose work later became the subject of much debate. Most people called it the Myrdal Commission, after its chairman.[37] There was disagreement as to what instructions it should receive. The nonsocialists wanted to restrict its research work to short-term issues related to the actual end of the war. The Social Democrats wanted to bring up the long-term issue of a structural rationalization of the business sector, in the hope of avoiding postwar capitalist crises and the wasting of labor and capital. The nonsocialist members of the First Chamber voted against the Social Democrats' plans. They defended the existing free economic system, which was to the best advantage of Sweden and should not be exchanged for what the Liberals called "another, untried system of a more monopolistic and bureaucratic nature, merely because dogmatists who are out of touch with reality recommend it."[38] The Agrarian party, which introduced a motion not to appoint the commission at all, argued that the technical studies already under way were sufficient for the time being.[39] But because of their majority position, the Social Democrats pushed through their proposal to give the commission a broad research task. The existing wartime consensus among the grand coalition parties had suffered its first setback.

In the work of the commission, two issues in particular caused differences of opinion. These were the two pivotal elements of the economic planning ideology: the expansionist unemployment policy and the question of structural rationalization of the business sector. The most famous expression of the Social Democrats' pessimistic economic expectations is the forecast worked out by the Myrdal Commission, which turned out to be incorrect. To counteract the expected depression, the commission rec-

[37] Lewin 1967, pp. 241–262.
[38] FK 2 TU utl (statements of the Special Committee), no. 13, p. 14.
[39] Ibid., p. 16.

ommended a large-scale program to stimulate buying power, according to the familiar pattern. How was it possible for this program to cause controversy as late as during the 1940s? Hadn't the nonsocialists accepted the expansionist unemployment policy? The answer is the simplest imaginable. A heavy majority of the nonsocialist members of the Myrdal Commission came from an older generation, from the sizable minority – especially within the Conservative party – who strongly opposed the radicalization of bourgeois liberalism.

On the issue of streamlining the structure of the business sector, the differences of opinion were even more serious, and here the nonsocialist members of the Myrdal Commission were also representative of their younger party colleagues. This conflict immediately came to light when the Myrdal Commission tried to define its tasks more exactly. The Social Democrats could cite the outcome of the parliamentary debate to support their view that long-term structural issues should also be dealt with, which the nonsocialists opposed. But the Social Democrats imposed their view.

The nonsocialists soon had reason for new complaints that the Myrdal Commission, in the words of the newly established liberal newspaper *Expressen,* had become an "executive organ for the postwar program of the Swedish labor movement."[40] In about a dozen members' bills, the Social Democrats attempted to initiate studies of the various structural problems in the business sector. The most important of these was the insurance bill, which, amazingly, left out the categorical demand for nationalization of the insurance industry contained in *The Postwar Program of the Swedish Labor Movement.* The Myrdal Commission voiced its warm approval of the bills when asked to comment on them. In addition, several people, including the commission chairman himself, were cosponsors and commission members at the same time. The controversial issues that could not be discussed in the grand coalition government were now being handled by the Myrdal Commission, which functioned as a kind of Social Democratic shadow government. This detour by way of the commission enabled the Social Democrats to keep the coalition government in existence for a few more months without betraying their economic policy ideology.

The nonsocialist press sharply attacked what it called these "nationalization bills." "The Social Democratic assault by means of the Myrdal Commission and the massive use of members' bills in Parliament has triggered a much-needed counteroffensive on several fronts, which ought to awaken the public to a realization of what precious assets are at stake," *Svenska Dagbladet* wrote. "The Swedish people have not borne heavy personal and pecuniary burdens for six years to protect our external freedom,

[40] *Expressen,* 12 Feb. 1945.

177

in order that our internal freedom is to be suffocated by a totalitarian state oppression which begins with 'economic democracy' and 'economic planning,' only to lead inevitably to a system of intellectual and material coercion."[41] But the Social Democrats were little impressed by "bourgeois expressions of opinion these days. . . . Their screams against nationalization are as shrill as they can be."[42] As the nonsocialist attacks mounted, there was a growing Social Democratic countercampaign against what *Morgon-Tidningen* called "propaganda noises."[43] The nonsocialist camp, on the other hand, criticized Social Democratic agitation in favor of the parliamentary members' bills in roughly the same terms. They opposed the mass submission of members' bills, "accompanied by thundering drum rolls in the Social Democratic party press and party propaganda."[44] After the temporary silence of the first wartime years, the debate on economic planning was again heating up with an intensity reminiscent of the most emotional debates during the Great Depression.

Social Democratic press support for the "parliamentary assault" became even stronger after Gunnar Myrdal became editor of *Tiden*. This was because the party journal now began a regular column called "*Tiden's* Industrial Critique," which energetically carried out the recommendation of *The Postwar Program of the Swedish Labor Movement* by undertaking its own industry-by-industry analysis of the structure of Swedish business.

And the political parties were not the only ones to shake their chains, to borrow a phrase from Wigforss's memoirs.[45] There were also noticeable attempts by certain interest organizations to assert their independence from the state and emancipate themselves from wartime economic regulation. In the labor market, a meatpacking workers' strike had been settled while a major labor dispute in the engineering industry had just broken out. These two industrial actions have been described as "a direct reaction against wartime 'loyalty' and voluntary labor market regulation."[46] The wartime political truce was obviously in a very advanced state of decay.

The mass submission of Social Democratic members' bills brought the debate on the future of the grand coalition government to a decisive stage. There was strong opinion among Social Democrats in favor of ending the coalition. But one factor that complicated the picture was that among the small group who considered the continuation of the grand coalition government a possibility was Prime Minister Per Albin Hansson himself, who still regarded the principle of unanimity and consensus solutions as an

---

[41] *Svenska Dagbladet*, 14 June 1945.
[42] *Morgon-Tidningen*, 17 Mar. 1945.
[43] Ibid., 16 July 1945.
[44] *Expressen*, 26 June 1945 ("Vi diskuterar").
[45] Ernst Wigforss, *Minnen III. 1932–1949* (Stockholm: Tidens förlag, 1954), p. 246.
[46] Heckscher 1951, p. 252.

ideal. Step by step, however, he became persuaded that such cooperation was not possible without sacrificing key demands in the postwar program. He was thus finally compelled to change his mind. The Liberal party agreed with the Social Democrats, although this party also included a group who appealed for caution and for attempts to prolong the grand coalition government. The Conservatives and to an even greater extent the Agrarians, however, indicated a willingness to continue the grand coalition.[47] The Communists repeated their invitations to work together with the Social Democrats, but these offers were rejected, not infrequently in downright derisive language.

Gunnar Myrdal had been a central figure in the process that led to the breakup of the wartime truce among the parties. He was also the man who gave the early postwar period its name. In a lecture late in July 1945, Myrdal declared that the labor movement stood at the beginning of its "harvest time."[48] The long-expected cabinet reorganization occurred on 31 July. The new, purely Social Democratic government adopted *The Postwar Program of the Swedish Labor Movement* as its policy declaration. *Stockholms-Tidningen*'s comment on the newly appointed government, still led by Hansson, is typical of the nonsocialist reaction: "It cannot be concealed that a broad segment of nonsocialist opinion regards certain portions of (the new government's) program with pronounced mistrust and considers it important for the country to be on its guard against the nationalization fanatics."[49]

Fundamental differences of opinion on economic ideology had once again emerged after a temporary cease-fire caused by extraordinary circumstances. The political truce and the consensus in favor of wartime economic regulation was now at an end. Harvest time and domestic political disputes awaited.

2. A LIMIT TO GOVERNMENT POWER

Never before had the supporters of the private business sector felt so threatened.[50] The Social Democrats might make their distinctions between nationalization and economic planning. They might state as their condition that they would only intervene in the business sector if it did not satisfy the needs of the labor movement. But under any circumstances, the only result would certainly be that the role of the state in the Swedish

[47] Olof Ruin, *Mellan samlingsregering och tvåpartisystem. Den svenska regeringsrågan 1945–1960* (Stockholm: Bonniers, 1968), pp. 130–162.

[48] "Prof Myrdal: Arbetarrörelsen står inför skördetiden," *Stockholms-Tidningen*, 30 July 1945.

[49] Ibid., 1 Aug. 1945.

[50] Lewin 1967, pp. 263–347. For the most part, I have listed here the primary sources of direct quotations only.

economy would expand, and the free-market economy would be further restricted.

And the really serious thing was that the Social Democratic government had a parliamentary position that enabled it to implement its economic policy program without bothering about what the nonsocialist parties said. This was because even after the 1944 election, the Social Democrats enjoyed a parliamentary majority; in the First Chamber they had an absolute majority, and in the Second Chamber they occupied exactly half the 230 seats, but given the 15 Communist seats they could count on a majority for the postwar program there too.

What can a potential loser do in such a situation? There was no opportunity for logrolling as there had been for Per Albin Hansson during the 1930s, when he used a brilliant political maneuver to reshape the political majority in Sweden. The expected policy decisions of the government and Parliament would constitute stable majority decisions that satisfied the first preference of the Social Democrats. There was no reason for the Social Democrats to deviate from such a promising and certain path.

Nor did it appear possible to split the Social Democrats by means of some elegant amendment to the political agenda, as Arvid Lindman had once done, using this strategy to catch the Liberal majority party off guard on the suffrage issue. The labor movement stood united. The work of producing the postwar program had brought the party together as the war drew to a close.

But the opportunities for strategic action were not entirely exhausted. In close cooperation with the private business sector, the nonsocialist minority undertook countermeasures that may be interpreted in our analytical language as a return to the most basic issue in strategic manipulation of the agenda – questioning whether the majority was qualified to make a decision of the kind that was planned. In each subsequent step in the political agenda, they could be outvoted because of their minority position. But defining the territory in which the majority exercises full control was a question of rights, which could not be decided by voting, the nonsocialists believed. Like freedom of speech, freedom of the press, and freedom of assembly, the right of private ownership was also a right that the majority could not abolish. There was an intimate connection between intellectual rights and economic ones. If economic freedom was violated, intellectual rights were also in the danger zone. The state should practice restraint in its exercise of power. Only if the powers of government and Parliament were limited could democracy and prosperity be preserved.

In other words, the strategy of the nonsocialists and the business sector was based on using arguments to persuade their opponents that they were not qualified to pursue their economic policy. If this failed, their fallback strategy was to generate strong enough public opinion to force the Social Democrats to give up their policy. They were aware that an enormous opinion-molding campaign was required to achieve this aim. But they were prepared to make the major effort that was needed. A campaign of ideological counterpropaganda against the labor movement began. For four years, from the publication of *The Postwar Program of the Swedish Labor Movement* in 1944 until the 1948 election, it left its mark on Swedish politics.

The nonsocialist critique of economic planning was conducted on two different levels: a theoretical critique that can be grouped into two categories, the freedom argument and the efficiency argument; and day-to-day political commentary including critical positions on the details of Social Democratic economic policy. The theoretical critique dominated the debate that followed the publication of the Social Democratic postwar program. At the same time, somewhat overshadowed by their lofty ideological overviews, the nonsocialists presented a day-to-day political polemic. Under the impact of currency and monetary policy pressures and, it should be added, the government's radical tax proposal, day-to-day political issues moved into the spotlight in 1947. In the 1948 election campaign, theoretical and day-to-day political arguments were woven together into a violent nonsocialist attack on the government. The nonsocialists referred to the policy actually being pursued and its economic consequences as a planned economy policy of the type the Social Democrats had professed in their postwar program. A few examples of the leading lines of thought among the critics of the planned economy and the reactions and behavior of the nonsocialists and the business sector vis-à-vis the government's economic policy follow.

The business community was fully aware that it would have to launch an information and propaganda program on an unprecedented scale in order to block Social Democratic plans for a structural rationalization of the business sector under state supervision. In May 1944, a counterpropaganda plan was discussed within the so-called Executive Club, consisting of the heads of the major international companies in the Swedish engineering industry. The secretary of the club declared that "I have the general impression that our countermeasures and counterpropaganda adhere too closely to old, ingrained habits. We appoint investigative commissions that, in keeping with venerable Swedish civil service tradition, produce profound investigations which admittedly possess authoritative weight, but which will be of relatively insignificant value for the simple reason that in the final stage of the political power game they are left unheeded. We will hold dignified and thoughtful speeches, in which the danger of undermining private enterprise is illustrated in somber phrases. But in our campaign for self-preservation, we will neglect to make use of the power of modern propaganda. It is a mistake to believe that we can influence the decisions of the political inner circles without a strong effort to mold public opinion. In other words, to drive home what we have proved by means of research, . . . we must make use of mass propaganda."[51]

In response to this call for mass propaganda, an organization called the Swedish Industry and Commerce Foundation financed such magazines as *Vecko-Nytt* and *Obs!* as well as the printing of books and pamphlets and the translation and publication of foreign antisocialist literature on an unprecedented scale. The campaign argued unremittingly on behalf of the virtues of limited government and the deleterious effects of economic planning. Prime Minister Hansson nicknamed this entire propaganda machine "the economic planning opposition" (*planhushållningsmotståndet* or PHM). The issue of the purposes and the financing of PHM propaganda became a debate within a debate during the economic planning dispute of the harvest years.

One of the most successful measures undertaken by the Swedish Industry and Commerce Foundation, in terms of public impact, was the translation and publication of F. A. Hayek's *The Road to Serfdom*. This work, extremely well received in the nonsocialist camp, was of enormous importance to the Swedish debate. Hayek was convinced that the supporters of the economic planning would abstain from their experiment if they only realized the consequences of the system. *The Road to Serfdom* was written as a pedagogical document. People would soon be returning from the war. The demand of the day would be "full employment." This demand would come to seem so important that everything else would have to be subordinate to it. But such a notion, Hayek emphasized, was the most fertile soil for an economic planning system. In peacetime, a free society should never become dependent on a single purpose. This also applied to the most important of all domestic political issues – the struggle against unemployment. If people demanded that full employment be achieved "at any price," they had succeeded in providing a justification for setting in motion the disastrous process of central planning. As a result, democracy would eventually collapse with unfailing certainty. In brilliant and passionate prose, Hayek appealed to people to stand up for limited government in order to ensure the survival of freedom and democracy, instead of embarking upon the disastrous economic planning experiment.[52]

Hayek's argument set the pattern for the theoretical critique of economic planning during the "harvest time." *Göteborgs Handels- och Sjöfartstidning* expressed concern that the state was pushing ahead "with the

[51] Sven Anders Söderpalm, *Direktörsklubben. Storindustrin i svensk politik under 1930- och 1940-talen* (Rabén & Sjögren; 12 TemaTeori 1976), p. 115.

[52] F. A. Hayek, *The Road to Serfdom* (Chicago: University of Chicago Press, 1944).

force of a flooding river."[53] *Stockholms-Tidningen* referred to the period as "the age of deification of the state."[54] *Svenska Dagbladet* feared "the state as an autocratic tyrant."[55] The nonsocialist parties, the leading men of the business community, the entire nonsocialist press, and the PHM organizations continuously whipped up an increasingly rancorous agitation against Social Democratic expansion of the state.

The efficiency argument, the second main theme of the nonsocialists' theoretical critique of economic planning, was subordinate to the freedom argument not only in importance but also in logical terms. It was something of an axiom of liberal philosophy that the coercion resulting from economic planning would also lead to inertia, waste, and inefficiency. The nonsocialists warned that the Social Democrats had an excessive faith in the ability of the state. In brief, the most common arguments can be summarized as follows. State economic operations would result in rigidity and bureaucracy. Economic planning would not encourage the power of initiative, entrepreneurship, and wealth formation, which were the driving forces of prosperity. "Superior intellects" able to predict the country's needs could not be found when such needs were not allowed to be expressed by means of free price formation. In a planned economy, people would not observe the necessary frugality when using government money; inflation would be unavoidable. Free foreign trade would be restricted or disappear, and with it one of the primary sources of Swedish prosperity.

On the day-to-day political level, the nonsocialists and the business community kept a continuous watch for any step the Social Democrats took toward implementing *The Postwar Program of the Swedish Labor Movement*. As we have seen, the confrontation began within the Myrdal Commission at an early stage, when the Social Democrats used their majority position to force the commission to add to its agenda the issue of state participation in streamlining the structure of the business sector. How should the nonsocialist parties and the representatives of business react to what they regarded as this Social Democratic abuse of power? Should they continue to participate at all in the official peacetime planning process? This question was asked within the board of directors of the Confederation of Swedish Industries. Some people wanted to withdraw business-sector representatives from this process. Continued participation would mean submitting to the paper work, bureaucratic supervision, registration, and regulation that the private business sector saw as its main task to resist.

But the most influential business leaders argued that in spite of all this, the business community should continue to take part in the peacetime

[53] *Göteborgs Handels- och Sjöfartstidning*, 4 Mar. 1947.
[54] *Stockholms-Tidningen*, 14 Dec. 1947.
[55] *Svenska Dagbladet*, 3 June 1947.

planning process. To succeed in their main strategy of making the Social Democrats abstain from their economic policy plans, it was necessary to have public opinion on their side. Only a broad popular reaction could force the Social Democrats to retreat. It was thus of fundamental importance to have popular support for every aspect of their strategic action. According to the minutes of the Confederation, "A refusal by the group of businessmen to participate in the work of the (commission) would be perceived as an obstruction that would not elicit any sympathy from the public."[56] As a result, they decided to continue. But, as one nonsocialist member of the Myrdal Commission later declared, they only remained and agreed to continue their research assignment "in order not to endanger future cooperation."[57]

The pressures continued. When the Myrdal Commission proposed steps to combat restraints on competition in the business sector, business people found it difficult to argue against letting the government perform investigations and register cartels; opposition against such fact-finding measures might be interpreted as an attempt by representatives of private business to defend abuses.

The business community used the same reasoning when the numerous economic commissions of inquiry were appointed; aside from those mentioned previously, initiated as a result of members' bills in the 1945 session of Parliament, Myrdal – now minister of commerce – appointed some commissions of inquiry at his own initiative, the most important being the furniture industry commission. Others, dealing with the electrical and construction industries, were based on members' bills in Parliament. The business community allowed itself to be represented in these commissions too, as members and experts; participation at an early stage would give them "an opportunity to develop in advance a definition, desirable from the standpoint of industry," of the issues to be dealt with.[58]

According to the postwar programs of the Conservatives and Liberals, the main defense against a peacetime depression was not public jobs but capital spending by companies themselves. In the same way, from a political standpoint, investments and production by companies were also the best defense against the state expansionism of the Social Democrats. With their energetic postwar reconstruction efforts, businessmen wanted to show that it was unfair and unjustified to underestimate the ability of private enterprise to maintain production and employment. Social Democratic mistrust also turned out to be wrong. Business entered an unprecedented boom period. "Productive labor" triumphed over "bureaucracy."

[56] Söderpalm 1976, p. 120.
[57] Harald Nordenson, "Myrdalskommissionens eftermäle," *Ekonomisk Revy* (1946): 4.
[58] The minutes of the Federation of Swedish Industries as quoted in Söderpalm 1976, p. 121; also pp. 127–128.

And after all, was it not wisest to follow the same line of action on the issue of the structural problems of business? On this controversial issue, was it not best to try to show through action that Social Democratic criticisms were unjustified, rather than pursuing a sterile policy of protest? As a consequence, businessmen themselves began to deal with the structural problems of various industries. As one empirical study puts it, the very existence of a government-appointed commission of inquiry spurred industry to efforts that would otherwise not have taken place.[59]

But there was a limit to how far business was willing to go to head off the Social Democrats. When the government proposed that the existing state commissions of inquiry on structural rationalization of the business sector be replaced by a permanent "sectoral council," the business community no longer wished to take part. The Confederation of Industries flatly rejected efforts by a government minister, Karin Kock, to begin negotiations on this issue. Business leaders were not willing to let themselves be pushed too far by Social Democratic economic policy experiments. They became increasingly bitter at what they regarded as a Social Democratic policy of extortion. There was no lack of threatening speeches about investment strikes and flight of capital if the Social Democrats tried to go any further with their interference in the structural rationalization of the business sector. The idea of sectoral councils was shelved.[60]

The business community thus used a combination of accommodation and firmness, sometimes cooperating and sometimes obstructing, in order to defend the principle of limited government as opposed to an expanding role for the state in economic planning.

By way of summary, the results of the government-appointed commission studies on ways to restructure the business sector and increase its efficiency were surprisingly modest recommendations, far less radical than the nonsocialists had feared and the Social Democrats had hoped for at the end of the war. Only a single commission report proposed nationalization – the report of the oil industry commission. But not even this industry was nationalized. The government explained this by citing Sweden's acute currency problems. Otherwise the commissions merely proposed changes of a technical nature such as greater specialization, improved personnel training, the formation of sales and purchasing organizations, quality labeling of goods, and changes in tariff levels.

The failure of the Social Democrats on the issue of state participation

---

[59] *Branschrationalisering. Mening, metoder, möjligheter* (Studieförbundet Näringsliv och Samhälle, 1958), p. 226. Cf. *Expressen*, 12 Feb. 1945: "It is thus not necessary to deny that public attention may speed a solution to the issue in a beneficial manner, hastening private intervention."

[60] Lewin 1967, p. 327.

in the structural rationalization of the business sector could not be concealed. They had, admittedly, stated that they had an undoctrinaire attitude toward the proper balance between the state and the market: Macroeconomic efficiency would be the decisive factor in choosing organizational structure. But when their research on the business sector resulted in hardly any expansion of the state, this outcome too obviously contradicted people's expectations at the end of the war. *Dagens Nyheter* was ironic in its assessment of the retreat of the Social Democrats in their economic policy: "To be undoctrinaire means, in the Social Democratic vocabulary, to be able to take back what you've said at any time and say just the opposite."[61]

In 1947 the failure of a depression to materialize, combined with an expansionist policy, resulted in serious inflation and pressures on the country's foreign currency reserves. The government was forced to begin negotiations with the nonsocialist parties and business organizations in order to bring about economic stabilization in Sweden. But these negotiations broke down, mainly because the Social Democrats refused to admit their role in causing the prevailing problems. Once again, the nonsocialists declared, their fears that economic planning would lead to inflation had been proved correct. But this time, difficulties had turned out to be far greater than during the 1930s. The nonsocialists set in motion a so-called misrule propaganda campaign against the government's handling of economic policy. Headlines like "Central Planners' Fiasco," "Planless Economic Planning," "Economic Planning in All its Glory," "The Crisis of the Central Planners," "Economic Planning Without a Plan" and "The Failure of Economic Planning" appeared on the editorial pages of nonsocialist newspapers.

The 1948 preelection debate began one year before the actual vote took place. "In twelve months, the Swedish people will vote in an election that for good reason is expected to be one of the most important in our country during this century," Ohlin wrote in 1947.[62] As early as April of that year, *Morgon-Tidningen* had already predicted that the Second Chamber election of 1948 would be a decisive trial of strength in Swedish politics. "This means," the newspaper continued, "that until then we will have a permanent election campaign. Public debate will be a bludgeoning match"[63] – an apt description of political debate in Sweden during 1947–1948.

The election itself was dramatic. The Liberals more than doubled their voter strength, but the party's major victory occurred mainly at the expense of the Conservative and Agrarian parties. The Social Democrats

---

[61] *Dagens Nyheter*, 7 July 1949.
[62] Bertil Ohlin, "Tolv månader till valet," *Folkpartiet* no. 6 (1947): 3 and 19.
[63] *Morgon-Tidningen*, 2 Apr. 1947.

lost only a few tenths of a percent of the electorate. The Communists suffered a disastrous loss, a reaction against the Soviet-inspired coup in Prague earlier that year. Voter turnout rose sharply; industrial workers in particular, who favored the Social Democrats,[64] voted in larger numbers. The Social Democrats managed to stay in power. They could still count on a majority in Parliament for their government manifesto, *The Postwar Program of the Swedish Labor Movement:* In the First Chamber the socialist bloc (Social Democrats and Communists) had 87 seats against 63 for the nonsocialist parties. In the Second Chamber, the socialists had a 120-to-110 advantage.

The insignificant shift in strength between the two blocs after such a long and hard ideological struggle was undeniably something of an anticlimax. It was as if the Swedish people, as during the tariff dispute, did not wish to give more than a noncommittal answer to questions that overwrought politicians found so vital.

But political passions had found their outlet in the election campaign. Most observers agreed that there was a rapid improvement in relations between the blocs after the election. In the words of Ernst Wigforss, "milder air" characterized the political climate; this change was immediately apparent in the fall 1948 economic policy session of Parliament and in the general policy debate of 1949.[65] The government also took a number of steps to improve its relations with the business community: The so-called Thursday Club was established as a forum for discussions on economic issues among the government, public agencies, and the business community, and the government appointed commissions of inquiry to review the structure of the tax system and examine whether it was possible to use general methods instead of detailed regulation in government economic policy. A new institute was established – Studieförbundet Näringsliv och Samhälle (SNS), known today in English as the Center for Business and Policy Studies.

These attempts to rally all political forces and to create a broadly based program of economic stabilization naturally concentrated people's interest in these efforts. The retreat of the Social Democrats on the structural rationalization issue could thus occur in a less sensational manner than might otherwise have been the case. The Social Democrats decided, in the shadow of this new interest in economic stabilization and political cooperation, that they would no longer try to push through the radical economic policy embodied in their postwar program.

[64] Leif Lewin, Bo Jansson, and Dag Sörbom, *The Swedish Electorate 1887–1968* (Stockholm: Almqvist & Wiksell, 1972), pp. 147–148.
[65] Wigforss 1954, pp. 392ff.; Lewin 1967, p. 358, n. 7.

This section has presented the nonsocialist critique of the planned economy during the "harvest time," depicting it as a strategy that successfully prevented the Social Democrats from introducing the economic policy for which they in fact had a majority. But this way of looking at the matter does not mean that the critique of economic planning by the nonsocialists and the business community should be regarded as sheer tactics. Some debaters, of course, may have exaggerated the danger of nationalization, for tactical reasons. But there can be no doubt that nonsocialist party representatives, the nonsocialist press, and the business community were strongly convinced that their critique of the planned economy was justified. Much of it was based on an honest concern for the preservation of freedom and prosperity in a planned economy.

In other words, there was an intimate relationship between ideology and strategy in the economic planning debate of the "harvest time" years. The strategy of denying the government's qualifications for controlling economic life is not a strategy that can be used by anybody, regardless of his ideological preferences. This strategy is, in itself, an expression of a particular ideological view. The defense of limited government is a means for liberalism to combat socialism and, at the same time, its ideal of the good society.

3. THE ASSURANCE GAME

Why did the Social Democrats abstain from carrying out the structural rationalization of the business sector under state leadership they had promised in their government policy declaration, even though after the 1948 election they still had a majority in favor of these plans?

In our analysis using game theory, we will let the two main alternatives available to the Social Democrats be either to abstain from or to implement the state-led structural rationalization of the business sector. For the nonsocialists and the business community, the question will be whether they should participate in or obstruct the postwar planning process. Under Social Democratic auspices, this process also came to include an analysis of the long-term structural problems of the business sector and thus functioned as the economic survey that, in the Social Democratic view, should precede economic planning by the state.

The best alternative for the Social Democrats would, of course, be that they succeeded in implementing their policy. This presupposed cooperation by the opposing side, which possessed vital knowledge of conditions in the business sector. This outcome is given a value of $+2$ for the Social Democrats (lower left-hand quadrant in Table 6.1). The nonsocialists and the business community regarded the economic planning system that would result from this policy as the worst imaginable alternative (-2).

The best alternative for the nonsocialists and the business community

188

Table 6.1. *The planned economy game*

	Nonsocialists and business community	
	Participate in postwar planning	Obstruct postwar planning
Social Democrats Abstain from state-led structural rationalization	0, 0	−2, +2
Implement state-led structural rationalization	+2, −2	−1, −1

would be if they did not have to make any concessions at all to the Social Democratic postwar planning process, while at the same time the Social Democrats abstained from their plans for structural rationalization of the business sector under state leadership. The relatively free-market economy of the interwar period would be preserved. As with the Social Democrats, the best alternative for the nonsocialists and the business community is assigned a value of +2 (upper right-hand quadrant). To the Social Democrats, the preservation of the social system of the interwar period and incomplete utilization of production factors appeared to be the worst alternative (−2).

The next best alternative for both sides would be if the nonsocialists and the business community admittedly cooperated in examining the structural problems of the business sector, but for the result of this survey to be that the Social Democrats did not consider it necessary to carry out their plans (upper left-hand quadrant). To the nonsocialists and the business community, such cooperation would entail a genuine sacrifice of economic policy ideals. They would be subjecting themselves to paper work and bureaucratic supervision, registration, and regulation, which they had hoped to escape when the war ended and which they firmly believed would not promote growing prosperity but on the contrary work against it. But if the Social Democrats could be persuaded, in the long term, to give ground on the issue of state participation in structural rationalization, this outcome would undoubtedly be very satisfactory. Arguments for both alternatives – to participate or obstruct – could thus be mustered, and we have seen how the leading figures in the business community weighed the choice between these two strategies. When we weigh together the advantages and disadvantages of the outcome described by the combination in

189

the upper left-hand quadrant, we can assign them a total value of 0 for the nonsocialists and the business community.

Similarly, a reconstruction of Social Democratic calculations for the outcome in the upper left-hand corner would also be a 0. The participation of the business community would admittedly enable them to bring about a survey of the business sector, but the result would still be that they abstained from far-reaching state intervention. It would not be entirely impossible to justify such a policy, either: The Social Democrats had emphasized in their postwar program that the state would only intervene when the business sector failed. Theoretically, of course, the survey could lead to the finding that no state intervention was necessary. The alternative of abstaining from intervention would, in that case, not be inconsistent. But it was naturally far less harmonious with socialist expectations during the "harvest time" than the alternative of carrying out structural rationalization of the business sector under state leadership.

What would finally happen if neither side compromised? The agitated mood during the harvest-time economic planning debate indicated that a genuine collision between the blocs was the most likely outcome. Both camps frantically banged their heads bloody in the clash between liberalism and socialism, between freedom and nationalization. In the end, this could certainly not lead to anything but a political and economic crisis. Without taking into account the large-scale investment and employment program being undertaken by the business sector, the Social Democratic government pursued an expansive economic policy resulting in major inflationary and currency problems. Without taking into account the labor movement's calls for economic information and employee participation in managing the business sector, all radical proposals such as the sectoral council idea were flatly rejected; there was no lack of talk about an investment strike and flight of capital to other countries. Everyone stood to lose from such an inflation, foreign currency, and capital spending crisis. This outcome was the next worst alternative for both sides (−1), albeit not quite as repugnant as total economic planning was to the nonsocialists and the business community, or uncontrolled capitalism was to the Social Democrats.

Given this assignment of utility values, we are again facing an example of the "prisoners' dilemma." If both sides follow their primary ideological preferences and choose "implement" and "obstruct" respectively, the result is a collision and a crisis, which is a bad alternative for both. But even if they compromise and agree to their second preferences, there are incentives for both to abandon the upper left-hand quadrant: The hope of a +2 instead of a 0, and the fear of a −2 instead of a 0 inevitably drive the players toward the crisis in the lower right-hand quadrant, which of course is the equilibrium point in the "prisoners' dilemma."

Economic planning

But this is not what happened. After the 1948 election the two sides achieved a reconciliation that corresponds most closely to the situation described in the upper left-hand quadrant. There was a compromise instead of a crisis.

Does this mean that game theory fails in this case? We have of course argued earlier that the strength of this type of analysis is that, given the actors' ability to behave rationally, it clearly points out whether there is a solution to a particular game and in that case what it is. In our table, the "prisoners' dilemma" has a solution, albeit not a very happy one, in the lower right-hand quadrant. In reality, the two sides settled for the solution described in the upper left-hand quadrant. So does game theory fail to explain the outcome of the economic planning dispute? Or on this issue, do we have to assume that the prerequisites for our analysis were not fulfilled – that is, that the politicians did not act rationally?

The answer is no to both questions. Our analysis of the economic planning dispute makes it worthwhile to penetrate more deeply into rational choice theory. No case has been the object of such exhaustive treatment in the literature as the "prisoners' dilemma." In this methodological literature, we also find an explanation as to why the economic planning debate of the "harvest-time" years led to a compromise instead of a crisis, to the upper left-hand quadrant instead of the lower right-hand one.

Of the many suggestions in the literature that have attempted to explain decisions on collectively better outcomes of the "prisoners' dilemma" than the equilibrium solution, which is unpleasant for both sides, let us examine the model for the "assurance game" developed by Jon Elster.[66] Before

[66] Jon Elster, *Forklaring og dialektikk. Noen grunnbegrepper i vitenskapsteorien* (Oslo: Pax, 1979), pp. 76ff. and 84ff.; Elster, *Ulysses and the Sirens. Studies in Rationality and Irrationality* (Cambridge: Cambridge University Press, 1979), pp. 18ff. and 141ff. See also William H. Riker, "Political Trust as Rational Choice," in *Politics as Rational Action. Essays in Public Choice and Policy Analysis*, ed. Leif Lewin and Evert Vedung (Dordrecht: Reidel, 1980), pp. 1–24; Amartya K. Sen, *Choice, Welfare and Measurement* (Oxford: Blackwell, 1982), pp. 62ff. and 74–83; Anatol Rapoport and Albert M. Chammah, *Prisoner's Dilemma: A Study in Conflict and Cooperation* (Ann Arbor: University of Michigan Press, 1965); Anatol Rapoport et al., *The 2 × 2 Game* (Ann Arbor: University of Michigan Press, 1976); C. Taylor, "Responsibility for Self," in *The Identities of Persons*, ed. A. Rorty (Berkeley and Los Angeles: University of California Press, 1976). The "metagame" theory presented by Nigel Howard, *Paradoxes of Rationality: Theory of Metagames and Political Behavior* (Cambridge, Mass.: MIT Press, 1971) means that the matrix is expanded so that one player makes his choice while taking into account the various alternatives that the other player may conceivably choose; surprisingly enough, the equilibrium solution will then be different and more advantageous than in the original, simple matrix. Howard's theory has, however, generally been rejected by researchers; see, for example, Michael Taylor, *Anarchy and Cooperation* (New York: Wiley, 1976), pp. 64–68. See also the textbook presentations in William H. Riker and Peter C. Ordeshook, *An Introduction to Positive Political Theory* (Englewood Cliffs, N.J.: Prentice-Hall, 1973), pp. 223ff., 250ff., and 296ff.; Steven J. Brams, *Game Theory and Politics* (New York: The Free Press, 1975), pp. 30–39 and 48–49; Robert Abrams, *Foundations of Political Analysis: An Introduction to the Theory of Collective Choice* (New York: Columbia University Press, 1980), pp. 191ff., 292, and 306–325.

Table 6.2. *The "prisoners' dilemma" and the "assurance game"*

		N			N	
		A	E		A	E
S	A	0, 0	−2, +2		+2, +2	−2, 0
	E	+2, −2	−1, −1		0, −2	−1, −1

we attempt to apply this model empirically, it should be pointed out that when we – like others working with rational choice theory – speak of the "rationality" of the actors, this does not mean that they need be "selfish," something that was previously often attributed to this type of analysis. If altruism is part of an actor's preferences, it is of course rational of him to act in such a way as to satisfy this altruism, that is, so that the other players are rewarded. Love is an example of such an altruistic game. Giving away presents may be another example; the act of giving itself creates happiness, which may be even greater than the receiver experiences.

Elster's model is, however, more interesting than trying to transform prisoners into altruists who are eager to minimize each other's punishment. He speaks not of "altruism" but of "solidarity." Solidarity is defined as "conditional altruism." Unlike altruism, solidarity is not based on an unconditional, individual ethical conviction. Solidarity means that a person behaves in a certain way *on the condition that everyone else also does the same.* No player is assumed to choose altruism on his own initiative if he is not sure that his opponent also does so.

On the basis of Elster's argument, in Table 6.2 we can let the Social Democrats (S) and the nonsocialists and business community (N) choose between two strategies, "altruism" (A) and "egoism" (E). The left-hand matrix in the table shows our old acquaintances: In the "prisoners' dilemma" the best choice is to behave egoistically yourself while your opponent behaves altruistically; the next best choice is for both to behave altruistically; the third best is for both to be egoists; and the worst is to behave altruistically while the other person behaves egoistically. This means that egoism is the dominant strategy chosen by both players. So the result is found in the lower right-hand quadrant – in other words, a situation to which both of them assign a lower value than the situation where both of them choose altruism (upper left-hand quadrant). The fact that individual rationality can thus lead to collective irrationality is, of course, the whole point of recommending a decision-making model like the "prisoners' dilemma."

In the "assurance game" shown in the right-hand matrix of Table 6.2, the preferences of the actors are the same, except that their two first preferences are switched around. There is no dominant strategy here. "Altruism" leads either to the best outcome, $+2$, or to the worst, -2. This strategy should only be chosen if the other player does the same. If the other player should, on the other hand, choose the egoistic strategy, the result is the worst outcome of all. In the "assurance game," where everyone chooses altruism, the solution in the upper left-hand quadrant is completely stable, because it is not in anyone's best interest to break out of a situation that everyone classifies as the highest of the available options.

So how will an actor know whether his opponent will choose altruism or egoism? The answer can be given in two steps. First, there has to be communication between the players. The specific prerequisite in the "prisoners' dilemma" is precisely that no communication is permitted. In the "assurance game," on the other hand, we allow the players to communicate; as rational actors, they can then calculate the consequences of choosing the egoistic strategy, and this persuades them to switch to the altruistic strategy instead. When the "prisoners' dilemma" changes to the "assurance game," this means, put simply, that we let the prisoners out of their cells and let them deliberate with each other for the purpose of finding a strategy for their common good.

This approach it not, however, sufficient to create stability. It is conceivable that after their deliberations, the prisoners will return to their cells and try to fool each other. Obviously there is much to be gained from such fraudulent behavior: If the other person chooses altruism and you yourself revert to egoism, you would improve your utility value from 0 to $+2$. In order for this solution to stick, it is thus necessary to express solidarity in concrete form by upgrading the outcome in the upper left-hand quadrant to the first preference of both players, moving down to second place the situation where you yourself are egoistic and your opponent altruistic. The realization that by practicing solidarity you can improve not only the other player's position but also your own leads to a change in preference ordering. Elster's concept, which can be described as an empirical hypothesis on how it is possible to achieve collective rationality in a "prisoners' dilemma," thus assumes that communication between the players leads to an awareness of the system, which is expressed in a change of preference ordering and a switch from a "prisoners' dilemma" to an "assurance game."

If we now return to Swedish political reality, it is striking how different the prerequisites were for rational political action during the tariff dispute of the 1880s, where we also encountered a "prisoners' dilemma," compared with the economic planning dispute of the 1940s. During the tariff dispute, what was missing was communication between the players. It is true that there were also proposals during the tariff dispute aimed at escaping the dilemma by moving from confrontation to compromise and appointing a commission of inquiry, thereby removing the issue from the political agenda. But this proposal was rejected in no uncertain terms; the two sides were not prepared to compromise but were determined to pursue their respective arguments until the opponent had been defeated. Despite an equally strong ideological passion during the economic planning dispute of the 1940s, however, the actors realized that it would be devastating to push the dispute to extremes. In 1947, serious concern about an imminent crisis began to spread. Both sides began to realize that their calculations had been wrong. Both camps took steps to make the necessary cooperation possible.

The Social Democrats realized that they had calculated wrong by underestimating the strength of the nonsocialists and the business sector. They had underestimated the purely economic skills of the business sector in dealing with postwar problems; their expectations of a depression had been totally discredited. They had also miscalculated their opponents' ability to conduct a political battle. They had, admittedly, said that they were prepared for resistance to state intervention in the business sector. But the PHM propaganda had been a counterattack of enormous strength, which the Social Democrats could not have imagined in their wildest fantasies.

The nonsocialists and the business community, for their part, realized that they had calculated wrong by underestimating the political strength of the labor movement. They had counted on a change of regime in 1948; *Dagens Nyheter* even celebrated an election victory in advance by mistakenly announcing that the Social Democrats had lost power (the same thing happened again a few weeks later when Dewey failed to dislodge Truman in the U.S. presidential election).[67] In the 1948 election, the Social Democrats successfully mobilized voters from their most loyal constituency, industrial workers. The nonsocialists' confidence in victory was replaced by resignation at the prospect that the Social Democrats might stay in power for many years. They had to adjust to this fact. Cooperation immediately became a more attractive alternative.

Unlike the politicians who took part in the tariff dispute, the main actors in the economic planning dispute finally made peace after years of irreconcilable struggle. When no one seemed able to achieve his first preference – either the intended planned economy or a market economy guaranteed by a change of regime – both sides were ready to reassess their strategies to avoid an unnecessarily bad collective solution.

[67] Herbert Tingsten, *Mitt liv. Tidningen 1946–52* (Stockholm: Norstedts, 1963), pp. 151–152.

Economic planning

A comparison with the tariff dispute shows, finally, how you can get stuck in the "prisoners' dilemma" and how you can get out of it. For years, the politicians who took part in the tariff dispute had managed to avoid the worst collective solution by "being silent" on the tariff issue. Their nondecision strategy is an example of a successful "assurance game" aimed at protecting Oscarian society against the threat of parliamentary democracy. But finally this silence was broken. The tariff issue rapidly became the dominant political litmus test; M.P.'s became more intensively committed to implementing their actual program than to scoring points in an abstractly phrased critique of the imperative mandate. In other words, there was a change of preference in the course of the dispute. Members of Parliament changed their preferences from the order indicated in the right-hand matrix in Table 6.2 to the order indicated in the left-hand matrix. The "assurance game" fell apart and was replaced by the "prisoners' dilemma."

The opposite occurred during the planned economy dispute. It began with an open confrontation according to the left-hand matrix of Table 6.2. But the realization that the game was moving toward an E–E result even though both sides preferred A–A persuaded the actors to change their preferences – but in the opposite direction from what had been the case during the tariff dispute. Concern for the political system was more important than implementing the points in an economic policy program. The politicians involved in the economic planning dispute were thus able to escape from the "prisoners' dilemma" and shift to an "assurance game." If they had continued to insist on their first preferences, they would have generated forces that they could not control. Swedish politics would have moved inexorably into a crisis situation that no one wanted. In that case, it was better for both sides to begin cooperating in order to prevent this evil. The establishment of cooperation was an expression of collectively rational political action.

A postelection editorial entitled "The Business Sector and Us" in the Social Democratic ideological journal *Tiden* asked this exact question: How should the party "bring about the good cooperation between the state and the business sector that everyone says is necessary?" Superficially, the chances might seem small; during the economic planning dispute, liberalism had "taken heart" and become "aggressive." It might seem "as if the prospects of a rapprochement and cooperation between the two camps are small and less than they have been for a long time." But "perhaps this is not necessarily true," the editorial writer continued. For what would be the consequences if the business sector continued to be "cocksure" and "straightforward" and rejected cooperation with the Social Democrats? "A cocksure viewpoint presupposes a belief in total success. If the conditions for this do not exist, an all-or-nothing attitude can never lead to gain

195

for one's own interests, no matter how deserving these might be – at most, they may lead to difficulties for one's supposed opponent, which in the long run will also become difficulties for everyone." These difficulties would, in turn, trigger economic planning measures – but economic planning of a kind that no one wanted, not even the Social Democrats. Economic regulation of *this* kind, in response to a crisis, was what could be expected from continued confrontation; it would not arise because anyone wanted it but would "simply be the result of powerlessness, of 'objective' inability to stop forces that could not be stopped." And, the editorial concluded, "it ought to be admitted and be just as clear that in our camp, we have no less reason for reflection." The least desirable alternative would be economic planning triggered by crisis, "economic planning that would be led only by circumstance and not by people, which we would be forced into but would not control."[68]

Contemporary source material on the deliberations leading to the establishment of the assurance game in Swedish politics after the 1948 election thus came very close to the language of game theory analysis.

4. THE RIGHTS METHOD

The Social Democratic retreat on the issue of a state-supervised structural rationalization of the business sector did not, however, mean the acceptance of the decision rule that the nonsocialists and the business sector cited as arguments for a limitation of government. The Social Democratic position was the result of deliberations on what was politically suitable. They did not agree for a minute that in principle there were certain limits to whether a politically elected majority was qualified to intervene in the economy. The right of private ownership was not an inalienable right, exempt from the exercise of majority rule, as the nonsocialist side maintained.

The legal foundation of the nonsocialists' rights argument against Social Democratic state expansionism was fragile: It consisted only of Chapter 16 of the 1809 Constitution, which was both famous and difficult to interpret. It stipulated that the king should not take away anyone's "property, movable or real, without trial and verdict in the manner prescribed by the laws and legal statutes of Sweden." As early as the late 1930s, the Conservatives had tried to bring about increased constitutional protection of private ownership rights. They introduced identical members' bills in both chambers calling for "introduction and affirmation in the Constitution of the fundamental principles of our current society in such a way that they may not be set aside without a change in the Swedish

---

[68] Per Åsbrink, "Näringslivet och vi," *Tiden* (1948): 449–455.

Economic planning

Constitution. The main principles that should be included here are: free-dom of association, assembly, speech and religion and the right of per-sonal property."[69] A parliamentary commission of inquiry proposed an amendment to Chapter 16, which went a long way toward satisfying the wishes of those who submitted the members' bill; among other things, it proposed stronger protection of economic freedom and private owner-ship.[70] The commission report did not lead to any legislation, however. During the economic planning debate of the "harvest time," Chapter 16 in its original form was all there was to fall back on.

It was, of course, difficult to use. The first point of contention was whether it was only binding on "the king" – that is, the government as the executive power – and not on the laws passed by the government and the Parliament together. Another question concerned whether the rule only forbade arbitrary deprivation of property in specific cases or also con-fiscation that affected all citizens equally, through law or otherwise.[71] If the latter were not also the case, one could ask what protection of prop-erty the Constitution actually provided.

The nonsocialists nevertheless tried to use a rights argument during the economic planning dispute of the 1940s when they fought Social Demo-cratic plans to transform the economy. During the debate on the 1947 tax bill, they criticized the proposed estate tax on legal grounds. The Conser-vatives and Liberals regarded the proposed tax as violating Chapter 16. In its official comment, the Svea Appeals Court used the same argument. Since the breakthrough of parliamentary government, this constitutional rule was regarded as also applying to legislation adopted jointly by the king and Parliament. What was viewed as a confiscatory tax proposal must consequently be adopted in the form of civil law and not in the sim-pler form of tax law. And the Appeals Court added: "But in a state that still has certain pretensions to be considered a constitutional state, it can never be without significance if, for good reason, a group of citizens has come to feel they are without rights, no matter how small this group is, indeed not even if it is a matter of a single person." This rights argument was repeated in the official comments of other appeals courts, certain other public agencies, and the Taxation Committee of Private Commerce and Industry. The Conservatives and Liberals characterized the estate tax proposal as an assault by the majority on the small minority who had to pay. *Svenska Dagbladet* wrote that "the majority has ruthlessly taken advantage of its position of power." *Dagens Nyheter* varied the theme of

---

[69] Mot FK 1938:128; quotation from p. 4 (Domö et al.) and AK 232 (Bagge et al.).

[70] *Betänkande med förslag till ändrad lydelse av § 16 regeringsformen* (SOU 1941:20).

[71] Ibid., p. 99 (Memorandum attached as Appendix 2 to the report); Ulf Brunfelter and Mats Svegfors, *Grundlag och egendomsskydd* (Västervik: Akademilitteratur, 1977), pp. 32–44.

denying that the majority was qualified to restrict the protection of property by maintaining that the proposal was not presented in the election campaign, so that the government lacked the mandate to carry out such a policy. But most of the Social Democratic proposal was adopted by Parliament. After the vote, the Conservative leaders of both chambers took the unusual step of having their objections recorded in the minutes. They declared that important parts of the tax bill "not only violate generally accepted legal principles" but were also "likely to hold back the growth of prosperity in our country." These objections were underscored by the mass concurrence of the Conservative M.P.'s.[72]

When the Royal Commission on Constitutional Matters was appointed in 1954, other constitutional problems besides the issue of protecting minority rights occupied the center of interest. Only because of members' bills – this time from Liberal party M.P.'s – was protection of minority rights added to the subjects to be studied by the commission. The sponsors of the members' bills said they hoped that rules would be added to the Constitution that "express the fundamental principles of the Swedish concept of law, for example, protection of private ownership rights."[73]

Then during the 1970s, when the old Swedish Constitution was replaced by a new one, the issue of protecting the rights of minorities became one of the most controversial topics of debate among the parties. As the various constitutional reforms were carried out, the increasingly inflamed issue of minority protection was juggled to new commissions of inquiry. No fewer than four commissions dealt with the issue, and there were two more commissions on freedom of speech.[74]

The Royal Commission of Constitutional Matters, chaired by Rickard Sandler, proposed, among other things, the establishment of rights to property and protection against expropriation. As for the strength of this protection, it proposed that the constitution only be required to contain a ban on retroactive penal legislation. When the commission report was being circulated for comment, this proposal was heavily criticized; according to its critics, including those in legal circles and business-sector organizations, a larger number of rights should enjoy constitutional protection or be subject to restrictions only by a qualified majority.

In 1972 the Commission on the Constitution chaired by Valter Åman

[72] Nils Elvander, *Svensk skattepolitik 1945–1970. En studie i partiers och organisationers funktioner* (Stockholm: Rabén & Sjögren, 1972), pp. 26–66, esp. pp. 38–39, 43, 51, 58, and 62. The sources mentioned are as quoted by Elvander.

[73] Mot FK 1958:B 155 (Ohlin et al.) and AK 218 (Ohlin et al.).

[74] On the decision-making process, see Erik Holmberg and Nils Stjernquist, *Grundlagarna* (Stockholm: Norstedts, 1980), pp. 14ff. Only a few main features of these developments will be mentioned here. The issue is currently the object of a research project at my department headed by Karl-Göran Algotsson, whom I would like to thank for his valuable suggestions.

proposed a further broadening of the extent of protection of rights. There had been a clear divergence of views among members of the commission, which was finally resolved by an agreement. The Moderates and Liberals gave up their demand that only a qualified majority of Parliament could approve restrictions on civil rights. The Social Democrats, in turn, approved the continued practice of judicial review by the courts in such cases. In keeping with the wishes of the nonsocialists, the commission's proposal only stipulated traditional rights. The Social Democrats withdrew their previous demand that modern social welfare rights also be included in the Constitution. During the preparation of the government bill, this agreement among the parties fell by the wayside. The nonsocialist parties introduced members' bills calling for stronger constitutional protection of rights. But now, too, the decision was marked by a spirit of compromise. One important element of this compromise was that the whole issue of fundamental rights would be studied by a new commission of inquiry.

By this time the issue had become highly politicized and drew lively media coverage: The "IB Affair," which focused on the right of journalists to reveal official secrets, contributed to this. In this climate, the Commission on Rights and Freedoms, chaired by Hjalmar Mehr, the leading local Social Democratic politician in Stockholm, worked for two years. Among the commission's proposals was that so-called social welfare rights would be included in the Constitution as program declarations and that a number of new rights be added. The commission was unable to reach unity on the issue of the strength of protection of rights. A majority consisting of Social Democrats and Center party members believed that it sufficed to specify in the Constitution the purposes for which rights could or could not be restricted and to use the right of judicial review. The Moderates and Liberals demanded stronger guarantees against majority decisions on issues that infringe on the rights of minorities. They felt that it should be possible to limit various freedoms and rights only by using the same procedure as in changing the Constitution or by a qualified majority. The version approved by Parliament largely followed the majority proposal, but judicial review by the courts was not written into the Constitution.

In 1977 the government appointed a Commission on the Protection of Rights, with Gunnar Heckscher, a former Conservative party leader, as chairman. In this commission, the four largest parties managed to reach agreement on such matters as tightening the procedures for passing legislation that restricted people's rights. The Liberal minority government's bill followed this proposal and received parliamentary approval.

By way of summary, it is clear that despite the substantial increase in rights stipulated in the new Constitution, the nonsocialists and the business community have not been successful in having the right of private ownership recognized as a constitutionally protected right exempt from the decisions of simple majorities, as was their ambition. The Swedish Constitution contains very weak protection of property rights. It mainly states only that citizens are entitled to compensation "for loss" in cases of expropriation according to principles determined by law; that authors, artists, and photographers are ensured the copyright for their works; and that retroactive tax laws are forbidden.

This is how Swedish politics reflects the glow of the European ideological debate, more than two hundred years old, on how democratic decisions ought to be reached when the actors disagree. The problem is based on the dualism of the very ideological tradition from which the debate originates. On the one hand, the political philosophers who paved the way for the French Revolution maintained that the people had a sovereign right to rule. On the other hand, the same theoreticians argued that citizens had certain natural rights that no one could violate. Ensuing European and American constitutional developments have given very divergent answers to the question of how to balance these two irreconcilable principles properly against each other – how much we should restrict the decision-making authority of the majority or, putting it differently, how extensive and strong the protection of minorities should be. In Sweden, the Conservatives, Liberals, and business-sector organizations have turned out to be the foremost supporters of the rights method, whereas the Social Democrats have most strongly advocated majority rule. These political battle lines became increasingly clear the further the constitutional reform process moved away from the old minimalist wording of Chapter 16 toward today's very extensive catalogs of rights.

In this dialogue between the majority and minority line in the democratic ideological debate, Arrow's paradox and rational choice theory seem to throw light on the problem. As we have seen, majority decisions need not be an expression of a majority opinion, but may come about through strategic manipulation of the agenda. Far from reflecting firm, carefully considered majority wishes, these decisions may be reached by means of temporary, frequently haphazard coalitions aimed at promoting special interests that, in turn, are only supported by minorities. For this reason, leading researchers of the rational choice school argue, decision rules in a democracy should be arranged in such a way as to give minority interests maximum protection against temporary majorities – for example, through nonunicameral systems requiring duplication of decisions, division of power, multiparty systems, regional autonomy, independent judicial power, and strong protection of rights.[75]

[75] See, for example, William H. Riker, *Liberalism Against Populism: A Confrontation between the Theory of Democracy and the Theory of Social Choice* (San Francisco: Freeman, 1982).

Economic planning

Let us look at economic planning versus a market economy in this context. The political implication of Keynes and the theories that began to be practiced in Sweden with the 1933 crisis agreement has been state interventionism. Where the market failed, Swedish Social Democrats also reasoned, the state should go in and make sure that all production factors were brought to bear and used efficiently. The result has been an enormous public sector. The political implication of rational choice theory seems to be to save the good name of the market. It has been made clear that the state can fail, too. The effects of state intervention have not been as positive as people assumed. The coalitions that, in the name of majority rule, are pushing the West toward increasingly large public sectors will thus have to moderate their demands and accord greater respect to the market economy and especially to the right of private ownership. The latter is still the only reliable incentive for increasing prosperity. "Tomorrow capitalism!" shouts the most daring representative of the new school.[76]

What we actually have to choose from is, on the one hand, an ideal of a perfectly functioning market or an ideal of a perfectly functioning state, or, on the other hand, a reality consisting of an imperfect market or a reality consisting of an imperfect state. Actually it is a correct observation that the modern expansion of the state, legitimized by Keynesian theories, has been fueled by an excessively naive belief in the superior wisdom of the government and in the means by which collective decisions arise. But what is the alternative? Not the market as an ideal, but the market as a reality with many imperfections. In other words, the decisive issue is which alternative we believe is the least imperfect – the market (as it really is) or the state (as it really is). Now, as so often otherwise, it is the task of political science to point out that in political reality the choice is between two evils; it is not a choice between something "good" and something "evil." In choosing between such values, rational choice theory cannot make the decision. In relation to values held by political parties, this theory is a neutral analytical technique. Arguments for both camps, for the rights method and majority rule, can be found in its rich arsenal of ideas. It has thus been shown that majority rule is, all things considered, preferable in the long run to those actors who wish to maximize agreement between collective decisions and their own individual preferences, provided these actors do not know the likelihood that they will end up in a majority or minority position. If, on the other hand, the majority situation is known, as in the economic planning debate of the "harvest time," the legislator has to decide whether he wants to force the status quo on the actors by using the rights method or force changes on them by applying

[76] Henri Lepage, *Tomorrow Capitalism* (Peru, Ill.: Open Court, 1982). The French version, *Demain le capitalisme,* was first published in 1978.

majority rule. Every decision rule has its consequences on the outcome of the game of political issues. An imperfect market solution, along with its social consequences, does not enjoy stronger support in rational choice theory than an imperfect state and its social consequences.[77]

But even if two sets of values confront each other in the debate on majority rule versus the rights method, it is also possible to argue in utilitarian terms for your view. We have seen examples of this in the economic planning debate of the "harvest time" period. The Social Democrats believed, in principle, that a majority was qualified to intervene in the private business sector by means of regulation, but there might be practical reasons why it was unsuitable to attempt to do so. The effect might be a political or economic crisis that was worse than the status quo. In our analytical language, rational calculation meant making choices in order to end up in the upper left-hand instead of the lower right-hand quadrant. In rational choice theory, similar game theory arguments have been advanced as reasons for a minority – whether it prefers the rights method or not – to choose the alternative that results in the least bad outcome in the upper left-hand corner by abstaining from obstructing decisions pushed through by a majority. The issue in principle is whether minorities should obey any laws or other collective decisions that a majority forces through. There are undoubtedly instances in which obstruction is the most effective method of imposing one's will. But in trying to win by obstruction, it is easy to end up in the "prisoners' dilemma," writes one author in a famous essay in which he apparently assumes a game matrix of the kind we designed for the economic planning game (Table 6.1): It is in my interest that there be government by majority rule; it is also in my interest that decisions can be implemented at the lowest possible costs through voluntary observance of law; but it is not in my interest to obey in a particular case. I want social peace but am perhaps not prepared to make my contribution to maintain it. But if everyone reasons this way, the system ends up in crisis. What occurs is worse than it would have been possible to achieve through voluntary acceptance of a majority decision.[78]

Finally, let us tie together the threads of this section. We have stated

[77] Douglas Rae, "Decision Rules and Individual Values in Constitutional Choice," *The American Political Science Review* (1969): 40–56; Rae, "The Limits of Consensual Decision," ibid. (1975): 1270–1294. Cf. Chapter 5 where I point out that Rae's argument, as I interpret it here as against the rights method, is also aimed against the rule of unanimity. Cf. also the editorial in *Ekonomisk debatt* (1979): 506–507, in which Staffan Viotti, citing the American economist Demsetz, rejects the so-called Nirvana approach, by which he means making a misleading comparison between a particular system as it actually works and another as it ideally works.

[78] Brian Barry, "Is Democracy Special?" in *Rational Man and Irrational Society? An Introduction and Sourcebook*, ed. Brian Barry and Russel Hardin (Beverly Hills, Calif.: Sage, 1982), pp. 325–340.

that the rights method and majority rule are two separate themes in the democratic ideological tradition, which, in Swedish politics, have been pursued primarily by the nonsocialists and business community and by the Social Democrats, respectively. A second conclusion is that the conflict of views on whether a majority is qualified to make decisions admittedly encompasses many different rights, but that at its core is the attitude toward the right of private ownership. According to bourgeois liberal philosophy, a free-market economy based on the right of private ownership is the only sure guarantee of intellectual freedom as well.

The Swedish debate on the rights method has thus not taken place in a social and economic vacuum. Various groups have cited those decision rules that have tended to further their own interests, disguised as the public good. Nonsocialists believed that not only the fundamental principles of Swedish law but also the growth of prosperity was threatened by Social Democratic tax policy. But from the Social Democratic perspective, not only the principle of unlimited popular sovereignty but also an ambition to improve production conditions in the business sector justified state intervention in Swedish business. Unlike proportional representation, the rights method is thus not a decision rule that can be used by any party at all when this suits that party's position or strength. The rights method, at least in twentieth-century Swedish politics, belongs in a particular political camp. We previously stated that in the economic planning dispute there is a correlation between the actors' ideological view and strategic action; this correlation can be extended to include the actors' opinion of the decision rule. The nonsocialists defended the market economy by denying that the majority was qualified to intervene in the business sector, while citing the rights method. The Social Democrats wanted to introduce economic planning with the aid of majority rule, because they did not accept the nonsocialist notion that the qualifications of the majority should be limited in this way. Two consistent philosophies confronted each other during the economic planning debate. A disaster was imminent but was avoided because an assurance game was established. But this outcome does not mean that either side yielded in principle to the other on the issue of which decision rule was the right one.

7

The supplementary pension system

1. SAFETY NET OR "STRONG SOCIETY"?

Cooperation between socialists and nonsocialists continued. The Social Democrats exhibited a probusiness attitude. "The governing party's nationalization plans have been stowed away for a while," one nonsocialist newspaper wrote after the 1948 election. Now the thing to do was to get rid of lingering wartime economic regulation.[1] This wish was also fulfilled: During the 1950s one set of regulations after the other was abolished. The Swedish economy underwent a liberalization. A new forum was found for the continuing dialogue with business that the Social Democrats had initiated during their efforts to create a consensus on economic policy: The Thursday Club shut down and was replaced by occasional conferences at the Harpsund estate, which an industrialist had bequeathed to Sweden's prime minister as an official country residence. In this peaceful setting, the government could clear up problems and misunderstandings about economic policy. "The spirit of Harpsund" became a symbol of smooth cooperation between the state, represented by the Social Democratic government, and the business community.[2] "The recurring discussions at Harpsund between the government and representatives of the business sector and working life are one of several signs that a new spirit of cooperation is being created," wrote Stockholms-Tidningen, now a Social Democratic newspaper. "Wise people both within enterprise and the labor movement are working to gain a more comprehensive perspective on economic policy issues. They are trying to get rid of their political party blinders."[3] The Social Democratic journal Tiden published an extremely positive editorial comment on the development of this Harp-

---

[1] Dagens Nyheter, 25 Nov. 1948.
[2] Leif Lewin, Planhushållningsdebatten (Stockholm: Almqvist & Wiksell, 1967), pp. 348–366 and 383–384; Nils Elvander, Intresseorganisationerna i dagens Sverige, 2d rev. ed. (Lund: Gleerup, 1969), pp. 201ff. The book was first published in 1966.
[3] Stockholms-Tidningen, 23 Nov. 1958.

sund spirit. The magazine criticized the previous attitude of the la\
movement toward private enterprise as overly prejudiced and said nothin\
was more desirable than trying to "tear down the barriers that still giv\
an unnecessarily negative accent to the connections between the labor\
movement and the business community."[4] A series of articles in the Social
Democratic newspaper *Arbetet* criticized previous confrontational attitudes on economic policy, while describing the Harpsund spirit as "an
essential point of light in this ideological darkness."[5]

The business community evinced a corresponding willingness to cooperate. At the initiative of some younger company executives associated
with SNS – the organizational successor (as noted in Chapter 6) of the
PHM movement, which had mobilized opposition to economic planning
during the 1940s – a debate on "the ideology of the business sector" began.
Business people had to accept a new dividing line between state and business sector, banker Tore Browaldh maintained. It was vain to dream about
turning the clock back to the interwar economic system, not to mention
the period before World War I. It was no longer possible for business
people unilaterally to advocate an old-fashioned liberal concept of freedom, argued industrial leader Axel Iveroth. It was necessary to develop a
"broader concept of freedom." Defending rigid old positions only resulted
in misunderstandings between the Social Democrats and the representatives of the business community. We have to avoid the error of "seeing
around us what we wish or fear, instead of what is there and is happening," Browaldh continued. "Our information is filtered through a capri-
cious layer of censorship which often distorts reality. . . . Just as the shape
of the vessel, not the nature of the liquid, determines the shape of the
liquid, we adapt the information we receive on the basis of our thinking
and not vice versa."[6] They could not more clearly have stated their view
that improved knowledge of an opponent's preferences is a prerequisite
for wiser decisions; they could not more clearly have indicated their desire
to take the other side's preference into account – in short, they could not
have expressed more clearly their belief in the necessity of achieving collective rationality by means of an assurance game.

The Harpsund spirit – or "Harpsund democracy," as some people even
put it – nevertheless posed a problem, because the opposition parties were

[4] "Relationer i välfärdsstaten," *Tiden* (1958): 385ff.
[5] Paul Lindblom, "Den glömda planeringsdebatten," *Arbetet*, 18 Sep. 1958. The two subsequent articles were called "Planering med förhinder" and "Planering för bostadsbyggan-
det" and were published on 24 and 28 Sep. respectively.
[6] Tore Browaldh, "Företagen i en förändrad värld," in *Näringsliv och Samhälle I* (Stockholm: Studieförbundet Näringsliv och Samhälle, 1953), pp. 7–27; Axel Iveroth, "Företaget
och samhället" and "Ett företag värt att leva i," in *Näringsliv och Samhälle* II (Stockholm:
Studieförbundet Näringsliv och Samhälle, 1956), pp. 11–38; Tore Browaldh, "Företag, indi-
vid och samhällsutveckling," in *Ideologi för näringslivet?*, ed. Ulrich Herz (Stockholm: Studieförbundet Näringsliv och Samhälle, Studier och debatt, no. 4, 1958), pp. 21–34.

ssions. Was there not a risk that they would be
vernment and the business community reached
ments? Or in the words of one detached observer,
spaper *Arbetaren,* "What will the nonsocialist parties
people show tendencies toward becoming politically self-
decisive? The Liberal, Conservative and Center party will be
or less hanging in the air if business people, large and small
mer, produce their own political action program."[7] The situation
came even worse in 1951 when the Social Democrats formed a coalition
government with the Agrarians, which made it possible for the Social
Democrats to stay in power despite declining voter support. The Liberals
and Conservatives seemed completely outmaneuvered from political
power.

The economic boom also continued, as we have mentioned – as
strongly and steadily as cooperation between the state and the business
community. National income grew every year. The great mass of people
reached a living standard they could never have dreamed of. Aside from
Switzerland, Sweden enjoyed the highest living standard in the world.
Sweden had moved from poverty to prosperity.

Greater prosperity provided new impulses in the debate on political ideology. The parties asked themselves how the new wealth should be used
and distributed. What were the tasks of government in a country where
poverty had virtually been abolished? Faithful to their liberal market-oriented philosophy, the nonsocialists believed that the state should continue
to guarantee a "safety net" for people, but that beyond that, the individual
should benefit directly from the new wealth by being able to choose what
to do with his savings. The Social Democrats, on the other hand, believed
that the state had to continue expanding even in a rich country, because
only a "strong society" could satisfy the new demands that economic
growth entailed.

These two ideologies – the principles of a safety net and of a strong
society – later confronted each other in the supplementary pension dispute. This controversy dominated Swedish politics during the late 1950s.
The reason was not only disagreement on an important ideological issue.
Because the Liberal and Conservative parties felt that their support among
the electorate was increasing, they hoped to capture political power with
the help of this issue.

The new prosperity of the 1950s in Sweden led to an ideological revitali-
zation within the nonsocialist camp. For twenty years, the nonsocialists

---

[7] *Dagstidningen Arbetaren,* 5 Dec. 1957.

had more or less been on the retreat as the Social Democrats built up the Swedish welfare state. They had either participated in this reform task or had failed in their opposition to it. They had made more and more concessions, allowing the role of the state in the economy to grow in order to protect the weaker members of society. But now poverty was being abolished. This opened new opportunities to the market-oriented ideology. Liberal party chairman Bertil Ohlin found it "high time for us here in Sweden to begin a new chapter after the one primarily concerning social insurance has been largely completed in a year or so." What would be new was that people would no longer be so dependent on the state. "When everyone's income rises and society has created a safety net, it is up to people themselves to take additional steps – through insurance, savings or the like – to supplement it in a way they themselves find suitable. With rising living standards, the need for subsidies from society will also be less."[8]

One cornerstone of nonsocialist philosophy was to encourage personal savings. The individual himself should save money to finance supplementary forms of economic security and not shift these costs onto future generations. And now as earlier, individual capital formation – as opposed to state compulsion – was the best guarantee of higher prosperity and continued freedom. But the Social Democrats seemed to want to continue increasing the state's share of the economy, even when people's fundamental needs were satisfied. According to Ohlin, this is where two ideologies confronted each other: "one more socialistic and one liberal. The first of these looks on with equanimity as savers are badly treated and society weakens the incentives to save. Society solves a number of economic security problems but is also forced to take care of capital formation, due to excessive taxation. The other, more liberal approach would like to give society the task of arranging a safety net in those areas where experience shows that too many people will otherwise not be protected. But we would like to organize matters in such a way that the individual's own feeling of responsibility is mobilized when it comes to improving his economic security as well as solving his housing problems. This means making it worthwhile and attractive to save. This also means preserving the individual's primary responsibility for supporting himself and his family. Big Brother should not take care of everything for him and treat him like a legally incompetent person. . . . Given a rising national income in the future, a growing proportion of this income flows in to society if tax tables and taxation policy are unchanged. This means that the same percentage of the national income can flow into the state treasury as before,

[8] AK 1957:2, p. 21.

even if we gradually lower the tax burden on the citizenry. There has to be an end to the policy of continuously increasing the state's share of the national income."[9]

The Social Democrats had been forced to give up their plans for a major expansion in public ownership, Ohlin continued. It had also reluctantly been forced to abolish the other kind of state control – economic regulation. "But now they are pushing ahead on the third path – the path of tax socialism. With the help of taxation, the state is taking control of a larger and larger proportion of people's income. . . . The thrust of our efforts should thus be to stop the growth in the state's share of the national income and then reduce this relative share so that people will gain a greater opportunity to determine for themselves how they want to arrange their lives. . . . As the safety net – arranged by society – is put in place, the rest can and should be arranged by the individual himself using part of the resources that the continued increase in income places at his disposal."[10]

"How soon will we be well-off?" asked Ohlin in a 1955 article. Within twenty-five years, he believed, the living standard would be doubled. "This is a real revolution in our material living conditions. An end to poverty and need – because a certain level of prosperity is within the reach of everyone. How unimaginative and out of touch with reality socialist theorists seem, trudging along in their nineteenth century rut and chewing on the outdated socialistic doctrines of that age like children who refuse to give up their candy. We are in a new age, where the forces of progress which have carried us this far – and which have nothing to do with socialism – promise to make this development move even faster. On one condition: that we do not block the wheels of progress by unsuitable and unnecessary nationalization, burdensome regulation and taxes that discourage savings."[11]

Indeed, rising prosperity seemed to be linked with the successes of the nonsocialist economic philosophy. After the Social Democrats lost ground in the 1956 election, Ohlin wrote a triumphant article in the magazine *Vecko-Journalen* in which he declared that socialism had now missed its last chance. Due to better technology, greater human skills, and the growth of private capital formation, the poverty that once gave rise to the socialist struggle was being abolished. The Social Democrats thus had to speed up their socialistic transformation before prosperity became widespread and people thereby lost their desire for revolutions and embraced nonsocialist values. Everywhere in Western Europe during the 1950s,

[9] AK 1956:2, pp. 4–5.
[10] Ibid., pp. 13–14.
[11] Bertil Ohlin, "Hur fort blir vi välsituerade?" *Stockholms-Tidningen*, 28 Dec. 1955.

however, socialism seemed to be arriving "too late." Only in poverty-stricken Africa and Asia did socialism still have a chance, in the same way as socialism had arrived "in time" to be implemented in poverty-stricken Russia. "The real enemy of socialism" – this was Ohlin's main point – "is a high and rising standard of living with secure employment in a society with intellectual and economic freedom."[12]

Ohlin's reasoning was highly typical of his party. Liberal members' bills called for more favorable conditions for personal saving, so that all citizens could participate in Sweden's capital formation process. The rapid increase in the national wealth should become everyone's personal property, and the relative role of the state in the economy should be reduced. New social issues also justified a review of the Liberal party program, and a committee was appointed to revitalize the ideological debate on the opportunities open to the market-oriented ideology in a prosperous society.[13]

The Liberal press was heartened by what it perceived as an apparent correlation between the growth of national wealth and the success of non-socialist political philosophy. Just as liberalism had suffered setbacks around World War I because its program had been implemented and nothing seemed to be left to work toward, the Social Democrats were now experiencing the same setbacks. Prosperity led to new problems for which the Social Democrats were not ideologically prepared. "Before the gates of prosperity" – to quote a program brochure published by the Liberal party board – liberalism was now emerging victorious in election after election.[14]

The same soothing message was being dispensed by the Conservative party, which for the first time in decades was enlarging its share of the electorate. The opportunity for people in a newly prosperous Sweden to have a greater personal say in how to spend their income was expressed by the Conservative party in its vision of the property-owning democracy or "ownership democracy." Their main point was that the increase in national income made it possible for everyone to become a capital owner. Beyond the "basic security" guaranteed by the state – the Conservatives used this term as the equivalent of the Liberal phrase "safety net" – people should be responsible for their own living standard by saving money. The outdated social welfare policy of the age of poverty, with the state dispensing alms to the needy, would give way to a democracy in which ownership was spread among all categories of people. Through ownership, an inde-

---

[12] Ohlin, "Socialismens sista chans," *Vecko-Journalen* no. 39 (1956): 17.
[13] Lewin 1967, pp. 400–401.
[14] *Stockholms-Tidningen*, 27 Apr. 1954; cf. ibid. 17 July 1952; *Upsala Nya Tidning*, 11 Sep. 1952; Per Olof Hanson, "Liberalism contra socialism," *Karlstads-Tidningen*, 25 Mar. 1955; *Världen och vi på 60-talet. Liberala perspektiv* (Stockholm, 1959).

pendent, responsible, and egalitarian lifestyle among people was developing. The latter was essential; saving and capital formation should spread to all people. Tax exemption on savings should thus apply only to a small sum. The Conservative party's concept of saving for specific goals was intended especially for the broad masses. The Conservatives gave examples of the things that people should save for: a house, a summer cottage, a motorboat, a small business, and – above all – stocks. By owning shares of stock in Swedish companies, people were taking part in the country's capital formation. Owning stocks was the fastest way of becoming a "capitalist."[15]

Like the Liberal party, the Conservatives drew a firm line between the basic protection that the state provided each individual and the supplementary insurance policies and pension plans he himself should be responsible for. "At the bottom there should be a basic pension in the form of a national old-age pension that has been improved to the point where it can really be said to cover the cost of the most unavoidable human needs. People's opportunities to build additional security for their old age on top of this, and their willingness to do so, should be strengthened and encouraged. This may be done through collective agreements, individual job contracts or voluntary insurance policies or pension plans in traditional or new forms."[16] Freedom of choice – the absence of a compulsory supplementary pension system – was the most essential point. In a free country, the Conservatives considered it self-evident "that society organizes a system of basic mutual protection for its citizens but leaves it to them to build up their own supplementary protection in free cooperation or individually on the basis of the needs and wishes of the individual."[17]

The most important task of the Conservative party was to prevent the Social Democrats from carrying out their plans to expand the state even in the new prosperous society, where social welfare needs had now been satisfied. "We want to shrink the right of the national and local governments to dispose of people's earnings in order to expand their own domain. . . . The Conservative party is a tax-cutting party. It sees in rising production and income an opportunity to reduce the public sector's share of this income, but also sees a gradual easing of taxation as a prerequisite for the most rapid possible rise in production and income." The issue of supplementary protection must not become a way for the Social Democrats to make further increases in the power of the state over individuals. "Saying yes to an improved national old-age pension and an additional opportunity to arrange supplementary security for old age based on people's varying needs and situations is saying no to a compulsory pension

[15] Lewin 1967, pp. 389ff.
[16] Mot AK 1956:595, p. 5 (Hjalmarson et al.).
[17] Mot AK 1958 A:417, p. 5 (Hjalmarson et al.).

system with its rigid norms for payments and fees. It is a rejection of the concept of moving billions of kronor from working life and production to the disposal of the state, under the guise of a pension system."[18]

As was the case with the Liberal party, this declaration by the Conservative party chairman Jarl Hjalrson expressed the party's main policy as it appeared in its parliamentary members' bills as well as in party and press debates.[19] And as in the case of the Liberal party, the new economic situation triggered a revision of the Conservative party program. The party now carried out the change in its program that it had approved but not implemented at the end of the war. The new program was characterized by the concept of a property-owning democracy and the importance of personal savings and a market economy in ensuring a continued increase in prosperity.[20]

The Agrarian party, which changed its name to the Center party around this time, shared the view of the Liberals and Conservatives that the new prosperity would make it possible to cut back the public sector. The Center party, too, revised its program and asked, like its nonsocialist colleagues, what kind of social organization would best guarantee that the more rapid increase in prosperity would also result in greater personal freedom and not lead to oppression of the individual by large-scale industrialism or socialism. And the answer was a society with many small owners.[21] Center party chairman Gunnar Hedlund spoke of the potential for broader distribution of the kind of individual capital formation that was made possible by the new national wealth, in precisely the same terms as the other nonsocialist party leaders. If we regard the right of private ownership as the foundation of enterprise, "then it also seems vital that the right of ownership and economic influence should belong to as many individuals as possible. This automatically happens as more and more people can afford to acquire possessions." A small private business was one way of satisfying these wishes. Personal initiative and drive often had their best chance to develop in such a business.[22] Living standards were rising rapidly in Sweden during the 1950s. But taxes were rising even faster, and this trend now had to be stopped so that individuals could personally keep more of the growth in national wealth.[23] The Center party, too, submitted members' bills calling for measures that would promote savings and facilitate capital formation under private, not state auspices.[24]

[18] AK 1956:2, pp. 19–20 (Hjalmarson).
[19] Lewin 1967, p. 393.
[20] Lewin 1967, p. 395.
[21] Ibid., p. 402.
[22] AK 1958 A:2, p. 25; cf. AK 1958 B:2, pp. 23–24.
[23] AK 1959:2, pp. 57ff. (Hedlund).
[24] Lewin 1967, p. 403.

"Citizens should be guaranteed basic security by means of social welfare policy," according to one Center party bill. "After this basic security has been arranged through an improved national old-age pension, in our opinion the public sector should not prescribe that an individual should have a supplementary pension plan on top of this. Every citizen should have the personal freedom to decide for himself how he wishes to improve his economic security beyond his national basic pension."[25]

The new prosperity in Sweden opened new social welfare policy perspectives, another Center party member declared. In a society with high living standards, social welfare policy could be restricted to certain primary tasks: "basic security at the beginning of life," "basic security in case of unprovoked loss of income," and "basic security in old age. . . . Beyond these primary tasks, we must be very cautious when it comes to continuing along the path of reforms based on comprehensive subsidies. Nor should the state intervene in the economic affairs of individuals through coercive measures of the kind represented by a supplementary pension system."[26]

On the main ideological issue of the role of government in a newly prosperous Sweden, there was thus a striking degree of agreement in the views advanced by representatives of the Liberal, Conservative, and Center parties. The state had an obligation to give people basic protection in case of illness, accident, and unemployment and in old age. But beyond this basic security, people should have freedom of choice in deciding how to spend their growing income. As wealth increased, the need for protective social welfare measures diminished. As prosperity rose, the state's share of the national income ought to decrease. The good times were perceived as bourgeois liberalism's big chance to bring about a reduction in the role of the state in the economy. This was the essence of the ideological message presented by Sweden's nonsocialist parties during the economic boom of the 1950s.

In their practical political actions, however, the nonsocialist parties have behaved directly contrary to this doctrine. During every decade since the 1920s, they have not only accepted an expansion of the public sector at the expense of the private sector, but have also actively participated in this process through various reform proposals. As the national income has risen, in practice they have worked toward an increase in the public sector's share of it, not a decrease. New men with increasingly ambitious social welfare policy views have assumed the leadership of the nonsocialist parties; we saw an example of this when the younger generation of postwar nonsocialist politicians accepted the government's full-employment

[25] Mot AK 1958 A:421, pp. 4–5 (Hedlund et al.).
[26] AK 1959:16, p. 121 (Antonsson).

policy, which their parties had opposed only ten to fifteen years before. And this gradual shift in the preferences of the nonsocialist parties did not, by any means, come to a halt in the mid-1950s, when they envisioned a future in which prosperity would reduce the public sector's share of the national income. During the decades since then, this shift in preferences has instead accelerated. Today the nonsocialist parties approve of a far larger public sector than they did in the 1950s.

An examination of this contradiction between ideology and action might lead us to pay no heed whatever to the safety net doctrine, but to regard it only as an example of the kind of glittering rhetoric that lives its own life, out of touch with everyday political realities. A more sympathetic interpretation would say that the contradiction is due to the fact that nonsocialist politicians have gradually expanded the concept of the safety net and that over the years they have come to classify more and more human needs as belonging to the sphere in which the state should be responsible. But if the concept thus expands all the time, if the net keeps rising and rising along with national income, we might ask whether the nonsocialist ideology of a reduced public sector – even in relation to the situation in the 1950s – is ultimately self-canceling. The liberal principle ends up coinciding with the Social Democratic one. The safety net concept turns into its opposite – the principle of the strong society.

The doctrine that a strong society is needed to satisfy the new demands that greater prosperity brings with it has dominated Social Democratic theory since the 1960s. But the origins of this doctrine can be found in the ideological debate of the 1950s, when improving incomes also caused the Social Democrats to reappraise their ideological principles.[27]

The halt in the "harvest-time" offensive and the retreat on the industrial rationalization issue in connection with the 1948 election, followed by the erosion of voter support in the 1952 and 1956 elections, led to despair in the Social Democratic camp. The ideological situation in the party was far from satisfactory, many critical Social Democrats believed. The Social Democratic party had lost its hold on developments. Sweden was a prosperous country and had overcome the poverty and discontent that had once created the political branch of the labor movement. There was a widespread sense of well-being, and a growing number of voters were beginning to sympathize with the nonsocialist parties, which traditionally

---

[27] Cf. *Tage Erlanders memoarer 1955–1960* (Stockholm: Tiden, 1976), p. 258: "Palme and I were in the process of discussing our way to the ideology of the strong society. The idea, of course, was to create a society so strong that it could be an effective protection to its citizens. It was entirely in line with this ideology to let employees participate in creating large publicly administered funds." This quotation is taken from Erlander's summary of the pension dispute.

represented people who were relatively well-off. The Swedish people were becoming more and more bourgeois. In this situation, new guidelines for a socialist policy were needed. The Social Democratic postwar policy had long since had its day. But the government seemed to want to restrict itself to merely administering Sweden's growing prosperity, not intervening in order to demonstrate the capitalist production system. Instead of a socialist transformation of society, the government was devoting all of its energy to bringing about a political consensus on economic stabilization policy. The Social Democrats had become the "contented party," betraying their socialist ideology by governing in a coalition with the Agrarians. Because of a new kind of determinism, which assumed that socialism was automatically being implemented as a result of the annual increase in prosperity, the party had slid into the same paralysis as during the 1920s. The Social Democrats had had to pay too high a price for Harpsund democracy and cooperation with the business sector. Modern capitalism was not a greedy beast but a very suave and cooperative little bastard who could offer his coalition partner great material benefits but demanded "his soul in exchange." The Social Democrats now had to formulate a new goal for national development, a goal beyond the welfare state. Such a daring goal would pose a challenge to an electorate with increasingly bourgeois attitudes and would perhaps result in additional parliamentary setbacks, one Social Democratic debater admitted. But it would be more honorable for Social Democratic government policy to die with its boots on than to fade away from natural causes.[28]

As it turned out, a famous speech during Parliament's 1956 general policy debate by the party chairman himself, Prime Minister Tage Erlander, defined the new role of the Social Democrats in a society that had achieved economic prosperity. Its central line of thought also appeared in a small pamphlet entitled *The Policy of Progress* (Framstegens politik), which the party executive board found reason to present to the party congress.[29] Erlander said that the nonsocialists were correct in claiming that the rapid rise in income had fundamentally changed the prerequisites for political reform work – not least for the Social Democratic party, whose entire operation was based on people's discontent with the poverty and deprivation of the old society. Yet it was an exaggeration to say that the causes of this discontent had completely disappeared. There was still reason to feel some discontent. This applied to young people who could not obtain

---

[28] Torsten and Turid Eliasson, "Det belåtna partiet?" *Tiden* (1957):165ff.; "Åderförkalkad eller bara trött?" *Libertas* no. 4 (1955):3–4; "Socialdemokrati, storfinans och ödestro," *Libertas* no. 3–4 (1954):3–4; *Folket*, 29 Nov. 1954; *Arbetet*, 3 Apr. 1955; *Aftontidningen*, 14 Oct. 1952; *Nyheterna*, 5 Oct. 1956; Jörn Svensson, "Planering för vad?" *Arbetet*, 8 Oct. 1958; Nils Evander, "Sotdöden eller ättestupa för socialdemokratin?" *Arbetarbladet*, 30 Oct. 1956.

[29] Lewin 1967, p. 407.

the housing they wanted and handicapped people whose economic security problems had not been resolved. Fortunately, this discontent only applied to limited groups of the population, and it should thus have proved possible to bring people together to solve these problems. But a new kind of discontent had replaced the old. "There is . . . a discontent that is of an entirely different type not at all reminiscent of the discontent that once led to the emergence of the (labor movement). . . . This is a discontent that I would like to characterize as the discontent of great expectations. Full employment and a social welfare safety net and a standard of living that has climbed rapidly from one year to the next have created a new confidence about the future among us all, but they have also created a rising impatience that things don't move faster than they do. When you are accustomed – as we are in the full-employment society – to having a decent income not only today, not only next week and next month, but also envision it before you from year to year, you target your demands toward things that involve longer commitments both for the individual and for society." In the new welfare economy, the state's economic commitments must increase in order to meet rising demands for roads, medical care, housing, and education.

For this reason, Erlander considered it totally unreasonable to say, as did the Conservatives, that "25 percent of the Swedish people's income, neither more nor less, should go toward public expenditures. . . . Full employment increases the pace of progress, but it also means a rise in demands and expectations. Both individuals and society then need to weigh alternatives against each other, manage their resources and economize. We cannot satisfy all wishes. There will be plenty of discontent, but it is a discontent of another type than previously. It is, as I have already said, a discontent of numerous expectations, and in fact it is not something we should be sorry about." On the contrary, to a socialist it has to be gratifying that people have raised their expectations in this way. "People's demands and dissatisfaction with things as they are, their impatience about the future, have always been a powerful driving force in the process of social change." All the nonsocialist talk about how an expanded public sector threatened freedom seemed to Erlander totally out of touch with reality.[30]

The Social Democrats thus drew a conclusion about rising prosperity that was diametrically opposed to that of the nonsocialists – that widespread economic security and prosperity did not make state intervention less important at all. On the contrary, in the new welfare economy people's expectations were of such a nature and on such a scale that only the state could satisfy them. The nonsocialists made the mistake of not view-

[30] FK 1956:2, pp. 23ff.

ing social change in a dynamic perspective, the Social Democrats believed. The nonsocialists' thinking was stuck in the insecurity of the liberal economy, and they could thus not imagine anything more important for the individual than to acquire capital and thereby protect himself from temporary loss of income from gainful employment. But in the Sweden of the 1950s, there was economic security and full employment. Consequently, people's wishes came to encompass an entirely different type of issue. People were no longer discontented about poverty and unemployment, but about such things as insufficient opportunities to obtain higher education, larger apartments, and better medical care for the mass of people. To satisfy these wishes, the state had to be given a new and more ambitious role.

As we have mentioned, the first application of this new ideological principle was the Social Democratic proposal for a compulsory supplementary pension system. The Social Democrats could not accept the nonsocialist view that the tasks of the state should be restricted to ensuring people an economic safety net. It was, in itself, gratifying that everyone agreed "that the elderly should receive decent basic protection, that we all agree that we and society will shoulder the not insignificant economic burdens that the national basic pension reform entails. . . . It is strange, however, that it should not have been possible to reach unity on going a bit further" and letting the state also be responsible for supplementary protection. If this protection was to be sufficiently effective, covering all citizens and also enabling them to change jobs between various areas in which separate pension plan agreements might have been reached, it was necessary for the state to guarantee the supplementary pension. People were no longer content to have a guaranteed economic safety net. "Why? Because in a full-employment society, we need protection that enables us also to maintain the standard of living we have achieved." A government guarantee of standard-of-living maintenance should be the new social welfare policy. Wealthy Sweden could afford this step. Replying to nonsocialist concern that future generations could not afford to pay heavy fees to the compulsory supplementary pension fund, the prime minister assured them that there would be room in the economy "to implement both the basic national pension and a pension plan that supplemented the rest of the social insurance system according to modern principles."[31]

The fact that the supplementary pension would be compulsory by no means implied any restriction on people's freedom. Now, as earlier, the Social Democrats believed that freedom could be realized *through* the state. As the Social Democrats saw it, the liberal concept of freedom was once again playing tricks on the nonsocialists: They had always believed

---

[31] AK 1958 A:17, p. 44 (Erlander).

that an expansion of the state entailed a loss of freedom, when in fact only the state could liberate people from the discontent they felt because their new expectations could not be satisfied fast enough. An expansion of the state, we could say using rational choice terminology, entailed a Pareto-style optimal solution that increased everyone's satisfaction. It was no longer possible to cling to the way of thinking that had prevailed in the interwar period, in the words of Erlander's close associate and later successor, Olof Palme, who played an important part in formulating the principle of the strong society. In those days, people lived with unemployment and mass poverty. "Today's young people are growing up in a society with full employment, a rising standard of living and substantial socioeconomic security. They consider this something completely natural. This gives them much greater freedom than earlier generations enjoyed – freedom to choose how they will shape their lives. . . . Paradoxically, [young people] use their greater freedom to make heavier commitments for the future and for long-term expenditures. Young people, too, commit themselves to housing costs, training courses, starting a family, buying a car and many other consumer durables that people often buy on installments and pay off. A sudden drop in income means something of a disaster for such a person. That person views this as real poverty, even if his family – or he or she – can actually afford their daily bread. Creating a sturdy safety net sounds good, but a safety net that will mean 300 kronor a month when the system is completed is not much to live on in a city like this. Our entire modern social welfare policy has thus aimed at guaranteeing, on top of the safety net, a reasonable maintenance of living standard in order to avoid this kind of sudden drop in income. Providing a safety net, a minimum standard, was the problem of the 1930s. Maintaining our living standard is the goal of the 1950s." The Conservatives "missed the boat" in the 1930s, Palme continued. They had now discovered this. But "with all their talk of safety nets," the nonsocialists were getting out of step with developments for a second time. They did not realize that the state had an obligation also to guarantee people a normal economic level and the maintenance of a high living standard, even in old age.[32]

The Social Democrats used the ideology of the strong society to legitimize the continued expansion of the government even in a prosperous welfare economy. People's new expectations regarding better roads, hospitals, and educational institutions and maintenance of a high living standard in old age required a larger, not a smaller role for the state. If people bought more cars, the road network had to be expanded. In the affluent society – to use the term employed by John Kenneth Galbraith, who came to occupy a position among Swedish Social Democrats during the 1960s

[32] FK 1958 A:17, p. 163.

similar to that of Keynes in the 1930s – "society" had to intervene to supplement existing amenities in proportion to individual demand. A critical reader wonders, however, what is meant in this context by "society." The Social Democrats answered the question by blurring together different concepts or playing a word game: They systematically confused "society" with "the state." By using the former term to mean the latter, they tried to engender a positive attitude toward the state among their listeners and readers, by pretending that collective solutions always had to mean state solutions. Remarkably enough, the nonsocialist parties also used this terminology, as the previously quoted comments from their leaders indicate. In this respect, the nonsocialists appear to have been completely tamed by the power of Social Democratic verbiage over thought.[33] But roads, hospitals, and education can be financed by user fees; they do not have to be paid for by tax money. The new expectations of people in a welfare economy can be satisfied by means of joint but voluntary arrangements without expanding the state. This applies, not least, to the design of a supplementary pension system. The entire insurance system can said to be based on the concept of voluntary association instead of state coercion. It also soon became clear that collective solutions are conceivable without state involvement, when the nonsocialist opposition presented its alternative on the supplementary pension issue.

2. APPEALING DIRECTLY TO THE PEOPLE

Bertil Ohlin, the Liberal party chairman, had mixed feelings about the political scene in which the supplementary pension issue was now unfolding. As hopeful in the long term as the development of a welfare economy may have seemed to the head of a nonsocialist party, the day-to-day political situation seemed all the more frustrating. For despite the fact that more and more voters were abandoning the Social Democrats, that party managed to cling to power. The built-in time lag in the bicameral system was part of the reason: The First Chamber, with its longer terms of office, was renewed in stages by an indirect election system, with local political bodies casting the votes. This practice perpetuated the majority the Social Democrats had enjoyed at their peak. Their successful coalition strategies were another reason: By sharing power with the Agrarian party, despite election setbacks the Social Democrats could count on a parliamentary majority for their proposals. Through their discussions with the business community at Harpsund, the government was ensured of support for the main lines of its economic policy among organizations that otherwise, for

[33] The quotations appearing earlier in this section are taken from AK 1956:2, pp. 4–5 and AK 1957:2, p. 21 (Ohlin); mot AK 1958 A:417, p. 5 (Hjalmarson et al.) and mot AK 1958 A:421, pp. 4–5 (Hedlund et al.).

ideological reasons, would have cooperated with the nonsocialists. And on the supplementary pension issue, the Social Democrats were now not hesitating to take advantage of their position, which they could only maintain through strategic manipulation, to strengthen further the role of the state in the economy and in relation to the individual.

If it merely waited for a government bill and a parliamentary vote, the nonsocialist opposition could already register a defeat. But as so many times before, the potential loser did not wish to accept such a passive role. The strategy the opposition now devised was based on detaching the supplementary pension issue from the agenda of the chambers and submitting it directly to the voters for their consideration. In 1954, after nonsocialist pressure, Parliament had given its first round of approval to a constitutional amendment entitling a minority to call an advisory referendum. After the various party proposals on a supplementary pension system had been worked out, the Liberals and Conservatives asked that the issue be subjected to a referendum in keeping with the pending constitutional amendment. This strategy offered many advantages. First, they hoped that in this way they could win on the issue itself; during the 1950s those who wanted to expand the state's coercive powers over the people were losing support among the Swedish electorate. Second, a referendum campaign would relentlessly expose the ideological split that existed within the governing coalition: Like the Liberals and Conservatives, the Agrarian party supported the principle of the safety net, whereas the Social Democrats supported their own concept of the strong society. The coalition could not reasonably survive after a divisive referendum. The government would be forced out of office and a nonsocialist government would get a chance to assume power. One fortunate circumstance in this context was that the Agrarians had previously supported the call for an expansion of the referendum system. The party could not now decently abandon this view. In other words, the referendum strategy was not only a means of getting one's way on an important ideological issue. It was part of a larger plan by the nonsocialist opposition to maneuver itself out of the powerless position in which Harpsund democracy and the red–green coalition had left it. With ill-concealed delight, the Liberals and Conservatives awaited the government's reaction to the referendum demand.

The prime minister tried to dodge the demands for a referendum. During the parliamentary debate, he replied that the supplementary pension issue was particularly unsuitable for a referendum because of its technically complex nature.[34] Public opinion itself must have seemed even more unsuitable to Erlander, however. An opinion poll commissioned by the Social Democratic party confirmed its worst fears; in March 1957 a larger

[34] AK 1957:2, pp. 32–33.

percentage of Swedes were favorably disposed toward the Liberal and Conservative party line on the supplementary pension issue than toward the Social Democratic line, even among the Social Democrats' own sympathizers.[35] Or as one researcher summarized the difficulties of the Social Democrats during this period: "The Social Democratic adversity ultimately lay in the fact that few voters, even among their own active members, shared the party leadership's view on the expansion of the public sector and the resulting consequences for taxes, capital formation, supplementary pension systems etc."[36]

But finally the Social Democrats could not resist this pressure on the referendum issue. They went along with the Liberal and Conservative parties,[37] even though both Erlander and Hedlund realized the risks this posed to their government coalition, which both of them wished to continue, although Hedlund was then heading a party that was increasingly split on its support for the coalition government.[38] The Liberals and Conservatives now had to take maximum advantage of the nonsocialist trend that was sweeping across a newly prosperous Sweden. The Social Democrats' concession on the referendum issue resembles the business community's reluctant participation in the postwar planning process of the 1940s that was dominated by the Social Democrats: Demands that the people should be allowed to have their say or be given more information are proposals that cannot be rejected without making you look democratically compromised, as if you were defending abuses.

On 26 March 1957, the government thus decided that a referendum on the supplementary pension issue would take place – not, however, in keeping with the pending constitutional amendment, as the nonsocialist opposition wished, but according to existing regulations. The government was thus trying to seize the initiative in the political game. By doing so, the government and a majority of Parliament would be able to formulate all of the alternatives that would be presented to the voters, even that of the nonsocialist opposition. This move was the topic of a particularly tumultuous parliamentary debate. The Liberal and Conservative party chairmen appealed to the government to reconsider its position in a democratic spirit and allow the opposition to formulate its own alternative. But the

[35] Stig Hadenius, "Partiers beslutsprocess och tjänstepensionsfrågan," *Statsvetenskaplig Tidskrift* (1965): 351, n. 16.

[36] Björn von Sydow, *Kan vi lita på politikerna? Offentlig och intern politik i socialdemokratims ledning 1955–1960* (Stockholm: Tiden, 1978), p. 138.

[37] Cf. Erlander's own words: "The members of this chamber know that I was very hesitant about using the referendum system on this issue. I went along with the Conservatives and Liberals after very energetic requests from these parties." AK 1959:16, pp. 94–95.

[38] Von Sydow 1978, pp. 131–139; Gustaf Jonasson, *I väntan på upbrott? Bondeförbundet/ Centerpartiet i regeringskoalitionenas slutskede 1956–1957* (Uppsala: Acta Universitatis Upsaliensis, 1981).

government refused to budge. Immediately after the parliamentary vote, the Liberals and Conservatives recorded in the minutes their protest against what they perceived as the majority's abuse of its power over the minority.

The referendum would concern three alternative proposals. Line 1 was the alternative supported by the Social Democrats, the Swedish Trade Union Confederation (LO), and the Communists and entailed a compulsory supplementary pension system based on fees that were to be paid through one's employer to a large state fund, with indexed pension payments to be linked to a person's fifteen "best years." Line 2 was supported by the Agrarian/Center party and was based on the option of starting a voluntary pension plan based on ordinary actuarial principles. Line 3 was recommended by the Liberals, the Conservatives, the Swedish Employers' Confederation, the Swedish Federation of Crafts and Small Industries, and the Swedish Union of Clerical and Technical Employees in Industry (whose parent confederation, the Central Organization of Salaried Employees, remained neutral). Like Line 2, Line 3 was based on voluntary association, but it emphasized collective bargaining agreements that might be reached by labor and management. The three alternatives each formed a national committee, with LO chairman Arne Geijer as the chief representative of Line 1, the Agrarian party's Professor Sten Wahlund as chairman of Line 2, and the head of the National Social Welfare Board, Ernst Bexelius, as chairman of Line 3.

The referendum was held on 13 October 1957, and the votes were distributed as follows: (the third column gives the breakdown if the blank ballots are excluded)

Line 1	45.8%	47.7%
Line 2	15.0%	15.6%
Line 3	35.3%	36.7%
Blank ballots	3.9%	———

All three sides claimed victory. The sponsors of Line 1 pointed out that they had the largest number of votes; the Line 2 committee compared its results with the Agrarian party's low percentage of the vote in the 1956 Second Chamber election; and the sponsors of Line 3 argued that the two alternatives that recommended a voluntary solution had together received an absolute majority. The difficulties of transforming individual preferences into unambiguous collective decisions have rarely been illustrated so clearly in Swedish political history.

Exactly as the nonsocialist opposition had expected, the referendum resulted in a government crisis. Both the Social Democrats and the Agrarians believed they had received the support of public opinion for their sharply divergent alternatives. The Center party decided to leave the government, whereupon the entire government resigned. The next step in the Liberal and Conservative calculation failed, however. The king admittedly asked Ohlin and Hjalmarson to form a nonsocialist three-party government, but the attempt came to naught because of Center party chairman Gunnar Hedlund's reluctance to switch immediately from one coalition to another. Erlander was asked once again to become Sweden's prime minister, and a pure Social Democratic government took office. The new government immediately began to work out a supplementary pension bill according to the compulsory alternative. It looked as if the Liberal and Conservative parties were about to lose the supplementary pension dispute in spite of everything.

The battle was not yet lost, however, because the Social Democrats could count on a majority only in the First Chamber, not in the Second. The government began negotiations with the three nonsocialist parties on the supplementary pension issue, but their differences were too great to reconcile. The prime minister said he wanted a consensus solution but added that there was no other basis for this than the compulsory pension alternative. The Liberal party chairman replied that all sides had to be willing to compromise if there was to be talk of a consensus solution. The chances of consensus became even smaller when it was learned that, in the midst of the negotiations, the government was continuing to draft its own bill.

Now Ohlin took a surprising step that would greatly reduce the prospects of a nonsocialist victory in the supplementary pension dispute. He proposed accepting the passage of supplementary pension legislation, but said that this legislation should be optional – that is, it should contain a provision entitling individuals or groups to withdraw from the system outlined in the law. The proposal was based on a theoretical concept of the function of referendums in a democracy. The main lines of policy were now tied to the results of the referendum. The task of politicians was to find a solution that best satisfied this outcome. Under these circumstances, it was improper to continue insisting on one's own conviction or that of one's party. It was a question of behaving in such a way that everyone's interests were satisfied. "We in the Liberal party believe that in any event we are obligated to take into account the public opinion that emerged from different quarters during the referendum, not just the opinion that voted for one line or the other."[39] But this move was subjected to strong criticism from all of the other parties – by the Social Democrats because it did not consistently maintain the principle of compulsory pensions and by the other nonsocialist parties because the doctrine of the safety net was weakened by the passage of a supplementary pension law.

[39] AK 1958:17, p. 122.

The supplementary pension system

The optional legislation policy thus turned out to be something as remarkable as a compromise product that was rejected by all sides except for its author. It was supported by the Liberal party only.

When the government bill was introduced and Parliament voted on it, as expected the proposal won approval in the First Chamber but was rejected by the Second Chamber.

In this situation Tage Erlander, who thought he detected a shift of voter opinion to his advantage as a result of the referendum campaign, renewed his attack. He asked for the dissolution of the Second Chamber and a new election. This request was granted. The day was long past when the king could resist such a request from the prime minister, although in some newspapers and magazines with ties to the Liberal and Conservative parties, the thought that the king both could and should have said no to the dissolution actually surfaced.[40] A prime minister had only resorted to dissolution twice before: during the tariff dispute in 1887 and during the Palace Yard crisis of 1914.

The outcome of the extra election of 1958, which was dominated entirely by the supplementary pension issue, illustrated with extreme clarity the division of the Swedish people in two equally large camps, neither one enjoying a majority; the election resulted in an exact balance between nonsocialists and socialists. There were major shifts within the nonsocialist camp. The Liberal party, which had obviously had a hard time making voters understand its compromise-oriented prolegislaiton policy, suffered heavy losses while the Conservatives and the Center party gained ground. The Social Democrats picked up 5 new seats in the Chamber. This meant that the nonsocialists had 115 seats and the socialists 116, but because the Speaker – a Social Democrat – was not entitled to vote, the figures in the upcoming vote on the government's supplementary pension bill would be 115 to 115.

Erlander was now as little inclined as before to compromise and give up the idea of making the system compulsory. The regular local elections in September 1958 continued the trend seen in the extra Second Chamber election; the Liberal party lost even more support, and the other parties picked up seats. Various forces within the Liberal party now tried to bring about "a leftist solution." *Dagens Nyheter* and *Expressen* urged the Lib-

[40] "In an exhaustive editorial on 15 January 1958 I tried, with the help of an account of parliamentary practice in English-speaking countries, to show that the king could not oppose a request by the government for dissolution of a chamber and a new election. It is possible that my study helped lead to the abandonment of the idea of using the king in the game surrounding the pension issue," wrote one of Karl Staaff's intellectual disciples, Herbert Tingsten, in his memoirs (*Mitt liv. tio år 1953–1963* [Stockholm: Norstedts, 1964], p. 230), while giving us yet another example of his teacher's technique of trying to prove what is the "living constitution" in Sweden using arguments taken from a practice that is considered to exist in English-speaking countries.

eral party to seek a settlement with the Social Democrats. When this did not materialize, *Dagens Nyheter* abstained from its traditional recommendation to its readers to support the Liberal party. This decision eventually led to the newspaper's isolation from the Liberal party and to the resignation of editors Herbert Tingsten and Kurt Samuelsson. A number of individual M.P.'s also lobbied for cooperation with the Social Democrats instead of a deal with the Conservatives and Center party.

Then in January 1959, Liberal party M.P. Ture Königson of Gothenburg declared that he could not consider voting no to the government's proposal if it were paired against that of the Conservatives or the Center party.[41] Now that the Liberal party's policy had been turned down by the electorate, in the final parliamentary vote he preferred to abstain. Königson expressed regret that it had not been possible to reach an agreement between the Liberals and the Social Democrats. His declaration attracted enormous attention. It meant, of course, that the voting situation changed: No longer 115 to 115, the result would now be 115 to 114. Königson rejected an appeal not to carry out his plans to abstain, out of consideration for his voters. He was no more willing than the M.P.'s during the tariff dispute of the 1880s to submit to any imperative mandate, either from his voters or his party. A member of Parliament ought to "vote according to his convictions and not let irrelevant considerations play any part."[42]

Until the very last, the Liberal party chairman fought the government bill. He attempted to bring about a technical coordination of the nonsocialist parties' motions, so that the government bill could be rejected by Parliament in any case. Among the steps that were considered was to force a vote on individual sections of the law, but this attempt failed due to the negative attitude of the Center party chairman. Hedlund declared that it would be possible to achieve unity among the nonsocialist parties only if the Liberal party gave up the element of coercion that existed in its modified proposal. In all essential respects, the Center stuck to Line 2 from the referendum.

All members of the Second Chamber were present during the dramatic vote on the evening of 14 May 1959. The compulsory supplementary pension system was approved by 115 votes to 114, with 1 abstention.

The Liberals and Conservatives had failed in their attempt to stop the

[41] In November 1958, Per Edvin Sköld had begun to negotiate separately with Königson on the supplementary pension issue. Sköld found that Königson would probably not vote with his party if it refused to bargain with the Social Democrats. To determine the situation in greater detail, the Social Democratic and Liberal leaderships began negotiations. Neither side made enough concessions to permit a compromise, however. On 8–10 January this was publicly confirmed when the Liberals declined to engage in official bargaining. A little over ten days later, Königson made his announcement. Von Sydow 1978, p. 328.

[42] AK 1959:16, p. 94.

Social Democratic supplementary pension proposal. What was more, their larger plan to drive the Social Democrats out of office lay in ruins. In the regular election of 1960, both the Liberals and Conservatives – this time especially the Conservatives – suffered setbacks, while the Social Democrats came out ahead. The supplementary pension dispute reversed the trend in the Swedish electorate. As the 1960s began, the nonsocialists had lost the entire increase in their voter base that they had picked up since the 1948 election.

3. COMPULSORY SUPPLEMENTARY PENSIONS ARE APPROVED

Why did Parliament approve a compulsory supplementary pension system, despite the fact that this proposal had been rejected by a majority not only of nonsocialist sympathizers but also of Social Democratic ones? This question can be divided into three separate problems. First, how could the opposition force a government decision on a referendum even though Prime Minister Erlander opposed this decision rule in principle? Second, why did as many as 46 percent of the voters support a compulsory pension system despite the fact that considerably fewer had sympathized with this alternative previously? Third, how could this minority among the voters, albeit a strong one, be transformed into a majority decision on a compulsory supplementary pension system in Parliament?

We will analyze the first problem, the decision to hold a referendum, in the customary manner using a game matrix. It will be a larger matrix than we have previously used in this book, because we have not two but three actors: the Agrarians/Center party (A); the Social Democrats (S); and the two nonsocialist opposition parties, the Liberals and Conservatives (O); the Communists supported the Social Democratic policy. The choice is between two alternatives: a parliamentary decision (p) and a referendum (r). Utilities ranging from $+2$ to -2 have been distributed on the basis of the parties' preferences regarding both the two alternative decision rules, their desired coalition partners and their desire for a good reputation in the eyes of the public. In simplified terms, the Agrarians primarily wanted a referendum and continued coalition with the Social Democrats, even though this coalition was losing popularity. The Social Democrats wanted a parliamentary decision and a continued coalition with the Agrarians. The nonsocialist opposition wanted a referendum and a coalition with the Agrarians. All of these players feared compromising themselves in the eyes of the electorate by appearing to be the lone opponent to the demand for a referendum. (A systematic presentation of the distribution of utility values is provided in n. 43.) Unfortunately it is not possible to find positive evidence in the material for all of these rankings. Only a few alternatives

Table 7.1. *The game of the referendum decision on the*
supplementary pension issue – order: A–S–O

	O			
	p		r	
	Sp	Sr	Sp	Sr
A p	−1, +2, −1	−1, +1, −1	−1, +2, −1	−2, −1, +1
r	−1, +1, −1	+2, −1, −2	+1, −2, +2	+2, −1, +2

were relevant in the game surrounding the supplementary pension issue; an actor rarely states his views, for example, on which of two unreasonable alternatives he prefers. In this situation the researcher is left to reconstruct the actors' complete preference orderings from other statements, using circumstantial reasoning.[43]

This gives us the matrix that appears in Table 7.1. If we begin by reconstructing actor A's deliberations, we find that A has a dominating strategy r (preferring one of the alternatives −1, +2, +1, +2 to one of the alternatives −1, −1, −1, −2). Actor O also has a dominating strategy r (preferring one of the alternatives −1, +2, +1, +2 to one of the alternatives −1, −1, −1, −2). Actor S can choose between a maximax strategy p, which he prefers if he is a risk taker (+2, +1, +2, −2), or a minimax strategy r, which he prefers if he is a more cautious general (+1, −1, −1, −1).

A's dominating strategy focuses interest on the lower row of the matrix and O's dominating strategy on the upper part of the matrix. If S chooses

[43] These preferences are written in the following order: Agrarians, Social Democrats, opposition. r = referendum. p = parliamentary decision. For example, rpr means that the Agrarians support a referendum, the Social Democrats prefer a parliamentary decision, and the opposition wants a referendum.

	A	S	O
+2 (best decision rule and best coalition)	rrp	ppr	rpr
	rrr	ppp	rrr
+1 (majority for best decision rule but undesirable coalition)	rpr	rpp	prr
		prp	
−1 (majority for undesirable decision rule)	ppp	rrr	ppp
	rpp	prr	ppr
	prp	rrp	rpp
	ppr		prp
−2 (alone against referendum)	prr	rpr	rrp

Table 7.2. *The final game between
the Agrarians and the Social
Democrats before the referendum
decision*

		S	
		p	r
A p		−1, +2	−2, −1
r		+1, −2	+2, −1

p, he obtains a utility of −2. If he chooses r, his utility is −1. As a rational actor, S then chooses the latter. The lower quadrant at the far right of the matrix is the solution to the game. All the players back the referendum method.

Empirically speaking, it was O's dominant strategy that first led to results. What all the players feared most was to see their democratic image compromised by being the sole opponent to the demand for a referendum; the lowest utility, −2, applies to all the actors exclusively in case of such an outcome.

But once O had introduced the referendum demand on the agenda, in practice O had also exhausted his role. Because a decision to hold a referendum was a government task − even if, in fact, it might have parliamentary consequences − the continued decision-making process became a game between A and S. To be able to follow the actors' calculations more clearly, we will detach the relevant squares and utilities from the right-hand portion of Table 7.1 and concentrate on the behavior of A and S. We then see that A still has a dominant strategy r, whereas S can choose between a maximax strategy p and a minimax strategy r. Tage Erlander's decision-making situation is similar to that of Gustaf V in the parliamentarism game. The king also had to choose between a maximax or a minimax strategy, and in the end he yielded and accepted parliamentary government, having realized his opponent's dominant strategy. In the same way, Erlander now settled for the referendum alternative (−1 in the lower right-hand quadrant in Table 7.2) in order to avoid the worst loss (−2 in the lower left-hand quadrant). But this was a heavy sacrifice. To Tage Erlander, a referendum was just as distasteful a decision rule as parliamentarism was to Gustaf V.

So it might appear as if A and O had won acceptance of their primary wish by bringing about a referendum on the supplementary pension issue.

But a referendum can be structured in many ways. On the coalition issue, A and O had different preferences: A still wished to retain his coalition with S, and O wanted cooperation with A. Consequently, A now presented a referendum model that would protect the government coalition as much as possible, even though A and S had different objective opinions on the supplementary pension issue. The referendum would be arranged in accordance with existing law, not the pending constitutional amendment, and the coalition government would thus enjoy maximum influence on the wording of the referendum. After having managed to place the issue on the agenda, O lost the initiative. The referendum decision was only a half-victory for O (and a half-defeat for S). The real winner was A, which got both his referendum and a chance to protect his coalition with S. We will return to the question of how A would achieve the latter purpose.

Our theoretical analysis thus means that in the final game, A took the initiative away from O and S submitted to A in the realization that A had a dominating strategy that S could not oppose without suffering even greater losses. Is there any empirical evidence for this conclusion? This question is obviously crucial, but before we answer it, let us approach the same conclusion by means of an additional game theory argument.

From the beginning, the Social Democrats were counting on a parliamentary decision (p) and the nonsocialist opposition wanted a referendum in accordance with the pending constitutional amendment (a). So

$$
\begin{array}{ll}
S & p \\
O & a
\end{array}
$$

The Agrarians resolved their dilemma between their preferences as to decision rule and coalition partner, respectively, by recommending a referendum in accordance with the existing constitution (c). So

$$
\begin{array}{ll}
S & p \\
O & a \\
A & c
\end{array}
$$

No actor had a majority for his proposal. The ranking among the proposals was as follows:

$$
\begin{array}{ll}
S & pca \\
O & acp \\
A & cap
\end{array}
$$

In pair-by-pair comparisons, it turns out that A's first preference is the Condorcet winner: c wins by 2 to 1 when compared with both a and p.

So how did the Condorcet winner emerge? Let us return to the question of empirical evidence.

The supplementary pension system

In Tage Erlander's memoirs and in the biography of Gunnar Hedlund, the same event is singled out as the one that finally clinched the decision to hold a referendum: Indeed, Erlander quotes directly from the Hedlund biography (stating the single objection that the event was incorrectly dated). Let us do the same:

Every day the government ate lunch in a small dining room in the Chancery Building and usually brought up issues at that time that did not require a formal cabinet session. This might be an uncontroversial appointment or a piece of business that a minister decided on his own but still wanted to inform his colleagues about.

It was at such a completely ordinary lunch one Thursday in May *(should be March)* 1957. Lunch usually lasted between 1 and 2 P.M. As usual, Gunnar Hedlund was late – shortly after 1:30 he came trudging in, looked impassive, sat down and was served his entrée and glass of milk.

Ten minutes later, Civil Service Minister Sigurd Lindholm got up and said he was expecting an official visit at 2:00 and wanted to prepare for it.

"Alright," said Erlander, "but before you go ... is there anyone who has any issue to bring up?"

"Yes," said Hedlund, "I have a little issue...."

"Sit down, Lindholm, and let's hear it."

"Well," said Hedlund, "I wonder how it is with the constitutional amendment on advisory referendums...."

"Well," said Erlander, fidgeting, "what about it?"

"I've been thinking about something," said Hedlund. "Isn't it true that you need *one*-third of the members plus one in each chamber to approve a referendum?"

Justice Minister Herman Zetterberg nodded yes.

"So who formulates the questions?" Hedlund wondered. "I've been thinking about that."

It became silent for a moment. Then Zetterberg said, "The people who demand the referendum."

"Well," said Hedlund, "I've been thinking about the...."

"So what is it?" Erlander exclaims. "Is there anything special about that?"

"If there happens to be one-third plus one," Hedlund continued, "who don't think the questions are good but demand a referendum and want the questions formulated differently ... Can that happen?"

Zetterberg nodded.

It became quiet again.

"If yet another group of members is joined by a few members who have changed their minds, and together they make up one-third plus one, and they demand a referendum and want to formulate the questions, then there will be several questions."

"What?" Erlander shouts. "But that won't work, will it? It hasn't been carefully thought out."

The whole proposal had been torpedoed in a minute or so. Zetterberg was forced to inform Parliament that the expected referendum bill would not be forthcoming (for reaffirmation). The Conservatives and Liberals became very angry, because they had pursued the demand for a new referendum system very energetically. This episode illustrates Hedlund's brilliance and ability to see alternative strategies quickly and assess the consequences. His legal experience was also helpful.[44]

But, it should perhaps be repeated, Erlander was already mentally prepared, so to speak, for the decision to use the existing rule instead of the pending constitutional amendment. He had searched high and low for a way out of a procedure that seemed in principle to be dubious in a representative democracy and was also strategically unfavorable. Erlander did not dare to oppose the referendum alone, but he went along with the demands of his coalition partner. But in the end, these demands assumed such a shape that the referendum alternative suddenly appeared less distasteful than before.

The answer to the second problem – how the Social Democrats could then attract 46 percent of the votes for their proposal despite the fact that support for it had been far weaker during the spring – is partly connected with the answer to the first. The government enjoyed an advantage because of its power to formulate the questions, including the opposition's alternative. The dispute concerned such terms as "freedom of choice," "constant purchasing power," and "collective bargaining agreements." The last term was inserted against the will of the nonsocialists in the text of their alternative. Furthermore, not two but three alternatives were presented to the voters. Hedlund's was called "Line 2," indicating that it was some kind of middle view between 1 and 3, even though objectively speaking it was the one that deviated most from the Social Democratic line. Research has shown that during the campaign, the two governing parties also took advantage of the opportunity offered by the three alternatives to avoid polemics against each other and thus avoid further weakening their coalition: Instead of criticizing each other, the Social Democrats and Agrarians focused far greater attention on Line 3.[45]

Finally, the referendum campaign also had a mobilizing effect on the Social Democratic faithful. Line 3 enjoyed the strongest support among those who declared their preference early. But Line 1 deprived Line 3 of its lead as the campaign wore on, as the number of undecided voters diminished sharply. Those who became active were mainly Social Democrats; their support for Line 1 increased from 29 percent to 80 percent during the campaign. In terms of social class, this group consisted primarily of industrial, construction, and unskilled workers.[46] A party apparently did not have to bend to the winds of public opinion that were

[44] Jorma Enochsson and Roland Petersson, *Gunnar Hedlund* (Stockholm: Norstedts, 1973), pp. 99–100; Erlander 1976, pp. 173–174.
[45] Björn Molin, *Tjänstepensionfrågan. En studie i svensk partipolitik* (Gothenburg: Akademi Görlaget, 1965), pp. 157 and 161.
[46] Bo Särlvik, *Opinionsbildningen vid folkomröstningen 1957* (SOU 1959:10), pp. 36, 103, and 105.

believed to be blowing. These winds could be turned through active opinion molding.

But no matter how successful the Social Democratic campaign was, it was not sufficient to create a majority for the proposal. The third problem remains to be dealt with – how it was finally possible to achieve a parliamentary majority in favor of a compulsory system.

Once again we see an expression of Erlander's singlemindedness. By dissolving the Second Chamber and declaring a new election, he wanted to achieve in Parliament the same improvement in his position that he had now won among the voters in the referendum. The election was also successful, albeit not quite enough. The balance of votes looked like it would be 115 to 115. In this situation, forces beyond Erlander's own control finally came to his rescue. The growing support within the Liberal party for a "leftist solution," which as we have indicated the Social Democrats were not slow to try to take advantage of, finally led to Königson's defection and a Social Democratic victory. Not since the days of Steam-Kitchen Olle had a single member of Parliament played such a crucial and dramatic part in a major political controversy.

The potential loser's strategy had failed. The mutual disagreements among the nonsocialists and the Liberal party's change of views in the hope of achieving a consensus solution are in strong contrast with the Social Democrats' consistent commitment to a compulsory supplementary pension system. By means of a combination of ideological conviction and strategic tenacity, as well as a goodly portion of luck in the final round, the prime minister outmaneuvered the Liberal party chairman's referendum strategy. The supplementary pension issue was to be Tage Erlander's greatest political victory and Bertil Ohlin's greatest defeat. As a result, the Liberal party once again assumed the second-ranking position in the nonsocialist opposition behind the Conservatives, which it had occupied before 1948.

4. THE REFERENDUM METHOD

In one respect, the disputes about the supplementary pension system in the 1950s and the planned economy in the 1940s had opposite outcomes. During the 1940s, the Social Democrats retreated on the actual issue of state involvement in the rationalization of the business sector, without thereby acceding to the decision rule that the nonsocialists perceived as justifying a limitation of state power. During the 1950s, on the other hand, the Social Democrats yielded to nonsocialist wishes as to the decision rule and arranged a referendum, but then took advantage of this to lead the party to a major victory on the issue itself. But their concession on the referendum method was tactical. Just as with the rights method, they were skeptical of the referendum method as a way that decisions should be made in a representative democracy.

In fact, the Social Democrats and the nonsocialists agreed that referendums should normally not play any prominent role in Sweden's political life. In this book we have been able to see how from the very beginning, from the first signs of a breakthrough for the popular will, Swedish democracy consistently followed the representative method instead of the direct method of popular influence. The opinions of the representatives of the Swedish people, not public opinion, were supposed to provide the basis for government decisions. It never crossed the minds of legislators that the people themselves should act as a decision-making body without the influence and mediation of elected representatives. The imperative mandate was emphatically rejected.

The first time that the concept of a referendum was put forth was during the suffrage debate.[47] David Bergström submitted a members' bill proposing that the issue of universal suffrage be subjected to a referendum. The bill, which was rejected, can be put in the context of the generally extraparliamentary work of the suffrage movement, with its mass petitions, people's parliaments, and so forth.[48]

For the Left, too, representative government was the constitutional ideal. This view, however, did not prevent referendums from being considered justified under particular circumstances. So far referendums have been used four times in Sweden. After the suffrage issue had been pursued to a successful conclusion and the Swedish system of government had been completely democratized, in 1922 an advisory referendum on alcoholic beverages was arranged. The result was a disappointment for the prohibitionists, who had expected a major victory. The Swedish people followed its old habit of responding roughly "fifty–fifty" to the politicians' questions: The prohibition proposal was rejected by 50.9 percent to 49.1 percent of the votes cast. One consequence was that the Liberals split into a Prohibitionist party and an antiprohibition Liberal party.

In 1955 a second referendum was arranged – on the issue of switching from left-hand to right-hand traffic. The merely advisory nature of the referendum and the fact that the members of Parliament were the decision makers became dramatically clear when Sweden made the actual transition to right-hand traffic some years later, despite the fact that no fewer than 82.9 percent of the voters had favored retaining left-hand traffic.

The third referendum was the one on the supplementary pension sys-

[47] For a historical account through the mid-1960s, see Gunnar Wallin, "Folkomröstningsinstitutet," in *Samhälle och riksdag II. Historisk och statsvetenskaplig framställning utgiven i anledning av tvåkammarriksdagens 100-åriga tillvaro* (Stockholm: Almqvist & Wiksell, 1966), pp. 261–358.
[48] See n. 45 above.

tem. As indicated earlier, dividing the issue into three alternatives helped very much to confuse the interpretation of the results. To some extent, the entire referendum system was compromised by the experience of the pension dispute. After all, the vote had not fulfilled the hopes of the nonsocialists, and the Social Democrats had been skeptical from the beginning. In 1960, Parliament rejected the pending constitutional amendment at the suggestion of Social Democratic and Center party spokesmen. "We were all a little caught up in referendum romanticism a few years ago," Prime Minister Erlander later declared. This statement appears in a study that summarizes the evolution of Social Democratic views by saying that during their long period in office after World War II they "acquired a successively harsher attitude toward the referendum system."[49]

The pattern of the supplementary pension dispute repeated itself in the most recent referendum in Sweden. In March 1980 a referendum was held on the issue of nuclear power, something that the opponents of atomic energy, headed by Center party chairman Thorbjörn Fälldin, had advocated for many years. Once again, three alternatives were presented instead of two. Once again, the problems of interpreting the results were formidable. Once again, all parties believed they could claim victory by means of appropriate comparisons and combinations.

The renewed interest in referendums during the 1940s was expressed in members' bills from all three nonsocialist parties during the 1948 session of Parliament. In 1954 these bills resulted in parliamentary approval of a pending constitutional amendment, whose inglorious fate we have followed until its rejection by Parliament in 1960. These members' bills consistently stressed that the representative system was the one that should normally be applied. But the referendum system might have a corrective effect on the political rigidity that arose in Sweden because the same party tended to occupy a permanent leading position. According to the Conservatives, referendums would enable the people to assume a larger role and responsibility for social reforms, which tended to intervene increasingly in their lives. "Precisely because these (reforms) are so invasive, it is a reasonable demand that full knowledge of the people's views be created. In this way, citizens gain a chance to exercise an influence without being narrowly tied to classes or parties." In itself, stability was an asset to a democracy, the Liberals believed. "But if stability is an advantage, the rigidity associated with it may be a danger. Why does a person vote for a particular party instead of for another? In many cases it is because he once got the notion that for one reason or another, he ought to vote for that party and continues to do so even after the original reason has ceased to be valid. Obviously doubts about the position of a majority of the people

---

[49] Wallin 1966, pp. 344 and 351.

on a certain issue arise especially easily when the difference between majority and minority in Parliament is insignificant. In principle it is thus fully justified to let the people themselves express their view." The Agrarians stated that the drawbacks that were always associated "with government by a majority party or a majority coalition" were growing because the parties were developing into large organizations that primarily represented certain social classes. This was obviously written before the establishment of the red–green coalition of 1951–1957.

"When governing power is in the hands of a party closely linked with a particular social class and its majority is narrow, the remainder of the people are disinclined to silently accept the decisions it makes. As a result of this, political conflicts become sharper. In such cases, a referendum becomes a safety valve through which political pressure can be eased."[50]

The fear of Social Democratic dominance is evident throughout these members' bills, because they were written under the influence of the planned economy debate of the "harvest time." The nonsocialists' interest in referendums originates from the same ideological world as the rights theory, with whose help they tried to block Social Democratic plans to expand the supervisory powers of the state. On the one hand, as in the Agrarian party's bill, they worried that the class interests of Social Democratic voters were one-sidedly favored by the prevailing election and party system. On the other hand, as in the Liberal bill, they found it hard to understand the reasons that made Social Democratic voters give their party a renewed vote of confidence and could not suppress the assumption that it was a question of voting purely by habit. Under any circumstances, they wanted to weaken the position of the socialist majority by, as the Conservatives put it, letting the people speak out directly about "invasive social reforms" in the quiet hope that state interventionism would receive substantially weaker support if the manifestation of will was not tied closely to official party policies. Like the rights theory, the referendum method was a way, albeit a weaker one, for the nonsocialists to protect the minority against the socialist majority.

The Social Democrats had a cooler attitude toward the referendum method. As we have seen, the Liberal party chairman's demand for a referendum on the supplementary pension issue was refuted by Tage Erlander in the parliamentary debate on grounds that the issue was especially unsuitable for a referendum because of its complex nature. At an internal party meeting with the Social Democratic parliamentary delegation, Erlander spoke more freely from the heart. The choice of a decision rule was not neutral in relation to the ideology that a person wanted to further,

---

[50] Mot 1948 FK:9 (Andrén et al.), 140 (Bergvall et al.), and 215, quotations from pp. 12 and 14 (Näsgård and Persson); AK:17, quotations from pp. 4–5 (Håstad, Skoglund, and Hjalmarson), 245, quotations from pp. 4–5 (Ohlin et al.) and 350 (Johansson i Mysinge et al.).

The supplementary pension system

Erlander believed. A referendum favored the nonsocialist view of society. "Referendums go together with a different form of government than the parliamentary system. Under a coalition government of the Swiss type, no objections can be aimed at the referendum system. On the other hand, it is obvious that referendums are a strongly conservative force. It becomes much harder to pursue an effective reform policy if reactionaries are offered the opportunity to appeal to people's natural conservatism and natural resistance to change. The enthusiasm of conservative parties for the referendum system is thus certainly related more or less consciously to the fact that it provides an instrument for blocking a radical progressive policy." But perhaps nonsocialist hopes were exaggerated in spite of everything, Erlander added. The Social Democrats were not lacking in opportunities to return the fire. "There are certainly many issues of importance to us where we could create a large public opinion in favor of rather far-reaching demands, given our propaganda apparatus and with the help of the trade union movement."[51]

The opponents of the Social Democrats had also pointed out that the referendum method may have conservative effects, but they saw this as something good. For a time during the work of preparing the 1922 referendum, a highly unusual coalition of Social Democrats and Conservatives existed. They did not hide the fact that they were compelled by widely divergent motives. One of the spokesmen of the reformist Conservatives stressed that the prerequisites for referendums had changed completely due to the constitutional reform. The referendum system had previously been intended as an arbitrator between the chambers, which were elected according to completely different systems. Such a procedure was contrary to the constitution then in use. Now the issue was completely different: Both chambers were democratically elected. Referendums could thus serve a new function. They could "have a moderating and restraining effect" if the decision makers should go too far in one direction or another. The system could counteract abrupt changes in opinion and help smooth out party differences.[52]

If we look at our own age, the 1980s, with its economic crises and government budget deficits, we again find the referendum method being advocated as a way of counteracting an excessively large public sector. "In Sweden, public expenditures will soon reach 70 percent of GDP, while in Switzerland they are less than 25 percent," says economist Assar Lindbeck. "This makes one ask whether this is because Swedes and Swiss have completely different preferences, different value systems. Or is it because we have here two democracies that 'happened' to choose two different types

[51] Von Sydow 1978, pp. 165–166.
[52] FK 1919:53, pp. 15ff. (Sam Clason).

of constitutional rules? Switzerland has a permanent coalition govern‐
ment, referendums, a federal system. Sweden has keen competition
between governments receiving around 50 percent of the votes, no bind‐
ing referendums and a more centralized system. If the difference in the
size of the public sector is due to the choice of constitution, we cannot
help discussing how we should design the rules of the game in relation to
what we want to accomplish."[53]

In the nonsocialist arguments for the referendum method, we hear an
unmistakable refrain from the idyllic Oscarian days, the dream of inde‐
pendent formation of opinion without propaganda and pressure from
political parties. If the voice of the people could make itself heard without
manipulation by politicians, it would favor a nonsocialist trend among
voters. This notion would cost the nonsocialists dearly during the supple‐
mentary pension dispute, when it led the proponents of Line 3 to tone
down their party images. As a consequence, their alternative was over‐
shadowed by the determined party propaganda of the Social Democrats.

The Social Democrats, too, have a heritage from the Oscarian age. But
the party system does not disturb *them*. They regard political parties as
necessary opinion-molding instruments. The Social Democrats slam the
brakes on the popular will, so to speak, in a different way. The untamed
popular will, to which nonsocialists pin their hopes, is precisely what
Social Democrats fear, because its outcome can deprive M.P.'s of their
freedom of action and opportunity to pursue an ideologically correct pol‐
icy. Tage Erlander rejected any notion that smacked of the imperative
mandate as energetically as M.P.'s ever did during the tariff dispute of the
1880s.

This tension between a radical Social Democratic leadership that
wanted to expand the public sector and a more conservative attitude
among Social Democratic voters continued after the supplementary pen‐
sion dispute. In the late 1960s, incidentally, the attitudes of the leaderships
of all Swedish parties stood to the left of voter attitudes; the system resem‐
bled a field where ears of grain – or voters – were bent by a wind toward
the left. By the late 1970s, the image of a fan is more suitable. On the left
side of the political scale, party leaders were still pulling their followers
strongly to the left; the leaders of the Center and Liberal parties occupied
essentially the same position on the left–right spectrum as their voters,
while the leadership of the Moderates was to the right of its voters.[54]

[53] "Assar Lindbeck om ny politik: Vi måste ändra systemen!" *Svenska Dagbladet*, 17 Feb.
1983.
[54] Sören Holmberg, *Riksdagen representerar svenska folket. Empiriska studier i represen‐
tativ demokrati* (Lund: Studentlitteratur, 1974), p. 87; Jörgen Westerståhl and Folke Johans‐
son, *Medborgarna och kommunen. Studier av medborgerlig aktivitet och representativ folk‐
styrelse. Rapport 5 från kommunaldemokratiska forskningsgrouppen. Ds Kn 1981:12*
(Stockholm: Liber, 1981), pp. 86–87.

The supplementary pension system

By way of summary, the referendum method can be described as one of the decision rules of the minority – whether we are referrring to the suffrage supporters of the 1890s, the prohibitionists of the 1920s, the nonsocialist opposition of the 1950s, or the antinuclear movement of the 1970s. Outside the closed doors of the decision-making body, out among the masses of people, they believe that public support for their own cause is more positive. A referendum is thus regarded as leading to victory whereas the verdict of the decision-making body spells defeat. It is consequently logical that the Social Democratic party, which has been more successful than its competitors in running the government and Parliament, is also the party that has adopted the most negative attitude toward the referendum method.

8

Nuclear power

1. MARCHING INTO THE NUCLEAR POWER SOCIETY

Government–business cooperation and the economic boom both continued. The Social Democratic party, which dominated the Swedish state,
established increasingly intimate ties with the business sector, especially
with major companies. Under the leadership of Tage Erlander and banker-
industrialist Marcus Wallenberg, the Swedish economy experienced a
golden age that made the Swedish living standard the highest in the world
during the 1960s. The chairman of the Swedish Trade Union Confederation and the director of the Swedish Employers' Confederation toured the
United States together and gave speeches about "the Swedish Model,"
which involved centralized collective bargaining agreements and a labor
–management relationship marked by cooperation and consensus. The
Social Democrats supported a liberal economic policy aimed at furthering
growth, accelerating the restructuring process, stimulating expansive economic forces, and facilitating the mobility of labor from low-wage companies threatened with bankruptcy to the most profitable economic sectors. Industrial profits and employee pay climbed at a record pace. In such
a flourishing economic climate, no one seemed to benefit from conflict; it
appeared as if continued consensus was to everyone's advantage.[1]

[1] When the "golden age ended" is a matter of debate. One event marking the beginning
of the end was a major mine workers' strike at the state-owned iron ore company LKAB in
the winter of 1969, followed by an increase in wildcat strikes in other industries. Another,
more profound change, of course, was the 1973–1974 oil crisis. Under any circumstances,
both the atmosphere of cooperation and the economic boom had ended by the mid-1970s,
when the Social Democrats had to step down and hand over power to the nonsocialists. The
foremost expression of the Social Democratic view of economic policy during the "golden
age" is *Samordnad näringspolitik* (Stockholm: Tiden, 1961). Otherwise, see Leif Lewin, *Planhushållningsdebatten* (Uppsala: Almqvist & Wiksell, 1967), pp.423–477; Nils Elvander, *Skan-
dinavisk arbetarrörelse* (Stockholm: Liber, 1980); Walter Korpi, *Arbetarklassen i välfärd-
skapitalismen: arbete, fackförening och politik i Sverige* (Stockholm: Prisma, 1978); Assar
Lindbeck, *Svensk ekonomisk politik. Problem och teorier under efterkrigstiden* (Stockholm:
Aldus/Bonniers, 1968).

Nuclear power

In the end, however, growth itself came to be questioned. Progress had its price. It led to the so-called moving van policy – government-sponsored training and incentives to relocate from economically depressed areas to those with labor shortages – which was viewed somewhat less favorably by those who were subjected to it than by those who had devised it. Such concepts as structural rationalization, large-scale production, and high technology lost some of their allure. In their place came the "green wave," which propelled the Center into the role of leading opposition party, capturing 25 percent of the vote in 1973. The party responded to the ideology of growth with an ecological philosophy, advocating greater attention to the environment, small-scale production units, and regional balance.

The nuclear energy issue is what eventually gave this new ideology its explosive political power. During their initial stages in the 1950s and 1960s, efforts to create a Swedish nonmilitary atomic power industry attracted no criticism. In 1970 and 1971 a virtually unanimous Parliament approved the construction of eleven nuclear reactors. But in 1973 the tide of public opinion shifted. Center party chairman Thorbjörn Fälldin, having been persuaded of the hazardous nature of nuclear power, started a virtual crusade to "stop the march into a nuclear power society." Those usually singled out as his initial sources of inspiration are Professor Hannes Alfvén, a Nobel prize winning Swedish physicist, and Birgitta Hambraeus, a Center party M.P. strongly influenced by Dr. Alfvén. Her 1972 parliamentary interpellation on the safety hazards of this new source of energy began a new chapter in Swedish nuclear energy policy. With the Center party as the leading opinion molder, assisted by the Left party Communists and such extraparliamentary groups as Friends of the Earth, the Environmental Center, the Field Biologists, and Alternative City, a powerful opposition to Swedish nuclear energy policy began to make itself heard. The exceptionally rapid emergence of the antinuclear movement during 1973–1975 has been described as an opinion-molding process that, "in terms of commitment and size during the postwar period, can only be compared with the supplementary pension dispute of the late 1950s." Energy policy became even more dramatic as a result of the 1973–1974 oil crisis, which triggered an international recession. In 1975, when it was again time for Parliament to take a position on government energy policy, a powerful new dimension of conflict had been established in Swedish politics. It cut straight through the traditional left–right spectrum of opinions on the role of the state in the business sector. After extensive "energy policy deliberations" within the parties, the Social Democrats, Moderates, and Liberals placed themselves in one camp along this new dimension of conflict, arguing that Sweden should keep its nuclear reactors in spite of everything. These parties were not, however, entirely unaffected by antinuclear arguments and there were subtle differences between their respective views. In the other camp were the Center party and the Left party Communists, who opposed all use of nuclear power. During this period, the only way to find people who advocated a large-scale expansion of nuclear reactors in Sweden was to go outside the walls of Parliament to a third group – the Swedish business community.[2]

In the introductory remarks to their 1975 government bill on energy matters, the Social Democrats declared that energy policy, like other policy areas, had to be subordinated to general welfare and be designed in such a way as to promote, in the best possible way, the social aims that the labor movement was trying to implement. Given this approach, the government bill was an argument – albeit far from carefree or superficial – for continued growth and the values that could be achieved as a result. For a long period of its history, Sweden had been self-sufficient in energy. When industrialization took place in the late nineteenth century, it was necessary to import fuel despite the rapid expansion of domestic hydroelectric power. At first, coal dominated Sweden's dependence on foreign fuel. After World War II, oil made its breakthrough as the dominant source of energy. Starting at a very insignificant volume, it climbed to 40 percent of total energy consumption and then reached 70 percent during the 1970s. A consistent feature of economic development had been that the rate of growth in energy consumption had continued to rise. During what Swedes called the "record-breaking years" of the 1950s and 1960s, energy consumption had climbed 4 to 5 percent annually. But Sweden had achieved an enormous improvement in living standards: Between 1950 and 1973 the aggregate value of industrial production in real terms had risen 2.8 times, while the number of working hours fell by 17 percent; 2 million new dwellings had been built since 1950; freight volume had increased from 14 to 44 billion metric ton-kilometers; the number of cars had risen from a 0.25 to 2.3 million; the public sector had expanded at a rate that had doubled the number of national and local government jobs, which now amounted to 900,000. Prime Minister Palme, chief sponsor of the government bill, declared that it was "unquestionable that the increased use of energy has been of great importance to the positive changes in society that I have indicated here."

---

[2] Sören Holmberg, Jörgen Westerståhl, and Karl Branzén, *Väljarna och kärnkraften* (Stockholm: Liber, 1977), quotation from p. 49; Pelle Isberg, *Svensk kärnkraft? En kärntekniker kommenterar debatten* (Stockholm: Natur och Kultur, 1976), pp. 13–60; Sigfrid Leijonhufvud, *Ett fall för ministären* (Stockholm: Liber, 1979), pp. 24–48; Lars Liljegren, *Ska vi dagtinga med förnuftet? Om energin och framtiden* (Stockholm: Tiden, 1977), pp. 11–32; Evert Vedung, *Kärnkraften och regeringen Fälldins fall* (Stockholm: Rabén & Sjögren, 1979), pp. 14ff.

But now a new situation had arisen. If not before, then during the oil crisis eyes had been opened to the dangers of thoughtlessly continuing to exploit the world's energy resources. The government now had to take a firmer grasp of developments by means of a continuous energy-planning process with recurring control stations for new decisions. The year 1985 had been chosen as the target point for medium-term planning. The government declared that its future energy policy would rest on four cornerstones.

First, the growth in energy consumption had to be slowed down. A large-scale energy-saving program was launched. The government proposed a new target for the size of energy consumption. A commission of inquiry on energy requirements had sketched four different alternatives for future energy use: unlimited or slower growth in the Swedish economy, either with or without nuclear power. In the Social Democratic leadership's "deliberations" with ordinary party members on energy issues, the prime minister had noticed that people seemed to understand the need to do something about the uninterrupted rise in energy consumption, even if this meant a lower rate of growth in private consumption. Solidarity with the third world, which needed access to energy to raise itself out of poverty, was another argument for a change in direction. The government thus proposed that Sweden's goal should be to bring down the annual increase in energy consumption from 4 to 5 percent to 2 percent. The proposal thus did not entail a reduction in energy use. It did not even mean an attempt to remain at an unchanged level. Its boldly proclaimed goal was to *reduce the rate of increase* in energy consumption, a phrase that may remind some people of the "newspeak" used by the politicians in Orwell's *1984*. Yet there is reason to describe this goal as radical. At the time, no other country in the world had imposed such a limit on itself. Attempting to achieve sudden changes in developments is rarely a successful form of political behavior. To slow the increase in energy consumption, the government also proposed an amendment to Chapter 136a of the Building Act, specifying that the establishment and expansion of energy-intensive industry would be subject to government review.

The second cornerstone of the new energy policy was an active oil policy. For obvious reasons related to economic conditions, supplies, and security policy, it was necessary to reduce dependence on oil, especially from the Middle East. The government proposed steps toward this end.

The government referred to the third cornerstone as "a secure power supply." Given existing technology, there were three main sources of energy: hydroelectric power, oil, and nuclear power. The accelerated expansion of hydroelectric power capacity during the 1950s and 1960s had been of major importance to Sweden's development into an advanced, prosperous industrial state. Out of consideration for the environment, the harnessing of additional rivers should now be deferred. For the reasons just mentioned, oil ought to play a decreasing part in Sweden's future energy mix. Nuclear power thus seemed to occupy a crucial position, especially because even by international standards, Sweden's uranium deposits at Ranstad were significant in size. They could cover the country's requirements for several hundred years. But nuclear power had its controversial safety problems. Of course, the prevailing opinion among the experts was that these risks were "very small," according to the prime minister. Palme also argued that more progress had been made on solving the problems of nuclear waste than in handling the by-products of other industries. But there was still one reason for the government not to propose an extensive, long-term program of nuclear expansion – namely, "the hesitancy that people feel about such a step." Olof Palme thus did not state that he himself felt any hesitancy. He was referring to public opinion. In its summary, the government bill made similar use of the third person: "At the same time, many people feel hesitant about a massive nuclear power program." What Palme seemed to be saying was that on such an important and controversial issue as nuclear power, the politicians had to await the approval of public opinion before they made their decision. But on the other hand, Palme did not want to say that people who opposed nuclear power were right in arguing that if there were now hesitancy about nuclear power, it should be brought to a halt. He strongly emphasized what devastating consequences a phasing out of nuclear power would have on employment, the economy, and social welfare policy. His conclusion was that two reactors should be added to the previously approved eleven-reactor nuclear energy program. This was described as a cautious policy aimed at preserving "genuine freedom of action so that, as our knowledge becomes greater and more certain, we still have alternative courses of action to choose from, in order to ensure our energy supply." The risks that might be associated with extensive, long-term nuclear power programs "do not, however, entail any obstacles to a limited-scale nuclear power program such as Sweden is now discussing," the prime minister assured Parliament.

The fourth and final cornerstone of the policy was international cooperation. It may seem somewhat contradictory to decry both rising oil prices and the poverty of the third world, as Olof Palme did. Oil income primarily benefited developing countries. But the prime minister pointed to the instability in the world currency market caused by higher oil prices and the fact that not all developing countries benefited from oil prices; many were poor in both oil and other raw materials. The oil crisis had created new sources of conflict. Many developing countries were certain to attempt to solve their energy policy problems by using nuclear power. There were risks that nuclear materials might be diverted to the production of atomic weapons. Finally, the prime minister linked the issue of international environmental problems with those of international solidarity and disarmament. The effects of energy consumption on climate were another reason why there was a great need for international cooperation. Sweden has an important part to play in this area.[3]

In all essential respects, the Moderates supported the energy policy of the Social Democrats. Not without qualms, they acceded to the goal of slowing down the increase in energy consumption to 2 percent annually. But this goal was not in first place in the Moderates' preference ordering, any more than it was for the Social Democrats. They expressed themselves very clearly on this matter: "We are not prepared to accord the 2 percent goal priority if it should turn out that this endangers our chances of maintaining the full employment or the economic growth on which there is unity among the political parties in our country." Economic growth required higher energy use. Here, too, the Moderates expressed themselves with great clarity: "There is an obvious correlation between a country's material well-being and its energy consumption." To achieve the 2 percent goal, the Moderates were willing to participate in various energy-saving programs. But they firmly opposed the government's plans to amend Chapter 136a – here their agreement with the Social Democrats on energy policy had to give way to the more fundamental conflict dimension related to the power of the state over the business sector. And no matter what happened to energy consumption in the industrialized countries, global energy consumption would increase under any circumstances, the Moderates asserted, for this was a prerequisite if poor countries were to be able to raise their living standards to the level that those in the rich countries regarded as self-evident.

The Social Democrats also received the support of the Moderates on the other three cornerstones of their energy policy: a reduction in oil dependence; a secure energy supply including the retention of nuclear power; and international cooperation to master the economic, environmental, and security policy consequences of energy use. The Moderates said yes to the proposal on thirteen reactors and added that contingency planning for a possible further increase in energy production should assume the form of a fourteenth reactor. The safety problems of nuclear power installations required close attention, they declared, and continued research should occupy a central role in energy policy. But experience showed that accident hazards were "small," radioactivity resulting from the expansion of nuclear power capacity represented "only a fraction of natural background radiation," and a major reactor accident, although "theoretically conceivable," was "very unlikely." Because hydroelectric power capacity, for environmental reasons, should only be expanded very

---

[3] Prop 1975:30; quotations from pp. 8, 10, 15, 17–18, and 19.

cautiously and the percentage of overall energy consumption represented by oil should decline, the conclusion was that the predicted increase in energy consumption would be satisfied mainly by the use of nuclear power.[4]

The nuclear power issue had split the nonsocialist bloc. The Moderates said this was unfortunate. To the Liberals, the situation posed an even greater dilemma, because they considered the prospect of "middle party cooperation" with the Center as especially important. What position should the Liberals adopt on nuclear power? The opinions expressed at the Liberal party's own round of internal deliberations on energy policy could be interpreted in different ways. The literature points to party secretary Carl Tham as the man who finally indicated a way out. Even if there might be reasons to support the Social Democratic proposal, in Tham's opinion the Liberal party should not move too far away from the Center party and too close to the Social Democrats. The Liberals recommended a nuclear program with eleven reactors.[5]

Unrestrained growth was not a Liberal ideal; like the Center, the Liberals believed that energy policy "must be subordinated to ecological requirements." Like other parties, they believed that a slowdown in the growth of energy consumption was necessary. But according to the Liberals, it was possible to follow this path further than the government had proposed. They unveiled an even more ambitious energy-saving program than the one stipulated in the government bill. It said that the increase in Sweden's energy consumption could be held at 0.5 percent below what the Social Democrats and Moderates had proposed. Energy was, of course, necessary for growth. "But this correlation is not so simple or clear in a highly industrialized country of Sweden's type." Energy-saving programs also required technological development, which in itself would generate employment. The government's proposed amendment to Chapter 136a of the Building Law was rejected by the Liberals as well as the Moderates; an independent board should instead give the government its opinions on industrial investments. The necessary research on energy saving should also include the energy sources that the Center party talked so much about – solar and wind energy. But when it came to the most controversial issue, the future of nuclear power, the Liberals and the Center had clearly different views. The Liberal leadership seemed to have no doubts whatever that it was necessary to keep using nuclear power during the next few years. Thoughts of immediately phasing out Sweden's nuclear reactors, such as the Center party advocated, were totally absent from the Liberal members' bill.

[4] Mot 1975:2029; quotations from pp. 1–2 and 17.
[5] Liljegren 1977, pp. 28ff.; Vedung 1979, p. 15 (Vedung cites Liljegren); Isberg 1976, p. 59; Leijonhufvud 1979, p. 39.

Nuclear power

The Liberals nevertheless admitted that the Center, their fellow "middle party," was correct in saying that uncertainty regarding the problems of nuclear waste had increased rather than decreased since Parliament had voted its approval of the eleven-reactor program. When the Social Democrats and the Moderates had admitted the same thing, they had drawn the conclusion that Sweden could not make any major new commitment to nuclear power but had to stay at roughly the level of its commitment to date. To achieve a balance between energy production and use, they had proposed thirteen reactors. The conclusion reached by the Center party and the Left party Communists, instead, was that this uncertainty should lead to a phasing out of nuclear power. For their part, the Liberals believed that the only reasonable consequence was to stick to the existing eleven-reactor program. This position, and no other, entailed freedom of action on the nuclear power issue, the Liberals asserted in a lively polemic against the Social Democratic and Moderate proposal. Like the Social Democrats, the Liberals preferred to present their arguments against nuclear power in the third person, but they did so using a choice of words that corresponded closely with the Center party's "small is beautiful" philosophy. "The existing opposition to nuclear power is related not only to fears about the safety aspects of waste disposal problems etc. It has to do with people's reactions to various risks and with their attitude toward large technological systems."[6]

The Social Democrats, Moderates, and Liberals thus argued from their varying positions that despite its safety problems, nuclear power must be retained at least in a medium-term planning perspective until 1985. Energy consumption could not be allowed to increase without limit. Nor was it conceivable any longer to satisfy Sweden's energy needs through a massive nuclear power program. The hazards of nuclear power could not be ignored. The exploitation of the earth's energy resources had to be controlled. But there could not be any question of now quickly phasing out Swedish nuclear reactors. Such a step would fundamentally damage the prosperity of the Swedish economy – even the Center party had to realize this. Calling for a rapid phaseout was thus nothing but "nuclear opportunism," Prime Minister Palme believed. It meant leaving it to others to make the difficult decisions, in the hope of being able to attract votes for one's make-believe game.[7] Palme apparently believed that this was something completely different from his own self-proclaimed willingness to pay heed to criticisms of nuclear energy. The chairman of the Moderates criticized the advocates of a nuclear phaseout who withdraw "from the work of society or indulge in dreams, in which the romanticized ideal of

---

[6] Mot 1975:2031; quotations from pp. 1, 4, and 21–22.
[7] RD (Proceedings of Parliament) 1975:91, pp. 140, 146–147, and 151.

the old agrarian society replaces the reality of the industrial society."[8] And despite his interest in middle-party cooperation, not even the chairman of the Liberal party could refrain from openly criticizing Center party members when he saw them demonstrate together with the Communists in support of dismantling nuclear power: "Last Saturday they walked together on the streets. . . . There were many idealists here, but also political weathervanes. Their words are simplifications."[9]

The Center party rejected the notion that keeping the Swedish nuclear power program at a level of eleven or thirteen reactors would mean preserving freedom of action. Only five of the eleven approved reactors were already in operation. Implementing Parliament's old decision by loading nuclear fuel into the other six reactors would thus dramatically increase dependence on nuclear power; if the Social Democrats and Moderates got their way, this dependence would grow by an additional two reactors. Such a policy "meant that our freedom of action is lost," the Center party wrote in its members' bill. "If we have 13 nuclear reactors and a situation where nuclear power accounts for 40 percent of electricity production, it is practically impossible to stop their operation and phase out nuclear energy."

Sweden's nuclear power must be phased out by 1985, because it was too risky a source of energy: This was the firm opinion of the Center party. For this reason, "the five reactors now in operation or trial operation must be replaced with other energy sources and with energy-saving measures. . . . The other six reactors approved by a majority of Parliament must be employed for other use."

Was it not possible to overcome the hazards, as the other parties hoped? The Center party believed this was hardly likely. The safety demands were extreme. The party accepted no disagreement whatsoever among those who assessed the safety of atomic energy. Its statement, often repeated on later occasions, was: "As long as a unanimous corps of researchers and experts cannot guarantee that the serious hazards related to nuclear power production can be mastered in a way that ensures complete safety, we cannot commit ourselves to nuclear power."[10] The pragmatic arguments and probability estimates that were employed in other public ventures could not be used in dealing with nuclear power. Whether the hazards "are large or small is indifferent, because the consequences are so terrible," the Center party's main spokesman asserted in the parliamentary debate.[11] "The hazards of nuclear power are of a different dimension," declared Thorb-

---

[8] Ibid., p. 112 (Bohman).
[9] Ibid., p. 120 (Helén).
[10] Mot 1975:2030; quotations from pp. 3 and 16–17.
[11] RD 1975:91, p. 51 (Sjönell).

jörn Fälldin in the verbal duel between himself and Olof Palme that marked the culmination of the parliamentary debate. "These hazards not only concern our own generation but to an even greater degree, coming generations. This is why we have to ask ourselves the question: 'What right do we have to take these risks?' " Fälldin rejected the accusation of nuclear opportunism with strong indignation. The Center party's no to nuclear power applied under all circumstances. "Obviously this applies both when we vote here in Parliament and if we were ever sitting in a government. For this reason, we cannot take part in a government that presents proposals to expand nuclear power." The opposition questioned a government that tried to shift responsibility for nuclear power policy onto others. The government and a majority of Parliament bore the heavy responsibility of continuing the march into a nuclear power society, which the Center party wanted to stop.[12]

As for slowing down the increase in energy use, the Center party believed it was necessary to go as far as limiting the growth rate to 1 percent a year. This did not, by any means, threaten prosperity to the extent the "nuclear power parties" claimed, said the Center party, citing an American study. A low rate of increase in energy use was instead thought to lead to a somewhat higher degree of employment. The government's energy-saving program was insufficient, the party believed. The Center proposed a heavier commitment to energy-conservation investments. The proposed steps to reduce Sweden's oil dependency were described as "the most positive thing in the government bill." The section on power supply was influenced by the party's criticism of nuclear energy. The ultimate basis of energy production has to be the earth's energy balance. The various energy sources must not be subjected to the "ruthless exploitation" that was now taking place. We have to move toward using renewable energy sources: wind, sunlight, geothermal energy. If as much were spent on tapping these resources as had been spent on developing nuclear power, these energy sources would become realistic alternatives. And during the period of transition required to develop these alternative energy sources, there was a very large amount of energy to be extracted from the country's peat bogs. As for international energy cooperation, the Center party specifically stated that most funds should be devoted to developing alternative, renewable energy sources. It strongly warned of the connection between the use of nuclear energy and the buildup of nuclear weapons.[13]

The Left party Communists supported the Center party's call for the dismantling of Sweden's nuclear power program as well as general efforts

[12] Ibid., pp. 109 and 142.
[13] Mot 1975:2030; quotations from pp. 26 and 2.

to dampen energy consumption and oil dependence. It said that Social Democratic, Moderate, and Liberal hopes of being able to master the safety problems of the atomic energy industry were unrealistic and irresponsible. The party emphasized that the expansion of the Swedish nuclear power program created a new and very serious dependence on foreign countries, especially the United States. Sweden's energy supply would be controlled by a superpower, which would decide through political channels what resources and services could be used.

But the Left party Communists also criticized the Center party's energy policy. Their members' motion had a grandiose Marxist perspective. The economic growth of the capitalist countries had now begin to run up against its outer limits. But a growth in the national economy as well as in energy supply was characteristic of capitalism. Its driving force was profit. Without growth, capitalism ended up in crisis. The Center party's program of trying to stop growth while keeping capitalism intact was called "idealistic and out of touch with reality." The stabilization that was now necessary in the economic and energy policies required much stronger direction than the Center party was prepared to provide: It necessitated a shift to socialistic central planning.[14]

Outside Parliament it was possible to find an even more positive view of nuclear power than the one espoused by what Thorbjörn Fälldin called the "nuclear power parties." For example, according to one nuclear engineer at the ASEA-ATOM corporation, the nuclear power parties had only superficially won a victory in the 1975 parliamentary vote on energy policy. On the contrary, the real winners were the opponents of nuclear power, who had lured all the parties away from a desirable, large-scale investment in Swedish nuclear power. "The result of the nuclear power debate in Sweden during 1973–1975 can be summarized briefly; the opponents of nuclear power won the battle." They had done so because of the energetic efforts of a handful of women and men whose untenable arguments now had to be refuted. It would be possible to turn around public opinion again by means of information. In a polemic pamphlet, the ASEA-ATOM engineer wanted to disseminate information about these opinion molders without thereby causing their many sympathizers to feel insulted; he wanted to write about "the seducers, not about the seduced." It was thus necessary to understand what the real energy policy problem was. It was not "whether Sweden needs 1 or 2 percent growth in energy consumption." He wanted to consign "this debate between Olof Palme and Thorbjörn Fälldin to the museum where it belongs." The real question was how to reduce oil dependence, and that problem was equally large

[14] Mot 1975:2034; quotation from p. 5.

whether energy consumption grew by 1 or 2 percent. The solution was an expansion of the nuclear power program. Atomic energy meant something revolutionary and new in human development and was the only thing that could lead the country out of the energy policy crisis that was in the process of paralyzing its economic and political system.[15]

The growing optimism of these statements harks back to the golden age of the 1960s and contrasts starkly with the resignation that followed the economic stagnation of the 1970s. Faith in progress had characterized the expansion of the Swedish nuclear power program from the start. It was manifested, for instance, in the study of Sweden's future electricity supply that the Swedish Central Power Supply Board (Centrala Driftledningen, or CDL) published in 1972, in which plans for the construction of twenty-four nuclear reactors were presented.[16] The energy policy bill approved by Parliament in 1975 admittedly brought about a revision of these plans, but the new study was still just as confident that "the use of uranium as fuel would provide a completely superior solution to the heating requirements of major cities" and that "environmental and safety factors very strongly favor nuclear power." As soon as the period covered by the parliamentary bill was over, the Swedish nuclear power program should be expanded. The conclusion of the new study was that "as early as the 1985 stage, it would be economically advantageous to install yet another nuclear reactor . . . beyond the 13 reactors included in the energy plan."[17]

In a rapid succession of books and articles, the advocates of an expanded Swedish nuclear power program argued their case. Their views can be classified into three areas, which strangely enough are exactly the same as those adopted by the opponents of nuclear power. But whereas the latter only saw the disadvantages of nuclear power, its advocates found nuclear power superior to other sources of energy in all three respects.

First and foremost, its advocates argued that nuclear power should be expanded because it was the safest source of energy. No other human activity was the object of such meticulous supervision as atomic energy. Very extensive data were available about the use of nuclear reactors around the world. Comparisons led to an unequivocal result. The hazards of nuclear power accidents were substantially lower than the hazards from virtually any other activity. In order for a reactor accident to have any perceptible effects, the water that carries off the heat from the reactor's fuel core had to leak out. This required several safety systems to collapse at the same time. Nothing anywhere near this serious had ever happened

---

[15] Isberg 1976; quotations from pp. 27, 30, 33, and 10–11.
[16] *Sveriges elförsörjning 1975–1990. 1972 års studie* (CDL, 1972).
[17] *Sveriges elförsörjning 1975–1985. 1975 års studie* (CDL, 1975); quotations from pp. 8, 12, and summary p. 3.

before. One study arrived at the conclusion that given seventeen reactors, such a leak would occur a maximum of once every thousand years. And in a maximum of one case out ten, the accident would be so large that the nuclear power plant would be damaged.

But if a nuclear power accident did occur, contrary to all probability, the consequences would not be nearly as serious as the opponents of nuclear power claimed in their unrestrained scare propaganda, full of false parallels with nuclear weapons explosions. A nuclear reactor could not explode in this way. "This is completely out of the question for reasons of physics. The damage from a nuclear power accident is limited to radiation damage." Radioactivity was not something that mankind had invented. Throughout history, man had been exposed to natural radiation from space and the crust of the earth, which was many times larger than the radiation created by nuclear power. The fear of plutonium was also exaggerated, according to a professor of chemistry who had handled this element on a daily basis for nearly twenty-five years. Accidents had admittedly occurred, but the consequences had been insignificant. During the war, twenty-five workers in Los Alamos had been exposed to plutonium dust. Twenty-three were still completely healthy; one had died of natural causes. The opponents of nuclear power spoke of genetic damage caused by nuclear power. In Sweden, researchers had exposed eighteen generations of mice to radioactivity and had looked for genetic damage. "Despite the fact that generation after generation of mice had received radiation doses exceeding by tens of thousands of times the doses that nuclear power plants would subject us humans to, it has not been possible to demonstrate any accumulated effects." The opponents of nuclear power considered it indefensible to use an energy source that left it to future generations to take care of its wastes. "It may be suitable to compare the consequences for future generations if fossil fuels should be used instead of nuclear power," was one dry comment made by a chief engineer at the State Power Board. Air pollution would be enormous and would have unforeseeable effects on the earth's climate and on future generations. "In contrast, the consequences of utilizing nuclear power can certainly be expected to cause negligible difficulties to future generations. It is thus not consistent to use ethical motives with reference to future generations as an argument against nuclear power plants if you simultaneously advocate the continued utilization of coal and oil."

The second reason to invest in nuclear power was environmental considerations. As we just saw, the advocates of nuclear power were inclined to bring up environmental issues even in their analyses of the consequences of using nuclear power. To a great extent, environmental destruction was the result of our use of energy, which destroyed forests, polluted the air and water, and affected the climate. Nuclear power, in contrast,

Nuclear power

was a clean source of energy that left nature intact. This fact was depicted as perhaps the most absurd feature of the nuclear power debate – that those who called themselves environmentalists and rode on the "green wave" opposed the most environmentally acceptable of all energy sources.

Finally, there were also economic reasons for using atomic energy. Nuclear power plants would by no means be unprofitable, as their opponents tried to argue. Nuclear power was undoubtedly the cheapest form of energy. Investing in nuclear power would also mean a major upswing for industry and employment in Sweden and would take advantage of its sizable uranium deposits. Did we not actually have an obligation to other countries – not least toward the third world, which desperately needed energy for its development – to do what we could to reduce the competition for the world's energy resources? "Self-imposed poverty and isolation" was not the right way for us to help make these people's lives happier and more bearable. The best way was by safeguarding the growth of Sweden's prosperity, so that goods and services would actually be created for distribution. A country as socially and technologically advanced as Sweden had good potential here to make a constructive contribution.[18]

How representative are these arguments? The best picture of the range of opinions on nuclear power outside Parliament can be obtained by going through the official comments of various interested parties on the report of the commission of inquiry on future energy requirements. If we examine these opinions, one group emerges that uses arguments of the kind we have indicated to advocate a high-energy alternative including the use of nuclear power. This main group, consisting of representatives of the business community, public enterprises, and power producers, wanted to expand the Swedish nuclear power program. Remarkably enough, the trade union movement, which also had an interest in industrial growth and full employment, did not belong to this circle.

In this section we have analyzed the first preference in the energy policy of the three groups of actors that we have singled out: The Social Demo-

---

[18] Jörgen Thunell, *Reaktorsäkerhet och olyckskonsekvenser* (CDL, 1974), p. 7; Bengt E. Y. Svensson, "Säkra kärnkraftsverk?" *Svenska Dagbladet,* 17 Feb. 1975; Svensson, "Oenigt om strålskada," ibid., 18 Feb. 1975; Tor Ragnar Gerholm, *Varför kärnkraft?* (Stockholm: KREAB, 1975), pp. 27ff., 39, and 47; Jan Rydberg, "Hur farligt är egentligen plutonium?" *Dagens Nyheter,* 4 Feb. 1975; Dag Jungnell, *Säkerhetsproblem i samband med plutonium* (CDL, 1974), pp. 11–12; Evelyn Sokolowski, *Kärnkraften. Principer och problem* (Stockholm: CDL/Ingenjörsförlaget, 1976); Jörgen Thunell, *Kol, olja, kärnkraft – en jämförelse* (Stockholm: CDL/Ingenjörsförlaget, 1975); Kåre Hannerz, *Kärnkraftens radioaktiva avfall* (ASEA-ATOM, 1974); Bengt Nordström, "Därför måste Forsmark byggas ut," *Svenska Dagbladet,* 8 Feb. 1975; Arnold Lundén, "Vision och verklighet i energidebatten," *Göteborgs Handels- och Sjöfartstidning,* 14 Feb. 1975; Bo Lehnert, "Både kärnkraft och nya energikällor," *Dagens Nyheter,* 23 Feb. 1975; Agnar Nilsson, "Hur farlig är strålningen?" *Svenska Dagbladet,* 25 Apr. 1975.

crats, the Moderates, and the Liberals wanted to keep nuclear power at least in a medium-term planning perspective; the Center party and Left party Communists wanted to dismantle it; and public enterprises and power companies wanted to expand it. But how does a more complete picture of the actors' preference orderings look? In concluding the section, we will attempt to characterize the nuclear power ideologies of the three groups by specifying the attitude of each group toward each of the alternatives to which one actor assigned a top-ranking position in the nuclear power debate.

Distinguishing the preference orderings of the extreme groups is easiest. No doubt, the expansion alternative seemed to the Center party and Left party Communists to be an even worse alternative than keeping nuclear power at the already agreed level. We can thus say that their preference order was phase out – keep – expand nuclear power.

In the same way, it is obvious that the dismantling alternative was the very worst alternative to the business community, whose ideology was a mirror image of that of the Center and Left party Communists. This group's preferences can thus be listed in the order expand – keep – phase out nuclear power.

What was the situation among the Social Democrats, Moderates, and Liberals? Should the extreme alternative "phase out" or "expand" take second place in their preference ordering? For the Social Democrats and Moderates, it is not especially difficult to state that the dismantling alternative was the one most peripheral to their arguments. Their ideology still largely bore the stamp of the progrowth philosophy. They depicted the hazards of nuclear power as small and possible to master. The phasing out of the nuclear power program was thus less irreconcilable with the energy policy arguments of the Liberals. But it is farfetched to claim that at that time, the Liberals would have preferred dismantling to expansion. There was an immense difference between the opinions of the Center party and of the Liberals. The Liberal statement that upholding the old decision to build eleven reactors entailed freedom of choice in energy policy was rejected without further ado by the Center party. The Liberal members' bill showed no understanding of the idea of phasing out nuclear power by 1985, and on some issues the Liberal criticism of nuclear power was more verbal than action oriented. While emphasizing that any classification entails a loss of information, but is justified if we wish to see the main outlines of the debate, we arrive at the conclusion that the preference ordering of the Social Democrats, Moderates, and Liberals at that time was keep – expand – phase out nuclear power. A couple of years later, the major nuclear power accident at Three Mile Island, near Harrisburg, Pennsylvania, would cause all the actors to shift their preferences in a direction more critical of nuclear power. In the subsequent debate, the

Nuclear power

Social Democrats, Moderates, and Liberals can be said to have switched around their second and third preference on the nuclear power issue.

By way of summary, the preferences of the actors on the nuclear power issue, as expressed when Parliament approved the 1975 energy policy bill, can be presented as follows:

> S + M + L: keep – expand – phase out
> C + LPC: phase out – keep – expand
> Business community: expand – keep – phase out

2. BINDING ONESELF

In the 1976 election campaign, Center party chairman Thorbjörn Fälldin was perceived as the self-evident nonsocialist candidate for prime minister.[19] The election successes of the Social Democrats during the supplementary pension dispute had been of a temporary nature. The main postwar trend, a shift of opinion in the direction of the nonsocialists, soon reasserted itself. Once the constitutional reform had introduced a strictly proportional voting system and a unicameral Parliament, no time lag in the composition of the First Chamber majority and no overrepresentation for the largest part could block the popular will. Slowly but surely, a nonsocialist election victory moved closer. In the 1973 election, as already mentioned, the Center party received a full 25 percent of the votes; the result was an exact balance between the blocs, with 175 seats for the nonsocialists and 175 for the socialists. The fact that such a deadlock could arise was an embarrassing oversight in the constitutional reform. As Parliament prepared for the 1976 election, the number of seats was reduced by one so that no repetition would be possible. The Social Democratic government stayed in office, but for three years an amazed world witnessed a demonstration of the lack of wisdom with which humanity is often governed: When Parliament voted on an issue where agreement between the socialist and nonsocialist blocs was impossible, it decided the matter by drawing lots. Would the trend of public opinion in favor of the nonsocialists continue in 1976, so that they could capture the last few additional votes they needed to form a nonsocialist government? Judging from the public opinion surveys, this shift in popular support was actually taking place. Early in 1976 the nonsocialists had a clear lead in the opinion

---

[19] This account is based on Holmberg, Westerståhl, and Branzén 1977; Vedung 1979; Leijonhufvud 1979; Olof Petersson, *Väljarna och valet 1976* (Stockholm: Statistiska Centralbyrån, 1977); Kai Hammerich, *Kompromissernas koalition. Person-och maktspelet kring regeringen Fälldin* (Stockholm: Rabén & Sjögren, 1977); Steven Koblik, *Sweden: The Unstable Balance. End of the Social Democratic Era in Sweden, 1973–80* (Claremont, Calif.: Pomona College, 1981), and a review of the newspaper debate with the help of the Press Archive, Department of Government, University of Uppsala.

polls, dramatically strengthened during the spring after support for the Social Democrats rapidly declined to less than 40 percent of the electorate.

But one issue cast a shadow over Thorbjörn Fälldin's candidacy for the post of prime minister – nuclear power. During the spring of 1976 he had repeated his nonnegotiable demand that nuclear reactors be phased out as a condition for his party's participation in a government. In a parliamentary debate in April, he uttered his famous words: "Let me say, so that there will be no misunderstanding: No ministerial post can be so desirable that I would be prepared to compromise my conviction."[20] He told the Center party Youth League, "This means that we will not participate in any government that begins to build any new nuclear power plant. We will not participate in any government that loads fuel into a new reactor, and we pose as a condition for participating in a government that work begin on a plan of preparedness for a gradual phasing out of the reactors that are in operation. This work must be pursued as intensively as possible and must take two or at most three years."[21] How would Fälldin, as the representative of a minority opinion, now be able to persuade the Moderates and Liberals to accept the Center party's phaseout policy? Would a nonsocialist government be able to pursue a joint atomic energy policy at all? The Social Democrats took advantage of every opportunity to question the credibility of the Center party chairman. No effort was spared so that the slogan "nuclear power opportunists" from the 1975 parliamentary debate would be kept alive. The Social Democratic press spoke openly of Fälldin's "bluffing" on the nuclear power issue. This obvious dilemma also seems to have had its impact on the voters. For although the nonsocialist bloc as a whole was strong, the Center party showed declining support from one opinion poll to the next. And this had been the case throughout Parliament's three-year term of office following the 1973 election. On the basis of figures from the Swedish Institute of Public Opinion Research, during the spring of 1976 there was speculation that Fälldin might lose his position as head of the largest nonsocialist party to Moderate chairman Gösta Bohman.

But outwardly, at least, the election strategists in the Center party leadership acted very calm. In an article entitled "Public Opinion Figures and Policy as the Election Approaches," party secretary Gustaf Jonnergård assured readers that "our (public opinion) figures are not good but our policy is good." The fact that the Center party had not succeeded in making people aware of its policy was "not any unique situation. It is an old truth that public opinion figures for the Center party between elections are lower than their election results." One explanation for this situation

---

[20] RD 1975/76:111, p. 141.
[21] *Protokoll från Centerns ungdomsförbunds förbundsstämma 1976*, p. 124.

was the small number of Center party newspapers. When the campaign took off, however, the Center party's policies would attract voter attention.[22] After their national conference in June, a summer lull descended on Center party policy makers. Whereas the Social democratic election machinery was working energetically to turn the tide of unfavorable opinion, the Center party chairman was harvesting summer hay and taking care of the sheep at his farm in Ramvik, northern Sweden.

The Social Democratic propaganda offensive yielded results. During the summer months, the Social Democrats experienced a strong recovery in voter support. The election debate now focused on areas where the Social Democrats were traditionally strong, such as the economy, employment, and social welfare issues. According to researchers who have analyzed opinion molding and voter behavior in the 1976 election campaign, during that summer it was "unclear whether energy issues would become a major theme in the election campaign."[23]

The situation changed as if by magic when Fälldin belatedly brought up the nuclear power issue again. At a press conference on August 25, which was broadcast by radio, the Center party chairman presented a far-reaching energy-saving program that would make it possible to phase out nuclear power by 1985. This move attracted enormous attention and turned nuclear power into the all-pervading issue during the remaining three weeks of the campaign. By means of interviews, researchers have established that the voters lost interest in the issues that favored the Social Democrats and became caught up in the nuclear power debate; the aggregate effect was that "a new issue, energy policy and nuclear power, moved ahead and became the biggest issue of the campaign."[24] An intensive debate on nuclear power was initiated on the editorial and news pages of the print media.[25] The Social Democratic recovery among the voters was interrupted; the trend once again shifted in favor of the nonsocialists; the Social Democrats once again lost sympathizers.[26]

If we only look at the contents of Fälldin's famous press conference of 25 August 1976, it is difficult to understand that it could have had such far-reaching consequences. This was because in principle, nothing was said at this press conference that had not already been said by the Center party: Nuclear power should be phased out by 1985, and the party did not want to participate in a government that loaded fuel into new nuclear reactors. But by repeating the demand for the dismantling of nuclear

[22] Gustaf Jonnergård, "Opinionssiffrorna och politiken inför valet," *Skånska Dagbladet,* 8 Mar. 1976.
[23] Petersson 1977, p. 200.
[24] Holmberg, Westerståhl, and Branzén 1977, pp. 45ff.
[25] Sören Holmberg, "Pressen och kärnkraften. En studie av nyhetsförmedling och debatt i 20 tidningar under 1976 års valrörelse," *Statsvetenskaplig Tidskrift* (1978): 211–238.
[26] Petersson 1977, p. 194.

power at the height of the election campaign, Fälldin publicly made a binding commitment on the nuclear power issue. This binding commitment had a maximum effect because it had been preceded by a long period of silence, during which the opposing side had gained ground and the Center party's credibility had been brought into question. All doubts about the party now vanished, and overnight the nuclear power issue became the main attraction of the election campaign. Timing is an important instrument in politics, as party secretary Jonnergård later argued. "We simply saved nuclear power until the right moment. We know, of course, that people can't get into every issue all at once."[27] But as one American researcher has said, Fälldin got plenty of help from the media in binding himself as categorically and dramatically as possible.[28]

By binding himself on the nuclear issue, Fälldin could achieve two purposes. First, he could try to escape from the role of potential loser in the election and lead his party to victory by dispelling any doubts about the credibility of the Center party on the nuclear issue. Viewed in this way, his nuclear power statement was an election argument of the ordinary kind: This is what I want to do, vote for me, and the world will become better. In a somewhat longer perspective, he could also use this binding commitment to attempt to escape from another role as a potential loser – in subsequent bargaining with his government coalition partners on the nuclear issue. He had given a signal to his presumptive cabinet colleagues that meant: Seek compromises on other issues, but I cannot budge on nuclear power after what I have now promised the voters. Whereas he succeeded in his first purpose, the latter was the one that would continue to make the political game dramatic. To those who have read the rational choice literature on binding oneself as a political strategy, this outcome is not a surprise.[29]

The blunting of the Social Democratic offensive was enough to ensure a nonsocialist victory in the election. The Social Democratic government resigned, and a nonsocialist one took office. It had been a long time com-

---

[27] Kaa Eneberg, "Gustaff Jonnergård – en taktiker till varje pris," *Dagens Nyheter,* 17 Oct. 1976. Jonnergård immediately denied certain parts of this interview. But this denial concerned something else – not the timing of Fälldin's nuclear power statement, but a statement that DN's journalist ascribed to him, to the effect that the Center party had known all along that a compromise on the nuclear power issue was unavoidable, but that for tactical reasons it had pretended to the voters that nothing of the kind would be considered. "We didn't know it in advance," Jonnergård declared in his denial. "The compromise could just as well have occurred in some other political field. Before the election we had good reason to hope that we could push through the Center's entire nuclear power policy." "Jonnergård: Jag blev felciterad," *Dagens Nyheter,* 18 October 1976.

[28] Koblik 1981, pp. 235–236.

[29] Thomas C. Schelling, *The Strategy of Conflict* (Cambridge, Mass.: Harvard University Press, 1960); Knut Midgaard, *Forhandlingsteoretiske momenter* (Oslo: Institutt for statsvitenskap, 1971), pp. 23–24.

Nuclear power

Table 8.1. *Changes in party strengths between the 1973 and 1976 elections, as a percentage of total votes*

	LPC	S	C	L	M
1973 and 1976 elections	−0.5	−0.9	−1.0	+1.7	+1.3

Source: Olof Petersson and Bo Särlvik, "När de borgerliga vann," *Statsvetenskaplig Tidskrift,* 1977, p. 79, table 2.

Table 8.2. *Changes in voting preference among swing voters in final stage of election campaign*

	LPC	S	C	L	M	Others	Total
Intended vote, according to survey							
23 August–5 September	5	25	16	28	23	3	100%
Actual vote	5	18	25	33	19	0	100%
Change	0	−7	+9	+5	−4	−3	

Source: Olof Petersson, *Väljarna och valet 1976* (Stockholm: Statistiska Centralbyrån, 1977), p. 190, table 4:36.

ing; forty-four years had passed since Per Albin Hansson formed his first cabinet during the Great Depression. While this obviously signified a very big change in Swedish politics, as Table 8.1 indicates it was the result of very small changes in the electorate: The shifts in each party's respective share of the votes was only between 0.5 and 1.7 percent. But this was the straw that broke the camel's back, giving a victory to the nonsocialists.

As indicated, the Center party lost exactly 1 percent of the votes, but the increase in the Moderates' and Liberals' share of the votes more than offset this loss. Without the dramatic developments during the final stage of the election campaign, however, the Center party's loss would have been even greater, as we can see in Table 8.2. Swing voters switched primarily to the Center party and in some degree to the Liberals; the Social Democrats lost the largest number.

Because these shifts were so small, every issue that can be shown to have determined people's decisions on how to vote was important to the election result. Nuclear power was such an issue – one of the most important – and it favored the Center party. For this reason, it can easily be argued, as the Social Democrats later did, that Thorbjörn Fälldin's self-binding strategy on the nuclear power issue provided the margin the nonsocialists needed to win their election victory.

There was never any doubt that the prime minister of the three-party nonsocialist coalition government would be Thorbjörn Fälldin. The Moderate party chariman became minister of economic affairs, and the Liberal chairman became labor minister. Negotiations on the formation of the government lasted for more than three weeks. Step by step, the parties agreed on policy guidelines and the distribution of ministerial posts. Not unexpectedly, the nuclear power issue turned out to be by far the hardest nut to crack. Only one hour before the party chairmen were scheduled to present their proposal to the Speaker of Parliament as to who should become the country's new prime minister did the three nonsocialist parties reach agreement.

It was clear from the government's policy declaration that the Moderates and Liberals had forced the Center party to make substantial concessions. The declaration did not promise any phasing out of nuclear power; it contained no pledges either to remove existing reactors from service or to interrupt the construction of planned reactors. On the other hand, the Moderates and Liberals had to go along with not allowing any new reactors to be loaded with nuclear fuel if the power company could not exhibit an acceptable agreement on reprocessing of spent nuclear fuel and also show how and where "completely safe final deposition" of the waste could take place. Barsebäck 2, Sweden's sixth nuclear reactor, which was ready for fuel loading, was exempted from this rule and could start operation, but it would have to be removed from service after one year if the owner could not show an agreement on how its waste would be handled. The policy declaration also announced that a major commission of inquiry on energy would be appointed in order to prepare material for new energy policy legislation to be approved by Parliament during 1978.

In other words, both sides had had to give and take; the negotiations had ended in a compromise. Fälldin admitted this himself when he declared that he "had not made it all the way" on the nuclear power issue. He had been compelled to go along with the loading of fuel into the Barsebäck 2 reactor, but in return he had won acceptance for safety regulations that would give Sweden's energy policy a new long-term direction.

This defense is strange. The self-binding strategy means, as we know, that compromises are out of the question. Fälldin had now agreed to a departure from his nuclear power policy just the same. In that case, it does not help that the reasons for a compromise may be very rational and that long-term gains may seem more important than a temporary concession. For by binding himself, Fälldin had declared in advance that he would forswear any participation in such forms of collective decisions. The critics of the Center party, headed by the new opposition leader, Olof Palme,

258

consequently shouted "A betrayal!" A public debate on morality and political strategy began; it would last for years to come.

The new government soon had its hands full with Sweden's economic problems. Instead of the "set table" that the Palme government had declared it was handing over to the Fälldin government, it turned out that the country was in an economic crisis. Large-scale loans were raised abroad, at the same time as the government was trying to implement such nonsocialist ideological principles as lower marginal tax rates and incentives for people to buy stocks and more widespread ownership of productive resources.

But inexorably, like a time bomb, new nuclear reactors were completed. In the winter of 1978 the State Power Board applied for permission to load fuel into the Forsmark 1 and Ringhals 3 reactors. By this time the rule stipulated in the government's policy declaration about completely safe final storage of spent fuel had resulted in a law, known as the Stipulations Act, that spelled out the conditions under which new reactors could be loaded with fuel. The State Power Board believed that in its application, it had fulfilled the requirements of the law as to final storage of nuclear waste. The Moderates and Liberals were of the same opinion. But the Center party had the opposite view. Fälldin postponed the decision time after time. Beginning in the late summer of 1978 the party chairmen – Fälldin, Bohman, and Ola Ullsten (who had recently succeeded Per Ahlmark as head of the Liberal party) – were once again completely enmeshed in nuclear power negotiations. It seemed harder and harder for Fälldin to go along with additional compromises, all the more so after December 1977 when he had had to accept the continued operation of Barsebäck 2 on the basis of a reprocessing argument, which the Moderates and Liberals but not the Center party had found acceptable. Were any additional compromises politically possible for Fälldin?

At the end of September, the government rejected the State Power Board's application. But the government's explanation for its action specified that additional geological test drilling in Sweden's bedrock was considered necessary in order to establish that safety requirements of the Stipulations Act were being fulfilled. If this were done and the Nuclear Power Inspectorate found the results acceptable, the government would approve the application to load fuel into Forsmark 1 and Ringhals 3.

The media immediately depicted this "drilling hole compromise" as a veiled yes to the loading of fuel; Fälldin was presented once again as "the loser" and the government's decision as a repeat of his "betrayal." At a televised press conference, an obviously hard-pressed Thorbjörn Fälldin, sweat pouring from his forehead, tried to parry the attacks of journalists, while Gösta Bohman and Ola Ullsten expressed their satisfaction with the agreement. Bohman even believed that the applicants had already fulfilled "99 percent" of the safety requirements laid down by the government. When the minister of energy, Center party member Olof Johansson, heard these words he ordered a memorandum distributed at the press conference that contained *his* interpretation of the drilling hole compromise. This memorandum required that extremely far-reaching requirements be fulfilled in order for an application to be approved. The energy minister's behavior caused great irritation among Moderates and Liberals. New discussions among the government parties became necessary. But by now, there was no longer any chance of consensus. After the enormous effort required to reach the drilling hole compromise, there was no political strength left to find new solutions. To the surprise of many, Ullsten was particularly inflexible. On 5 October 1978, the government resigned. The first nonsocialist cabinet in forty-four years had not been able to survive through its regular three-year term. Fälldin and the opponents of nuclear power had, at least in a short-term perspective, failed to stop the march into the nuclear society.

This did not, however, mean that nuclear power ceased to play a major role in Swedish politics. The nuclear reactor accident at Three Mile Island in 1979 had a very significant impact. In the ironic words of Tage Danielsson, a nuclear power opponent and writer/actor well known for his satirical revues and films, "an unlikely event turned out to be a real one." The Social Democrats, Moderates, and Liberals now shifted preferences in a direction more critical to nuclear power and agreed to the idea of holding a referendum on the issue. The Center party and Left party Communists had toyed with the idea of such a referendum for a long time, because as potential losers in the parliamentary arena they thought they had more to gain if the decision were referred instead to the public arena. Just as in the case of the supplementary pension referendum, the results of the nuclear power referendum were difficult to interpret because not two but three alternatives were presented to the voters. What is more, the supporters of all three alternatives declared that their own alternative meant a phasing out of nuclear power. Line 1 and Line 2 specified, however, that this would take place only after the reactors already approved had been completed and had been used throughout their economic and technological lifetime. According to Line 3, supported by the Center party and Left party Communists, Sweden's atomic reactors would be phased out within ten years. Objectively speaking, it was hard to see any difference among the three "nuclear power parties." The Social Democrats, who for election strategy reasons wanted to distance themselves from the Moderates, made an amendment to the agenda and demanded that in addition to stating their opinion on nuclear power as such, the people should also say whether they thought nuclear reactors should be owned

Table 8.3. *The nuclear power game*

	Fälldin	
	Swerve	Not swerve
Bohman–Ullsten Swerve	0, 0	−1, +1
Not swerve	+1, −1	−2, −2

by the state and local governments, as opposed to private power companies. The Moderates could not accept this, but instead they formulated
their own alternative – Line 1 – while the Liberals, on the other hand, saw
no obstacles to working with the Social Democrats on behalf of Line 2.
The result of the referendum, which was held in March 1980, was that
Line 1 received 18.7 percent of the votes, Line 2 got 39.3 percent, and Line
3 attracted 38.6 percent. The day after the referendum, the voters, politicians, and media completely lost interest in the issue that had dominated
Swedish politics for half a decade. The nuclear power issue was relegated
to the periphery of the political game. Eventually Parliament approved the
construction and use of twelve reactors, specifying that they were later to
be shut down successively, the last one "no later than the year 2010."[30]

3. THE DECISIONS TO LOAD NUCLEAR REACTORS

Why was Thorbjörn Fälldin prepared as prime minister, on certain conditions, to load fuel into new nuclear reactors despite the fact that in the
1976 election campaign he had categorically committed himself to the
phasing out of nuclear power? Let us subject the deliberations of the actors
on the nuclear power issue to our customary game theory analysis. We
will first examine the decision in the fall of 1976 that led to the loading
of fuel into Barsebäck 2, and after that the decision in the fall of 1978 that
led to the collapse of the tripartite nonsocialist government.

The decision-making process within the government is what interests
us. For this reason, we will ignore the opposition and place Bohman–
Ullsten on one side as row players and Fälldin on the other side as the
column player. Their utility values can be seen in Table 8.3. For reasons
that will soon become clear, we will call the alternatives "not swerve,"
which means that you stick to your view of nuclear power, and "swerve,"
meaning that you deviate from this view.

[30] Prop 1979/80:170 and 1980/81:90, quote from appendix 1, p. 287.

The best outcome for both sides is to be able to avoid swerving while the opponent swerves (+1 in the lower left-hand quadrant for Bohman–Ullsten, + 1 in the upper right-hand quadrant for Fälldin). The outcome that is next best for both sides is for both to swerve in order to make a compromise possible (upper left-hand quadrant). What alternative is the worst and what is the next worst? During the fall 1976 negotiations on the formation of a government, Bohman and Ullsten (actually his predecessor Ahlmark) were willing to make concessions to Fälldin's tough safety requirements in order to avoid a head-on collision with Fälldin on the nuclear power issue, which would have prevented the formation of a nonsocialist government (lower right-hand quadrant). In Fälldin's case there are contradictory statements. Before the election, he had eliminated the compromise alternative by means of his self-binding strategy. After the election, however, he spoke the language of compromise, justifying his willingness to go along with the loading of fuel at Barsebäck 2 by saying that he had admittedly not made it all the way but had come part of the way: Being in the government was important in itself because it enabled his party to influence policy on matters that included nuclear power. In other words, the ordering between the worst and next-worst alternatives for Fälldin switched after the election: Before the election the "swerve" alternative was the worst, after the election the alternative of a collision was the worst. Because what we are explaining here is the decision in fall 1976, let us allow the latter set of views to be represented in the matrix. The lower left-hand quadrant will be the very worst alternative – both for Fälldin and for Bohman–Ullsten.

By reconstructing the actors' preferences in this way, we have arrived at a game that, alongside the "prisoners' dilemma," is the most famous in the literature of game theory – the game of "chicken." It can be illustrated by a daredevil game that young people in California supposedly played in the late 1950s. They would drive two cars straight toward each other at high speed; the first one to swerve was the "chicken." If you wanted to look really brave, you threw your steering wheel out the window. This demonstrated to your opponent that you couldn't swerve, which forced him to do so in order to avoid a head-on collision. The utility values in Table 8.3 reflect the drivers' evaluations of the various outcomes of this game resulting from different combinations of the alternative courses of action, "not swerve" and "swerve."

Our interpretation of the nuclear power game in the fall of 1976 is that the nonsocialist party chairmen were involved in a chickenlike game when it came to making your opponent swerve from his previous path on the nuclear power issue and thereby – if total submission on the part of the opponent was not now within reach – make possible a compromise and the formation of a government.

Nuclear power

Unlike the "prisoners' dilemma," both players in "chicken" have a shared worst alternative that they can avoid through cooperation. In the "prisoners' dilemma," on the other hand, we know that a player only experiences the worst alternative if he chooses the cooperation alternative while his opponent does not.

Also unlike the "prisoners' dilemma," there is no dominant strategy in "chicken." Two quadrants are in equilibrium in this game: the lower left-hand and upper right-hand quadrants. If the Bohman–Ullsten side drives straight ahead, Fälldin should swerve; if Fälldin drives straight ahead, Bohman–Ullsten should swerve.

The most significant difference between the "prisoners' dilemma" and "chicken" is that in "chicken" the punishment for refusal to cooperate is greater than the loss can be if you cooperate. This fact has led to extensive discussions of one empirical application of this game – the study of super-power conflicts. Are the U.S. and Soviet arms buildups and conflicts a "prisoners' dilemma" or a "chicken" game? If the former is the case, developments are moving inevitably toward something that no one wants. The gravity of the situation may thus seem to justify a minimax strategy. But on the other hand, if politicians are minimax players, the threat of a nuclear war, which comprises the lower right-hand quadrant here, is actually an effective method for averting war. Under any circumstances, there is reason to emphasize that the instability of the cooperation strategies in both the "prisoners' dilemma" and "chicken" may cause the players to choose not to cooperate, something that has particularly devastating consequences in "chicken."

Unlike the "prisoners' dilemma," there is thus no solution to "chicken." Who wins and who loses depends on what risks the actors are prepared to take. Bluffing, threats, ultimatums, and – not least – binding oneself are methods intended to force your opponent into submission. But using such tricks is not without risk: It can easily lead to self-induced failure. This need to make decisions while uncertain of your opponent's reactions is very obviously a part of the conditions under which our politicians work, and the "chicken" game is thus usually considered a very realistic model of the political game, with its singular mixture of rationality and drama.[31]

During the bargaining that followed their 1976 election victory, all three nonsocialist party chairmen also felt very strong pressure to reach

[31] Anatol Rapoport, *Two-Person Game Theory* (Ann Arbor: University of Michigan Press, 1966), pp. 137ff.; Steven J. Brams, *Game Theory and Politics* (New York: The Free Press, 1975), pp. 39–50; Robert Abrams, *Foundations of Political Analysis. An Introduction to the Theory of Collective Choice* (New York: Columbia University Press, 1980), pp. 193ff.; Jon Elster, *Ulysses and the Sirens. Studies in Rationality and Irrationality* (Cambridge: Cambridge University Press, 1979), pp. 121ff.; Glenn H. Snyder and Paul Diesing, *Conflict among Nations: Bargaining, Decision Making, and System Structure in International Crises* (Princeton, N.J.: Princeton University Press, 1977), pp. 44–45.

agreement on immediate formation of a government. After such a long period of Social Democratic rule, nonsocialist voters expected a great deal from a three-party government. The party chairmen were being forced to form a government under virtually any conditions. At the same time, their differences on the nuclear power issue were public knowledge. After lengthy negotiations, a compromise was finally achieved: The actors moved away from the threatening lower right-hand quadrant up to the upper left-hand one. In the end, Fälldin did not allow his self-binding during the election campaign to prevent him from taking this step. The "betrayal" debate that followed was the price he had to pay for this maneuver.

After this, let us move on to the negotiations during the fall of 1978. At that time, conditions were partly changed. By means of the drilling hole compromise, Fälldin tried once again to end up in the upper left-hand quadrant. But this time he did not succeed. Two years of the betrayal debate had undermined the credibility of the Center party. Fälldin's concern was no longer just to "save the government." He also had to "save the party." The media nevertheless characterized the agreement not as a compromise but as a capitulation on Fälldin's part, as if – to put it differently – he were not in the upper left-hand quadrant but in the lower left-hand one. In other words, Fälldin had become the chicken. In this political situation, that was more than the Center party could tolerate. By handing out his memorandum at the press conference, the energy minister – figuratively speaking – helped Fälldin to throw his steering wheel out the car window. The self-binding strategy was restored. Because his opponent was considered likely to "drive straight ahead" and Fälldin had sacrificed his ability to steer, a collision was inevitable. The game ended in the lower right-hand quadrant.

The conditions of the game were, however, different during the fall of 1978, not only for Fälldin but also for Ullsten. The latter had begun to play with the thought of being able to form a pure Liberal party government if the three-party government should collapse. The lower right-hand quadrant no longer seemed so threatening to him at all (and Table 8.3 no longer indicates Ullsten's preferences). Whereas Bohman, who was ideologically furthest away from Fälldin, continued his procompromise policy for strategic reasons, Ullsten's strategic interests caused him to switch to a harder line even though ideologically he was closer to Fälldin. A final pronuclear gesture on the part of Ullsten was enough finally to trigger the collapse of the government.[32]

This was no happy solution for Thorbjörn Fälldin. He had been forced

---

[32] Olof Petersson, *Regeringsbildningen 1978* (Stockholm: Rabén and Sjögren, 1979); Vedung 1979, pp. 63 and 76.

to help bring about an outcome that gave him lower utility values than were theoretically possible, despite the fact that he was not forced into this by the logic of the decision-making situation, as in the "prisoners' dilemma." The explanation is that Fälldin's self-binding strategy, though in practice abandoned two years earlier, continued to cast its shadow over his calculations and prevented him from choosing in such a way as to minimize his losses. In other words, the nuclear power issue illustrates the dangers of the self-binding strategy and how it tends to get in the way of rational political action, as we have defined it here – not to cling inflexibly to your original preferences but instead to maneuver so that you at least get something, when you cannot get everything. As long as you only have the support of a minority, you simply cannot make a binding ideological commitment and at the same time try to get into the government by forming coalitions with others who oppose your views.

4. THE WEIGHTING METHOD

What finally happened is what it says in the textbook: The majority got its way. The minority did not succeed in stopping the march into the nuclear power society. But it was a close call. In rational choice theory, some have argued that in decision-making situations such as the one described here, the will of the minority *ought* to be able to win and that the right collective decision on the nuclear power issue would have been for Bohman–Ullsten to swerve for Fälldin.

Let us begin our analysis of the arguments for this point of view by recalling the prerequisites for the nuclear power game during the fall of 1978. The government controlled 180 seats against 169 seats for the opposition. The Moderates had 55, the Center party 86, and the Liberals 39 seats. To win, all three coalition parties thus had to vote the same way. It was enough if one governing party withdrew its support to enable the opposition to win instead. A majority decision within the government would result in a defeat in the parliamentary vote.

The government parties thus had to reach agreement on a common policy. But who should yield to whom? Steven Strasnick has argued that it is possible to understand such problems by closely examining the different actors' preference orderings. On the next few pages we will apply Strasnick's analytical technique to the Swedish nuclear power issue. As indicated in the analysis of ideologies in the first section of this chapter, their preference orderings looked as follows (we will now ignore all the other actors and concentrate on the decision-making problems of the government parties):

> Fälldin: phase out – keep – expand nuclear power
> Bohman–Ullsten: keep – expand – phase out nuclear power

Ideology and strategy

To make our presentation easier, let us introduce the following symbols:

A = Fälldin
B = Bohman–Ullsten
x = phase out nuclear power
y = keep nuclear power
z = expand nuclear power

The preference orderings are:

A: xyz
B: yzx

A prefers x and B prefers y. But what is the right collective decision? Both A and B prefer y to z, and according to so-called Pareto optimality, the collective preference is also y over z, which is written yPz. But in choosing between x and z and between x and y, A and B disagree. Using Arrow's terminology, we can either abandon the transitivity rule or else let one of the actors become a "dictator."

Let us, for example, adhere to the transitivity rule; and let us permit the collective to be indifferent in the choice between x and y, that is, xIy. Because yPz and xIy, according to the transitivity rule xPz also follows. The point here is that while A has this particular preference ordering and puts x ahead of z, B prefers z to x. Yet the collective preference is xPz. In other words, A's preferences are decisive, or as we say in rational choice jargon, A is the dictator whose preferences come before the other player's. On the nuclear power issue, this would imply that in choosing between phasing out (x) and expanding (z) nuclear power, Fälldin's opinion should be allowed to decide the matter.

Arriving at a decision in this way by submitting to the will of a dictator may seem unfortunate. Strasnick maintains, however, that in situations such as the one depicted here, it may actually be something desirable. He begins his argument in favor of this view by questioning another of Arrow's conditions – that collective decisions should only be made dependent on the order in which individuals rank their preferences. "This condition rules out consideration of what are customarily called 'preference intensities,'" Strasnick writes. "After all, it is argued, why should the collective choice in a situation where competing individuals are only mildly committed to one alternative over another be automatically the same as in a similar situation where one of the individuals now has a desperate need for some alternative and everyone else is lukewarm?"

When it comes to reaching a decision based on such preference orderings as those stated here, we humans are not equally enthusiastic about the outcome of all pair-by-pair comparisons among the alternatives, Stras-

266

nick believes.[33] But to establish such differences in level of commitment, we need a theory about what is meant by giving "higher priority" to a particular decision over another. Strasnick formulates the following principle: "The only acceptable social choice procedure is that which prefers in each choice situation the alternative favored by the individual who would be left worse off if his preference were not satisfied."

Does this mean that Fälldin's policy of phasing out nuclear energy (x) should be preferred to Bohman–Ullsten's proposal to keep nuclear energy at its then-current level (y)? According to Strasnick's decision rule, we should draw this conclusion if alternative y is worse for Fälldin than the phasing-out alternative is for Bohman–Ullsten, indicated by the symbols $x_B > y_A$. If we wish to follow Strasnick's argument in a stringent manner, we must furthermore be able to show that the utility of a victory has to be greater for A than for B, that is, that $x_A > y_B$.

We thus finally arrive at the following:

$$x_A > y_B > z_B > x_B > y_A > z_A \qquad xPy \text{ and } xPz$$

The first part of this formula involves comparing the utility of x and y to the various actors, as we just discussed. After this come the rankings according to B's original preference ordering. Then we make the comparison just discussed, $x_B > y_A$, and finally there is a comparison according to A's original ranking of y and z. According to this line of reasoning, x should be chosen over y (and also x over z). The collective decision should be xPy. Fälldin's phasing-out policy should be preferred to Bohman–Ullsten's status quo alternative.[34]

---

[33] Strasnick also proves that given certain conditions that resemble those presented by Arrow, it is possible to work out a well-defined decision rule that takes advantage of such comparisons. Unlike Arrow, Strasnick thus proves that a decision rule that fulfills these prerequisites actually exists.

[34] The reason that the simpler decision-making principle does not suffice is that we face a situation where Strasnick's decision rule is to be applied for the first time. This is because in deducing his principle, Strasnick assumes the existence of at least one situation where the more demanding prerequisites are fulfilled. Once we have found such a case, the simpler decision rule is generally applicable.

On the nuclear power issue, it would thus have been possible to argue that Fälldin's wishes should have been allowed to decide the matter with the help of an alternative method. We could then have let the decision between x and z comprise the so-called first-time case – that is, if $x_A > z_B$ and $x_B > z_A$, the collective outcome is xPz. After this, according to Strasnick, it suffices to compare the individuals' evaluation of their own preferences as not being satisfied. xPy would then follow if we can show $x_B > y_A$. In principle, this method is less demanding:

$$x_A > z_B > x_B > y_A > z_A \qquad xPz \text{ and } xPy$$

but in our special case the practical differences between the two methods are probably paper thin.

The argument summarized here is taken from Steven Strasnick, "The Problem of Social Choice: Arrow to Rawls," *Philosophy and Public Affairs* (1976): 241–273; quotations from pp. 245 and 262. I would like to extend my thanks to Jörgen Hermansson of my department for our stimulating discussions of Strasnick's theory.

Table 8.4. *Intensity of voter commitment on the nuclear power issue*

	Category[a]				
	1	2	3	4	5
No. of people interviewed	904	483	274	468	249
% who consider the nuclear power issue one of the absolutely most important issues or a fairly important issue	79	45	22	41	58

Note: The same pattern emerges when the attitude of voters toward nuclear power is measured using two other indicators. I would like to thank Olof Petersson of my department for being kind enough to extract the data for this table for me from his study of the 1976 election.

[a]The categories define responses to the proposal "Stop the expansion of nuclear power." 1 = Good proposal: very important that it be implemented; 2 = Good proposal: fairly important that it be implemented; 3 = Doesn't matter very much; 4 = Bad proposal: fairly important that it not be implemented; 5 = Bad proposal: very important that it not be implemented.

In his discussion of what is the right decision rule when actors' preferences cross each other as they did on the nuclear power issue in Sweden during the mid-1970s, Strasnick thus puts his finger on the so-called intensity problem: Votes should be weighted so that the actor who is most intensively committed is not ignored; the vote of the person who has the most to lose if defeated should weigh heaviest.

What do we know empirically about the actors' level of commitment on the nuclear issue? We have already mentioned that Fälldin personally embraced it with extraordinary enthusiasm. But was this generally true of the opponents of nuclear power? Can we also say whether they were more intensively committed than the supporters of nuclear power?

Actually we can, thanks to the extensive interview studies that political scientists carried out at the time of the 1976 election. In Table 8.4 we see that the groupings at the extremes of opinion on the nuclear power issue – both the people who thought it was very or fairly important to stop the expansion of nuclear power and those who thought it was very or fairly important not to stop it – were more intensively involved in the issue than other groups. But the U curve is asymmetrical: A larger proportion of the opponents than of the supporters of nuclear power considered these proposals important. The opponents of nuclear power were more intensively involved than its supporters.

The same situation can also be illustrated using data from another study of the 1976 election; Table 8.5 shows the correlation between involvement

Table 8.5. *The voters' assessment of important
election issues: percentage who mentioned energy
and nuclear power policy*

LPC	S	C	L	M	% of all interviewees
29	12	45	19	13	21

in the nuclear power issue and party sympathies. Researchers asked the voters whether there was any issue in the upcoming election that was especially important to them. Of all voters surveyed, 52 percent mentioned one or more such issues. Energy and nuclear power policy emerged as the most important issue. It was mentioned by 21 percent of these voters; no other issue was mentioned as often. The difference among the various party sympathizers was clear. No fewer than 45 percent of Center party sympathizers mentioned this issue, whereas the corresponding figure for the Social Democrats was only 12 percent. The Moderates showed almost as little interest, whereas the figure among Liberal sympathizers was somewhat higher. Among the supporters of the other antinuclear party, the Left party Communists, interest was substantially higher.[35]

We can thus conclude that the opponents of nuclear power were more intensively involved in the issue than its advocates. Does this also mean that we should follow Strasnick in according special weight to their vote and letting the opponents of nuclear power win the game?

Strasnick is remarkably brief in his normative arguments. As the perceptive reader will already have noted, he considers it sufficient to agree with Rawls's criterion for an acceptable decision rule: The person who should be favored is the one who has the most to lose if his preference is not satisfied.

Rawls's – and Strasnick's – arguments stand or fall on the assumption that the world consists of minimaxers, who want to minimize their losses. To Gustaf V during the Palace Yard crisis and Tage Erlander as he faced the decision about a referendum on the supplementary pension issue, it was rational to choose a minimax strategy, because they were aware of their opponents' preference ordering and could figure out that otherwise they would suffer maximum losses. But when we are compelled to make our calculations under the veil of ignorance without information about the consequences to us of our own behavior, there is nothing that says that we should follow a minimax strategy. Everything depends on what risks we are prepared to take. We can instead choose a maximax strategy

---

[35] Holmberg, Westerståhl, and Branzén 1977, pp. 40ff., esp. table 3, p. 43.

and design a society with big differences between people, in the hope of ending up on the sunny side of life ourselves. The veil of ignorance is no guarantee of the adoption of a rule system that will promote social equality or minimize losses in society. If we wish to promote such values, we must find our normative arguments outside game theory's closed world of value-neutral strategies.

Strasnick's contribution is that he has shown how we can compare the intensity of involvement by various actors through an analysis of the preference orderings of individual actors. This important achievement was, for a long time, regarded as impossible. But what conclusions we should draw from the fact that different groups have different levels of involvement in a particular issue is a more difficult normative problem than Strasnick seems to think.

The problem of intensity has been debated throughout the ideological development of democracy. By what right a more weakly committed majority can force its will on an intensely committed minority is a classic question. The leading modern work in this area is Robert Dahl's *A Preface to Democratic Theory*. If A prefers x and B prefers y and we are supposed to decide who wins, there are certainly many of us, Dahl writes, who would like to know how intensive are the wishes of each side. What is more reasonable than to let the intensively committed person get his way, even if he represents a minority? Not merely counting but also weighing votes may be a better way of turning individual preferences into collective decisions. For simple majority rule is a primitive method of making decisions. Strictly speaking, it only says something about the first preference of a majority. Dahl's work takes the form of a discussion of the possibility of finding a new method that would also take into account the fact that political alternatives may be embraced with varying degrees of commitment by citizens. But in the end, Dahl is forced to give up. There is no way to compare the intensity of different citizens' preferences, he believes. Who should decide when the majority should concede to a minority? How can we record and compare intensity? In what way can we protect ourselves from abuses, for example in the form of citizens who exaggerate their intensity in order to gain advantages? And even though today we actually do have theoretical techniques like Strasnick's and there are empirical measuring methods such as public opinion surveys for comparing the intensity of different citizens' preferences, we are compelled to admit that none of them is of practical use in day-to-day political work. The use of these methods is limited to retrospective scholarly analysis of how the political game was played. No matter how faulty it may be, simple majority rule seems irreplaceable. But Dahl makes one recommendation. He advocates a constitutional system with a maximum distribution of power on different levels and to different bodies, so that an intensive minority has as many opportunities as possible to assert itself against the majority.[36] In general, those researchers who have focused on the intensity problem have followed the same line.

In practice, it is not possible to make comparisons between the intensity of various actors' political commitment, another researcher writes. We can only compare the intensity of our own feelings, "and it is precisely this kind of comparison that leads to logrolling, where an individual trades his vote on an issue of relative low intensity for him, in return for support on an issue about which he feels more strongly."[37]

Only a constitutionally guaranteed, far-reaching distribution of power prevents oppression on the part of the majority, one of the leading theoreticians of rationalist political science also writes. Only in this way can we promote the possibility that in the long run, collective decisions will reflect individual preferences in a correct way.[38]

And these possibilities are also often present in political reality, to shift once again from theoretical analysis to empirical description. This need not depend only on the skill of minority representatives in the political game. Sometimes the constellation of actors' preferences may be such that it is rational for the majority to let the minority do what it wants. Free possession of weapons in the United States is an example of this. A majority of Americans, both in the Republican and Democratic parties, are against free possession of weapons. A minority of the population – for example, weapons dealers and members of rifle clubs – is for it. Those in the latter group are more intensively committed to the issue and can let it determine how they vote. Those in the former group are lukewarm and let other issues determine their choice of party. The parties thus have everything to lose by bringing up the issue of regulating the possession of weapons on the agenda. Their decision thus concurs with the wishes of the intensively committed minority.[39]

The intensity problem is the Achilles' heel of democracy. When Arrow ignores it and only requires collective decisions in keeping with the ranking of individual preferences, regardless of how strong these are, he builds

[36] Robert A. Dahl, *A Preface to Democratic Theory* (Chicago: University of Chicago Press, 1956), esp. pp. 49–50, 82–83, 90–119, and 124–151.

[37] J. Roland Pennock, *Democratic Political Theory* (Princeton, N.J.: Princeton University Press, 1979), pp. 394ff.; quotation from p. 396.

[38] William H. Riker, *Liberalism Against Populism: A Confrontation between the Theory of Democracy and the Theory of Social Choice* (San Francisco: Freeman, 1982).

[39] The opportunities for special interests to assert themselves despite their minority position were discussed at a 1979 conference whose proceedings were edited by Michael J. Malbin, *Parties, Interest Groups, and Campaign Finance Laws* (Washington, D.C.: American Enterprise Institute, 1980).

a distorted model of how democratic decisions should ideally be made.[40] But perhaps, in spite of everything, this is the only practical possibility. The weighting method would probably create greater problems than it would solve. Our own conclusion is that there is no solution, at least for the present, to the intensity problem.

In the political history of Sweden, two separate constitutional traditions run together on this problem. On the one hand Swedes pay homage to the principle of political equality and demand that every citizen's vote should be worth the same; universal and equal suffrage and parliamentarism are expressions of this view. At the same time, they counteract this principle by the mere fact of allowing those who have particularly strong interests in some issue to organize in order to advance their causes by extraparliamentary means. And this principle of freedom of association is considered as holy as universal and equal suffrage. What is more, when special interests are affected, they are given extra influence; they are allowed to sit as members of commissions of inquiry and are asked to contribute their written comments on commission reports and to take part in implementing decisions. Perhaps it is this mixture of political egalitarianism and consideration for special interests or, if we wish, parliamentary and corporative forms of decision making, that makes it possible to maintain good relations in society.

"Staaff or De Geer?" – this is how the question was posed during the constitutional crisis of the 1910s in Sweden. By unifying and bringing together different groups, preferably by means of agreements and compromises, the father of the 1866 parliamentary reform had tried to run the country while taking special interests into account. Per Albin Hansson would later follow in De Geer's footsteps in the conviction – to quote Fredrik Lagerroth, a professor of political science – "that if there is a majority, then it acts wisely by paying heed to what a strong minority has to say." The gap between this and Staaff's constitutional ideals was enormous, with Staaff instead calling for majority rule, parliamentarism, and a party government in an adversary relationship with the opposition.[41]

Is one of these ways of making decisions more correct than the other? In the fall of 1978, would the government have been less respectful of

---

[40] It should be noted, however, that in an essay as early as 1967 Arrow admitted that basing decisions exclusively on rankings of individual preferences might be an unnecessarily narrow decision rule. In many cases we actually had information that made it possible to compare the intensity of different actors' preferences – "I am better off under conditions x than you under conditions y." It remains to be seen, Arrow concluded, whether such observations can lay the foundation for a usable rational choice theory. Kenneth J. Arrow, "Values and Collective Decision-making," in *Philosophy, Politics and Society,* ed. Peter Laslett and W. G. Runciman (Oxford: Blackwell, 1967), pp. 213–231.

[41] Gunnar Rexius, "Parlamentarismen och svensk tradition," *Svensk Tidskrift* (1917):181–193; Fredrik Lagerroth, "Staaf eller De Geer? Till frågan om vårt levande statsskicks typologi," *Statsvetenskaplig Tidskrift* (1943): 1–33, quotation from p. 26.

citizens' preferences if, in the spirit of Per Albin Hansson, it had engaged in *logrolling*, with nuclear power as one of several issues in one agreement – something that party secretary Jonnergård incidentally seems to have considered[42] – instead of in a desperate attempt to achieve a *compromise* on the nuclear power issue alone? No, we can hardly say so. Allowing the opponents of nuclear power, through Fälldin, to push through their first preference in exchange for concessions from the Center party on other issues would not have been any more wrong than letting Per Albin Hansson's minority party push through its first preference on unemployment policy in 1933, in exchange for agricultural protectionism (or letting Bramstorp push through his first preference on agricultural policy in exchange for supporting the Social Democratic unemployment policy).

The spirit of De Geer and Per Albin Hansson still hovers over Swedish politics, even though Karl Staaff's majority rule is the main principle. This means that no one need give up hope just because he is in a minority. If his preferences are strong enough, his vote may end up weighing more heavily than that of others, provided he is prepared to pay the price and his counterpart is willing to bargain. The weighting method is not a decision rule that can generally replace majority rule. Nor is it possible to argue in principle that the influence of different actors should be related to how much they have to lose in a defeat. But the weighting method is a decision rule that a potential loser can bring up, under certain circumstances, when trying to extricate himself from the threat of defeat.

On the nuclear power issue, however, Thorbjörn Fälldin did not succeed in doing this.

[42] See n. 27 above.

9

Employee investment funds

1. OWNERSHIP AND WELFARE ECONOMICS

Socialism derives its specific character and problems from its attitudes toward ownership.

The ideologies of the nineteenth century sometimes described ownership as the mainspring of progress, at other times as the root cause of the miseries of the class system. The former position was espoused by representatives of bourgeois liberalism, an ideology closely associated with the industrialization process. The latter was the view of socialist theorists, who generally believed that it would be necessary to interfere with the right of private ownership in order to create a happier society in the future. Karl Marx developed this view into a provocative theory of industrial development. He taught that mass poverty made it impossible for capital owners to find customers for all their products. As a result, violent crises would arise in the capitalist system. In the end the system would be hit by a major catastrophe, in which the economically exploited workers would seize power and transfer industrial companies to public ownership. Toward the end of the nineteenth century, practically all Social Democratic parties embraced this program.

In Sweden, the early Social Democrats put all their energy into political reforms unrelated to the ownership of capital. Together with the Liberals, they struggled for universal suffrage and parliamentary government. Only when these wishes had been fulfilled at the end of World War I was "socialism placed on the agenda," as they put it. But it now turned out that the Social Democrats were far from ready to mount an action against the right of private ownership. The party ended up in a state of paralysis and ideological confusion. How much room for a socialistic action program actually existed when the expected disaster did not materialize and private ownership of capital thus survived? Didn't an increase in the prosperity of the workers actually mitigate against the underconsumption cri-

274

sis, which, in turn, was a prerequisite for their assault on capitalism? The whole 1920s passed without the party being able to escape from this dilemma.

As we know, the solution was offered by the new economic policy of the 1930s, which preserved the right of private ownership while showing a method for sharply increasing state influence on the economy, spearheaded by an expansionist unemployment policy. The Social Democrats abandoned doctrinaire socialist theory in favor of a more pragmatic approach. As long as private enterprise could generate full employment, it could be tolerated. Nationalizations should only take place in cases where capitalism had failed. This new method was considered superior to the old nationalization doctrine, and not only because it provided practical guidance for immediate programs that were in keeping with the traditional Marxist theory of underconsumption as the cause of economic crises. Ernst Wigforss, the architect of the new policy, also considered it more effective than the nationalization of companies, because selective nationalization was insufficient to pull the business sector "out of the free market and its chaos," whereas the measures now being undertaken gave the state a central hold over the entire economy. Consequently "to some extent and perhaps not such a small extent," the party was embarking in a new ideological path when it now abandoned the state ownership policy and adopted an "economic planning" or "welfare" policy.[1]

Large-scale government expenditures, designed to supply purchasing power to the broad mass of people and build up a welfare economy, created a new problem – inflation. As early as the end of the 1930s, Sweden experienced rapid inflation, as the nonsocialist critics of a government welfare policy had warned from the start. And during the 1940s, when the Social Democrats once again mistakenly predicted a difficult crisis for capitalism, Sweden's inflationary and foreign exchange problems became alarming. The Social Democratic government continued to stimulte purchasing power even though the economy was flourishing. Did economic conditions thus place limits on welfare policy? Was it necessary to abstain from further social welfare reforms and pay raises in order to avoid runaway inflation?

During the 1950s two economists at the Swedish Trade Union Confederation (LO), Gösta Rehn and Rudolf Meidner, came forward with a theory aimed at helping to solve this problem. The government should continue to pursue its welfare policy, they believed, but should control inflation by the withdrawal of purchasing power, in the form of a high-taxation policy. High taxes should be aimed primarily at companies whose profits had grown during the economic boom. Corporate profits

---

[1] Leif Lewin, *Planhushållningsdebatten* (Uppsala: Almqvist & Wiksell, 1967), pp. 74–75.

should be squeezed from two sides. A high-taxation policy was one. The other was a trade union principle known as the wage policy of solidarity. This meant that the unions would not only seek the highest possible pay increases consistent with employment and investment goals, but would also demand equal pay for equal work, regardless of the ability of a company to pay its labor costs. The wage policy of solidarity was aimed at achieving a narrower range of wages: Workers in highly productive companies would abstain from taking out all that was possible in terms of pay hikes, while workers in less productive firms would receive the same high level of wages and salaries as the others. Rehn and Meidner were aware that this economic pressure would cause difficulties for less profitable companies and perhaps even lead to bankruptcies. But this was not entirely negative; wage and salary policy thus became part of the structural rationalization process. To make it easier for the business sector to adapt to this process, Sweden required a very ambitious government program on labor market policy, possessing the large resources needed to move people from low-paying, unproductive companies and industries to the efficient high-paying enterprises of the future. The program thus presupposed the existence of expanding companies that enjoyed good profits.

The emergence of the wage policy of solidarity and the government's new labor market policy reflected great consistency in terms of the history of ideas. The victory of welfare policy over ownership policy (that is, nationalization) in the early 1930s meant that the Social Democrats had committed themselves not to abolish private capitalism but to save it, to make it efficient. Such ambitions were further accentuated by these new efforts to promote structural rationalization. Or as Gösta Rehn put it: The goal of the welfare state was "to realize what the free market should be able to realize according to its pretensions, but cannot."[2]

The pace of structural rationalization was stepped up and the Swedish economy flourished during the liberal 1960s. But one problem remained unsolved; indeed, it actually grew along with the profits of the most successful companies. The problem can be expressed in its briefest form as follows. The wage policy of solidarity did, of course, result in more equitable incomes. But it also favored the stockholders in the most successful companies, because their employees abstained from demanding pay increases as large as would have been possible.

Rudolf Meidner was asked by LO to study this problem. In his report, Meidner began with the observation that "wage restraint by highly paid categories of employees may lead to additional profit increases in expansive companies and thereby speed the rate of growth in the wealth of their

[2] Lewin 1967, pp. 367ff., 412ff., and 419ff.; Gösta Rehn, "Arbetsmarknadspolitik som samhällsidé," in *Femton år med Tage Erlander. En skrift till 60-årsdagen 13 juni 1961*, ed. Olle Svensson (Stockholm: Tiden, 1961), p. 80.

owners." Particularly during the 1960s with their favorable economic growth rate, there had been a palpable increase in wealth and in the concentration of power in the business sector. Meidner had no great faith in the chances of coming to grips with this situation by using traditional political methods. It would, of course, be possible to step up pay raises further, but this would result in lower corporate capital spending and thus a slower rise in living standards. So-called clearing funds would make it possible to redistribute labor costs in a way that favored the most profitable companies to a lesser degree than at present, but such a system would not give employees any larger share in newly generated wealth. Higher corporate taxation would have the same long-term negative effects as additional pay hikes. A profit-sharing system linked to each individual company violated the concept of wage solidarity, because it would only favor those who worked in especially profitable companies. Programs to promote savings were not considered capable of increasing the net savings rate. A broader distribution of stock ownership was deemed unlikely to result in any broadening of decision-making power over the busienss sector.

For these reasons, Meidner now presented his proposal for a system of employee investment funds.[3] He said that the funds should encompass a number of companies. They should be collectively owned and also include an equalization fund that would gather and distribute the returns from all their shareholdings. Meidner expressed a strong commitment to the principle of *collective* ownership. Fund systems that allowed the payment of individual dividends to their shareowners went against their real purpose, in his view. They were part of bourgeois ideology with its cult of individual freedom and lack of interest in genuine social equality. "Among liberal economists, social romantic notions are so strong that to them; the thought of depriving individual employees of the right to use 'their' share freely is repugnant, indeed irreconcilable with 'an economic order based on freedom.... ' Within the trade union movement, which derives its strength precisely from its collective nature, opposition to collectivist solutions cannot reasonably be equally strong."

Meidner went on to develop this ideological perspective. The wage policy of solidarity was pushed more and more into the background of his analysis; equalization of wealth and economic democracy were his central theme. The introduction of employee investment funds was thus described

---

[3] Employee investment funds were not a completely new idea among the Social Democrats. For their earlier intellectual history, see Erik Åsard, *LO och löntagarfondsfrågan. En studie i facklig politik och strategi* (Stockholm: Rabén & Sjögren, 1978), and Berndt Öhman, *Solidarisk lönepolitik och löntagarfonder. SOU 1982:47*, pp. 115–146. I would like to extend my thanks to Erik Åsard of my department and Berndt Öhman at the University College of Örebro for their many stimulating opinions on this chapter.

as "a technique for successively transferring the ownership of productive capital from private owners to the employee collective." He said that employee funds would, "in the long term, own more than half the shares of the major Swedish companies." "A power vacuum will arise when private capital owners lose the central role they occupy today" – the employee funds would give the unions a new task here.

In other words, Meidner was reviving the old ownership policy, which was part of the Social Democratic ideological tradition. Because welfare policy no longer seemed to provide a practical path to economic equality, pragmatism called for a reexamination of ownership as a means to that end. Meidner alluded to the radical currents of the early 1970s, which were generating impatience among the trade unions: "Right now in Sweden, we are experiencing a strong wave of trade union demands for greater influence and a greater role in decision making as well as a shift in power relations within companies to the benefit of the employees." If greater codetermination by means of welfare policy and ownership policy were posed as alternatives, "the choice would certainly fall on the former alternative," Meidner admitted. "The concept of labor as the basis of the right of codetermination is more firmly rooted in the traditions of the labor movement than is the concept of employee power through ownership." But why choose? It ought to be possible to pursue both these policies at the same time. They could "support and complement each other." A necessary step in the development of economic democracy was "a successive change in ownership structure."[4]

Some rapid jumps through the history of Social Democratic ideas enable us to see how different positions and lines of action succeed each other like links in a logical chain. With great effort, the Social Democrats freed themselves from the Marxist economic disaster theory, with its categorical demands for nationalization. But by pumping out more purchasing power, their new policy – with its more flexible attitude toward ownership – generated other problems. They tried, in turn, to solve these by means of even more advanced economic policy operations until the employee investment fund proposal, though based on modern wage and labor market policy, once again turned ownership policy into a day-to-day political program of action.

The concept of employee investment funds has historical roots outside as well as inside the Social Democratic tradition. Granting employees a share in company profits is in no way irreconcilable with a nonsocialist view of society. On the contrary, by providing employees with a stake in

---

[4] Rudolf Meidner, with Anna Hedborg and Gunnar Fond, *Löntagarfonder* (Stockholm: Tiden, 1975); quotations from pp. 10, 83–84, 99, 107, and 119–120. The employee investment fund debate has already been the topic of extensive scholarly treatment. A lengthy list of references can be found in Öhman 1982.

a company's profits, nonsocialists have seen an opportunity to demolish the foundations of socialist class struggle and make the workers into allies in defending the market economy. John Stuart Mill pursued this line of reasoning further and played the same role for bourgeois liberalism as Karl Marx played for social democracy. Profit sharing made it possible to devleop a new and harmonious relationship between workers and capital owners, Mill argued. It was a method by which crude capitalism would be civilized and conflicts would be replaced by cooperation. The liberal concept of profit sharing led to experimentation during the late nineteenth century, and during the 1880s an international congress on profit sharing was even held in Paris. But the idea had a hard time becoming genuinely widespread; many a capitalist was unwilling to lower his own earnings by profit sharing, and trade unions also rejected the concept of shared ownership.[5]

In Sweden, however, the nonsocialist parties – opposed by the trade unions – continued to advocate giving employees a stake in company profits. The Liberal party was a particularly strong supporter of the idea. It was, incidentally, on the basis of initiatives from this party that the government appointed a commission of inquiry on employee investment funds in 1975.[6] During the many postwar revisions of party programs, what the Moderates refer to as the principle of "ownership democracy" has been continuously advocated by all three nonsocialist parties: Sweden's growing national wealth should be spread to as many people as possible; assets should be owned by private individuals and not by the state or other collective bodies; personal savings and, not least, stock ownership should be promoted; and taxation policy should be designed to encourage individual entrepreneurial initiatives. The arguments of the nonsocialist parties and the business community emphasized the desirability of reversing the trend toward concentration of capital in business and of spreading the ownership of stocks. The systems of profit sharing between owners and employees that have been adopted by numerous banks and other companies in Sweden in recent years are examples of the kind of development the nonsocialists want to support. Another example is the system of mutual funds introduced by nonsocialist governments during the 1970s, which provided tax advantages up to a certain level, thereby persuading a substantial number of people to save money in the form of share trust units and thus participate in corporate capital formation.

---

[5] Åsard 1978, pp. 16–17.

[6] Because of the strong political disagreements between the blocs, this commission of inquiry was discontinued before arriving at any proposal. The work of the commission is analyzed by Erik Åsard in his book *Kompromiss eller konfrontation? Politik och strategi i den statliga löntagarfondsutredningen 1975–1981* (Uppsala: Department of Government, University of Uppsala, 1984).

The conflicts that exist on the issue of employee investment funds thus do not consist of one camp being *for* and the other camp being *against* this system. All parties would like to promote the distribution of owner- ship to broad categories of employees. The difference is that the Social Democrats and Communists want collective funds, with trade unions as the dominant ownership group, in which individuals are not entitled to remove their trust units from the fund. The nonsocialists, in contrast, want a fund system based on personal ownership and allowing the indi- vidual full rights to dispose of his or her trust units. Both sides deny that the other side's proposal will result in any real broadening of decision- making power: The Social Democrats are convinced that major capitalists will maintain their power of ownership in the business sector even if there are a larger number of individual stockholders. The nonsocialists, in turn, view trade-union-owned collective funds as the worst conceivable form of concentration of power.

Meidner's thoughts on employee funds were strongly supported by LO. "This is how we will deprive the capitalists of their power!" the trade union movement magazine *Fackföreningsrörelsen* declared. In an inter- view in this magazine, Meidner said, "We would like to deprive the old capital owners of their power, which they exercise by virtue of their own- ership. All experience indicates that systems of employee influence and monitoring are insufficient.... It is my firm belief that only functional socialism is sufficient to achieve a far-reaching change in society."[7]

After an extensive study and information campaign during the fall, a somewhat reworked version of Meidner's report was presented to the 1976 LO congress. It essentially repeated Meidner's views, but it contained more specific proposals. It set the profit share at 20 percent of corporate earnings and declared that the tasks of the funds would be "comprehen- sive" while the new Codetermination Act (or Act on Employee Partici- pation in Decision Making) would apply more to internal conditions in a company. The report set a lower limit of fifty and an upper limit of one hundred employees. At first the stock voting rights of the funds would be exercised by trade union locals, later by a comprehensive fund, with union locals enjoying the right to make and veto proposals.[8]

The debate at the trade union confederation congress was lively. The LO Executive gave Meidner's central concepts its unqualified endorse- ment. "The employee investment funds will change our economy in the direction of greater democracy and greater employee influence," LO chairman Gunnar Nilsson declared in his speech presenting the proposal. "They will counteract the concentration of private ownership and power

---

[7] *Fackföreningsrörelsen* no. 19 (1975); quotations from pp. 11 and 17.
[8] *Kollektiv kapitalbildning genom löntagarfonder. Rapport till LO-kongressen 1976.*

that is occurring today."[9] A number of technical problems still remained to be studied, the LO Executive stated in its official opinion, but the general guidelines specified in the report should now be approved. The congress followed this proposal.[10]

The Social Democratic party, on the other hand, was unprepared for the intensive debate on employee investment funds that had now begun. The party leadership observed a silence that one researcher labeled "almost deafening." Olof Palme avoided the subject as much as possible, instead speaking of its complexity and importance. He said that it would be unsuitable to interfere in internal trade union debate and that it was necessary not to force a solution too quickly. Above all, the party leadership objected to the broad ideological perspective of Meidner's report – the fact that the author's analysis of the wage policy of solidarity extended through the entire problem of ownership. We should concentrate on welfare problems, which people were familiar with, said Sten Andersson, the party secretary. "If we are going to make people understand why we want to pursue a particular policy in an area, we should start with the problem as they experience it, and not at the other end with the power problem. They are uninterested in that, and consequently we cannot win their support in solving the problems that we are trying to solve."[11]

As a result, the two branches of the Swedish labor movement pursued two different strategies in the 1976 election campaign: The trade union branch pursued an ownership policy while the Social Democratic party pursued its traditional welfare policy. The subsequent defeat of the Social Democrats was due in part to the employee fund issue.[12]

It was obviously necessary to close ranks once again. The party and LO appointed a joint task force to study the fund issue further. In 1978 this body presented its report, which was completely different in tone from the earlier reports. Even in the introduction, the report declared that the proposal it was presenting would "not fundamentally change the economic and political environment in which companies will function. Their operations will continue to be governed by the market." The report added, "The purpose of employee investment funds is not to deprive current capital owners of their assets. Nor is their purpose to limit the dividends on shares in such a way that it will become less attractive for individuals in the future to supply risk capital to the business sector." The report thus proposed compensation for profit sharing, in such a way that the fund system did not intrude on the room for dividends to individual stockhold-

---

[9] *Landsorganisationens nittonde ordinarie kongress 1976*, p. 709.
[10] Ibid., p. 733.
[11] Åsard 1978, pp. 160ff.; quotation from p. 162. Åsard took the Sten Andersson quotation from Swedish Radio, Program 1, 5 Oct. 1975.
[12] Section 2 below.

ers. But how could a profit-sharing system with full compensation lead to more equitable distribution of wealth? And how can a proposal not designed to deprive current capital owners of their assets be reconciled with Meidner's plan to transfer ownership of productive capital successively from private owners to employees on a collective basis? The ideological retreat represented by the new proposal could not be concealed.

The structure of the fund system was based on the previous study but was softened on important points; in addition to the compensation rule, the size limits were changed in such a way that profit sharing would only occur in major companies with at least five hundred employees. There would also be legal guarantees that companies would not change their dividend policies in ways that would put individual minority interests at a disadvantage. The fund system would be organized into regional representative assemblies; employee representatives on the boards of companies would be appointed on an equal basis by local employees and the assemblies, and companies outside the system would be assessed a separate fee, payable to a codetermination fund. The report also proposed a system of two nationwide development funds, one with a "public-sector majority" and the other with an employee majority, supplemented by regional development funds.

Most important, the 1978 report was characterized by a new argument for employee funds, replacing the ideological call for a dismantling of private capitalism. This new motive was to contribute to capital formation in companies. The country's economic situation had drastically deteriorated. Savings and capital spending were falling, Sweden was running a trade deficit, and unemployment was climbing. It was necessary to reverse this trend and once again increase the rate of capital formation. If Sweden did not want a further increase in private wealth because the necessary savings would occur on a private basis, an employee investment fund system was needed.[13]

The report naturally caused considerable confusion when it was discussed at the Social Democratic party congress in 1978. A long series of speakers criticized the party board, which in principle supported the report's proposal to establish regional development funds but did not believe that the overall proposal of the task force was such that it could now provide the basis for a political decision. Was the party leadership trying to remove the entire employee fund issue from the upcoming 1979 election campaign? asked one delegate to the congress, who submitted a motion to the effect that the employee fund issue should "be accorded a prominent place in the (party's) 1979 election manifesto." Others spoke of

---

[13] *Löntagarfonder och kapitalbildning. Förslag från LO-SAPs arbetsgrupp 1978*, pp. 5–6 (quotation) and 40.

their "doubts" about the direction in which the party was moving, of "the excessively unclear" statements of the leadership, of statements that could "give rise to different interpretations, which partly conflict with each other," of terminology that was too "vague" and required "clarifications." "Ever since Meidner presented his proposal, (the employee investment fund issue) had awakened enthusiasm and hopes." But when it turned out that the party leadership "was faltering," it was "not so strange that interest declined. . . . Then came the election defeat, which was perhaps a result of this rambling." Others concurred. Party workers would certainly never quite regain their enthusiasm again; one speaker referred to "all the discontented people out in our organizations." The proposal had been "watered down and now, this year, it doesn't look as if even an inch of it is left."[14]

The employee fund proposal was further studied by a new joint task force, including LO and Social Democratic party representatives. In 1981 this group presented a concrete proposal for a fund system; no further research would be needed. According to this proposal, the funds would be financed in two ways: by raising the employer-financed supplementary pension (ATP) fee by an amount equivalent to 1 percent of payroll, and by imposing a profit-sharing fee of 20 percent of company earnings above a certain level. The money in the funds would be invested as equity capital in the business sector. The capitalist system's one-sided emphasis on profit maximization would thereby be supplemented by other, welfare-related goals. If major companies obstructed the system by not carrying out new share issues even though there were good economic reasons for soliciting new equity capital, the trade union local could initiate such issues. An employee investment fund would be established in each county. Various organizational models were discussed; the essential thing was that the decision-making bodies for the funds would have "a clear employee majority" and that "employee influence forms the basis for the funds," not "citizens' influence." This reasoning largely coincided with a proposal presented as early as June 1980 by the LO and Social Democratic party representatives in the government-appointed commission of inquiry on employee investment funds.[15]

Was the new proposal closer to Meidner's bold ideas of 1975 or the toned-down proposal of 1978? The 1981 report carefully avoided providing an answer on this crucial point. The entire line of reasoning of the report presupposes a fundamental change in the owenrship structure of the business sector; companies would gain "new owners and new goals." The important thing now was "to increase employee influence in the busi-

---

[14] *Socialdemokratiska Arbetarepartiets tjugosjunde kongress 1978*, pp. 269–321.

[15] *Arbetarrörelsen och löntagarfonderna. Rapport från en arbetsgrupp inom LO och socialdemokraterna 1981*; quotations from pp. 85, 105, and 107; Åsard 1984.

ness sector (through) ownership." "The right to buy shares is not being limited in any respect." At the same time, the proposal was presented as a continuation of traditional Social Democratic policy: The funds were compared with the ATP system, which had made it possible to finance the welfare policies of future decades; in fact, the employee investment funds would strengthen the market economy by spreading power to new owners and supplying new savings.[16]

The report was discussed at the next LO congress and the Social Democratic party congress, which both took place in 1981. Its lack of ideological clarity allowed room for different interpretations, which enabled practically all speakers to concur in the respective statements of the LO Executive and the party board, which both approved the report. The restoration of unity in the labor movement was the important thing – or as one speaker put it, "During the summer we have all noted with pleasure that the party and LO have exactly the same opinion on this issue. A parallel reading of the statements of the party board and the LO Executive confirms this. This heartening unanimity stands in positive contrast to the situation we experienced during 1976, the year of the last LO congress."[17]

These manifestations of unity, which in fact concealed different ideological viewpoints, began to look almost absurd when they were combined with an open mandate to the party leadership to continue handling the employee investment fund issue. They made a distinction between the "principles" behind the funds, which would now be firmly established, and their "technical design." But, as one researcher has pointed out, in practice this distinction was difficult to maintain.[18] The freedom of action that Olof Palme requested was also "substantial," with regard to both the design and the timetable of the fund system.[19] Only a few objections were heard. One speaker opposed the party board's request for "carte blanche from the congress freely to cut, change and amend the employee fund proposal" and warned that on one previous occasion the labor movement had been "overridden" by a party leaderhsip that was excessively timid and willing to compromise. Another delegate said Olof Palme resembled "a scared mouse" when he was questioned by television and radio reporters on whether employee investment funds threatened the capitalist mar-

---

[16] *Arbetarrörelsen och löntagarfonderna*, quotations from p. 54; *LO 80-rapporten. Rapport till LO-kongressen 1981*, p. 81.

[17] *Landsorganisationens tjugonde ordinarie kongress 1981*, pp. 803–857, quotation from p. 842; *Socialdemokratiska Arbetarepartiets tjugoåttonde kongress 1981*, pp. 7–49, and *partistyrelsens utlåtanden* (statements of the party board), pp. 35–46.

[18] Öhman 1982, p. 168.

[19] *Landsorganisationens tjugonde ordinarie kongress 1981*, p. 1430.

ket economy.[20] But other speakers supported the open mandate, often in enthusiastic terms, and both congresses approved it.

In a major address to the LO congress, Olof Palme turned both the lack of ideological clarity and the open mandate into something positive, into an expression of the strength of the party and of its firm commitment to return to government and "bring order to the country." The upcoming 1982 election cast its shadow over his speech. At any price, the party chairman wanted to avoid fueling nonsocialist campaign efforts and stimulating scare propaganda about huge funds that would suffocate people's desire to work and create bureaucracy and a lack of freedom in Sweden. The Social Democrats should run their election campaign, he argued, in such a way that the nonsocialists would fail to make headway with this kind of propaganda. In this context it was important to take advantage of the Swedish people's earlier good experience of the big ATP funds, which – far from curtailing freedom – had helped finance pensions, housing, schools, and hospitals. If the employee funds were described in this way, they ought not to be capable of scaring anyone, he said.

According to Palme, the recession necessitated the establishment of employee investment funds to ensure capital formation in the business sector. "That is what we should have the funds for. There is no dogmatism behind this, but rather the conviction that we have to set aside money for investments in order to safeguard jobs and prosperity." In an economic downturn, this welfare policy by no means contradicted an ownership policy, because without changing ownership conditions, we would not "be able to achieve the necessary rallying of forces to manage our economic problems." A continued concentration of power over the business sector in a few hands would "be contrary to people's feeling of fairness and justice." Employee investment funds were a guarantee of productive investments; "employee funds don't move to Liechtenstein." Given this strategy, the economic recession actually helped rescue the Social Democrats from their ideological difficulties. It provided a concrete and meaningful argument for an ownership policy, while at the same time this policy was toned down, becoming merely one part of a general antirecession program.

Palme kept returning to the upcoming election. No matter how much the nonsocialists and the business sector now agitated against employee investment funds, history showed that sooner or later, they would surrender to the labor movement's offensive. The labor movement would have to "bear the main responsibility for lifting Sweden out of recession." In this perspective, it was "important that we preserve our ability to carry

[20] *Socialdemokratiska Arbetarepartiets tjugoåttonde kongress 1981,* pp. 15 and 23.

out a constructive dialogue, to give and take" in order to gain the broadest possible support for the employee investment fund concept. This was why Palme now requested "substantial maneuvering room" in continuing to deal with the issue. "It is an expression of strength and self-reliance that we have said all along that we are open to discussion on the technical design of the employee funds."[21]

The long task of ideological preparation was completed. The party and the trade union movement had reached agreement on a joint proposal for an employee investment fund system. But it was a manifestation of unity that actually incorporated a variety of ideological notions; it was a consensus built up amidst continuously shifting viewpoints and arguments. The original fighting spirit had been followed by doubts. In report after report, the unions and the party had swung back and forth between more radical and more modest proposals for intervention in capital ownership. After LO's ruddy determination of 1975–1976 had given way to the party's pale cast of thought two years later, the desire for revenge following its election losses now impelled the party leadership to regain some of its original fighting spirit. But it was unclear *what* it was fighting for, because at the same time the party leadership had extracted an open mandate to create the broadest possible consensus for a program to lead Sweden out of recession. The leadership was convinced that nonsocialist propaganda against the funds was dangerous, and it tried in every way to tone down the radical character of the fund proposal. The Social Democratic party leadership only reluctantly ventured out during the election campaign to defend the reincarnated version of its old ownership policy.

2. THE "OUTSTRETCHED HAND"

The Swedish people did not approve of the idea of collective employee investment funds. As early as 1975, the first year of the debate, public opinion polls began charting the attitudes of the public. Repeated and frequent surveys using the same phrasing of the questions generated a unique store of source material, which enables us to follow in detail the vicissitudes of public opinion on the fund issue. The public's negative perception of collective employee investment funds can be seen, for instance, in a compendium of thirteen surveys during the period 1975–1980, published in 1981. During these six years, public opinion had been remarkably stable. An average of 64 percent of interviewees believed that employee ownership in the business sector should be increased by means of funds that featured individually owned shares, while only 19 percent preferred trade-union-

---

[21] *Landsorganisationens tjugonde ordinarie kongress 1981*, pp. 1426–1432. As to the comparison with the 1932 party congress, see *Socialdemokratiska Arbetarpartiets tjugosjunde kongress 1978*, p. 273.

dominated collective funds. A number of different versions of the questions yielded a similar picture. The main trend that was measurable was a slight strengthening of opposition to collective funds over time. If the material was broken down along party lines, it turned out that even among Social Democrats and LO union members, a majority preferred the concept of individual profit sharing to collective funds. A system of employee investment funds featuring individual share units was preferred by a majority of Sweden's nonsocialists. Among Social Democrats, opinion was evenly divided.[22]

From the very beginning, the chairmen of the nonsocialist parties had sharply attacked proposals to create collective employee investment funds. This theme had played a prominent part in the early stages of the 1976 election campaign, before nuclear power attracted everyone's attention. The Center party chairman had warned that employee investment funds would lead Sweden in the direction of "Eastern bloc socialism." The Moderate party chairman had criticized "fund socialism" as irreconcilable with freedom and democracy, and the head of the Liberal party had declared that the employee fund proposal should "be thrown in the waste basket." As election researchers have shown, this antisocialist propaganda was successful, as so many times previously in Swedish history. The issue of nationalization and employee investment funds was one of the three issues on which the voters felt that the Social Democrats projected a more negative image in 1976 than in 1973.[23]

With great persistence, the nonsocialists had stuck to this successful antisocialist propaganda, stepping it up further as the 1982 election approached, because the Social Democrats had left the research stage behind them and were ready to implement their ideas. Business organizations, led by the Swedish Employers' Confederation, hurried to the assistance of the nonsocialist parties in a massive propaganda effort against the proposed employee investment funds. A spirit of consensus between the business community and the state, as represented by the labor movement, had prevailed during the 1950s and 1960s. It was superseded by a political mood more reminiscent of the tough ideological disputes on economic planning of the nonsocialist propaganda days in the 1940s.

Would the outcome of the employee investment fund issue be that Olof Palme once again failed to recapture power from the nonsocialists?

The Social Democratic party leadership was acutely aware of what a liability the employee investment fund issue constituted for them among

[22] *Sex års fondopinioner 1975–1980. Aktiespararnas skriftserie nr 12* (Sveriges Aktiespar-ares Riksförbund, 1981).
[23] Olof Petersson, *Väljarna och valet 1976* (Stockholm: Statistiska Centralbyrån, 1977), pp. 197ff.; Sören Holmberg, Jörgen Westerståhl, and Karl Branzén, *Väljarna och kärnkraften* (Stockholm: Liber, 1977), pp. 45ff.

Table 9.1. *Percentage of time devoted to different issues by the parties themselves and as shown on the television news programs Rapport and Aktuellt, 1982 election campaign*

	LPC		S		C		L		M	
	Own image	TV image	Own image	TV image	Own image	TV image	Own image	TV image	Own image	TV image
Employment and the economy	28	21	31	34	40	20	33	32	33	16
Taxes and deductions	10	24	4	9	9	12	6	6	18	26
Nuclear power and energy	7	0	0	1	3	2	3	1	0	0
Employee investment funds	5	3	6	24	21	17	23	15	24	19
Social welfare issues	18	13	37	11	7	13	11	9	5	7
Other issues	32	39	22	21	20	36	24	37	20	32
Total	100	100	100	100	100	100	100	100	100	100
N	172	38	136	138	161	86	91	87	144	88

Source: Kent Asp: *Sveriges Radios bevakning av 1982 års valrörelse* (Gothenburg: Department of Government, University of Gothenburg), table 2.

the voters. There was strong internal criticism against the proposed funds within the party. Professor Assar Lindbeck, a well-known economist, attracted the most attention by resigning from the Social Democratic party because of its stance on the fund issue.

The party leadership did not, however, intend to fall willingly into the trap that the nonsocialist parties and the business organizations were now laying. As a potential loser, Olof Palme did two things to avoid defeat. First, he adopted a policy of not talking so much about the funds in the election campaign, but instead talking more about social welfare issues, employment, and the economy. Table 9.1 shows what a low profile the Social Democrats maintained on the employee investment fund issue, compared with the picture given by the nightly television news programs *Rapport* and *Aktuellt* and by the nonsocialist parties.[24]

As the reader will recall, silence is not an unfamiliar strategy in Swedish political history. It was used in the 1880s, when M.P.'s tried to avoid letting voter opinon bind them to a particular view on the tariff issue. But as the table indicates, Palme could not maintain total silence on the issue throughout the election campaign. His second technique was to apply the strategy we referred to in Chapter 1 as "adjusting one's motion." The Social Democrats attempted to assuage the massive public opinion opposed to employee investment funds by trying to make the funds look like an expression not of the unpopular ownership policy but of its traditional welfare policy. The shift of policy during the 1930s had not meant the categorical rejection of all changes in ownership, but a transition from a doctrinaire to a pragmatic approach to ownership. Even within the framework of welfare policy, there might also be reason to intervene in ownership conditions when other methods turned out to be without effect.

Considering his far-reaching pledges of "employee power" by means of the fund system, Palme's strategy was bold. He took maximum advantage of the open mandate he had been given to tone down the fund proposal further. His rhetorical skills once again triumphed when he declared that he wanted to offer "an outstretched hand" to the nonsocialists. This was more than an expression of hope that a dispute that he appeared to be losing would come to an end; he was also implying that out of concern for the best interests of the country, everyone should join forces to lead the country out of recession. The public should regard him as a national father figure, not as a socialist agitator. The image of the outstretched hand was also intended to tone down even further the far-reaching ambitions of the employee investment fund proposal. Implicit in this image is

---

[24] I would like to thank Sören Holmberg and Kent Asp at the Department of Government, University of Gothenburg, who have granted me permission to publish Tables 9.1, 9.2, and 9.3.

Table 9.2. *Election issues, 1976, 1979, and 1982 – percentage of total replies given in which each issue is mentioned as important in choosing a party*

Interview question: Think about this year's election. Are any issue or issues important to you in deciding which party you intend to vote for in the parliamentary election on September 19?

	1976	1979	1982
Employee investment funds	4	3	22
Employment	5	14	21
Economic policy	4	7	10
Social welfare policy/medical care	6	3	9
Family policy	9	7	6
Taxation	9	13	6
Pensions/old age care	5	4	6
Environmental issues	3	4	5
Ideological issues (socialism/capitalism)	13	4	3
Energy and nuclear power	21	21	2
Housing policy	1	4	2

Note: Seventy-five percent of interviewees (2,087 people) answered the question by mentioning one or more issues as important in choosing a party in 1982. A total of 4,069 such replies (= percentage base) were given by the 2,087 people who answered the question.
Source: Sören Holmberg: *Valundersökning 1982* (Gothenburg: Department of Government, University of Gothenburg), table 22.

that the person making the proposal is willing to bargain and make concessions. If Palme considered it possible to reach agreement with the nonsocialists, whose antifund attitude was well known to everyone, the voters would thus understand that the proposal could not be so revolutionary.

But the nonsocialists did not accept the outstretched hand. They said that they did not wish "to negotiate on the introduction of socialism." They were now also more unwilling than before to discuss even changes of a more limited kind. They consistently rejected every such invitation.

The Social Democrats won the election. They received 45.6 percent of the vote and formed a minority government. They declared that they had now received the mandate of the electorate to introduce employee investment funds. Tables 9.2 and 9.3 indicate, however, that both the strategy of silence and the outstretched hand had failed in their purpose. In the 1982 election campaign, the voters considered employee investment funds the most important issue of all; in dramatic fashion it switched places with the nuclear power issue, which had occupied first place in the 1976 and

Table 9.3. *Opinions on the policy of each party on three issues, 1979 and 1982 – difference between percentages of positive and negative opinions*

Issue	LPC		S		C		L		M	
	1979	1982	1979	1982	1979	1982	1979	1982	1979	1982
Employee investment funds	−10	−17	−4	−25	−1	+10	−1	+9	−4	+13
Employment	+2	+1	+25	+34	+4	−4	+9	−8	−5	−8
Taxation	−6	−8	+5	+6	+3	+3	+5	+2	−1	−2

Source: Sören Holmberg: *Valundersökning 1982* (Gothenburg: Department of Government, University of Gothenburg), table 24.

1979 campaigns. The tables also show that voters had a very negative opinion of Social Democratic policy on the fund issue in 1982 and, more-over, a substantially more negative opinion than three years earlier, whereas their opinion of the attitudes of nonsocialist parties toward the funds was clearly favorable in 1982. In contrast, voter opinion of Social Democratic employment policy was very positive. The Social Democrats won the 1982 election *in spite of* their employee investment fund propos-als, not because of them.

Now came the time in the history of the fund issue described by one Moderate M.P. as "the period of silent hurrying."[25] Three internal study commissions were appointed by the prime minister's office to prepare a government bill. Per-Olof Edin, chief economist of the Metal Workers' Union, was the driving force. At the same time, Palme repeated his offer from the election campaign regarding the "outstretched hand." He was just as interested now as previously in not being identified with any mili-tant "fund socialism" that would be pushed through Parliament against rigid nonsocialist opposition with the smallest possible majority and only with the support of the Communists. A settlement across bloc lines was preferable. The nonsocialists once again saw no reason to "bargain about the introduction of soicalism." They felt that the prime minister was showing "a fist" rather than "an outstretched hand."

This entire bargaining procedure is reminiscent of the way Palme's political mentor, Tage Erlander, maneuvered during the supplementary pension dispute. After the referendum, which had done little to make the situation clearer, Prime Minister Erlander invited the chairmen of the nonsocialist parties to bargain, but added that no other basis for these

[25] RD 1983/84:53–54, p. 4 (Tobisson).

negotiations was conceivable except the Social Democratic policy of compulsory pensions. This move eventually resulted in a split in nonsocialist ranks and Ohlin's compromise attempt. On the employee investment fund issue, however, the nonsocialist front remained solid.

There were few leaks as to what was happening in the government's internal study commissions. The dominant event in the media during the winter of 1982–1983 was an interview with the finance minister, Kjell-Olof Feldt, in the business weekly *Veckans Affärer*. Feldt admitted that there were shortcomings in the Social Democratic proposal for employee investment funds and that it was uncertain whether a government bill could even be submitted before the 1985 election.[26] The interview resulted in an indignant debate in the Social Democratic press; Feldt maintained that his statements had been misinterpreted.

There was great uncertainty about the party's policy. The Social Democrats were "a party without an inner compass," one writer said in the party's ideological magazine *Tiden*. The party had "no underlying faith in the future, no obvious marching direction that gives strength and confidence. . . . Despite its talk of implementing the third stage of democracy, codetermination in worklife and the employee investment funds are not being accompanied by any inspiring dreams of the future, but instead are in the nature of temporary defenses, two more examples of fine-tuning justified by redistribution policy."[27]

An editorial in *Tiden* complained that the nonsocialists had not accepted the outstretched hand; their mistrust seemed too strong "even if the leadership of the labor movement were prepared to postpone the employee investment funds, a move we would support in that case." And the editorial writer added, with resignation, "It is not encouraging to have to pursue such a central issue on the basis of the hope that people have already become tired of it."[28]

The foremost expression of internal Social Democratic criticism of the party's employee investment fund policy was an editorial in *Stockholms-Tidningen* in the spring of 1983 under the startling headline "Was the fund concept wrong right from the start?" "There have been eight years of intensive debate, a major state commission of inquiry and three of our own proposals, involving major revisions from one to the next. If, after all this, we have still come no further than to say that fundamental ideological as well as crucial technical issues are still unresolved and the 'temporary' solution we present is not even related to our own earlier proposals but to another, older system (the National Pension Insurance Fund)

[26] *Veckans Affärer* no. 42 (1982).
[27] Anders Isaksson, "Ett parti utan inre kompass," *Tiden* (1983); quotations from pp. 207 and 209.
[28] Arne Helldén, "Återfinn den 'lyckade' reformismen," *Tiden* (1983): 336.

– then we should certainly ask ourselves if perhaps there was nevertheless something wrong with the idea itself." The newspaper saw the explanation for the clumsy handling of the fund issue in "poor preparedness within the labor movement, both in ideological and practical terms, for a debate on ownership." Certain problems related to wages and capital formation could presumably be solved. "That would be nice. Otherwise we believe that practical proposals should be deferred – until the labor movement has had a more impartial discussion of what it wants to accomplish."[29]

The newspaper could not more clearly have given failing marks to the old-but-new policy the party was now following.

However, LO continued to push impatiently for employee investment funds. At the June 1983 congress of the Municipal Workers' Union, LO chairman Stig Malm called on the government to show its decisiveness by introducing a fund system that would take effect the following January. The very next day, Prime Minister Palme informed the LO chairman that a government bill on a fund system would be submitted to Parliament during its upcoming fall session.

During the summer, the government's internal commissions presented their recommendations. The government maintained a rapid pace in its preparations: The period allowed for written comments on the commission reports was so short that the nonsocialist parties protested, and a number of organizations only commented on some of the proposals. The Draft Legislation Advisory Committee also opposed the way the matter was handled: It was "critical of the fact that an issue of such great importance in principle and with such controversial features has been handled in such a way."[30] Only the day after the committee met, the government submitted its bill on employee investment funds to Parliament.

The bill proposed five funds, whose task would be to manage part of the money in the National Pension Insurance Fund. Each fund would have nine board members, of which at least five would represent employee interests. Their assets would be invested primarily in the stock market and would come from a profit-sharing tax and from a special portion of employer-financed supplementary pension fees. Profits below a certain level were exempted from the profit-sharing tax.

Compared with the LO–Social Democratic proposal of 1981, the government bill represented a major ideological retreat. Its most striking feature was the limited scale of the fund system now being established. It could be assumed that the employee investment funds would eventually own a maximum of 10 percent of total market capitalization on the Stock-

[29] *Stockholms-Tidningen,* 12 Apr. 1983.
[30] Lagrådets protokoll (proceedings of the Draft Legislation Advisory Committee), 3 Nov. 1983, prop 1983/84:50, p. 144.

holm Stock Exchange, making them a large stockholder but far from being "the dominant owner," the holder of "more than half the shares in major Swedish companies," the new power group that would take the place of private capitalists, and so forth, as the advocates of fund systems had previously envisioned. The bill also limited the influence of the funds on individual companies: The board of an employee investment fund could not acquire shares in a listed company if this step gave the fund 8 percent or more of the voting power in that company. Nonsocialist propaganda to the effect that the proposal was only the first step toward a completely socialistic business sector was effectively rejected: A ceiling was placed on the amount of money each fund board would receive. The amount would rise each year until 1990, after which there would be no further payments; the funds would stop being expanded. Or in the words of Olof Palme, "This proposal is not the first step. It's *the* step." This was a categorical statement, whose purpose was admittedly to calm the non-socialists, but it was hardly consistent with the pragmatism with which Palme otherwise argued that the employee investment funds could be reconciled with Social Democratic welfare policy. Quite possibly, a pragmatic view of ownership in the future could find reasons for even greater intervention in the business sector if the market economy should undergo serious strains.

Another remarkable feature of the bill was that it required the fund boards to pursue a yield-oriented investment policy. In other words, the funds would operate according to exactly the same capitalistic principles as private companies. The text of the government bill showed not a trace of the visionary thoughts in the 1981 LO–Social Democratic report, which stated that one purpose of the funds would be to supplement profit maximization with other welfare goals. Also abandoned was the idea expressed in the 1981 report that trade union locals would be entitled to force companies to issue new shares.

The preamble of the bill followed Olof Palme's adjustment strategy. It presented the employee investment fund proposal as a genuine expression of welfare policy. It stated that by far its most important task was to lead Sweden out of recession. This presupposed that it would be possible to combine slow growth in costs and prices with low unemployment. Now that profits in the business sector were again beginning to climb, it was important that prices and costs did not accelerate again. To avoid such a development, steps should be taken to prevent the rise in profits from resulting in additional concentration of power and ownership in business. Employee investment funds were thus being proposed now. "This is the decisive and fundamental reason why the government is presenting its proposal." But employee ownership should be "clearly limited. This should be reflected in a limit on the employees' ownership stake in any individual company. But it also leads to the conclusion that the total size of the funds should be limited in the manner proposed by the fund group. Their expansion should thus come to an end when they have achieved their intended volume in 1990." And to avoid the tiniest suspicion that the Social Democrats had reverted to some kind of doctrinaire ownership policy, the finance minister himself specified how the employee investment fund proposal should be interpreted in terms of the history of ideas. He repeated this argument in the parliamentary debate: "Employee investment funds are a way of adding to the welfare society in a difficult period when new redistribution and stabilization policy initiatives are needed to deal with our problems. Employee investment funds are a way of strengthening the fundamental community of interests that has existed for so many years in our country in our approach to work, production and savings. The introduction of employee investment funds is thus a reform in the traditional Social Democratic and reformist spirit."[31]

It is hard to believe that this is what people expected at the enthusiastic trade union and party congresses of 1981, when they had gathered strength for the long election campaign ahead. The party leadership had stretched its open mandate to the very limit, both by restricting the volume of the fund system and by watering down its goals.

To the nonsocialist parties, the government's behavior after the 1982 election must have entailed a strategic dilemma. Two alternative courses of action were available. One was to make a triumphant announcement of their own ideological victory and the actual retreat of the Social Democrats. The other was to ignore the retreat and continue their antisocialist drumfire. They chose the latter course. They once again rejected the outstretched hand, with both the nonsocialist parties and the business organizations refusing to accept an invitation from the government late in the summer of 1983 to discuss the possibility of an agreement on the fund issue. On the contrary, they prepared a huge antifund demonstration against the government. In other words, they acted in the same way as the court circles around Gustaf V during the prelude to the Palace Yard crisis. Then as now, the government had been forced into retreat; at that time the issue had been defense. Staaff had offered his outstretched hand to the prodefense groups in his Karlskrona speech. This had been brusquely rejected and instead, the prodefense sentiment in the country had been exploited by the Farmers' March. In the same way, the critics of the employee investment fund system pretended not to see the changes in the actual situation, but instead decided to take maximum advantage of the strong antifund sentiments in the country. On 4 October 1983, 80,000 or

---

[31] Prop 1983/84:50, quotations from pp. 35, 52, and 56; RD 1983/84:53–54, pp. 49 (Feldt) and 91 (Palme).

Table 9.4. *Attitude toward government bill on employee investment funds in November 1983 (percent) – initials indicate party sympathizers and LO union members, respectively*

	M	L	C	S	LPC	LO	All
For	1	4	1	40	55	28	18
Against	93	82	89	26	24	44	61
Don't know	6	14	10	34	21	28	20

Note: Number of people interviewed: 2,664
Source: SIFO-Indikator, 1983:6.

perhaps 100,000 people gathered in Stockholm to express their criticism of collective employee investment funds, although one Social Democratic source reported counting only 27,600 demonstrators.

And the negative public opinion figures on employee investment funds continued to pour in. After the government bill had been introduced, the Swedish Institute of Public Opinion Research (SIFO) asked voters to answer this question: "If you were a member of Parliament, would you vote for or against the bill on employee investment funds?" The results can be seen in Table 9.4. Only 18 percent of interviewees would have voted for the bill and a full 61 percent against it, while 20 percent replied "Don't know." The distribution of views among the sympathizers of various parties showed a strongly critical attitude toward the fund system among the nonsocialist parties. Among Social Democrats, 40 percent supported the fund bill and 26 percent opposed it. Only among Left party Communist sympathizers was there a majority in favor of the fund bill. Criticism of the funds was also remarkably strong among LO union members. The following explanation was provided by SIFO itself: "Ironically enough, opposition to the funds is greater among LO members than among Social Democratic sympathizers. This is partly because there are many nonsocialists among LO members. If LO members were M.P.'s, 28 percent would vote for the bill, 44 percent would vote against it and 28 percent do not know how they would vote."[32]

The two-day-long parliamentary debate on the employee investment fund issue began on 20 December 1983. During the debate, which completely followed party lines, the party delegations indicated their mass concurrence with their chairmen's speeches; to demonstrate an unbroken nonsocialist front, the nonsocialist party chairmen also indicated their concurrence with each other. The Social Democrats repeated that the

[32] *SIFO-Indikator*, 1983:6, p. 9.

employee investment funds were part of a carefully conceived plan to lead Sweden out of the recession. A spreading of economic influence to employees by means of collective funds was necessary, both to achieve slower cost increases as a goal of economic stabilization policy and with reference to capital formation in the business sector. The nonsocialists painted the hazards of socialistic tendencies in loud colors and warned that collective funds would restrict freedom and lead to bureaucracy. They specifically promised that the funds would be abolished if there were a nonsocialist victory in the next election; and only the day after the bill was approved, they announced that they had appointed a task force that would present a phaseout plan well before that election. The nonsocialists regretted that the Social Democrats were now implementing a proposal that so obviously went against the will of the Swedish people. The Social Democrats expressed regret that although their own side had been continuously prepared for negotiations with the opposition, the nonsocialists had rejected their outstretched hand. When the bill was put to a vote, it won on the strength of Social Democratic and Communist votes, while the nonsocialists voted against it.[33]

One incident that attracted attention during the parliamentary debate was the critical words about the fund system which Finance Minister Kjell-Olof Feldt scribbled down on a scrap of paper while sitting in Parliament, and which a reporter from *Stockholms-Tidningen,* a Social Democratic newspaper, happened to see and photograph:

> Employee funds are junk, okay,
> But now we've dragged them all this way.[34]

This bit of doggerel became the rather inglorious concluding remark in the Social Democratic handling of the fund issue. Now they wanted to get the issue off the agenda at any price; it was time to stop – this was not the first step, but "*the* step." The party had extricated itself as hastily as possible from its experiment with the ownership policy. Noticeably relieved, it could return to a consistent, traditional Social Democratic welfare policy.

3. ENACTMENT OF THE COLLECTIVE EMPLOYEE INVESTMENT FUND SYSTEM

Why did the nonsocialists reject the hand that Olof Palme stretched out to them? Why was no agreement reached on employee investment funds, despite the prime minister's repeated offer of negotiations? As with the

[33] RD 1983/84:53–54, pp. 3–203 and RD 1983/84:55, pp. 4–66.
[34] *Stockholms-Tidningen,* 21 Dec. 1983.

Table 9.5. *The Social Democratic calculation in
the employee investment fund game*

	The nonsocialists	
	Adjustment	Confrontation
The Social Democrats Adjustment	+2, +1	−1, −1
Confrontation	+1, −2	−2, +2

other issues considered in this book, we shall try to give a comprehensive answer using a game theory analysis. The model that will be presented focuses attention on the interplay between the actors: The decision that will finally be made on an issue depends both on the opposing player's choice of strategy and on one's own action. The final result depends not only on what proposals are actually presented, but above all on how these are interpreted, or misinterpreted, by the opposing player.[35]

For the Social Democrats (Table 9.5) the cooperation that would be the result if both sides adjusted to each other was the best alternative (upper left-hand quadrant). And even if a general settlement could not be achieved, an agreement with the middle parties (Center and Liberals), or with one of them, was originally considered far from impossible. More generally, the upper left-hand quadrant can be described as "the Swedish model," with cooperation across the lines separating the two political blocs. The confrontation alternative thus appeared less attractive, because it threatened such cooperation. Only after extreme hesitation did the party give in to LO's desire to push for an employee investment fund system. Meidner's original proposal (lower left-hand quadrant) thus came only in second place in the Social Democratic preference ordering. Above all, the party wanted to avoid an antinationalization campaign (lower right-hand quadrant); the labor movement had painful experience of what such campaigns could mean and in the 1982 election campaign once again tasted some of this bitter medicine. In this case, some adjustment to the nonsocialists, which is roughly what happened as a result of the parliamentary vote in December 1983, was actually preferable (upper right-hand quadrant).

In the judgment of the Social Democrats, the antinationalization policy

[35] Glenn H. Snyder and Paul Diesing, *Conflict Among Nations: Bargaining, Decision Making, and System Structure in International Crises* (Princeton, N.J.: Princeton University Press, 1977), pp. 37–48 and 107–182; Knut Midgaard, "Co-operative Negotiations and Bargaining: Some Notes on Power and Powerlessness," in *Power and Political Theory: Some European Perspectives*, ed. Brian Barry (New York: Wiley, 1976), pp. 117–137.

298

Table 9.6. *The nonsocialist calculation in the*
employee investment fund game

	The nonsocialists	
	Adjustment	Confrontation
The Social Democrats Adjustment	+1, +2	−1, −1
Confrontation	+2, −2	−2, +1

in the lower right-hand quadrant was the first preference of the nonsocialists. They could not interpret the categorical nonsocialist rejection of the outstretched hand in any other way. The Social Democrats were not convinced that all the nonsocialist rhetoric in favor of the Swedish model actually expressed the first preference of the nonsocialists; in their judgment, this was instead the second preference of the nonsocialists (upper left-hand quadrant). The worst alternative for the nonsocialists was, of course, the original Meidner plan (lower left-hand quadrant). This plan was worse than the solution finally adopted by Parliament (upper right-hand quadrant).

So the problem facing the Social Democrats was that the fund issue put them on a course that threatened to pull Swedish politics away from the Swedish model – which, as we saw in Chapter 8, was also being undermined by other conditions. Their entire continued handling of the fund issue was designed to avoid such a development. The strategy of the outstretched hand can be described as a Social Democratic adjustment strategy aimed at adapting to nonsocialist views and thereby, if possible, restoring a climate of cooperation according to the Swedish model.

As Table 9.5 indicates, "adjustment" was also a dominating strategy for the Social Democrats (+2 or −1 was preferable to +1 or −2 respectively). The nonsocialists thus should have understood that the Social Democrats would choose this alternative. As rational actors, they should then also have preferred "adjustment" to "confrontation" in order to achieve a +1 instead of a −1. The Swedish model could thereby be saved.

The nonsocialists did not perceive the game in this way at all, however. Contrary to what the Social Democrats assumed, the nonsocialists primarily wanted to defend the Swedish model (upper left-hand quadrant in Table 9.6); on the other hand, they did not believe – analogously with the judgment of the Social Democrats – that their opponent preferred this outcome; they assumed that the Social Democrats accorded the Meidner funds first preference (lower left-hand quadrant) and the Swedish model second place (upper left-hand quadrant). If the Swedish model could not be maintained, a consistent defense of the market economy by means of a tough antinationalization policy was the nonsocialists' second preference (lower right-hand quadrant); they realized that such a campaign was what the Social Democrats wanted most to avoid. Giving in entirely to the Meidner funds (lower left-hand quadrant) was the worst alternative for the nonsocialists, worse than the decision reached in December 1983 (upper right-hand quadrant).

An analysis of the utility values in Table 9.6 shows that the nonsocialists had to choose between a maximax strategy ("adjustment") or a minimax strategy ("confrontation"). In the same way, in the judgment of the nonsocialists, the Social Democrats had a choice between a minimax strategy ("adjustment") and a maximax strategy ("confrontation"). What is rational action in such a situation? As the reader will recall from accounts of earlier games, this depends entirely on what risks we are willing to take. The nonsocialists were not willing to take any risks. At this point, they believed that they had had too much bad experience of what happened when you bargained and made agreement with the Social Democrats. Most recently, the tax agreement reached on the so-called wonderful night of 24 April 1981 between the two middle parties and the Social Democrats, causing the Moderates to resign from the three-party nonsocialist government, had turned out to be a disappointment. The nonsocialists felt deceived by the Social Democrats. Now they could, admittedly, see a series of retreats by the Social Democrats. But was this enough? The Social Democrats had of course not capitulated, but still had some form of employee investment funds in their program. As long as the Social Democrats did not entirely remove the funds from the agenda until after the 1985 election, the nonsocialists did not dare make any agreements. The chairmen of the nonsocialist parties openly declared that they did not trust Olof Palme as a bargaining partner. They consequently preferred to turn down his invitations flatly and aim instead at reversing the decision to introduce collective employee investment funds after the hoped-for nonsocialist victory in the 1985 election. The nonsocialists were not willing to take the risk of being hit by maximum losses if they adopted an adjustment strategy and then, for instance, the Social Democrats enlisted Communist help in pushing through a far-reaching fund proposal in any event. The nonsocialists thus chose the minimax strategy and adopted a policy of confrontation.

If we then put together what the Social Democrats believed about themselves (Table 9.5) and what the nonsocialists believed about themselves (Table 9.6), we get the situation shown in Table 9.7. The combination of the Social Democrats' dominating strategy of "adjustment" and the nonsocialist parties' minimax strategy of "confrontation" led to parliamentary approval of the government bill, which we find in the upper right-

Table 9.7. *The employee investment fund game,*
with the Social Democrats' and nonsocialist
parties' own respective preferences

	The nonsocialists	
	Adjustment	Confrontation
The Social Democrats Adjustment	+2, +2	−1, −1
Confrontation	+1, −2	−2, +1

hand quadrant. But as we see, this quadrant by no means represented the best solution; this would have come about if both sides had followed the adjustment strategy and restored the climate of cooperation represented by the Swedish model (+2 for both sides in the upper left-hand quadrant). Mutual mistrust now prevented an assurance game of the kind that paved the way for cooperation after the tough dispute on economic planning in the 1940s. The nonsocialists were not sure what Olof Palme meant by his invitations for cooperation. They were not convinced that the outstretched hand really meant that the Social Democrats preferred cooperation according to the Swedish model. Thus, they followed the confrontation policy even in dealing with the watered-down proposal, which Parliament approved in December 1983.

4. THE PARTY DISCIPLINE METHOD

Why did Parliament approve the introduction of collective employee investment funds, even though a majority of citizens were against this proposal? In this section we will provide an explanation that we hope is somewhat less trivial than the observation that, on this issue, the M.P.'s were obviously not representative of the Swedish people. We will show that even though a majority of citizens disapproved of the decision by a majority of M.P.'s, the M.P.'s in each party delegation behaved in a way that was representative of their respective voters. Whereas in the previous section we examined the actors' strategies, calculations, misunderstandings, and defeats, in this section we will shift our interest, in keeping with our principle for structuring each chapter, to the rule system that enables a minority to push through decisions against a majority of public opinion, while strictly observing democratic principles.

Table 9.8 shows public attitudes toward the government bill on

Table 9.8. *Attitudes toward the employee investment fund bill among people who voted for the different parties*

	In favor	Against	Don't know	Total
Nonsocialists	0	8	0	8
Social Democrats	3	2	3	8
Communists	1	0	0	1

employee investment funds during the fall of 1983, as measured by SIFO.[36] Given the size of the parties and the distribution of public opinion on the funds, seventeen units provide the best approximation of the influence of the participants: 8 for the nonsocialists, 8 for the Social Democrats, and 1 for the Left party Communists.[37] In highly politicized issues such as employee investment funds, and in most issues generally, the first step in the parliamentary decision-making process is to establish the party line. As we see, this presents no problem for the nonsocialist parties. They are all opposed to the funds. (The breakdown of units by party is Moderates, 4; Conservatives, 3; and Liberals, 1.) Nor do the Left party Communists have any problems. The party is in favor of employee investment funds, although a more detailed analysis of the SIFO figures shows that the majority in favor of the funds in this party was as small as 55 percent. The Social Democrats, on the other hand, were divided: three units in favor, three "don't knows," and two units against. The party had to seek unity. In this internal game, too, the majority principle functions as the decision rule. It is unclear from the pattern of units but clear from the SIFO material that the group in favor of the funds was a few percentage points larger than the "don't know" group. If the party's parliamentary delegation wanted to vote in accordance with the majority of Social Democratic citizens who had expressed an opinion on the issue, it should thus have supported the fund bill. This was also what happened, of course.

After the parties have thus adopted a position, the next step is the actual parliamentary vote. The four units in favor of the fund system have now suddenly become nine and have thereby turned into a majority, as com-

[36] Table 9.4 above.
[37] This analytical technique can be found, for example, in James M. Buchanan and Gordon Tullock, *The Calculus of Consent: Logical Foundations of Constitutional Democracy* (Ann Arbor: University of Michigan Press, 1962), pp. 220ff., and Ingemar Ståhl, "En ekonomisk teori för blandekonomin," *Erfarenheter av blandekonomin. Uppsatser och diskussioner vid Dahmén-symposiet om den svenska blandekonomin Saltsjöbaden 18–19 oktober 1976* (Stockholm: Almqvist & Wiksell International, 1977), pp. 54–55. SIFO director Hans Zetterberg pursues the same arguments in connection with his figures in *SIFO-Indikator*, 1983:6, p. 4.

pared with the eight remaining units opposed to the funds. A combination of party discipline and the majority principle enables a minority to push through a collective decision against the will of the majority.

Some nonsocialists, however, intimated that the parliamentary vote approving the employee investment funds was not the result of entirely honest procedures. One Moderate M.P., for example, put on a big show of indignation at the fact that the finance minister wanted to implement something he did not believe in, only in order to be "obedient to his party."[38]

Let us ignore what Finance Minister Feldt believed deep down – we cannot know this – and ask the question in terms of principles: Is it an expression of dishonesty to vote contrary to one's conviction in Parliament? As far as we can understand, the only possible way of answering this question with a categorical yes is to imagine that political parties did not exist and to surrender ourselves to the Oscarian dream of M.P.'s who are independent of their voters and autonomously form an opinion on political issues, without taking anything else into consideration. This world vanished as early as the tariff dispute of the 1880s, which began the transformation of Swedish representation theory and elevated the political parties to the role of organizers of the political game. Since then we have been guided by two principles, the majority method and the party discipline method, which sometimes collide, as they did on the employee investment fund issue.[39] We thus need not assume at all that any "dishonesty" was part of the game when the majority that passed the fund bill was being put together. Given the opinion found in the various parties, the approval of the bill was simply a logical result of the decision rules that the Swedish Parliament follows.

For a potential loser, such collisions between the majority method and the party discipline method can serve as a lever that helps him to achieve a favorable decision, even though he lacks majority support for his proposal. In terms of principles, we encounter a problem here, which is discussed in detail in Chapter 10 – Weber's discourse on ultimate ends and responsibility. Ideological conviction drives people to devote themselves to politics in order to create a better society. But as long as we do not enjoy dictatorial power and as long as we are not interested in only a sin-

[38] RD 1983/84:55, p. 9 (Gennser).
[39] The difficulties that arise when the minority principle is combined with the party discipline method are thoroughly discussed by the foremost theoretician of Swedish parliamentarism, Karl Staaf, *Det demokratiska statsskicket. Jämförande politiska studier* II, ed. Nils Edén and Erik Staaff (Stockholm: Wahlström & Widstrand, 1917), pp. 180–202 and 305ff. For discussion by modern political scientists, see Hanna Fenichel Pitkin, *The Concept of Representation* (Berkeley and Los Angeles: University of California Press, 1967), pp. 147ff., and J. Roland Pennock, *Democratic Political Theory* (Princeton, N.J.: Princeton University Press, 1979), pp. 335ff.

gle issue, we have to join forces in order to promote our ideas through collective action if we are to have any prospect of seeing them implemented. And in this context, the need arises to achieve unity within the collective, to adapt the wishes of different groups on different issues to each other. A responsible politician can thus not withdraw his support from the party without further ado, just because it follows a different policy on a particular issue than he would have wanted. The relevant consideration is whether his opposition to the party is of such crucial importance that he is prepared to take the consequences on other issues that a defeat for the party on a particular issue may lead to. This is the ethical dilemma that a politician must constantly live with, and whose solution varies depending on the weight of the issues and the parliamentary consequences.

Parliament's enactment of a collective employee investment fund system provides yet another illustration of the main problem in rationalist political science: the difficulties of turning individual preferences into collective decisions and the opportunities that a minority has to make its influence felt in politics. During the democratic experimentation of the past one hundred years, we have obviously formualted far too many conditions – and far too many irreconcilable conditions – that we want democratic decision rules to fulfill. This has made it difficult to maintain an overview of politics and has created numerous opportunities for the skilled tactician. For normatively oriented theory, the situation is less than satisfactory. Perhaps it will be the major task of political science researchers during the next decade to work out a more stringent theory on how we should behave when making collective decisions in a democracy.

10

Strategic action in politics

1. MANEUVERING ROOM IN POLITICS

The concept of politics as rational action was defined in the introductory chapter of this study in two steps: first, as the ability of politicians to rank their preferences; and second, as the ability to act strategically – that is, to maneuver in such a way that as many of their preferences as possible can be realized at the present time, without thereby diminishing their long-term prospects.

On the basis of this definition, we have been able to follow our politicians as they have used strategic action to further their own positions on a number of major controversial issues in Sweden during the past century. The exclusive pursuit of their first preference has rarely been the best way for these actors to promote their interests. But by modifying their preferences in various ways, linking them with other issues, referring them to other decision-making bodies, maintaining silence about them, or – on the few occasions when this is considered suitable in spite of everything – by uncompromisingly arguing their case in order to force their opponent into retreat, the winners of these games have managed to increase their influence on impending decisions.

What should be our attitude toward such strategic action in politics? Is it an acceptable means of achieving political goals? Or is it a morally dubious undertaking that only reinforces our "contempt for politicians," to use a phrase that is fashionable in Sweden today?

World literature overflows with condemnations. Politicians are described as unscrupulous cynics and ruthless frauds, who conceal their real motives behind a facade of beautiful phrases. A typical example is provided by the words with which Shakespeare allows the son of the murdered king to characterize Macbeth:

> I grant him bloody,
> Luxurious, avaricious, false, deceitful,

Ideology and strategy

Sudden, malicious, smacking of every sin
That has a name.[1]

Of the two types of behavior often criticized, calculation and lying, only the first will be discussed here. The question of whether it is permissible to lie in politics or break election promises or abandon agreements with other politicians has led to lively debate to which our research contributes little original material.

Approaching politics from a rationalist perspective, however, provides much insight into the kind of manipulation of the agenda in the form of planning, calculation, and trade-offs between wishes that we refer to as strategic action. Three problems will be discussed in this chapter. First, we will summarize our previous explanation as to why strategies arise in politics at all. Second, we will join rationalist theoreticians in asking if there is anything we can do about this situation. Third, we will specify a normative approach to strategic action in politics.

The political game in the major controversial issues that we have discussed in this book has consistently been analyzed from the perspective of the potential loser, that is, from the standpoint of the person(s) who would have lost if simple majority rule were strictly applied to the original preferences of the actors. This somewhat unusual approach has been chosen to emphasize the possibility of alternative courses of events in history. The research concept behind the study assumes that history is not determined by fate, but created by rational actors, equipped with a will to influence developments and with an ability both to order their preferences and to act strategically.

This perspective means that we do not deceive ourselves into thinking that politicians can do what they want. To be successful, a politician must thoroughly analyze the various prerequisites of each game – for example, those of an economic and social nature – and carefully distinguish between what can and what cannot be influenced.

This fact can be illustrated by the suffrage issue early in this century. At the time, social trends seemed to be going against the Right. Rapid industrialization was enabling more and more workers to fulfill the property or income qualification to vote. Their party sympathies were for the Left. In one election district after another, Conservatives were being replaced by leftists (primarily Social Democrats or Liberals) under the majority system of representation. The Conservatives feared that in the long term, their party would be wiped out or in any case wither away into an insignificant remnant. In this situation, Arvid Lindman intervened. He managed,

---

[1] William Shakespeare, *Macbeth*, act 4, scene 3.

306

through great political and strategic skill, to switch this trend onto another, less threatening track. Unlike his more reactionary fellow Conservatives, Lindman understood that it was not possible to halt the expansion of working-class political influence, which was the consequence of social trends. But this did not mean that the influence of the workers had to have such a strong impact as the majority method of representation implied. Proportional representation would yield a better outcome for the Conservatives, and the game surrounding the broadening of the suffrage is the story of how Lindman, as the potential loser, managed to engineer a split in the Liberal majority party and stitch together a new majority that supported proportional representation. The rising Left consequently ended up with smaller representation than it would otherwise have enjoyed, and the Conservatives were guaranteed that under any circumstances they would be represented in proportion to their strength in the electorate. Lindman could not stop industrialization, nor did he wish to. But by intervening as he did, he could make sure that the political damage to his party would be less than it otherwise might have been.

We thus assume that in general, there is a certain amount of maneuvering room in politics. This freedom of action need not be large; the concept of maneuvering room also implies that there are limits to what can be done. The task of the politician is to find out where these limits are located, thereby discover what alternatives are available to him, and then work to achieve the alternative that most closely matches his preferences. No matter how narrow the actors' maneuvering room may often appear, they usually have a chance to do *something* to influence the decision in one direction or the other. When only a single alternative is thought to exist, this is almost always due to the limits of human imagination.

Actually, it would also have been possible to develop this thesis in a history book written from the perspective of the potential winner instead of the potential loser. For the person who is winning usually also has alternatives; he can choose to win in one way or another. But the history of winners has already been written many times, and all too often, so many explanations are piled on top of each other that the chance that something completely different might have occurred is forgotten. It is thus easier to see that there is maneuvering room in politics if we view history from the perspective of the potential loser, because the reconstruction of his calculations contains precisely the chance that something else besides the probable can be realized.

If we stay for just a moment with Lindman and the suffrage issue, we soon realize that the idea of maneuvering room in politics is not based on *one* prerequisite, but on two. One is our earlier observation, actually obvious and indeed trivial, that only the most rigid fatalists would deny: Politics is, at the same time, dependent and independent of social trends.

Social events such as industrialization, urbanization, and bureaucratization determine neither directly nor indirectly how political decisions will look. As a minimum, we must ascribe to politicians, based on their preferences, at least the ability to hamper or promote developments. They can, moreover, often change them.

The other prerequisite is considerably more advanced. It has surprised us during the past twenty years and given us new, counterintuitive knowledge about the political decision-making process. It explains why strategies arise in politics. In order for Lindman to succeed, it was of course not sufficient that he had the opportunity to play with different principles of political representation in an industrial society. He also needed maneuvering room in the decision-making body to persuade it to support the idea he finally decided to pursue. It is easy for us to imagine that strategic maneuvering room existed in earlier ages, when plotting princes competed for power with all imaginable ruthlessness and corrupt M.P.'s let themselves be bought by the French and Russian ambassadors. But how can there also be such maneuvering room in our own age, when the political game has been civilized in the form of definite rules for how collective decisions should be reached, and when the majority principle singles out the alternative that will win? The answer is that majority rule, exactly contrary to what we previously thought, does not always provide such unequivocal outcomes. Turning individual preferences into collective decisions is not at all a simple or automatic process. The decisions reached with the help of majority rule need not correspond to the first preference of any majority of the decision makers. In his famous work on the voter's paradox, Kenneth Arrow showed this more exactly,[2] thereby laying the groundwork for a new branch of political science – rational choice theory, under whose influence this book was written.

So far in this book, we have abstained from expressing any opinion on the best kind of decision rule in a democracy. We have used the insight into the prerequisites of politics provided us by the voter's paradox to *explain* political decisions. The imperfections of majority rule allow room for strategic action in politics. These shortcomings are what give the potential loser a chance. Just as a politician can, to some extent, be described as free in relation to social trends, he can also to some extent be described as free in relation to the temporary majority bloc, even in a democracy. He can undermine this majority by means of skilled maneuvers and create a new majority in favor of an opinion that conforms more closely to his own preferences. Our presentation has thus sought to

[2] Kenneth J. Arrow, *Social Choice and Individual Values* (New Haven, Conn.: Yale University Press, 1963). The book was first published in 1951.

explain collective decisions by analyzing the ideological preferences and strategic action of politicians.

How does one go about undermining a majority? We have learned from rational choice theory that proposals introduced for voting by a majority need not always be "stable," as the term goes. If we only count first preferences, we may obtain far too superficial an image of what the actors really want. If we look at their entire preference ordering, we sometimes discover how different wishes collide in such a way that proposals go in circles; their ranking does not fulfill the transitivity requirement. In such a situation, there is an incentive for the actors to modify their original preferences and cooperate in presenting a new proposal for a majority position, thereby improving their utility values.

When Arrow originally presented this finding – rooted in the ideas of the Enlightenment philosopher Condorcet – he encountered skepticism among political scientists, who saw the voter's paradox as a mere academic game of numbers without relevance to political reality. But as research has moved ahead, this skepticism has ceased and we have increasingly begun to understand the fundamental importance of the paradox to the way we make decisions in a democracy. Collective decisions do not fall down from the heavens when we invoke the name of the people. They emerge from a continuous give-and-take among bargaining minorities.

By looking at the legendary crisis agreement between the Social Democrats and the Agrarians, in this study we have been able to provide a graphic example of how the voter's paradox can work. A straight application of majority rule in the spring of 1933 would have led to the defeat of the Social Democratic unemployment policy. But because the expected majority decision was unstable, Per Albin Hansson managed to bring about an agreement with the Agrarians, whereby the outcome for both sides was better than it otherwise would have been. His use of logrolling not only enabled Hansson to maneuver himself out of the role of potential loser. Because the resulting coalition lasted, he was able to set his party's stamp on the entire future of Swedish welfare policy and parliamentary government.

More generally speaking, maneuvering room arises in politics as soon as a politician weighs the consequences of modifying his preferences on some issue in order to improve his utility values. Arvid Lindman successively radicalized his suffrage proposal until the majority tipped in his favor and the government bill could pass. And the strategies are legion. This book is one big panorama of the opportunities available to politicians in this respect.

But these opportunities need not lead to victory. Our potential losers have not always been successful in their efforts. In about half the cases we have discussed, they have come up short. Therefore, we first have analyzed the actors' ideological preferences and their strategic action, and then have attempted to explain why they won or lost when the final decision was made.

Using some of the issues covered in the book, we will illustrate here how a potential loser can also fail in his strategies. The first case simply shows that politics is sometimes a zero-sum game, where one person's gains are balanced by another's losses. Someone has to lose, no matter how skillfully both camps pursue their game. In the late 1950s Bertil Ohlin, chairman of the Liberal party, tried to avoid a defeat in a parliamentary vote on the supplementary pension issue by asking that the issue instead be made the subject of a referendum. Ohlin had good reason to believe that he would win a referendum, and his request was so skillfully presented that his opponent, Prime Minister Tage Erlander, could not reject it without losing prestige with the voters. As we have seen, however, Erlander managed to establish a counterstrategy that turned around public opinion on the supplementary pension issue. Step by step, Erlander beat back the opposition's attack and strengthened his position so that the Social Democratic pension policy could be forced through, albeit with the narrowest possible voting majority. A failed attempt such as Ohlin's is easily reconcilable with rational choice theory; the application of this theory is by no means restricted to successful games.

The rational choice analytical approach can also be used to explain another type of failures – those that occur because the actors are completely inflexible and in which the results are dictated by forces they cannot control. Such cases are, in fact, classic examples of rational choice analysis; the "prisoners' dilemma" is the most frequently cited example of all in this theory. In our study, we interpreted the birth of the party system and of modern Swedish politics during the tariff dispute of the 1880s as a "prisoners' dilemma," in which M.P.'s helped undermine the Oscarian society and sow the seeds of our present-day parliamentarism and democracy. They did so against their will but nonetheless through rational calculation.

We thus realize from the "prisoners' dilemma" that even rational calculation designed to maximize one's utility values may lead to changes that none of the actors wishes. This fact is something of a challenge to the very assumption that politics is rational action. Researchers have thus found reason once again to ask whether we are capable of controlling events. Finding ways out of the "prisoners' dilemma" has become a central task of rational choice theory. Among the more interesting arguments is the proposal for a concept of collective rationality that does not stop with the short-term utility calculations of the actors, but also asks whether the outcome resulting from such calculations is actually the best conceivable one. Because this is not the case in the "prisoners' dilemma," there may be reason to reassess strategies and enter into a so-called assurance game, employing long-term cooperation to avoid a less desirable outcome. In this way, the actors can restore the maneuvering room they were in the process of losing because of the logic of the decision-making situation itself. The resolution of the tough ideological confrontations on economic planning during the 1940s was interpreted in this book as a shift from a "prisoners' dilemma" to an assurance game. And conversely, the breakdown of the M.P.s' nondecision strategy during the tariff dispute was interpreted as an example of how actors can be lured by their ideological commitment to work against their own best interests and maneuver themselves into a "prisoners' dilemma."

We can summarize this section with the following observations:

(1)   There are shortcomings in the ability of majority rule to turn individual preferences into collective decisions.
(2)   Politicians are rational actors who try to maximize their utility values.
(3)   Given (1) and (2), it is unavoidable that these actors will attempt to utilize the maneuvering room that arises because of the shortcomings of the decision rule in order to improve their positions by means of strategic action.

2. IN SEARCH OF A DECISION RULE

Our interest thus turns to the normative basis of our study. When majority rule turned out to contain such shortcomings, a lively debate arose within rational choice theory as to whether there is any other decision rule that more effectively eliminates the room for strategic action in politics. One British researcher expressed the matter as follows: When political life decays, leadership weakens, and the whole system of government is questioned, we have to go off "in search of a new decision rule."[3]

When we begin such a search, we should not forget the special prerequisites that apply to this process. The first is that the decision rule should fulfill Arrow's conditions or some other, similar conditions that leave no room for strategic action in politics. We never assume that there might be something desirable about politicians indulging in such action – something there is reason to return to later in this chapter. Second, we must not overlook the fact that majority rule was never launched as a counterweight to strategic action. This rule was instituted for completely different

---

[3] Nevil Johnson, *In Search of the Constitution: Reflections on State and Society in Britain* (Oxford: Pergamon, 1977), p. vii. See also Donald D. Searing, "Rules of the Game in Britain: Can the Politicians be Trusted?" *The American Political Science Review* (1982): 239–258.

reasons designed to promote social equality. One man – one vote, regardless of class and social standing, was the slogan of those parties that transformed authoritarian European states into modern democracies, inspired by the ideas of the French Revolution. If we now find a decision rule that is more resistant to strategy than majority rule, it is thus by no means certain that it is preferable. In the last analysis, we must of course make an assessment of what values this decision rule promotes and how important it is in this context that the opportunity for strategic action is less in one case than in the other.

Let us first see whether the alternative decision rules considered by our potential losers on the issues we have discussed afford better protection against strategies than majority rule. It should be emphasized that "alternative decision rules" need not, of course, refer to decisions according to any principle other than one man–one vote. This may be the case in the weighting method, in which the actors' influence is graded according to some scale of values – for example, how intensively committed various actors are on a particular issue. But it may also be merely a method for undermining a temporary majority to achieve another majority. This is the case with the Condorcet method, for instance, in which the final decision is made according to majority rule in any event.

The alternative decision rules are systematized in Table 1.7. We stated there that our reasoning about the voter's paradox was based on two tacit assumptions – that the actors enjoyed equal voting rights and that they disagreed. If their voting rights were different, enabling one actor to prevail over the other, no difficulties would arise. His proposal would become the collective decision. *Autocracy* as a decision rule was described as the most common rule we have had, and still have, in this world for making decisions on behalf of a group.

Nor is there any voter's paradox, of course, when the actors are unanimous in their views. They approve the policy on which everyone agrees. The concept of unanimity is of interest because of the idea of the *general will*. When there is disunity, a minority should not regard the outcome as a defeat, but as a source of information on what the right decision is. It should consequently change its opinion and support the majority policy. This decison rule, too, has played an important part in the political history of the past two centuries.

But in modern Sweden, neither autocracy nor the general will is a relevant decision rule, nor does either of them fulfill Arrow's conditions. For these reasons, both rules were eliminated from Table 1.7. If we had been interested in the normal and the potential winner and thus in majority rule, it would have been placed midway between these two decision rules in the table, "between the lone voice of the dictator in an autocracy and the 100 percent unanimity of the general will." Because we are, instead, interested in the exceptions and the potential loser, we instead listed some other decision rules here that those who wish to avoid defeat can try to pursue as an alternative to majority rule.

Of these alternative decision rules, one has lost its relevance during the period under study – the past 100 years – in the same way as autocracy and the general will. This is the *division-of-power rule*. It is, incidentally, the only one of the alternative rules that does not fulfill the two conditions of equal voting rights and disunity. The division-of-power rule purely formally accorded the king a special position compared with that of other citizens. This has now been abolished in the new Constitution, which stipulates that all power emanates from the people. But in practice, the division-of-power rule ceased to apply half a century earlier. As we have seen here, this occurred in a very remarkable way. The Constitution was not declared invalid; it was ignored. The winners did not demand a new Constitution; they requested that the system that had applied until then should be declared unconstitutional. The republicans did not demand the abolition of the monarchy; they retained the existing system but took away from the king those powers that are incumbent upon a monarch.

The decision rules that remain to be discussed are arranged in Table 1.7 in the following two categories:

> *Disagreement between parties and voters*
> The imperative mandate
> The referendum method
>
> *Disagreement among political parties*
> The proportional representation method
> The Condorcet method
> The party discipline method
> The weighting method
> The rights method

The rules in the first category are intended to govern the disunity that may arise between parties and voters. Should politicians be governed by the views of their voters or should they be allowed to act more independently? If the former were the case, perhaps researchers would find here the decision rule they are seeking: Given sufficiently detailed instructions from the voters, the politicians would have no maneuvering room for strategic action. The rules in the second category concern disunity among political parties and are arranged – Chapter 1 stated – according to the extent to which minorities would be favored compared with what would be the case if we used simple majority rule. Should policy be shaped exclusively by the wishes of the majority or should we also take into account the ability of minorities to defend their interests in various respects? In the previous section, we have already seen that the first principle, despite its presumed lack of ambiguity, can be set aside because a majority consists of minorities that may have an interest in changing their positions. But could more formal regulation of this minority influence by some decision rule perhaps counteract the element of strategy in politics?

We will begin this quick review of the seven rules with the *imperative mandate*. As the reader will recall, this decision rule was rejected in principle by everyone in the tariff dispute. But in the end it was cited in desperation by the free traders. To avoid a defeat in Parliament, where their opponents were gathering larger and larger support each year, the free traders attempted to bring about a decision among the voters that was to their own advantage.

In the same way, the *referendum method* has enabled the potential loser to pursue a strategy. Those who were in the process of losing the battle in Parliament hoped for stronger support if the issue could instead be referred to the people themselves for a direct decision. Because he believed that public opinion was on his side, Bertil Ohlin decided to demand that the supplementary pension issue be moved out of the closed chambers of Parliament and face the verdict of the people, while speaking in ironic terms of Erlander's anxiety about such a step. Far from being resistant to strategic action, both the imperative mandate and the referendum method have thus offered political actors greater strategic maneuvering room. It also seems inevitable that this should be the case, even if the politicians do not resort to such tactical feints as in Sweden's last two referendums on supplementary pensions and nuclear power, respectively. No matter how honestly we exert ourselves to analyze public opinion on a political issue, certain alternatives must finally be chosen to be voted on, and certain wording must be used. In this context, every attitude and every word affects the outcome of the referendum in one direction or the other. If we wish to find a decision rule that counteracts strategic action in politics, we cannot choose anything worse than letting the decision be preceded by an extra election campaign on the issue, for election campaigns are the time when politicians have the largest room of all for strategic action.

A discussion of the rules with whose help we try to achieve agreements among contending political parties is actually just as discouraging. Majority rule was the original basis for the method used in choosing representatives of the people. The parties that were losing voter support eventually realized, however, that *proportional representation* would be more advantageous for them. But this did not make the election of representatives a simple and automatic process. Strategic considerations affected attitudes toward methods of representation. It has consistently been the minority that has sought to strengthen its position with the help of proportional representation. At the time of the historic decision on manhood suffrage early in this century, this applied to the Conservatives, who, not without reason, anticipated that their position in industrial society would become weaker and weaker. Twenty years earlier and sixty years later it was the Liberals, because during these periods *they* were at a disadvantage. And in the same way, the Conservatives and Social Democrats have shifted viewpoints without allowing themselves to be prevented by any ideological qualms. In this way, the change in representation method has only been a means for politicians to act for the benefit of their party's interests.

The next decision rule, the *Condorcet method,* gives the minority some improvement in its position but has generated heated debate on political morality. Undermining unstable majorities and creating new coalitions have been condemned as unacceptable political chicanery. But on the other hand, the method has been defended both by practical politicians such as Per Albin Hansson and by rational choice theoreticians such as James Buchanan and Gordon Tullock as a way of achieving collective decisions that reflect the entire preference ordering of the actors in a truer and more correct manner. No one, on the other hand, has claimed that this method is a bulwark against strategic action. On the contrary, in itself it is often an incentive to strategic modification of preferences.

Like the Condorcet method, the *party discipline method* means that under certain circumstances a minority is able to impose its will against that of the majority – paradoxically, in the name of the majority. A majority of a majority provides opportunities for strategic manipulation.

As for the two remaining rules, the *weighting method* and the *rights method,* we can first ask whether they fulfill the equal voting rights criterion specified at the beginning. The weighting method implies, of course, that the preferences of certain actors should be accorded greater weight than those of others. The rights method means that certain interests should be exempted from majority decisions. Unlike the division-of-power rule, however, these methods do not grant special privileges to a particular individual or a particular group of actors. Instead, anyone can enjoy the advantages that these rules bring about. In other words, it is a matter of acting in such a way as to qualify for these rules – and this is a motive for strategic action. In the chapter on nuclear power, we concluded that in many cases the weighting method seems more appealing than simple majority rule, because it takes into account not only the order in which the actors rank their preferences, but also the intensity with which different actors embrace them. But it is equally obvious that it would be very difficult in practical political work to compare the intensity of the various actors' commitments. We pointed to the risk that actors might exaggerate their commitment, if we followed the principles of the weighting method, in order thereby to increase their political influence on an issue. In the chapter on economic planning, we said that in terms of

315

pure principle, the rights method is part of the democratic ideological tradition. On the other hand, there have been disagreements as to what rights
should be counted – the right of private ownership has been the most
controversial of these – and whether there has been a violation of rights
in a given case. As a consequence, the rights principle has not functioned
as an unequivocal, conclusive decision rule but as a particular type of argument that has turned out to be especially potent in political propaganda.

Thus none of the alternative decision rules makes strategic action
impossible, any more than majority rule does. And there is reason to add
the following important statement: *Modern research has been no more
successful in indicating any other decision rule that eliminates room for
strategic action in politics.*

In other words, do we finally have to give up, canceling our search for
a decision rule that makes strategic action impossible? This actually seems
to be the case, if we accept Arrow's criteria for decision making. But how
self-evident are they, in fact? Let us now ignore these requirements for a
moment and go back to the history of political ideas to examine how people in earlier periods looked at the conditions that collective decision
making ought to fulfill.

So as not to get lost while undertaking such a review, we are justified
in first raising our eyes a bit above the matters we have been discussing so
far. Majority rule and the alternative decision rules all belong to the same
family. Their common feature is that collective decisions are to be based
on the preferences of individual actors on individual issues. But things
need not be this way. In historical terms, this concept is young, contrast-
ing sharply with older assumptions. It can be found in the works of Condorcet, and it achieves its clearest expression under the utilitarians and
Bentham. Arrow is part of the same school; we can speak of a *Bentham–
Arrow decision principle*. Bentham expressly declared that "there is no
one who knows what is for your own interest so well as yourself," and
"the universal interest is simply the sum of the interests of the various
members who compose the society."[4]

For earlier thinkers, however, it seemed absurd that the general interest
would be achieved through such a simple summation of actors' preferences. When Plato founded his academy after the oligarchic revolt against
Athenian democracy in 404 B.C., he sowed the seeds of systematic Western
thinking on rhetoric, philosophy, and political science. Frustrated in his
own political ambitions and bitterly critical of all existing systems of government, Plato proclaimed that only those who possessed philosophical

---

[4] Hanna Fenichel Pitkin, *The Concept of Representation* (Berkeley and Los Angeles: University of California Press, 1972), pp. 198–199.

wisdom understood what was best for a society. Using his famous analogy of the underground cave, he argued that philosophers should govern, for the benefit of the people but by no means on their instructions. For ordinary people's notion of politics was as fuzzy as the shadow pictures on the wall of the cave, which the prisoners tried to interpret. Only those who had been up in the light knew how actual reality looked. In the same way, citizens were prisoners in the darkness of the sensual world, but it was possible to achieve insight by following the path of philosophy to the world of ideas.[5]

The independence of leaders in relation to their people, their duty to pursue the policy they found just, without being influenced by the people's demands, would be the main theme of political doctrine until the late eighteenth century, when the ideas we associate with Condorcet, Bentham, and Arrow began to spread. This tradition culminated with Edmund Burke, who condemned the budding ideas of democracy in his reflections on the French Revolution. As a member of Parliament, he developed his notion that a politician was deceiving his voters if he betrayed his judgment to follow public opinion; he told his voters in Bristol that he was obligated to "defend your interests against your opinions."[6]

This *Plato–Burke decision principle,* or as it is sometimes called, the Burkean theory of representation, thus means that a politician's own assessment of the facts should determine what position he takes, even if it does not coincide with the views of his voters. Because it is based on a criterion different from the Bentham–Arrow principle, it avoids being affected by the voter's paradox. We can point out that the Plato–Burke principle only moves the problem up from the voters' arena to the parliamentary arena, where the voter's paradox can recur. But the way out is again the same: When M.P.'s decide how they will vote, it is not a question of a simple aggregation of individual preferences, either. Within the party delegations, too, there is an influence from the respective party leaderships, aimed at establishing a particular line of action.

Given this background, it is remarkable to see how little attention the Plato–Burke principle receives in rational choice debate. The same applies to the whole classic mandate debate, where the supporters of this principle form one camp and those of the Bentham–Arrow view form the other. It is as if researchers in rational choice theory had completely cut off their

[5] Plato, *Skrifter. I svensk tolkning av Claes Lindskog. Tredje delen* (Stockholm: Gebers, 1922), pp. 275–311.

[6] Edmund Burke, *The Works. Volume the Second* (London: John C. Nimmo, 1899), p. 382. On Burke's relationship with his voters, see Ernest Barker, *Burke and Bristol. A Study of the Relations between Burke and his Constituency during the Years 1774–1780* (Bristol: Arrow-Smith, 1931).

links with the history of ideas.[7] Nor is it self-evident that the Plato–Burke principle should be regarded as "outdated" in a democracy and thus in some way unworthy of serious discussion. As we have seen, the conflict on the imperative mandate in Sweden did not at all lead to the abolition of the ban on such mandates. It was removed only during the latest reform of the Constitution, but this was not regarded as involving any actual change; it remains true today that an M.P. is free to work for the policies he deems correct, unbound by his voters.

As the basis of the third decision-making principle that we will take from the history of ideas, we will choose Niccolo Machiavelli, the Italian Renaissance political theorist who is usually credited with having founded political science as an independent discipline. Previously, Platonic or Christian-influenced thinking about politics was intimately interwoven with what was considered the "right" opinion in different contexts. The writings of Machiavelli, which are devoted entirely to the art of war and politics, single out the concept of strategy. For the first time, we encounter here a carefully thought out, instrumental approach to politics.[8] Machiavelli does, admittedly, have a primary goal that engages his passion – unifying Italy and driving out the barbarians. But what has given him his place in intellectual history is his unscrupulous advice on how a prince should behave to reap success from the plans he has devised. People talk about how important it is for a prince to be faithful to high ideals, Machiavelli writes, but everyone still knows that we evaluate him primarily on the basis of what he can achieve. The prince thus "cannot practice all those things for which men are considered good, being often forced, in order to keep his position, to act contrary to truth, contrary to charity, contrary to humanity, contrary to religion. Therefore he must have a mind ready to turn in any direction as Fortune's winds and the variability of affairs require, yet, as I have said above, he holds to what is right when he can but knows how to do wrong when he must." In short, when evaluating political action, in Machiavelli's words, we should look "only at their results."[9] With shocking honesty, Machiavelli had put into

---

[7] For a stimulating discussion, however, see an unpublished article by James Douglas at Northwestern University, *How Actual Political Systems Cope with the Paradoxes of Social Choice* (paper for International Institute of Applied Systems Analysis, Laxenberg, Austria). See also John R. Chamberlin and Paul N. Courant, "Representative Deliberations and Representative Decisions: Proportional Representation and the Borda Rule," *The American Political Science Review* (1983): 718–733. "Surprisingly," Chamberlin and Courant write, turning around our question, "the theory of representation has gone almost untouched by rational choice theorists."

[8] Sheldon S. Wolin, *Politics and Vision: Continuity and Innovation in Western Political Thought* (Boston: Little, Brown, 1960), pp. 195–238.

[9] Niccolo Machiavelli, *The Prince: Selections from The Discourses and Other Writings*, ed. John Plamenatz (London: Fontana/Collins, 1972), pp. 108–109. The book was written in 1513.

print an issue that court circles otherwise usually only whispered about. No matter how amoral his reputation may be, the issue he raises cannot be ignored. Its relevance has been continuously confirmed by world history.

If we also wish to choose a modern thinker who pursues this line of thought into our own era, it is natural to look at Max Weber. In his lectures entitled *Wissenschaft als Beruf* and *Politik als Beruf,* delivered in Munich in the revolutionary winter of 1919, Weber repeats Machiavelli's question. For those who are driven only by the passion for truth, science is the right career, no matter how uncertain it might seem. Weber views the conditions governing politics as distinctly different. Here a devotion to a cause is insufficient, "a sterile excitation" or "a romanticism of the 'intellectually interesting' running into emptiness.... It does not make a politician unless passion as devotion to a 'cause' also makes responsibility to this cause the guiding star of action." In Weber's well-known terminology, there are two kinds of ethics applicable to politics. One is the ethic of ultimate ends: Without feeling the call of an idea, without having a program to fight for, one can never accomplish anything in politics. The second is the ethic of responsibility: A politician must also take responsibility for the consequences of his actions, considering that he is involved in many issues. A politician strictly oriented toward ultimate ends soon finds that he lacks all semblance of influence. The ethic of responsibility then forces him to deviate from his convictions on some issues. But how far can he go along this path? Finding the right balance was the fundamental dilemma of politics, Weber stated. "No ethics in the world can dodge the fact that in numerous instances the attainment of 'good' ends is bound to the fact that one must be willing to pay the price of using morally dubious means or at least dangerous ones – and facing the possibility or even the probability of evil ramifications. From no ethics in the world can it be concluded when and to what extent the ethically good purpose 'justifies' these ethically dangerous means and ramifications."[10]

Just as in the Plato–Burke principle, in the *Machiavelli–Weber decision principle* something comes between actors' preferences and the decision: What an objective assessment of the issue is for the former, a responsibility for the success of many issues is for the latter. The Machiavelli–Weber principle thus does not lead to any voter's paradox either: One should always make the decision that, considering its ultimate ends, is deemed the most appropriate in a broader context. The Machiavelli–Weber ethic of responsibility is thus of interest for our continued discussion.

[10] *From Max Weber: Essays in Sociology,* ed. and trans. by H. H. Gerth and C. Wright Mills (New York: Oxford University Press, 1958); quotations from pp. 115, 121. The lectures were held in 1919. Gerth and Mills translated Weber's term *Gesinnungsethik* as "the ethic of ultimate ends."

In both the Plato–Burke and Machiavelli–Weber decision principles, the process of political decision making is thus presented as something far more sophisticated than a simple addition of individual first preferences on individual issues. We can discuss which of Arrow's conditions these two decision-making principles violate. They may be perceived as violating the "nondictatorship" condition, because the judgment of politicians is assigned a decisive role vis-à-vis that of the voters. They may also be regarded as deviating from the condition that decisions be independent of "irrelevant alternatives," because decisions are not derived exclusively from the way in which citizens order their preferences. But is a politician's own opinion on an issue really independent of what his voters think, or is his assessment of the consequences of a particular action "irrelevant" to the decision? In fact, such assessments are of crucial importance to our evaluation of the political process; indeed, the fact that politicians make such assessments can be described as the actual vital force of politics.

With Arrow's conditions, we not only have difficulties in the form of the voter's paradox and of maneuvering room for strategic action, which is not really conceptually manageable. We also have too superficial and mechanical an image of decision making. In this book, the consistent image of politics has been one of actors using the rules of order in attempts to manipulate the agenda to benefit their interests. The role of the politician as described in the Bentham–Arrow decision principle is that of the extreme one-issue politician, who only stares at each of the items on the agenda individually without seeing any connection between the different items, and who is completely uninterested in the order in which items are discussed. This is, of course, a completely unrealistic description of a politician. There is consequently reason, in our final section, to analyze the seemingly unavoidable political strategies in a different way, which does not leave them outside the model but assigns them their rightful place in our picture of political action.

By way of summary, we draw the following conclusions in this section:

(1) The room for strategic action made possible by the voter's paradox under majority rule and the existence of many issues is also found under every other known decision rule in the Bentham–Arrow family.

(2) In the history of political ideas, however, there are at least two decision-making principles that get around the voter's paradox, without making strategic action impossible. One is the Plato–Burke principle of representation. The other is the Machiavelli–Weber ethic of responsibility. Neither of these two principles prescribes that collective decisions should be based exclusively on the preferences of individual citizens.

Table 10.1. *Four roles for politicians*

	Ultimate ends	Responsibility
Free	Boström Palme	Lindman Hansson
Bound	Fälldin	Ohlin

3. REPRESENTATION AS TRUSTEESHIP

The three decision-making principles that the last section singled out in the light of intellectual history – the Bentham–Arrow, Plato–Burke, and Machiavelli–Weber principles – confront each other in Table 10.1. In the horizontal axis, we join Max Weber in asking whether a politician should allow himself to be led exclusively by his "ultimate ends" on each issue or whether he should also take "responsibility" for the consequences of his actions, considering that he is involved in many different issues. In the vertical axis, we join Edmund Burke in asking whether a politician should be "free" or "bound" by the opinions of his voters. The lower left-hand quadrant, which combines a belief in the ethics of responsibility with the view that a politician should be bound by his voters, denotes the Bentham–Arrow decision principle. If we move upward in the matrix, we encounter the Plato–Burke theory of representation. If we move to the right, we find the Machiavelli–Weber ethic of responsibility. This gives us four different roles for the politician, all of which have been represented in the political game in Sweden during the past hundred years. We will thus use as examples in the table the names of politicians who were potential losers in the political disputes we have covered.[11]

Our first case describes a politician who is characterized by the ethic of ultimate ends and stands free in relation to his voters. Only his own views determine the behavior of this politician; he does not give up his convictions either out of consideration for the consequences of his behavior or as a concession to his voters. This simple, clear position was represented by most M.P.'s during the tariff dispute. In the summer of 1887 they indignantly rejected the tactical maneuver of allowing the tariff issue to be buried in a commission of inquiry; the battle had to continue until either one camp or the other had been pushed back. The result was a disaster for the existing political system. Any claim that members of Parliament should

[11] The king and the division-of-power rule are omitted for the same reason as in the previous section. Ohlin was the potential loser on two issues. There are consequently six names in the matrix.

be bound by their voters was also summarily rejected; M.P.'s considered it their foremost duty to pursue their views independently for the benefit of the country.

The two most recent former leaders of the Social Democratic party sometimes expressed a similar position. On the supplementary pension issue, Tage Erlander – to turn to a potential winner – pursued his ultimate end against the resistance of the electorate and rejected all compromises. On the employee investment fund issue, Olof Palme consistently acted contrary to a majority of public opinion, albeit in this case it is not equally self-evident how his role as a politician should be classified. Obviously Palme was more "free" than "bound" – he specifically requested and received an open mandate in handling the issue. But was he guided more by "ultimate ends" than by "responsibility"? This is debatable. The whole adjustment strategy was designed to move closer to the nonsocialists in order to achieve a consensus. But unlike such earlier politicians as Arvid Lindman or Per Albin Hansson, Palme was not prepared to give up the party's position on the employee investment fund issue, as they had done with regard to the suffrage and agricultural free-trade issues, respectively. This lack of inclination to give up a cause and the will to stick to his convictions – it can be debated whether they were his own or LO's – lead us finally to place Palme in the square that combines a free position in relation to the voters with maintaining the ethic of ultimate ends.

This political role can be illustrated by the following two quotations – a Burkean-sounding statement that the late nineteenth-century Conservative leader E. G. Boström made to his voters and Olof Palme's request for an open mandate on the employee investment fund issue:

1. *If you do not get what you want, you will get what is better and more useful to you.*[12]
The congress should give the Social Democratic party leadership substantial room for maneuver in its continued handling of the employee investment fund issue.

After this, we move to the upper right-hand quadrant, where we meet two politicians who very successfully maneuvered themselves out of an expected defeat. Both Arvid Lindman and Per Albin Hansson considered

---

[12] The quotation, like the placement of Boström in the matrix, is not representative of his entire career as a statesman. It is true of the early Boström, the aggressive protectionist leader we have met in this study. But as prime minister during the 1890s Boström, in contrast, became famous for his tactical skill – for what Weber calls the ethic of responsibility. The Boström quotation serves here merely as an illustration of a line of reasoning on an issue of principle.

themselves free in relation to their voters, who undoubtedly had a different view on the respective issues of universal manhood suffrage and agricultural tariffs than the ones they themselves helped implement. They also
considered themselves free to deviate from their own convictions on these
issues. Their motives were related to the ethic of responsibility. Unlike the
M.P.'s during the tariff dispute, Lindman and Hansson found it completely absurd to go down with their ships like stubborn sea captains. On
the contrary, they considered it a politician's duty to ensure that the best
possible decision was made, now that their own program could not be
realized in its entirety. They expressed themselves in similar terms. Should
the government just sit as a silent witness to the bargaining of others when
everyone knew that the suffrage issue could not be resolved in exactly the
way proposed in the government bill, Lindman asked rhetorically. Was it
reasonable for the government to let itself be shunted aside without further ado by permitting others to manipulate their proposals, Per Albin
Hansson exclaimed.

2. *As every military man knows, there is occasionally reason to give
up one position, without losing sight of your goal, in order to gain
another.*

*If the government runs into opposition from a majority of Parliament,
it will have to consider what options the situation offers in order to assert
the wishes of public opinion.*

The lower right-hand quadrant combines the ethic of responsibility
with a commitment that binds political action to voter opinion. The views
of the electorate should provide the basis for action. The task of politicians is to find the solution that best satisfies various majority and minority
wishes. The contrast between this and the upper left-hand quadrant could
not be greater. While the politician in the latter quadrant exclusively follows his ultimate ends without concessions either to the voters or to the
views of other politicians, politicians in the lower right-hand quadrant
feel they have a responsibility to find the solution that best corresponds to
the opinion of the general public.

In both the economic planning and supplementary pension issues, this
political role was represented by Bertil Ohlin. During these two controversies, Ohlin believed that Social Democratic plans should be halted, one
reason being that these plans enjoyed no popular support. At the same
time, however, Ohlin was willing to follow the bidding of the ethic of
responsibility. After the successful popular uproar against economic planning, he helped bring about the reconciliation of 1948. After the supplementary pension referendum of 1957 he proposed, although this time
unsuccessfully, a compromise designed to satisfy the interests of everyone.

Ideology and strategy

The quotation that illustrates the political role in this quadrant is taken from the latter occasion:

3. *We in the Liberal party believe that ... we are obligated to take into account the public opinion that emerged from various quarters during the referendum, not just the opinion that voted for one line or the other.*

The lower left-hand quadrant, finally, eliminates the maneuvering room for various solutions that Ohlin wanted to safeguard, by predicating a binding commitment, this time based on a politician's own convictions, which he pledges in this way to defend faithfully. No considerations related to the ethic of responsibility justify any deviation in this case. Those who choose to play this political role are governed by the ethic of ultimate ends as much as the M.P.'s during the tariff dispute, but the independence from their voters that the latter politicians enjoyed has been replaced here by categorically binding election promises. In other words, here we encounter Bentham–Arrow inflexibility, without either ideological or strategic freedom of choice for the decision maker. One example from real political life is Thorbjörn Fälldin during the 1976 election. To illustrate this position, let us choose his famous preelection statement:

4. *No ministerial post can be so desirable that I would be prepared to compromise my conviction.*

If we thus move clockwise through the matrix, starting in the upper left-hand quadrant, we find a chronological pattern; the issues follow each other in time from quadrant to quadrant. We should not make too much of this observation. It is easy to find exceptions. As mentioned already, both Tage Erlander and Olof Palme can be classified in the same quadrant as Boström, thereby interrupting the chronology – just as the political parties have generally been notably cautious about making categorical self-binding commitments during the two election campaigns following 1976, apparently warned by the difficulties that affected Fälldin.[13] But we believe that the matrix nevertheless indicates two definite trends in time.

One is the trend from the ethic of responsibility to the ethic of ultimate ends. The trend toward voting more on the basis of political views has been a major theme of the changes in the electorate during recent decades; the ideological content of politics is playing a growing part in a voter's choice of party.[14] Deviations from election programs are condemned as a moral betrayal, something that only further increases "mistrust, and sometimes contempt, toward our political system," to quote a comment by one

[13] Cf. Leif Lewin, "Politikern behöver utrymme för taktik," *Svenska Dagbladet*, 7 July 1982.
[14] Olof Petersson, *Väljarna och valet 1976* (Stockholm: Statistiska Centralbyrån, 1977), pp. 128ff.; Sören Holmberg, *Svenska väljare* (Stockholm: Liber, 1981), pp. 223–291.

nonsocialist politician on the devaluation of the Swedish krona carried out by the Social Democratic government after the 1982 election.[15]

The second trend is for the position of politicians to become increasingly unfree in relation to the electorate. The media have probably played an essential role in this process. There is a vast difference between the old-style, respectful interviews with politicians we can see flash past us in old newsreels and today's gung-ho journalism, designed to bait politicians into making binding declarations of one kind or another. But the new style of the media, in turn, is probably only a sign of a more profound change in the Swedish representation system and the dissolution of political authority.[16] In one standard work on political representation, the author reflects that "it may be the more egalitarian a nation is in its general outlook, the more it feels that it is just as good as its rulers are, and perfectly capable of judging them, the less inclined it is to give them a wide range of discretion."[17]

In our terms, we would like to say that the trend from the ethic of responsibility to the ethic of ultimate ends and the trend from freedom to self-binding commitments for our politicians are what created the current debate on the impropriety of strategic action in politics. In our opinion, it was no chance occurrence that Fälldin ran into trouble after 1976. He had maneuvered himself into the Bentham–Arrow quadrant, thereby losing the freedom of action that politics requires of its practitioners.

Is there any solution? If there is, it is by no means uncomplicated. In any event, it cannot be formulated in any simple commands with whose help we attempt to turn back the clock to the ethic of responsibility and unbound mandates.

Burke's and Boström's arrogant statements to their voters would be hard to swallow today, quite apart from the fact that a politician who tried anything in that style would certainly not be reelected – a fate that, incidentally, Burke himself suffered as early as 1780. Yet today's discussion among political scientists and politicians on whether M.P.'s "represent people's views" seems grossly oversimplified. Representation is more than a matter of reflecting public opinion. There also has to be room for opinion molding in politics, for agitation against prevailing opinions or prevailing indifference. One of the difficulties of modern politics is to find the right balance between these two functions, or to put it another way, the right balance between Burke's and Bentham's positions.

---

[15] Bert Levin, "Sveket mot Sverige," *Svenska Dagbladet,* 22 Oct. 1982. Regarding the same accusation on the part of Olof Palme against Thorbjörn Fälldin for betrayed election promises, see Chapter 8.

[16] See, for example, Jörgen Westerståhl, "Från överhetstro till individualism," *Dagens Nyheter,* 15 Oct. 1982. Cf. "Ett nytt slags auktoritet," *Tiden* (1982):586ff. (editorial).

[17] Pitkin 1972, p. 213.

In the same way, there has to be a balance along the second dimension of our table, between the ethic of ultimate ends and the ethic of responsibility. Here, too, there is no reason to cultivate any extreme position. A politician without ideological conviction awakens our mistrust, and we ask on what grounds he is asking for our vote. We regard an "evangelist" who has no ambitions for political power as unfit to promote our collective interests. Herbert Tingsten expressed the dilemma as follows: "It is obviously impossible to make a judgment between these forms of ethics; on the contrary, all we can do is declare that the world needs them both and that besides, they are never rigidly separated in individual people; a politician needs a drop of idealism and utopianism, the anarchist and pacifist need a bit of realism and adaptability so as not to remain in silence and isolation. Kierkegaard and Ibsen's Brand can be cited by the men of ultimate ends, Lincoln, Gladstone and Franklin D. Roosevelt by the bearers of responsibility; in Strindberg's Master Olof and in the life work of Gandhi, we see the struggle between the concepts of ultimate ends and responsibility and the interweaving of the two."[18]

Our conclusion is thus that we ought to resist the trends we believe are distinguishable in our age and, without striving for any extreme positions, attempt to move upward and to the right in the matrix. The Bentham–Arrow quadrant at the lower left is unfortunately not only representative of current trends. It is also one of the most influential viewpoints in political science today. And although this model has been very useful in recent research on the reasons behind political decisions, it is not especially fruitful to a discussion on political morality. For instead of studying the balancing of opposing interests, which is the life blood of politics, it bypasses this issue in silence. But politicians are not the simple voting robots depicted in the Bentham–Arrow model. They are popular representatives with the responsible task of making decisions even in cases where the most desirable outcome cannot be achieved. This is where strategic deliberations become unavoidable in politics.

One could characterize what we have said so far as an attempt to make a virtue out of a necessity. We have found that, assuming rational actors and an understanding of the shortcomings of decision rules, strategic action is unavoidable in politics. Rather than say nothing about these strategies, as Arrow does, it is better to formulate a theory that expressly assumes that they exist, albeit as a necessary evil.

By way of summary, we will now take this viewpoint one step further and state that strategic action need not be a necessary evil, either. It is not merely unavoidable. It can represent something good in politics. To

[18] Herbert Tingsten, *Från idéer till idyll. Den lyckliga demokratien* (Stockholm: Norstedts, 1966), pp. 244–245.

understand the specific character of politics, we can compare it with nature. What distinguishes human action from biological evolution is that humans can say yes to unfavorable changes and no to favorable ones. Let us once more use rational choice theory to examine three alternatives – A, B, and C – in which C is better than B and B is better than A. We first allow these alternatives to describe a biological phenomenon – for example, three versions of a protein. We further assume that it is possible to go from A to B and from A to C in one step, but not from B to C. The natural selection process will then, without hesitation, accept the mutation that goes from A to B if it occurs first, without taking the time to wait for the better change from A to C. The step from A to B will thereby irrevocably destroy the possibility of achieving the optimum. If, on the other hand, A, B, and C represented alternative political actions, the best outcome would be achievable thanks to the ability of politics to calculate strategically and "await the right opportunity."

Let us imagine, alternatively, that A is better than B and C is better than A, and it is possible to go from A to B and from B to C in one step, but not from A to C. The natural selection process will then not be able to follow the indirect strategy of "one step back, two steps forward." There is no mutation for the worse in order to achieve the best. Only humans can work out intentions, purposes, and calculations. In this example, he can thus achieve the best outcome, C, while nature would stop at A.[19]

In strategic action, we meet human beings at their most potent, as rational and calculating creatures who are not blindly dependent on deterministic laws. By balancing opposing interests, setting priorities and planning, they are in a position to shape the future by their own will. Their freedom of choice is admittedly far from total. We have consistently argued in this book that one prerequisite for success is that they must thoroughly understand the limits of their opportunities. But we oppose the tendency of our own age to narrow these opportunities further, just for the satisfaction – in the name of a single-issue mentality or direct-democracy romanticism – of ensuring that politicians will enjoy no privileged position compared with other citizens. This ignores the special conditions associated with political tasks. At most, people begrudge politicians the freedom to participate in the occasional compromise, while hastening to assure us that this does not legitimize a Machiavellian lack of scruples in choosing political methods. How carefully considered is this morality? Isn't it possible to justify ruthless actions in our age, even such political murders as eliminating Hitler in the early 1930s? The new media style of trying to pin down politicians on detailed election promises, or citing public opinion

[19] Jon Elster, *Forklaring og dialektikk. Noen Grunnbegreper i vitenskapsteorien* (Oslo: Pax, 1979), pp. 62–63.

as reported by the pollsters – which is intended for the laudable purpose of monitoring the politicians in a critical fashion – is not the only villain of the piece. The most depressing thing of all is to hear politicians themselves moralizing over their opponents' tactical games, when they know they themselves would act the same, should the opportunity arise.

Giving our political elites a freer position than they enjoy in the Bentham–Arrow quadrant is only one of two elements of what I consider a more fruitful approach to the political decision-making process. The other element is to turn everyone into practitioners of the ethic of responsibility by encouraging citizens to become politically involved. Just as representation is not only a matter of reflecting opinion but also of molding opinion, democracy is not only universal suffrage but also an educational process in which everyone gains experience of the problems of decision making by holding positions of trust. I have maintained in earlier books that good government emerges from this interaction between opinion-molding politicians and actively participating citizens.[20] For only if we have an informed, politically involved citizenry with experience of practical politics can we dare to set the politicians free. Without public criticism and monitoring, a political "dictatorship" in Arrow's technical sense can easily slide into a genuine oligarchy. Involvement in civic affairs is likely to lead to greater public understanding of the importance of strategy in optimizing political decisions. Restoring respect for the independent judgment of decision makers – both on the issues via-à-vis supposed public opinion and as regards the consequences of various alternative actions – is thus, in Weber's words, restoring the notion of politics as a profession and a calling. A politician is not a delegate who votes according to his principal's instructions, without thinking about the consequences. He is a trustee who, in an interplay with the wishes of the voters, argues for his own convictions in the hope of persuading them. At the same time, however, a politician reserves the right to take into account the probable consequences of various actions before he makes his decision.

[20] *Folket och eliterna. En studie i modern demokratisk teori* (Stockholm: Almqvist & Wiksell, 1970); *Hur styrs facket? Om demokratin inom fackföreningsrörelsen* (Stockholm: Rabén & Sjögren, 1977).

Appendix

Table A.1. *Elections to Second Chamber of Parliament, 1872–1908*

A. 1872–1884

Year	Number of voters	% of men over 21 eligible to vote	% of eligible voters who cast ballots
1872	45,198	21.9	19.1
1875	49,765	23.0	19.5
1878	54,821	23.3	20.3
1881	66,591	23.6	23.7
1884	73,636	24.1	25.2

B. 1887 I–1908

Year	Number of voters	Protectionists, Right	Moderate free traders	Free traders, Left	% of men over 21 eligible to vote	% of eligible voters who cast ballots
1887 I	129,717	41.4	—	58.6	21.9	48.1
1887 II	95,874	46.8	—	53.2	22.2	35.9
1890	105,807	42.7	—	57.3	22.8	38.5
1893	126,615	39.4	25.9	34.7	23.7	42.4
1896	140,588	38.6	23.4	38.0	23.9	45.3
1899	136,945	53.2	—	46.8	25.4	40.3
1902	180,527	45.3	—	54.7	27.7	47.2
1905	217,323	45.3	—	54.7	30.6	50.4
1908	308,389	38.5	—	61.5	34.7	61.3

Sources: SOS Allmänna valen and Leif Lewin, Bo Jansson, and Dag Sörbom: *The Swedish Electorate 1887–1968* (Stockholm: Almqvist & Wiksell, 1972), p. 146.

Table A.2. Elections to Second Chamber of Parliament (P) and to local bodies (L) that chose First Chamber, 1910–1968; parliamentary (P) and local (L) elections, 1970–1982

Year	Type of election	Participating voters, absolute numbers	% of eligible voters who cast ballots	Relative distribution of valid votes									
				Moderates	Center party	Liberals	Christian Democrats	Social Democrats	Social Democratic Leftists	Socialists	Left party Communists	Others	Total
1910	L	455,289	49.3	39.5	—	39.8	—	19.9	—	—	—	0.8	100
1911	P	607,487	57.0	31.2	—	40.2	—	28.5	—	—	—	0.1	100
1912, 1914	L	597,399	54.8	40.8	—	32.5	—	26.6	—	—	—	0.1	100
1914, spring	P	763,423	69.9	37.7	0.0	32.2	—	30.1	—	—	—	0.1	100
1914, fall	P	735,485	66.2	36.5	0.2	26.9	—	36.4	—	—	—	0.0	100
1916, 1918	L	677,941	53.5	35.9	4.5	26.5	—	29.9	3.2	—	—	0.0	100
1917	P	739,053	65.8	24.7	8.5	27.6	—	31.1	8.1	—	—	0.0	100
1919	L	1,805,627	63.3	24.9	13.2	25.4	—	30.5	5.8	—	—	0.2	100
1920	P	660,193	55.3	27.9	14.2	21.8	—	29.7	6.4	—	—	0.0	100
1921	P	1,747,553	54.2	25.8	11.1	19.1	—	36.2	3.2	—	4.6	0.0	100
1922	L	1,091,348	38.2	31.8	11.9	17.1	—	32.9	1.8	—	4.5	0.0	100
1924	P	1,770,607	53.0	26.1	10.8	16.9	—	41.4	—	—	5.1	0.0	100
1926	L	1,483,450	49.8	28.9	11.7	16.1	—	39.0	—	—	4.1	0.2	100
1928	P	2,363,168	67.4	29.4	11.2	15.9	—	37.0	—	—	6.4	0.1	100
1930	L	1,827,953	58.2	28.4	12.5	13.5	—	41.4	—	2.8	1.2	0.2	100
1932	P	2,500,769	68.6	23.5	14.1	11.7	—	41.7	—	5.3	3.0	0.7	100
1934	L	2,103,034	63.6	24.2	13.3	12.5	—	42.1	—	4.0	2.8	1.1	100
1936	P	2,925,255	74.5	17.6	14.3	12.9	—	45.9	—	4.4	3.3	1.6	100

1938	L	2,616,646	66.0	17.8	12.6	12.2	—	50.4	—	1.9	3.8	1.3	100
1940	P	2,889,137	70.3	18.0	12.0	12.0	—	53.8	—	0.7	3.5	0.0	100
1942	L	2,902,037	66.8	17.6	13.2	12.4	—	50.3	—	0.1	5.9	0.5	100
1944	P	3,099,103	71.9	15.9	13.6	12.9	—	46.7	—	0.2	10.3	0.4	100
1946	L	3,342,832	72.0	14.9	13.6	15.6	—	44.4	—	—	11.2	0.3	100
1948	P	3,895,161	82.7	12.3	12.4	22.8	—	46.1	—	—	6.3	0.1	100
1950	L	3,836,082	80.5	12.3	12.3	21.7	—	48.6	—	—	4.9	0.2	100
1952	P	3,801,284	79.1	14.4	10.7	24.4	—	46.1	—	—	4.3	0.1	100
1954	L	3,837,387	79.1	15.7	10.3	21.7	—	47.4	—	—	4.8	0.1	100
1956	P	3,902,114	79.8	17.1	9.4	23.8	—	44.6	—	—	5.0	0.1	100
1958 (1 June)	P	3,864,963	77.4	19.5	12.7	18.2	—	46.2	—	—	3.4	0.0	100
1958 (21 Sep.)	L	3,899,040	79.2	20.4	13.1	15.6	—	46.8	—	—	4.0	0.1	100
1960	P	4,271,610	85.9	16.5	13.6	17.5	—	47.8	—	—	4.5	0.1	100
1962	L	4,068,550	81.0	15.5	13.1	17.1	—	50.5	—	—	3.8	0.0	100
1964	P	4,273,595	83.9	13.7	13.4	17.1	1.8	47.3	—	—	5.2	1.5	100
1966	L	4,425,179	82.8	14.7	13.7	16.7	1.8	42.2	—	—	6.4	4.3	100
1968	P	4,861,901	89.3	12.9	15.7	14.3	1.5	50.1	—	—	3.0	2.6	100
1970	P	4,984,207	88.3	11.5	19.9	16.2	1.8	45.3	—	—	4.8	0.4	100
1970	L	4,974,542	88.1	11.7	19.5	16.2	1.8	45.6	—	—	4.4	0.7	100
1973	P	5,169,002	90.8	14.3	25.1	9.4	1.8	43.6	—	—	5.3	0.5	100
1973	L	5,151,562	90.5	13.9	23.7	10.4	2.1	43.2	—	—	5.1	1.7	100
1976	P	5,457,043	91.8	15.6	24.1	11.1	1.4	42.7	—	—	4.8	0.3	100
1976	L	5,563,676	90.3	15.2	22.4	11.5	1.8	43.6	—	—	4.8	0.7	100
1979	P	5,480,126	90.7	20.3	18.1	10.6	1.4	43.2	—	—	5.6	0.8	100
1979	L	5,563,974	89.0	18.6	17.7	10.5	2.1	43.0	—	—	5.8	2.3	100
1982	P	5,606,603	91.4	23.6	15.5	5.9	1.9	45.6	—	—	5.6	2.0	100
1982	L	5,694,923	89.6	21.7	15.3	6.0	2.4	45.5	—	—	5.4	3.8	100

Appendix

Table A.3. Referendums

Year	Subject	% of voters taking part	Yes	No	Line 1	Line 2	Line 3	Blank
1922	Prohibition	55.1	49.1	50.9	—	—	—	—
1955	Right-hand traffic	53.2	15.5	82.9	—	—	—	1.6
1957	Supplementary pension system	72.4	—	—	45.8	15.0	35.3	3.9
1980	Nuclear power	75.6	—	—	18.7	39.3	38.6	3.3

Table A.4. *Distribution of seats in Parliament, 1912–1982*

Year	Conservatives	Center party	Liberal party	Social Democrats	Left Socialists	Socialists	Communists	Total
				A. First Chamber, 1912–1969				
1912	86	—	52	12	—	—	—	150
1914B	88	—	49	13	—	—	—	150
1915	89	—	47	14	—	—	—	150
1918	88	—	45	16	1	—	—	150
1921	37	19	40	51	—	—	3	150
1922	41	18	38	50	2	—	1	150
1925	44	18	35	52	—	—	1	150
1929	49	17	31	52	—	—	1	150
1933	50	18	23	58	—	1	—	150
1937	45	22	16	66	—	1	—	150
1941	35	24	15	75	—	—	1	150
1945	30	21	14	83	—	—	2	150
1949	24	21	18	84	—	—	3	150
1953	20	25	22	79	—	—	4	150
1957	13	25	30	79	—	—	3	150
1958B	16	24	29	79	—	—	3	151
1961	19	20	33	77	—	—	2	151
1965	26	19	26	78	—	—	2	151
1969	24	21	26	79	—	—	1	151

Table A.4. *(cont.)*

B. Second Chamber, 1912–1969

Year	Conservatives	Center party	Liberal party	Social Democrats	Left Socialists	Socialists	Communists	Total
1912	64	—	102	64	—	—	—	230
1914B	86	—	70	74	—	—	—	230
1915	86	—	57	87	—	—	—	230
1918	57	14	62	86	11	—	—	230
1921	71	30	47	75	5	—	2	230
1922	62	21	41	93	6	—	7	230
1925	65	23	33	104	—	—	5	230
1929	73	27	32	90	—	—	8	230
1933	58	36	24	104	—	6	2	230
1937	44	36	27	112	—	6	5	230
1941	42	28	23	134	—	—	3	230
1945	39	35	26	115	—	—	15	230
1949	23	30	57	112	—	—	8	230
1953	31	26	58	110	—	—	5	230
1957	42	19	58	106	—	—	6	231
1958B	45	32	38	111	—	—	5	231
1961	39	34	40	114	—	—	5	232
1965	33	35 + 1	43	113	—	—	8	233
1969	32	39	34	125	—	—	3	233

C. Unicameral Parliament, 1971–1982

Year	Moderate party	Center party	Liberal party	Social Democrats	Left party Communists	Total
1971	41	71	58	163	17	350
1974	51	90	34	156	19	350
1976	55	86	39	152	17	349
1979	73	64	38	154	20	349
1982	86	56	21	166	20	349

Table A.5. Swedish governments, 1867–1986

7 Apr. 1858–3 June 1870	L. De Geer I, minister of state for justice
3 June 1870–8 Apr. 1874	A. G. Adlercreutz, minister of state for justice
4 May 1874–11 May 1875	E. Carleson, minister of state for justice
11 May 1875–19 Apr. 1880	L. De Geer II, minister of state for justice; 20 Mar. 1876, prime minister
19 Apr. 1880–13 June 1883	A. Posse
13 June 1883–16 May 1884	C. J. Thyselius
16 May 1884–6 Feb. 1888	R. Themptander
6 Feb. 1888–12 Oct. 1889	D. A. G. Bildt
12 Oct. 1889–10 July 1891	G. Åkerhielm
10 July 1891–12 Sep. 1900	E. G. Boström I
12 Sep. 1900–5 July 1902	F. V. von Otter
5 July 1902–13 Apr. 1905	E. G. Boström II
13 Apr.–2 Aug. 1905	J. O. Ramstedt
2 Aug.–7 Nov. 1905	Ch. Lundeberg
7 Nov. 1905–29 May 1906	K. Staaff I, Liberal
29 May 1906–7 Oct. 1911	A. Lindman I, Conservative
7 Oct. 1911–17 Feb. 1914	K. Staaff II, Liberal
17 Feb. 1914–30 Mar. 1917	H. Hammarskjöld
30 Mar.–19 Oct. 1917	C. Swartz, Conservative
19 Oct. 1917–10 Mar. 1920	N. Edén, Liberal–Social Democratic coalition
10 Mar.–27 Oct. 1920	H. Branting I, Social Democratic
27 Oct. 1920–13 Oct. 1921	L. De Geer the Younger (to 23 Feb. 1921), O. von Sydow, caretaker government
13 Oct. 1921–19 Apr. 1923	H. Branting II, Social Democratic
19 Apr. 1923–18 Oct. 1924	E. Trygger, Conservative
18 Oct. 1924–7 June 1926	H. Branting III (to 24 Jan. 1925), R. Sandler, Social Democratic
7 June 1926–2 Oct. 1928	C. G. Ekman I, Prohibitionist–Liberal coalition
2 Oct. 1928–7 June 1930	A. Lindman II, Conservative
7 June 1930–24 Sep. 1932	C. G. Ekman II (to 6 Aug. 1932), F. Hamrin, Prohibitionist
24 Sep. 1932–19 June 1936	P. A. Hansson I, Social Democratic
19 June–28 Sep. 1936	A. Pehrsson i Bramstorp, Agrarian
28 Sep. 1936–13 Dec. 1939	P. A. Hansson II, Social Democratic–Agrarian coalition
13 Dec. 1939–31 July 1945	P. A. Hansson III, grand coalition (all parliamentary parties except Communists)
31 July 1945–1 Oct. 1951	P. A. Hansson IV (to 6 Oct. 1946), T. Erlander I, Social Democratic
1 Oct. 1951–31 Oct. 1957	T. Erlander II, Social Democratic–Agrarian coalition
31 Oct. 1957–8 Oct. 1976	T. Erlander III (to 14 Oct. 1969), O. Palme I, Social Democratic
8 Oct. 1976–18 Oct. 1978	T. Fälldin I, Conservative–Liberal–Center party coalition
18 Oct. 1978–12 Oct. 1979	O. Ullsten, Liberal
12 Oct. 1979–5 May 1981	T. Fälldin II, Conservative–Liberal–Center party coalition
22 May 1981–20 Sep. 1982	T. Fälldin, Liberal–Center party coalition
8 Oct. 1982–	O. Palme II (to 1 Mar. 1986), I. Carlsson, Social Democratic

Appendix

Table A.6. *Chairmen of Sweden's political parties*

A. General Electoral Association, name changed in 1938 to Conservative National Organization, in 1969 to the Moderate party

Arvid Lindman	1912–1935
Gösta Bagge	1935–1944
Fritiof Domö	1944–1950
Jarl Hjalmarson	1950–1961
Gunnar Heckscher	1961–1965
Yngve Holmberg	1965–1970
Gösta Bohman	1970–1981
Ulf Adelsohn	1981–1986
Carl Bildt	1986–

B. Agrarian party, name changed in 1957 to Center party

Carl Berglund i Gimnene	1913–1916
Erik Eriksson i Spraxkya	1916–1919
Johan Andersson i Raklösen	1919–1924
Johan Johansson i Kälkebo	1924–1928
Olof Olsson i Kullenbergstorp	1929–1934
Axel Pehrsson i Bramstorp	1934–1949
Gunnar Hedlund i Rådom	1949–1971
Thorbjörn Fälldin	1971–1986
Karin Söder	1986–

C. Liberal party, split in 1923 into the Prohibitionists and Liberals, merged again in 1934

Sixten von Friesen	1900–1905
Karl Staaff	(1904) 1907–1915
Daniel Persson i Tällberg (chairman of Five-Man Council)	1916–1917
Nils Edén	1917–1923

Prohibitionists

C. G. Ekman	1923–1932
Ola Jeppsson i Mörrum	1933–1934

Liberals

Eliel Löfgren	1923–1930
Ernst Lyberg	1930–1933
K. A. Andersson	1933–1934

Liberal party

Felix Hamrin (chairman of the council of representatives)	1934–1935
Ola Jeppsson (chairman of the executive committee)	1934–1935
Gustaf Andersson i Rasjön	1935–1944
Bertil Ohlin	1944–1967
Sven Wedén	1967–1969
Gunnar Helén	1969–1975
Per Ahlmark	1975–1978
Ola Ullsten	1978–1983
Bengt Westerberg	1983–

Appendix

Table A.6. *(cont.)*

D. The Social Democratic Labor party

Hjalmar Branting	1889–1925
Per Albin Hansson	1925–1946
Tage Erlander	1946–1969
Olof Palme	1969–1986
Ingvar Carlsson	1986–

E. The Social Democratic Leftist party, name changed in 1921 to the Communist party, split into Höglund and Kilbom factions in 1924, Communist party reestablished in 1929, name changed to Left party Communists in 1967

Social Democratic Leftist party

C. Vinberg and Z. Höglund	1917
Ernst Aström and Karl Kilbom	1918
Z. Höglund and Karl Kilbom	1919–1921
Nils Andersson i Borlänge	1921
Otto Nygren	1922–1923

Communist party

Z. Höglund	1921–1924

Communist party (Höglund faction)

Z. Höglund	1924–1926

Communist party (Kilbom faction)

Nils Flyg	1924–1943

Communist party

Sven Linderot	1929–1951
Hilding Hagberg	1951–1964
C. H. Hermansson	1964–1975
Lars Werner	1975–

Index

Index

Index

Index

Printed in the United Kingdom
by Lightning Source UK Ltd.
103088UKS00001B/77